# Risk Management: A Strategic Approach

# Risk Management: A Strategic Approach

Edited by
**Markel Armstrong**

Larsen & Keller
www.larsen-keller.com

Risk Management: A Strategic Approach
Edited by Markel Armstrong
ISBN: 978-1-63549-251-4 (Hardback)



Larsen & Keller
Published by Larsen and Keller Education,
5 Penn Plaza,
19th Floor,
New York, NY 10001, USA

**Cataloging-in-Publication Data**

Risk management : a strategic approach / edited by Markel Armstrong.
p. cm.
Includes bibliographical references and index.
ISBN 978-1-63549-251-4
1. Risk management. 2. Risk management--Technological innovations.
3. Management. 4. Strategic planning. I. Armstrong, Markel.
HD61 .R57 2017
658.155--dc23



Printed and bound in China.

For more information regarding Larsen and Keller Education and its products, please visit the publisher's website www.larsen-keller.com

# Table of Contents


**Preface** VII

**Chapter 1 Introduction to Risk Management** **1**
- i. Risk Management 1
- ii. Crisis Management 17
- iii. Risk 33

**Chapter 2 Different Types of Risk Management** **76**
- i. Enterprise Risk Management 76
- ii. Project Risk Management 86
- iii. Social Risk Management 88
- iv. Operational Risk Management 94
- v. Financial Risk Management 98
- vi. Fuel Price Risk Management 99
- vii. IT Risk Management 101

**Chapter 3 Theory Related to Risk Management** **122**
- i. Dragon King Theory 122

**Chapter 4 Analysis and Assessment of Risk Management** **132**
- i. Risk Analysis 132
- ii. Hazard Analysis 133
- iii. Fault Tree Analysis 136
- iv. Society for Risk Analysis 145
- v. Risk Assessment 146
- vi. Flood Risk Assessment 153
- vii. Own Risk and Solvency Assessment 156

**Chapter 5 Preventive Measures for Risk Management** **163**
- i. ISO/TC 223 163
- ii. Contingency Plan 165
- iii. Common Alerting Protocol 166
- iv. Currency Analytics 170
- v. Social Responsibility 171
- vi. Risk Pool 174
- vii. Risk Management Programme 176

**Chapter 6 Risk Management: Tools, Methods and Techniques** **177**
- i. Risk Management Tools 177
- ii. RIMS Risk Maturity Model 187
- iii. Event Chain Methodology 189
- iv. Risk Register 192

v. Predictive Analytics 194
vi. Delphi Method 210
vii. Monte Carlo Method 216
viii. Risk Breakdown Structure 230
ix. Control Self-assessment 236
x. Scenario Analysis 241
xi. Black–Scholes Model 243
xii. Value at Risk 257

**Chapter 7 Essential Aspects of Risk Management 268**
i. Risk Matrix 268
ii. RiskLab 270
iii. Precautionary Principle 271

**Chapter 8 Various Risk Management Softwares 283**
i. Actimize 283
ii. PillarOne.RiskAnalytics 285
iii. Logic Manager 288
iv. SureID 289

**Chapter 9 Risk Management: A Global Overview 293**
i. Institute of Risk Management 293
ii. Risk and Insurance Management Society 295
iii. Global Association of Risk Professionals 295
iv. Financial Risk Manager 301

**Permissions**

**Index**

# Preface

Risk management refers to the process of analyzing, assessing, identifying and prioritizing the risks involved or uncertainty of objects. It involves minimizing and controlling these unfavourable circumstances so that the business bears minimum to no loss. This book unfolds the innovative aspects of risk management which will be crucial for the holistic understanding of the subject matter. The topics included in it are of utmost significance and are bound to provide incredible insights to readers. In this text, constant effort has been made to make the understanding of the difficult concepts of risk management as easy and informative as possible for the readers. It will serve as a valuable source of reference for those interested in this field.

Given below is the chapter wise description of the book:

Chapter 1- The identification of the possible situations that can cause risks is known as risk management. It helps in the coordination of the resources in order to minimize and control the probability of any unfortunate event. It also seeks to minimize the effects of uncertainty on the performance of a business. This chapter will provide an integrated understanding of risk management.

Chapter 2- Enterprise risk management includes methods and processes that are used by companies to manage risks. It helps in providing frameworks for risk management. The other types of risk management included in this chapter are project risk management, social risk management, operational risk management, financial risk management, IT risk management etc. The topics discussed in the section are of great importance to broaden the existing knowledge on risk management.

Chapter 3- The basic theory that is related to risk management is the dragon king theory. It is used as a metaphor to refer to an event that is extremely large and has developed from a rare and unique situation. The topic discussed in this chapter is of vital importance, and provides the readers with a better understanding of risk management.

Chapter 4- Risk analysis is defined in a number of ways; the definitions usually depend on how risk analysis relates to other concepts. Risk management can be divided into two components, risk assessment and risk management. This section on analysis and assessment of risk management is an overview of the subject matter incorporating all the major aspects of the topic.

Chapter 5- The preventive measures for risk management are ISO/TC 223, contingency plan, common alerting protocol, currency analytics and social responsibility. ISO/TC 223 is a committee of international organization for standardization; the purpose of this was the protection of society from emergencies and disasters caused by intentional human activity. This section elucidates the crucial theories of risk management.

Chapter 6- There are mainly three types of risk tool and two of these are identified by their own approach while the third is the basis of project risk management. The types of risk tools are capital asset pricing model and probabilistic risk assessment. Event chain methodology, risk register and the Monte Carlo method are some of the other topics in this section. The chapter discusses the methods and techniques of risk management in a critical manner providing key analysis to the subject matter.

Chapter 7- The essential aspects of risk management are risk matrix, RiskLab and precautionary principle. Risk matrix is used during risk assessment and is used to define the level of risk that can be caused by an event while RiskLab is a research laboratory that conducts research on financial risk management. This chapter serves as a source to understand the major aspects of risk management.

Chapter 8- There are many econometric techniques that help in the process of financial risk modeling. Actimize provides prevention of financial crime and also provides risk management products and services to the financial service industry. Alternatively, the risk management software included in this chapter are PillarOne.RiskAnalytics, LogicManager and sureID. This section will provide an in-depth understanding of risk management softwares.

Chapter 9- The organizations and institutes working for risk management are Risk and Insurance Management Society, Institute of Risk Management, Global Association of Risk Professionals and Financial Risk Manager. Risk and Insurance Management Society is an association that dedicates itself to the practice of risk management. It has a number of nonprofit charitable entities and 3500 industrial entities. The chapter on organizations and institutes working for risk management offers an global overview of the subject matter.

Indeed, my job was extremely crucial and challenging as I had to ensure that every chapter is informative and structured in a student-friendly manner. I am thankful for the support provided by my family and colleagues during the completion of this book.

**Editor**

1

# Introduction to Risk Management

The identification of the possible situations that can cause risks is known as risk management. It helps in the coordination of the resources in order to minimize and control the probability of any unfortunate event. It also seeks to minimize the effects of uncertainty on the performance of a business. This chapter will provide an integrated understanding of risk management.

## Risk Management

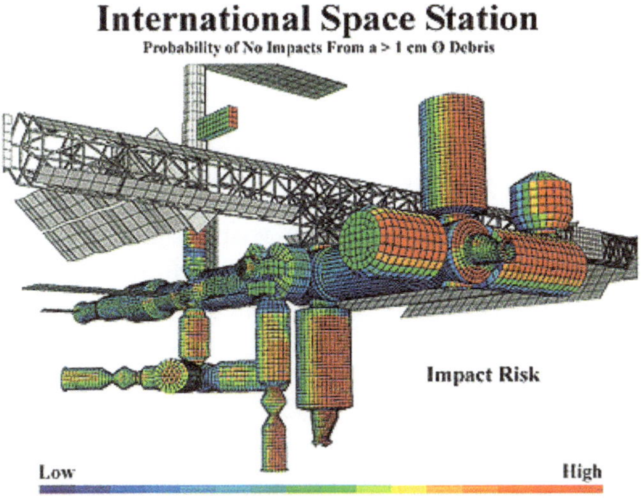


Example of risk management: A NASA model showing areas at high risk from impact for the International Space Station.

Risk management is the identification, assessment, and prioritization of risks (defined in ISO 31000 as *the effect of uncertainty on objectives*) followed by coordinated and economical application of resources to minimize, monitor, and control the probability and/or impact of unfortunate events or to maximize the realization of opportunities. Risk management's objective is to assure uncertainty does not deflect the endeavor from the business goals.

Risks can come from various sources including uncertainty in financial markets, threats from project failures (at any phase in design, development, production, or sustainment life-cycles), legal liabilities, credit risk, accidents, natural causes and disasters, deliberate attack from an adversary, or events of uncertain or unpredictable root-cause.

There are two types of events i.e. negative events can be classified as risks while positive events are classified as opportunities. Several risk management standards have been developed including the Project Management Institute, the National Institute of Standards and Technology, actuarial societies, and ISO standards. Methods, definitions and goals vary widely according to whether the risk management method is in the context of project management, security, engineering, industrial processes, financial portfolios, actuarial assessments, or public health and safety.

Risk sources are identified and located in human factor variables, mental states and decision making as well as infrastructural or technological assets and tangible variables. The interaction between human factors and tangible aspects of risk highlights the need to focus closely on human factors as one of the main drivers for risk management, a "change driver" that comes first of all from the need to know how humans perform in challenging environments and in face of risks (Daniele Trevisani, 2007). As the author describes, «it is an extremely hard task to be able to apply an objective and systematic self-observation, and to make a clear and decisive step from the level of the mere "sensation" that something is going wrong, to the clear understanding of how, when and where to act. The truth of a problem or risk is often obfuscated by wrong or incomplete analyses, fake targets, perceptual illusions, unclear focusing, altered mental states, and lack of good communication and confrontation of risk management solutions with reliable partners. This makes the Human Factor aspect of Risk Management sometimes heavier than its tangible and technological counterpart»

Strategies to manage threats (uncertainties with negative consequences) typically include avoiding the threat, reducing the negative effect or probability of the threat, transferring all or part of the threat to another party, and even retaining some or all of the potential or actual consequences of a particular threat, and the opposites for opportunities (uncertain future states with benefits).

Certain aspects of many of the risk management standards have come under criticism for having no measurable improvement on risk; whereas the confidence in estimates and decisions seem to increase. For example, it has been shown that one in six IT projects experience cost overruns of 200% on average, and schedule overruns of 70%.

## Introduction

A widely used vocabulary for risk management is defined by *ISO Guide 73:2009*, "Risk management. Vocabulary."

In ideal risk management, a prioritization process is followed whereby the risks with the greatest loss (or impact) and the greatest probability of occurring are handled first, and risks with lower probability of occurrence and lower loss are handled in descending order. In practice the process of assessing overall risk can be difficult, and balancing resources used to mitigate between risks with a high probability of occurrence but lower loss versus a risk with high loss but lower probability of occurrence can often be mishandled.

Intangible risk management identifies a new type of a risk that has a 100% probability of occurring but is ignored by the organization due to a lack of identification ability. For example, when deficient knowledge is applied to a situation, a knowledge risk materializes. Relationship risk appears when ineffective collaboration occurs. Process-engagement risk may be an issue when ineffective operational procedures are applied. These risks directly reduce the productivity of knowledge workers, decrease cost-effectiveness, profitability, service, quality, reputation, brand value, and earnings quality. Intangible risk management allows risk management to create immediate value from the identification and reduction of risks that reduce productivity.

Risk management also faces difficulties in allocating resources. This is the idea of opportunity cost. Resources spent on risk management could have been spent on more profitable activities. Again, ideal risk management minimizes spending (or manpower or other resources) and also minimizes the negative effects of risks.

According to the definition to the risk, the risk is the possibility that an event will occur and adversely affect the achievement of an objective. Therefore, risk itself has the uncertainty. Risk management such as COSO ERM, can help managers have a good control for their risk. Every companies have different level for their internal control, which leads to the different result for the different companies. For example, the framework for ERM components includes Internal Environment, Objective Setting, Event Identification, Risk Assessment, Risk Response, Control Activities, Information and Communication, and Monitoring.

## Method

For the most part, these methods consist of the following elements, performed, more or less, in the following order.

1. identify, characterize threats
2. assess the vulnerability of critical assets to specific threats
3. determine the risk (i.e. the expected likelihood and consequences of specific types of attacks on specific assets)
4. identify ways to reduce those risks
5. prioritize risk reduction measures based on a strategy

## Principles of Risk Management

The International Organization for Standardization (ISO) identifies the following principles of risk management:

Risk management should:

- create value – resources expended to mitigate risk should be less than the consequence of inaction
- be an integral part of organizational processes
- be part of decision making process
- explicitly address uncertainty and assumptions
- be a systematic and structured process
- be based on the best available information
- be tailorable
- take human factors into account
- be transparent and inclusive
- be dynamic, iterative and responsive to change
- be capable of continual improvement and enhancement
- be continually or periodically re-assessed

## Process

According to the standard ISO 31000 "Risk management – Principles and guidelines on implementation," the process of risk management consists of several steps as follows:

## Establishing the Context

This involves:

1. identification of risk in a selected domain of interest
2. planning the remainder of the process
3. mapping out the following:
    - the social scope of risk management
    - the identity and objectives of stakeholders
    - the basis upon which risks will be evaluated, constraints.
4. defining a framework for the activity and an agenda for identification
5. developing an analysis of risks involved in the process
6. mitigation or solution of risks using available technological, human and organizational resources.

## Identification

After establishing the context, the next step in the process of managing risk is to identify potential risks. Risks are about events that, when triggered, cause problems or benefits. Hence, risk identification can start with the source of our problems and those of our competitors (benefit), or with the problem itself.

- Source analysis – Risk sources may be internal or external to the system that is the target of risk management (use mitigation instead of management since by its own definition risk deals with factors of decision-making that cannot be managed).

Examples of risk sources are: stakeholders of a project, employees of a company or the weather over an airport.

- Problem analysis – Risks are related to identified threats. For example: the threat of losing money, the threat of abuse of confidential information or the threat of human errors, accidents and casualties. The threats may exist with various entities, most important with shareholders, customers and legislative bodies such as the government.

When either source or problem is known, the events that a source may trigger or the events that can lead to a problem can be investigated. For example: stakeholders withdrawing during a project may endanger funding of the project; confidential information may be stolen by employees even within a closed network; lightning striking an aircraft during takeoff may make all people on board immediate casualties.

The chosen method of identifying risks may depend on culture, industry practice and compliance. The identification methods are formed by templates or the development of templates for identifying source, problem or event. Common risk identification methods are:

- Objectives-based risk identification – Organizations and project teams have objectives. Any event that may endanger achieving an objective partly or completely is identified as risk.

- Scenario-based risk identification – In scenario analysis different scenarios are created. The scenarios may be the alternative ways to achieve an objective, or an analysis of the interaction of forces in, for example, a market or battle. Any event that triggers an undesired scenario alternative is identified as risk.

- Taxonomy-based risk identification – The taxonomy in taxonomy-based risk identification is a breakdown of possible risk sources. Based on the taxonomy and knowledge of best practices, a questionnaire is compiled. The answers to the questions reveal risks.

- Common-risk checking – In several industries, lists with known risks are available. Each risk in the list can be checked for application to a particular situation.
- Risk charting – This method combines the above approaches by listing resources at risk, threats to those resources, modifying factors which may increase or decrease the risk and consequences it is wished to avoid. Creating a matrix under these headings enables a variety of approaches. One can begin with resources and consider the threats they are exposed to and the consequences of each. Alternatively one can start with the threats and examine which resources they would affect, or one can begin with the consequences and determine which combination of threats and resources would be involved to bring them about.

## Assessment

Once risks have been identified, they must then be assessed as to their potential severity of impact (generally a negative impact, such as damage or loss) and to the probability of occurrence. These quantities can be either simple to measure, in the case of the value of a lost building, or impossible to know for sure in the case of an unlikely event, the probability of occurrence of which is unknown. Therefore, in the assessment process it is critical to make the best educated decisions in order to properly prioritize the implementation of the risk management plan.

Even a short-term positive improvement can have long-term negative impacts. Take the "turnpike" example. A highway is widened to allow more traffic. More traffic capacity leads to greater development in the areas surrounding the improved traffic capacity. Over time, traffic thereby increases to fill available capacity. Turnpikes thereby need to be expanded in a seemingly endless cycles. There are many other engineering examples where expanded capacity (to do any function) is soon filled by increased demand. Since expansion comes at a cost, the resulting growth could become unsustainable without forecasting and management.

The fundamental difficulty in risk assessment is determining the rate of occurrence since statistical information is not available on all kinds of past incidents and is particularly scanty in the case of catastrophic events, simply because of their infrequency. Furthermore, evaluating the severity of the consequences (impact) is often quite difficult for intangible assets. Asset valuation is another question that needs to be addressed. Thus, best educated opinions and available statistics are the primary sources of information. Nevertheless, risk assessment should produce such information for senior executives of the organization that the primary risks are easy to understand and that the risk management decisions may be prioritized within overall company goals. Thus, there have been several theories and attempts to quantify risks. Numerous different risk formulae exist, but perhaps the most widely accepted formula for risk quantification is: "Rate (or probability) of occurrence multiplied by the impact of the event equals risk magnitude."

## Composite Risk Index

The above formula can also be re-written in terms of a composite risk index, as follows:

composite risk index = impact of risk event x probability of occurrence

The impact of the risk event is commonly assessed on a scale of 1 to 5, where 1 and 5 represent the minimum and maximum possible impact of an occurrence of a risk (usually in terms of financial losses). However, the 1 to 5 scale can be arbitrary and need not be on a linear scale.

The probability of occurrence is likewise commonly assessed on a scale from 1 to 5, where 1 represents a very low probability of the risk event actually occurring while 5 represents a very high probability of occurrence. This axis may be expressed in either mathematical terms (event occurs once a year, once in ten years, once in 100 years etc.) or may be expressed in "plain English" (event has occurred here very often; event has been known to occur here; event has been known to occur in the industry etc.). Again, the 1 to 5 scale can be arbitrary or non-linear depending on decisions by subject-matter experts.

The composite risk index thus can take values ranging (typically) from 1 through 25, and this range is usually arbitrarily divided into three sub-ranges. The overall risk assessment is then Low, Medium or High, depending on the sub-range containing the calculated value of the Composite Index. For instance, the three sub-ranges could be defined as 1 to 8, 9 to 16 and 17 to 25.

Note that the probability of risk occurrence is difficult to estimate, since the past data on frequencies are not readily available, as mentioned above. After all, probability does not imply certainty.

Likewise, the impact of the risk is not easy to estimate since it is often difficult to estimate the potential loss in the event of risk occurrence.

Further, both the above factors can change in magnitude depending on the adequacy of risk avoidance and prevention measures taken and due to changes in the external business environment. Hence it is absolutely necessary to periodically re-assess risks and intensify/relax mitigation measures, or as necessary. Changes in procedures, technology, schedules, budgets, market conditions, political environment, or other factors typically require re-assessment of risks.

## Risk Options

Risk mitigation measures are usually formulated according to one or more of the following major risk options, which are:

1. Design a new business process with adequate built-in risk control and containment measures from the start.

2. Periodically re-assess risks that are accepted in ongoing processes as a normal feature of business operations and modify mitigation measures.
3. Transfer risks to an external agency (e.g. an insurance company)
4. Avoid risks altogether (e.g. by closing down a particular high-risk business area)

Later research has shown that the financial benefits of risk management are less dependent on the formula used but are more dependent on the frequency and how risk assessment is performed.

In business it is imperative to be able to present the findings of risk assessments in financial, market, or schedule terms. Robert Courtney Jr. (IBM, 1970) proposed a formula for presenting risks in financial terms. The Courtney formula was accepted as the official risk analysis method for the US governmental agencies. The formula proposes calculation of ALE (annualized loss expectancy) and compares the expected loss value to the security control implementation costs (cost-benefit analysis).

## Potential Risk Treatments

Once risks have been identified and assessed, all techniques to manage the risk fall into one or more of these four major categories:

- Avoidance (eliminate, withdraw from or not become involved)
- Reduction (optimize – mitigate)
- Sharing (transfer – outsource or insure)
- Retention (accept and budget)

Ideal use of these strategies may not be possible. Some of them may involve trade-offs that are not acceptable to the organization or person making the risk management decisions. Another source, from the US Department of Defense, Defense Acquisition University, calls these categories ACAT, for Avoid, Control, Accept, or Transfer. This use of the ACAT acronym is reminiscent of another ACAT (for Acquisition Category) used in US Defense industry procurements, in which Risk Management figures prominently in decision making and planning.

## Risk Avoidance

This includes not performing an activity that could carry risk. An example would be not buying a property or business in order to not take on the legal liability that comes with it. Another would be not flying in order not to take the risk that the airplane were to be hijacked. Avoidance may seem the answer to all risks, but avoiding risks also means losing out on the potential gain that accepting (retaining) the risk may have allowed.

Not entering a business to avoid the risk of loss also avoids the possibility of earning profits. Increasing risk regulation in hospitals has led to avoidance of treating higher risk conditions, in favor of patients presenting with lower risk.

## Hazard Prevention

Hazard prevention refers to the prevention of risks in an emergency. The first and most effective stage of hazard prevention is the elimination of hazards. If this takes too long, is too costly, or is otherwise impractical, the second stage is mitigation.

## Risk Reduction

Risk reduction or "optimization" involves reducing the severity of the loss or the likelihood of the loss from occurring. For example, sprinklers are designed to put out a fire to reduce the risk of loss by fire. This method may cause a greater loss by water damage and therefore may not be suitable. Halon fire suppression systems may mitigate that risk, but the cost may be prohibitive as a strategy.

Acknowledging that risks can be positive or negative, optimizing risks means finding a balance between negative risk and the benefit of the operation or activity; and between risk reduction and effort applied. By an offshore drilling contractor effectively applying HSE Management in its organization, it can optimize risk to achieve levels of residual risk that are tolerable.

Modern software development methodologies reduce risk by developing and delivering software incrementally. Early methodologies suffered from the fact that they only delivered software in the final phase of development; any problems encountered in earlier phases meant costly rework and often jeopardized the whole project. By developing in iterations, software projects can limit effort wasted to a single iteration.

Outsourcing could be an example of risk reduction if the outsourcer can demonstrate higher capability at managing or reducing risks. For example, a company may outsource only its software development, the manufacturing of hard goods, or customer support needs to another company, while handling the business management itself. This way, the company can concentrate more on business development without having to worry as much about the manufacturing process, managing the development team, or finding a physical location for a call center.

## Risk Sharing

Briefly defined as "sharing with another party the burden of loss or the benefit of gain, from a risk, and the measures to reduce a risk."

The term of 'risk transfer' is often used in place of risk sharing in the mistaken belief that you can transfer a risk to a third party through insurance or outsourcing. In practice if the insurance company or contractor go bankrupt or end up in court, the original risk is likely to still revert to the first party. As such in the terminology of practitioners and scholars alike, the purchase of an insurance contract is often described as a "transfer of risk." However, technically speaking, the buyer of the contract generally retains legal responsibility for the losses "transferred", meaning that insurance may be described more accurately as a post-event compensatory mechanism. For example, a personal injuries insurance policy does not transfer the risk of a car accident to the insurance company. The risk still lies with the policy holder namely the person who has been in the accident. The insurance policy simply provides that if an accident (the event) occurs involving the policy holder then some compensation may be payable to the policy holder that is commensurate with the suffering/damage.

Some ways of managing risk fall into multiple categories. Risk retention pools are technically retaining the risk for the group, but spreading it over the whole group involves transfer among individual members of the group. This is different from traditional insurance, in that no premium is exchanged between members of the group up front, but instead losses are assessed to all members of the group.

## Risk Retention

Involves accepting the loss, or benefit of gain, from a risk when it occurs. True self insurance falls in this category. Risk retention is a viable strategy for small risks where the cost of insuring against the risk would be greater over time than the total losses sustained. All risks that are not avoided or transferred are retained by default. This includes risks that are so large or catastrophic that they either cannot be insured against or the premiums would be infeasible. War is an example since most property and risks are not insured against war, so the loss attributed by war is retained by the insured. Also any amounts of potential loss (risk) over the amount insured is retained risk. This may also be acceptable if the chance of a very large loss is small or if the cost to insure for greater coverage amounts is so great it would hinder the goals of the organization too much. Risk retention or acceptance is common type of risk response on treats and opportunities.

Risk Management plan

Select appropriate controls or countermeasures to measure each risk. Risk mitigation needs to be approved by the appropriate level of management. For instance, a risk concerning the image of the organization should have top management decision behind it whereas IT management would have the authority to decide on computer virus risks.

The risk management plan should propose applicable and effective security controls for managing the risks. For example, an observed high risk of computer viruses could be mitigated by acquiring and implementing antivirus software. A good risk management plan should contain a schedule for control implementation and responsible persons for those actions.

According to ISO/IEC 27001, the stage immediately after completion of the risk assessment phase consists of preparing a Risk Treatment Plan, which should document the decisions about how each of the identified risks should be handled. Mitigation of risks often means selection of security controls, which should be documented in a Statement of Applicability, which identifies which particular control objectives and controls from the standard have been selected, and why.

## Implementation

Implementation follows all of the planned methods for mitigating the effect of the risks. Purchase insurance policies for the risks that have been decided to be transferred to an insurer, avoid all risks that can be avoided without sacrificing the entity's goals, reduce others, and retain the rest.

## Review and Evaluation of the Plan

Initial risk management plans will never be perfect. Practice, experience, and actual loss results will necessitate changes in the plan and contribute information to allow possible different decisions to be made in dealing with the risks being faced.

Risk analysis results and management plans should be updated periodically. There are two primary reasons for this:

1. to evaluate whether the previously selected security controls are still applicable and effective
2. to evaluate the possible risk level changes in the business environment. For example, information risks are a good example of rapidly changing business environment.

## Limitations

Prioritizing the *risk management processes* too highly could keep an organization from ever completing a project or even getting started. This is especially true if other work is suspended until the risk management process is considered complete.

It is also important to keep in mind the distinction between risk and uncertainty. Risk can be measured by impacts x probability.

If risks are improperly assessed and prioritized, time can be wasted in dealing with risk of losses that are not likely to occur. Spending too much time assessing and managing unlikely risks can divert resources that could be used more profitably. Unlikely events do occur but if the risk is unlikely enough to occur it may be better to simply retain the risk and deal with the result if the loss does in fact occur. Qualitative risk assessment is subjective and lacks consistency. The primary justification for a formal risk assessment process is legal and bureaucratic.

## Areas

As applied to corporate finance, *risk management* is the technique for measuring, monitoring and controlling the financial or operational risk on a firm's balance sheet, a traditional measure is the value at risk (VaR), but there also other measures like profit at risk (PaR) or margin at risk. The Basel II framework breaks risks into market risk (price risk), credit risk and operational risk and also specifies methods for calculating capital requirements for each of these components.

## Enterprise

In enterprise risk management, a risk is defined as a possible event or circumstance that can have negative influences on the enterprise in question. Its impact can be on the very existence, the resources (human and capital), the products and services, or the customers of the enterprise, as well as external impacts on society, markets, or the environment. In a financial institution, enterprise risk management is normally thought of as the combination of credit risk, interest rate risk or asset liability management, liquidity risk, market risk, and operational risk.

In the more general case, every probable risk can have a pre-formulated plan to deal with its possible consequences (to ensure *contingency* if the risk becomes a *liability*).

From the information above and the average cost per employee over time, or cost accrual ratio, a project manager can estimate:

- the cost associated with the risk if it arises, estimated by multiplying employee costs per unit time by the estimated time lost (*cost impact, C* where *C = cost accrual ratio * S*).
- the probable increase in time associated with a risk (*schedule variance due to risk, Rs* where Rs = P * S):
    - Sorting on this value puts the highest risks to the schedule first. This is intended to cause the greatest risks to the project to be attempted first so that risk is minimized as quickly as possible.
    - This is slightly misleading as *schedule variances* with a large P and small S and vice versa are not equivalent. (The risk of the RMS *Titanic* sinking vs. the passengers' meals being served at slightly the wrong time).
- the probable increase in cost associated with a risk (*cost variance due to risk, Rc* where Rc = P*C = P*CAR*S = P*S*CAR)
    - sorting on this value puts the highest risks to the budget first.
    - see concerns about *schedule variance* as this is a function of it, as illustrated in the equation above.

Risk in a project or process can be due either to Special Cause Variation or Common Cause Variation and requires appropriate treatment. That is to re-iterate the concern about extremal cases not being equivalent in the list immediately above.

## Medical Device

For medical devices, risk management is a process for identifying, evaluating and mitigating risks associated with harm to people and damage to property or the environment. Risk management is an integral part of medical device design and development, production processes and evaluation of field experience, and is applicable to all types of medical devices. The evidence of its application is required by most regulatory bodies such as FDA. The management of risks for medical devices is described by the International Organization for Standardization (ISO) in ISO 14971:2007, Medical Devices—The application of risk management to medical devices, a product safety standard. The standard provides a process framework and associated requirements for management responsibilities, risk analysis and evaluation, risk controls and lifecycle risk management.

The European version of the risk management standard was updated in 2009 and again in 2012 to refer to the Medical Devices Directive (MDD) and Active Implantable Medical Device Directive (AIMDD) revision in 2007, as well as the In Vitro Medical Device Directive (IVDD). The requirements of EN 14971:2012 are nearly identical to ISO 14971:2007. The differences include an Annex that refers to the new MDD and AIMDD, the requirement for risks to be reduced *as low as possible*, and the requirement that risks be mitigated by design and not by labeling on the medical device (i.e., labeling can no longer be used to mitigate risk).

Typical risk analysis and evaluation techniques adopted by the medical device industry include hazard analysis, fault tree analysis (FTA), failure mode and effect analysis (FMEA), hazard and operability study (HAZOP), and risk traceability analysis for ensuring risk controls are implemented and effective (i.e. tracking risks identified to product requirements, design specifications, verification and validation results etc.). FTA analysis requires diagramming software. FMEA analysis can be done using a spreadsheet program. There are also integrated medical device risk management solutions.

Through a draft guidance, FDA has introduced another method named "Safety Assurance Case" for medical device safety assurance analysis. The safety assurance case is structured argument reasoning about systems appropriate for scientists and engineers, supported by a body of evidence, that provides a compelling, comprehensible and valid case that a system is safe for a given application in a given environment. With the guidance, a safety assurance case is expected for safety critical devices (e.g. infusion devices) as part of the pre-market clearance submission, e.g. 510(k). In 2013, FDA introduced another draft guidance expecting medical device manufacturers to submit cybersecurity risk analysis information.

## Project Management

Project risk management must be considered at the different phases of acquisition. In the beginning of a project, the advancement of technical developments or the response to threats presented by a competitors projects, may cause a risk or threat assessment and subsequent evaluation of alternatives. Selection of a response presented by technology options, or competitor threats are important applications of risk management. Once a decision is made, and the project begun, more familiar project management applications can be used:

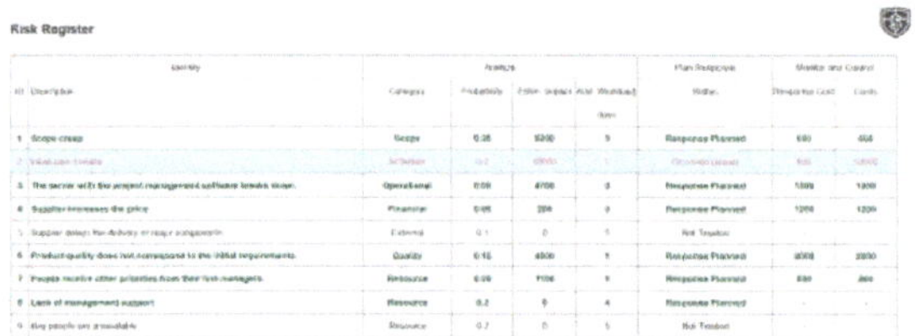


An example of the Risk Register for a project that includes 4 steps: Identify, Analyze, Plan Response, Monitor and Control.

- Planning how risk will be managed in the particular project. Plans should include risk management tasks, responsibilities, activities and budget.
- Assigning a risk officer – a team member other than a project manager who is responsible for foreseeing potential project problems. Typical characteristic of risk officer is a healthy skepticism.
- Maintaining live project risk database. Each risk should have the following attributes: opening date, title, short description, probability and importance. Optionally a risk may have an assigned person responsible for its resolution and a date by which the risk must be resolved.
- Creating anonymous risk reporting channel. Each team member should have the possibility to report risks that he/she foresees in the project.
- Preparing mitigation plans for risks that are chosen to be mitigated. The purpose of the mitigation plan is to describe how this particular risk will be handled – what, when, by whom and how will it be done to avoid it or minimize consequences if it becomes a liability.
- Summarizing planned and faced risks, effectiveness of mitigation activities, and effort spent for the risk management.

## Megaprojects (Infrastructure)

Megaprojects (sometimes also called "major programs") are large-scale investment projects, typically costing more than US$1 billion per project. Megaprojects include major bridges, tunnels, highways, railways, airports, seaports, power plants, dams, wastewater projects, coastal flood protection schemes, oil and natural gas extraction projects, public buildings, information technology systems, aerospace projects, and defense systems. Megaprojects have been shown to be particularly risky in terms of finance, safety, and social and environmental impacts. Risk management is therefore particularly pertinent for megaprojects and special methods and special education have been developed for such risk management.

## Natural Disasters

It is important to assess risk in regard to natural disasters like floods, earthquakes, and so on. Outcomes of natural disaster risk assessment are valuable when considering future repair costs, business interruption losses and other downtime, effects on the environment, insurance costs, and the proposed costs of reducing the risk. There are regular conferences in Davos to deal with integral risk management.

## Information Technology

Information technology is increasingly pervasive in modern life in every sector.

IT risk is a risk related to information technology. This is a relatively new term due to an increasing awareness that information security is simply one facet of a multitude of risks that are relevant to IT and the real world processes it supports.

A number of methodologies have been developed to deal with this kind of risk alongside adaptations of existing practices to new paradigms including agile risk management .

ISACA's *Risk IT* framework ties IT risk to enterprise risk management.

## Petroleum and Natural gas

For the offshore oil and gas industry, operational risk management is regulated by the safety case regime in many countries. Hazard identification and risk assessment tools and techniques are described in the international standard ISO 17776:2000, and organisations such as the IADC (International Association of Drilling Contractors) publish guidelines for HSE Case development which are based on the ISO standard. Further, diagrammatic representations of hazardous events are often expected by governmental regulators as part of risk management in safety case submissions; these are known as bow-tie diagrams. The technique is also used by organisations and regulators in mining, aviation, health, defence, industrial and finance.

## Pharmaceutical Sector

The principles and tools for quality risk management are increasingly being applied to different aspects of pharmaceutical quality systems. These aspects include development, manufacturing, distribution, inspection, and submission/review processes throughout the lifecycle of drug substances, drug products, biological and biotechnological products (including the use of raw materials, solvents, excipients, packaging and labeling materials in drug products, biological and biotechnological products). Risk management is also applied to the assessment of microbiological contamination in relation to pharmaceutical products and cleanroom manufacturing environments.

## Business Continuity

Risk management is simply a practice of systematically selecting cost-effective approaches for minimising the effect of threat realization to the organization. All risks can never be fully avoided or mitigated simply because of financial and practical limitations. Therefore, all organizations have to accept some level of residual risks.

Whereas risk management tends to be preemptive, business continuity planning (BCP) was invented to deal with the consequences of realised residual risks. Business continuity planning consists of measures that are proposed in the event of various natural disasters or other serious incidents affecting a company. The necessity to have BCP in place arises because even very unlikely events will occur if given enough time. Risk management and BCP are often mistakenly seen as rivals or overlapping practices. In fact, these processes are so tightly tied together that separation seems artificial. For example, the risk management process creates important inputs for the BCP (e.g., assets, impact assessments, cost estimates). Risk management also proposes applicable controls for the observed risks. Therefore, risk management covers several areas that are vital for the BCP process. However, the BCP process goes beyond risk management's preemptive approach and assumes that the disaster will happen at some point.

## Risk Communication

Risk communication is a complex cross-disciplinary academic field related to core values of the targeted audiences. Problems for risk communicators involve how to reach the intended audience, to make the risk comprehensible and relatable to other risks, how to pay appropriate respect to the audience's values related to the risk, how to predict the audience's response to the communication, etc. A main goal of risk communication is to improve collective and individual decision making. Risk communication is somewhat related to crisis communication.

## Digital and Internet

In the 2000s, the digital era brings a paradigm shift. Digital risks are risks of potential loss of information, breaches or privacy or confidentiality and/or loss of core services which are arising from increased dependency on information technology systems, digital information storage systems, Internet services and digital processes. As more businesses are advertising and providing services online, as with Apple Computers and its online iTunes store, businesses are becoming more dependent on their IT and Internet operations. It will become a major challenge for the new evolving executive role of 'digital' risk officer. Executives are accountable for both operational performance and achieving strategic objectives. There is now a need for executives to understand the direct alignment of digital risks with the strategic business goals of the enterprise. Digital risk management is the next evolution in 'digital risk and security strategies'. It is about re-defining corporate governance and 'digital perpetuation' and should form part of the digital risk management plan.

## Crisis Management

Crisis management is the process by which an organisation deals with a major event that threatens to harm the organization, its stakeholders, or the general public. The study of crisis management originated with the large-scale industrial and environmental disasters in the 1980s. It is considered to be the most important process in public relations.

Three elements are common to a crisis: (a) a threat to the organization, (b) the element of surprise, and (c) a short decision time. Venette argues that "crisis is a process of transformation where the old system can no longer be maintained." Therefore, the fourth defining quality is the need for change. If change is not needed, the event could more accurately be described as a failure or incident.

In contrast to risk management, which involves assessing potential threats and finding the best ways to avoid those threats, crisis management involves dealing with threats before, during, and after they have occurred. It is a discipline within the broader context of management consisting of skills and techniques required to identify, assess, understand, and cope with a serious situation, especially from the moment it first occurs to the point that recovery procedures start.

### Introduction

Crisis management is a situation-based management system that includes clear roles and responsibilities and process related organisational requirements company-wide. The response shall include action in the following areas: Crisis prevention, crisis assessment, crisis handling and crisis termination. The aim of crisis management is to be well prepared for crisis, ensure a rapid and adequate response to the crisis, maintaining clear lines of reporting and communication in the event of crisis and agreeing rules for crisis termination.

The techniques of crisis management include a number of consequent steps from the understanding of the influence of the crisis on the corporation to preventing, alleviating, and overcoming the different types of crisis. Crisis management consists of different aspects including:

- Methods used to respond to both the reality and perception of crisis.
- Establishing metrics to define what scenarios constitute a crisis and should consequently trigger the necessary response mechanisms.
- Communication that occurs within the response phase of emergency-management scenarios.

Crisis-management methods of a business or an organization are called a crisis-management plan. A British Standard BS11200:2014 provides a useful foundation for understanding terminology and frameworks relating to crisis, in this document the focus is on the corporate exposure to risks in particular to the black swan events that result in significant strategic threats to organisations. Currently there is work on-going to develop an International standard.

Crisis management is occasionally referred to as incident management, although several industry specialists such as Peter Power argue that the term "crisis management" is more accurate.

A crisis mindset requires the ability to think of the worst-case scenario while simultaneously suggesting numerous solutions. Trial and error is an accepted discipline, as the first line of defense might not work. It is necessary to maintain a list of contingency plans and to be always on alert. Organizations and individuals should always be prepared with a rapid response plan to emergencies which would require analysis, drills and exercises.

The credibility and reputation of organizations is heavily influenced by the perception of their responses during crisis situations. The organization and communication involved in responding to a crisis in a timely fashion makes for a challenge in businesses. There must be open and consistent communication throughout the hierarchy to contribute to a successful crisis-communication process.

The related terms emergency management and business continuity management focus respectively on the prompt but short lived "first aid" type of response (e.g. putting the fire out) and the longer-term recovery and restoration phases (e.g. moving operations to another site). Crisis is also a facet of risk management, although it is probably untrue to say that crisis management represents a failure of risk management, since it will never be possible to totally mitigate the chances of catastrophes' occurring.

## Types of Crisis

During the crisis management process, it is important to identify types of crises in that different crises necessitate the use of different crisis management strategies. Potential crises are enormous, but crises can be clustered.

Lerbinger categorized eight types of crises

1. Natural disaster
2. Technological crises
3. Confrontation
4. Malevolence
5. Organizational Misdeeds
6. Workplace Violence
7. Rumours
8. Terrorist attacks/man-made disasters

## Natural Crisis

Natural crises, typically natural disasters, are such environmental phenomena as earthquakes, volcanic eruptions, tornadoes and hurricanes, floods, landslides, tsunamis, storms, and droughts that threaten life, property, and the environment itself.

Example: 2004 Indian Ocean earthquake (Tsunami)

## Technological Crisis

Technological crises are caused by human application of science and technology. Technological accidents inevitably occur when technology becomes complex and coupled and something goes wrong in the system as a whole (Technological breakdowns). Some technological crises occur when human error causes disruptions (Human breakdowns). People tend to assign blame for a technological disaster because technology is subject to human manipulation whereas they do not hold anyone responsible for natural disaster. When an accident creates significant environmental damage, the crisis is categorized as *megadamage*. Samples include software failures, industrial accidents, and oil spills.

Examples: Chernobyl disaster, Exxon Valdez oil spill, Heartbleed security bug

## Confrontation Crisis

Confrontation crisis occur when discontented individuals and/or groups fight businesses, government, and various interest groups to win acceptance of their demands and expectations. The common type of confrontation crisis is boycotts, and other types are picketing, sit-ins, ultimatums to those in authority, blockade or occupation of buildings, and resisting or disobeying police.

Example: Rainbow/PUSH's (People United to Serve Humanity) boycott of Nike

## Crisis of Malevolence

An organization faces a crisis of malevolence when opponents or miscreant individuals use criminal means or other extreme tactics for the purpose of expressing hostility or anger toward, or seeking gain from, a company, country, or economic system, perhaps with the aim of destabilizing or destroying it. Sample crisis include product tampering, kidnapping, malicious rumors, terrorism, and espionage.

Example: 1982 Chicago Tylenol murders

## Crisis of Organizational Misdeeds

Crisis occur when management takes actions it knows will harm or place stakeholders at risk for harm without adequate precautions. Lerbinger specified three different types of crises of organizational misdeeds: crises of skewed management values, crises of deception, and crises of management misconduct.

## Crises of Skewed Management Values

Crises of skewed management values are caused when managers favor short-term economic gain and neglect broader social values and stakeholders other than investors. This state of lopsided values is rooted in the classical business creed that focuses on the interests of stockholders and tends to disregard the interests of its other stakeholders such as customers, employees, and the community

Example: Sears sacrifices customer trust

It has 3 stages -precrisis -acute -chronic and -conflict resolution

## Crisis of Deception

Crisis of deception occur when management conceals or misrepresents information about itself and its products in its dealing with consumers and others.

Example: Dow Corning's silicone-gel breast implant

## Crisis of Management Misconduct

Some crises are caused not only by skewed values and deception but deliberate amorality and illegality.

## Workplace Violence

Crises occur when an employee or former employee commits violence against other employees on organizational grounds.

Example: DuPont's Lycra

## Rumors

False information about an organization or its products creates crises hurting the organization's reputation. Sample is linking the organization to radical groups or stories that their products are contaminated.

Example: Procter & Gamble's Logo controversy

## Crisis Leadership

Alan Hilburg, a pioneer in crisis management, defines organizational crises as categorized as either acute crises or chronic crises. Erika Hayes James, an organizational psychologist at the University of Virginia's Darden Graduate School of Business, identifies two primary types of organizational crisis. James defines organizational crisis as "any emotionally charged situation that, once it becomes public, invites negative stakeholder reaction and thereby has the potential to threaten the financial well-being, reputation, or survival of the firm or some portion thereof."

1. Sudden crisis
2. Smoldering crises

## Sudden Crisis

Sudden crises are circumstances that occur without warning and beyond an institution's control. Consequently, sudden crises are most often situations for which the institution and its leadership are not blamed.

## Smoldering Crisis

Smoldering crises differ from sudden crises in that they begin as minor internal issues that, due to manager's negligence, develop to crisis status. These are situations when leaders are blamed for the crisis and its subsequent effect on the institution in question.

James categorises five phases of crisis that require specific crisis leadership competencies. Each phase contains an obstacle that a leader must overcome to improve the structure and operations of an organization. James's case study on crisis in the financial services sector, for example, explores why crisis events erode public trust in leadership. James's research demonstrates how leadership competencies of integrity, positive intent, capability, mutual respect, and transparency impact the trust-building process.

1. Signal detection
2. Preparation and prevention
3. Containment and damage control

4. Business recovery
5. Learning

## Signal Detection

Si Sense-making: represents an attempt to create order and make sense, retrospectively, of what occurs. Perspective-taking: the ability to consider another person's or group's point of view.

## Preparation and Prevention

It is during this stage that crisis handlers begin preparing for or averting the crisis that had been foreshadowed in the signal detection stage. Hilburg has demonstrated that using an impact/probability model allows organizations to fairly accurately predict crisis scenarios. He's recognized the greatest organizational challenge is 'speaking truth to power' to predict truly worst-case scenarios. Organizations such as the Red Cross's primary mission is to prepare for and prevent the escalation of crisis events. Walmart has been described as an emergency-relief standard bearer after having witnessed the incredibly speedy and well-coordinated effort to get supplies to the Gulf Coast of the United States in anticipation of Hurricane Katrina.

## Containment and Damage Control

Usually the most vivid stage, the goal of crisis containment and damage control is to limit the reputational, financial, safety, and other threats to firm survival. Crisis handlers work diligently during this stage to bring the crisis to an end as quickly as possible to limit the negative publicity to the organization, and move into the business recovery phase.

## Business Recovery

When crisis hits, organizations must be able to carry on with their business in the midst of the crisis while simultaneously planning for how they will recover from the damage the crisis caused. Crisis handlers not only engage in continuity planning (determining the people, financial, and technology resources needed to keep the organization running), but will also actively pursue organizational resilience.

## Learning

In the wake of a crisis, organizational decision makers adopt a learning orientation and use prior experience to develop new routines and behaviors that ultimately change the way the organization operates. The best leaders recognize this and are purposeful and skillful in finding the learning opportunities inherent in every crisis situation.

## Crisis Communication

The effort taken by an organization to communicate with the public and stakeholders when an unexpected event occurs that could have a negative impact on the organization's reputation. This can also refer to the efforts to inform employees or the public of a potential hazard which could have a catastrophic impact. There are 3 essential steps that an organization can take to prepare for and withstand a communications crisis: 1) Define your philosophy; 2) Assess your vulnerabilities; 3) Develop a protocol.

## Models and Theories Associated With Crisis Management

## Crisis Management Strategy

Crisis management strategy (CMS) is corporate development strategy designed primarily to prevent crisis for follow-up company advancement. Thus, CMS is synthesis of strategic management. It includes projection of the future based on ongoing monitoring of business internal and external environment, as well as selection and implementation of crisis prevention strategy and operating management. This is including current status control based on ongoing monitoring of the internal and external environment, as well as crisis-coping strategy selection and implementation.

## Crisis Management Model

Successfully managing a crisis requires an understanding of how to handle a crisis – beginning with before they occur. Alan Hilburg speaks about a crisis arc. The arc consists of crisis avoidance, crisis mitigation and crisis recovery. Gonzalez-Herrero and Pratt found the different phases of Crisis Management.

There are 3 phases in any Crisis Management as shown below

1. The diagnosis of the impending trouble or the danger signals.
2. Choosing appropriate Turnaround Strategy.
3. Implementation of the change process and its monitoring

## Crisis Management Planning

No corporation looks forward to facing a situation that causes a significant disruption to their business, especially one that stimulates extensive media coverage. Public scrutiny can result in a negative financial, political, legal and government impact. Crisis management planning deals with providing the best response to a crisis.

## Contingency planning

Preparing contingency plans in advance, as part of a crisis-management plan, is the first step to ensuring an organization is appropriately prepared for a crisis. Crisis-management teams can rehearse a crisis plan by developing a simulated scenario to use as a drill. The plan should clearly stipulate that the only people to speak to publicly about the crisis are the designated persons, such as the company spokesperson or crisis team members. Ideally it should be one spokesperson who can be available on call at any time. Cooperation with media is crucial in crisis situation, assure that all questions are answered on time and information on what was done to resolve the situation is provided. The first hours after a crisis breaks are the most crucial, so working with speed and efficiency is important, and the plan should indicate how quickly each function should be performed. When preparing to offer a statement externally as well as internally, information should be accurate and transparent. Providing incorrect or manipulated information has a tendency to backfire and will greatly exacerbate the situation. The contingency plan should contain information and guidance that will help decision makers to consider not only the short-term consequences, but the long-term effects of every decision.

## Business Continuity Planning

When a crisis will undoubtedly cause a significant disruption to an organization, a business continuity plan can help minimize the disruption. First, one must identify the critical functions and processes that are necessary to keep the organization running. This part of the planning should be conducted in the earliest stages, and is part of a business impact analysis phase that will signpost "How much does the organization stand to lose?" (Osborne, A. (2007). Practical Business Continuity Management. Business Management: Top tips for effective, real-world Business Continuity Management).

Each critical function and or/process must have its own contingency plan in the event that one of the functions/processes ceases or fails, then the business/organization is more resilient, which in itself provides a mechanism to lessen the possibility of having to invoke recovery plans (Osborne, 2007). Testing these contingency plans by rehearsing the required actions in a simulation will allow those involved to become more acutely aware of the possibility of a crisis. As a result, and in the event of an actual crisis, the team members will act more quickly and effectively.

A note of caution when planning training scenarios, all too often simulations can lack ingenuity, an appropriate level of realism and as a consequence potentially lose their training value. This part can be improved by employing external exercise designers who are not part of the organisational culture and are able to test an organizations response to crisis, in order to bring about a crisis of confidence for those who manage vital systems (Borodzicz, Edward P. (2005). Risk, Crisis & Security Management).

Following a simulation exercise, a thorough and systematic debriefing must be conducted as a key component of any crisis simulation. The purpose of this is to create a link and draw lessons from the reality of the simulated representation and the reality of the real world. (Borodzicz, 2005).

The whole process relating to business continuity planning should be periodically reviewed to identify any number of changes that may invalidate the current plan. (Osborne, 2007).

## Structural-functional Systems Theory

Providing information to an organization in a time of crisis is critical to effective crisis management. Structural-functional systems theory addresses the intricacies of information networks and levels of command making up organizational communication. The structural-functional theory identifies information flow in organizations as "networks" made up of members ". Information in organizations flow in patterns called networks.

## Diffusion of Innovation Theory

Another theory that can be applied to the sharing of information is Diffusion of Innovation Theory. Developed by Everett Rogers, the theory describes how innovation is disseminated and communicated through certain channels over a period of time. Diffusion of innovation in communication occurs when an individual communicates a new idea to one or several others. At its most elementary form, the process involves: (1) an innovation, (2) an individual or other unit of adoption that has knowledge of or experience with using the innovation, (3) another individual or other unit that does not yet have knowledge of the innovation, and (4) a communication channel connecting the two units. A communication channel is the means by which messages get from one individual to another.

## Role of Apologies in Crisis Management

There has been debate about the role of apologies in crisis management, and some argue that apology opens an organization up for possible legal consequences. "However some evidence indicates that compensation and sympathy, two less expensive strategies, are as effective as an apology in shaping people's perceptions of the organization taking responsibility for the crisis because these strategies focus on the victims' needs. The sympathy response expresses concern for victims while compensation offers victims something to offset the suffering."

## Crisis Leadership

James identifies five leadership competencies which facilitate organizational restructuring during and after a crisis.

1. Building an environment of trust

2. Reforming the organization's mindset

3. Identifying obvious and obscure vulnerabilities of the organization

4. Making wise and rapid decisions as well as taking courageous action

5. Learning from crisis to effect change.

Crisis leadership research concludes that leadership action in crisis reflects the competency of an organization, because the test of crisis demonstrates how well the institution's leadership structure serves the organization's goals and withstands crisis. Developing effective human resources is vital when building organizational capabilities through crisis management executive leadership.

## Unequal Human Capital Theory

James postulates that organizational crisis can result from discrimination lawsuits. James's theory of unequal human capital and social position derives from economic theories of human and social capital concluding that minority employees receive fewer organizational rewards than those with access to executive management. In a recent study of managers in a *Fortune* 500 company, race was found to be a predictor of promotion opportunity or lack thereof. Thus, discrimination lawsuits can invite negative stakeholder reaction, damage the company's reputation, and threaten corporate survival.

## Social Media and Crisis Management

Social media has accelerated the speed that information about a crisis can spread. The viral effect of social networks such as Twitter means that stakeholders can break news faster than traditional media - making managing a crisis harder. This can be mitigated by having the right training and policy in place as well as the right social media monitoring tools to detect signs of a crisis breaking. Social media also gives crisis management teams access to real-time information about how a crisis is impacting stakeholder sentiment and the issues that are of most concern to them.

The crisis management mantra of Lanny Davis, former counsellor to Bill Clinton is to "Tell it Early, Tell it All, Tell it Yourself". A strategy employed at the Clinton White House 1996 – 1998, to any breaking

Organisations should have a planned approach to releasing information to the media in the event of a crisis. A media reaction plan should include a company media representative as part of the Crisis Management Team (CMT). Since there is always a degree of unpredictability during a crisis, it is best that all CMT members understand how to deal with the media and be prepared to do so, should they be thrust into such a situation.

In 2010 Procter & Gamble Co called reports that its new Pampers with Dry Max caused rashes and other skin irritations "completely false" as it aimed to contain a public relations threat to its biggest diaper innovation in 25 years. A Facebook group called "Pampers bring back the OLD CRUISERS/SWADDLERS" rose to over 4,500 members. Pampers denied the allegation and stated that only two complaints had been received for every one million diapers sold. Pampers quickly reached out to people expressing their concerns via social media, Pampers even held a summit with four influential "mommy bloggers," to help dispel the rumour. Pampers acted quickly and decisively to an emerging crisis, before competitors and critics alike could fuel the fire further.

## Examples of Successful Crisis Management

### Tylenol (Johnson and Johnson)

In the fall of 1982, a murderer added 65 milligrams of cyanide to some Tylenol capsules on store shelves, killing seven people, including three in one family. Johnson & Johnson recalled and destroyed 31 million capsules at a cost of $100 million. The affable CEO, James Burke, appeared in television ads and at news conferences informing consumers of the company's actions. Tamper-resistant packaging was rapidly introduced, and Tylenol sales swiftly bounced back to near pre-crisis levels.

When another bottle of tainted Tylenol was discovered in a store, it took only a matter of minutes for the manufacturer to issue a nationwide warning that people should not use the medication in its capsule form.

### Odwalla Foods

When Odwalla's apple juice was thought to be the cause of an outbreak of E. coli infection, the company lost a third of its market value. In October 1996, an outbreak of E. coli bacteria in Washington state, California, Colorado and British Columbia was traced to unpasteurized apple juice manufactured by natural juice maker Odwalla Inc. Forty-nine cases were reported, including the death of a small child. Within 24 hours, Odwalla conferred with the FDA and Washington state health officials; established a schedule of daily press briefings; sent out press releases which announced the recall; expressed remorse, concern and apology, and took responsibility for anyone harmed by their products; detailed symptoms of E. coli poisoning; and explained what consumers should do with any affected products. Odwalla then developed - through the help of consultants - effective thermal processes that would not harm the products' flavors when production resumed. All of these steps were communicated through close relations with the media and through full-page newspaper ads.

### Mattel

Mattel Inc., the toy maker, has been plagued with more than 28 product recalls and in Summer of 2007, among problems with exports from China, faced two product recalls in two weeks. The company "did everything it could to get its message out, earning high marks from consumers and retailers. Though upset by the situation, they were appreciative of the company's response. At Mattel, just after the 7 a.m. recall announcement by federal officials, a public relations staff of 16 was set to call reporters at the 40 biggest media outlets. They told each to check their e-mail for a news release outlining the recalls, invited them to a teleconference call with executives and scheduled TV appearances or phone conversations with Mattel's chief executive. The Mattel CEO Robert Eckert did 14 TV interviews on a Tuesday in August and about 20 calls with individual reporters. By the week's end, Mattel had responded to more than 300 media inquiries in the U.S. alone."

### Pepsi

The Pepsi Corporation faced a crisis in 1993 which started with claims of syringes being found in cans of diet Pepsi. Pepsi urged stores not to remove the product from shelves while it had the cans and the situation investigated. This led to an arrest, which Pepsi made public and then followed with their first video news release, showing the production process to demonstrate that such tampering was impossible within their factories. A second video news release displayed the man arrested. A third video showed surveillance from a convenience store where a woman was caught inserting a syringe into a can. The company simultaneously publicly worked with the FDA during the crisis. This made public communications effective throughout the crisis. After the crisis had been resolved, the corporation ran a series of special campaigns designed to thank the public for standing by the corporation, along with coupons for further compensation. This case served as a design for how to handle other crisis situations.

## Examples of Unsuccessful Crisis Management

### Bhopal

The Bhopal disaster in which poor communication before, during, and after the crisis cost thousands of lives, illustrates the importance of incorporating cross-cultural communication in crisis management plans. According to American University's Trade Environmental Database Case Studies (1997), local residents were not sure how to react to warnings of potential threats from the Union Carbide plant. Operating manuals printed only in English is an extreme example of mismanagement but indicative of systemic barriers to information diffusion. According to Union Carbide's own chronology of the incident (2006), a day after the crisis Union Carbide's upper management arrived in India but was unable to assist in the relief efforts because they were placed under house arrest by the Indian government. Symbolic intervention can be counter productive; a crisis management strategy can help upper management make more calculated decisions in how they should respond to disaster scenarios. The Bhopal incident illustrates the difficulty in consistently applying management standards to multi-national operations and the blame shifting that often results from the lack of a clear management plan.

## Ford and Firestone Tire and Rubber Company

The Ford-Firestone Tire and Rubber Company dispute transpired in August 2000. In response to claims that their 15-inch Wilderness AT, radial ATX and ATX II tire treads were separating from the tire core—leading to crashes—Bridgestone/Firestone recalled 6.5 million tires. These tires were mostly used on the Ford Explorer, the world's top-selling sport utility vehicle (SUV).

The two companies committed three major blunders early on, say crisis experts. First, they blamed consumers for not inflating their tires properly. Then they blamed each other for faulty tires and faulty vehicle design. Then they said very little about what they were doing to solve a problem that had caused more than 100 deaths—until they got called to Washington to testify before Congress.

## Exxon

On March 24, 1989, a tanker belonging to the Exxon Corporation ran aground in the Prince William Sound in Alaska. The Exxon Valdez spilled millions of gallons of crude oil into the waters off Valdez, killing thousands of fish, fowl, and sea otters. Hundreds of miles of coastline were polluted and salmon spawning runs disrupted; numerous fishermen, especially Native Americans, lost their livelihoods. Exxon, by contrast, did not react quickly in terms of dealing with the media and the public; the CEO, Lawrence Rawl, did not become an active part of the public relations effort and actually shunned public involvement; the company had neither a communication plan nor a communication team in place to handle the event—in fact, the company did not appoint a public relations manager to its management team until 1993, 4 years after the incident; Exxon established its media center in Valdez, a location too small and too remote to handle the onslaught of media attention; and the company acted defensively in its response to its publics, even laying blame, at times, on other groups such as the Coast Guard. These responses also happened within days of the incident.

## Lessons Learned in Crisis Management

## Impact of Catastrophes on Shareholder Value

One of the foremost recognized studies conducted on the impact of a catastrophe on the stock value of an organization was completed by Dr Rory Knight and Dr Deborah Pretty (1996, Templeton College, University of Oxford - commissioned by the Sedgewick Group). This study undertook a detailed analysis of the stock price (post impact) of organizations that had experienced catastrophes. The study identified organizations that recovered and even exceeded pre-catastrophe stock price, (*Recoverers*), and those that did not recover on stock price, (*Non-recoverers*). The average cumulative impact on shareholder value for the recoverers was 5% plus on their original stock value. So the net impact on shareholder value by this stage was actually positive. The non-recoverers remained more or less unchanged between days 5 and 50 after the catastrophe, but suffered a net negative cumulative impact of almost 15% on their stock price up to one year afterwards.

One of the key conclusions of this study is that "Effective management of the consequences of catastrophes would appear to be a more significant factor than whether catastrophe insurance hedges the economic impact of the catastrophe".

While there are technical elements to this report it is highly recommended to those who wish to engage their senior management in the value of crisis management.

## Crisis as Opportunity

Hilburg proffers that every crisis is an opportunity to showcase an institution's character, its commitment to its brand promise and its institutional values. To address such shareholder impact, management must move from a mindset that manages crisis to one that generates crisis leadership. Research shows that organizational contributory factors affect the tendency of executives to adopt an effective "crisis as opportunity" mindset. Since pressure is both a precipitator and consequence of crisis, leaders who perform well under pressure can effectively guide the organization through such crisis.

James contends that most executives focus on communications and public relations as a reactive strategy. While the company's reputation with shareholders, financial well-being, and survival are all at stake, potential damage to reputation can result from the actual management of the crisis issue. Additionally, companies may stagnate as their risk management group identifies whether a crisis is sufficiently "statistically significant". Crisis leadership, on the other hand, immediately addresses both the damage and implications for the company's present and future conditions, as well as opportunities for improvement.

## Public-sector Crisis Management

Corporate America is not the only community that is vulnerable to the perils of a crisis. Whether a school shooting, a public health crisis or a terrorist attack that leaves the public seeking comfort in the calm, steady leadership of an elected official, no sector of society is immune to crisis. In response to that reality, crisis management policies, strategies and practices have been developed and adapted across multiple disciplines.

## Schools and Crisis Management

In the wake of the Columbine High School Massacre, the September 11 attacks in 2001, and shootings on college campuses including the Virginia Tech massacre, educational institutions at all levels are now focused on crisis management.

A national study conducted by the University of Arkansas for Medical Sciences (UAMS) and Arkansas Children's Hospital Research Institute (ACHRI) has shown that many public school districts have important deficiencies in their emergency and disaster plans (The School Violence Resource Center, 2003). In response the Resource Center has organized a comprehensive set of resources to aid schools is the development of crisis management plans.

Crisis-management plans cover a wide variety of incidents including bomb threats, child abuse, natural disasters, suicide, drug abuse and gang activities – just to list a few. In a similar fashion the plans aim to address all audiences in need of information including parents, the media and law enforcement officials.

## Government and Crisis Management

Historically, government at all levels—local, state, and national—has played a large role in crisis management. Indeed, many political philosophers have considered this to be one of the primary roles of government. Emergency services, such as fire and police departments at the local level, and the United States National Guard at the federal level, often play integral roles in crisis situations.

To help coordinate communication during the response phase of a crisis, the U.S. Federal Emergency Management Agency (FEMA) within the Department of Homeland Security administers the National Response Plan (NRP). This plan is intended to integrate public and private response by providing a common language and outlining a chain-of-command when multiple parties are mobilized. It is based on the premise that incidences should be handled at the lowest organizational level possible. The NRP recognizes the private sector as a key partner in domestic incident management, particularly in the area of critical infrastructure protection and restoration.

The NRP is a companion to the National Incidence Management System, which acts as a more general template for incident management regardless of cause, size, or complexity.

FEMA offers free web-based training on the National Response Plan through the Emergency Management Institute.

Common Alerting Protocol (CAP) is a relatively recent mechanism that facilitates crisis communication across different mediums and systems. CAP helps create a consistent emergency alert format to reach geographically and linguistically diverse audiences through both audio and visual mediums.

## People and Crisis Management

A group of international psychoanalysts startet in 1994 with a project to contribute to crisis management in the sense of managing conflicts between national groups. They called themselves *Partners in confronting collective atrocities*. They began their work with the so-called Nazareth-Conferences – based on the model of *Leicesterconferences* having been developed by the Tavistock Institute.

## Elected Officials and Crisis Management

Historically, politics and crisis go hand in hand. In describing crisis, President Abraham Lincoln said, "We live in the midst of alarms, anxiety beclouds the future; we expect some new disaster with each newspaper we read."

Crisis management has become a defining feature of contemporary governance. In times of crisis, communities and members of organizations expect their public leaders to minimize the impact of the crisis at hand, while critics and bureaucratic competitors try to seize the moment to blame incumbent rulers and their policies. In this extreme environment, policymakers must somehow establish a sense of normality, and foster collective learning from the crisis experience.

In the face of crisis, leaders must deal with the strategic challenges they face, the political risks and opportunities they encounter, the errors they make, the pitfalls they need to avoid, and the paths away from crisis they may pursue. The necessity for management is even more significant with the advent of a 24-hour news cycle and an increasingly internet-savvy audience with ever-changing technology at its fingertips.

Public leaders have a special responsibility to help safeguard society from the adverse consequences of crisis. Experts in crisis management note that leaders who take this responsibility seriously would have to concern themselves with all crisis phases: the incubation stage, the onset, and the aftermath. Crisis leadership then involves five critical tasks: sense making, decision making, meaning making, terminating, and learning.

A brief description of the five facets of crisis leadership includes:

1. Sense making may be considered as the classical situation assessment step in decision making.
2. Decision making is both the act of coming to a decision as the implementation of that decision.
3. Meaning making refers to crisis management as political communication.
4. Terminating a crisis is only possible if the public leader correctly handles the accountability question.
5. Learning, refers to the actual learning from a crisis is limited. The authors note, a crisis often opens a window of opportunity for reform for better or for worse.

## Professional Organizations

There are a number of professional industry associations that provide advice, literature and contacts to turnaround professionals and academics. Some are:

1. Turnaround Management Society (International / Focus on Europe)

2. Institute for Turnaround (England)

3. Turnaround Management Association (International)

4. Institut für die Standardisierung von Unternehmenssanierungen (Germany)

# Risk

Risk is the potential of gaining or losing something of value. Values (such as physical health, social status, emotional well-being or financial wealth) can be gained or lost when taking risk resulting from a given action or inaction, foreseen or unforeseen. Risk can also be defined as the intentional interaction with uncertainty. Uncertainty is a potential, unpredictable, and uncontrollable outcome; risk is a consequence of action taken in spite of uncertainty.

Risk perception is the subjective judgment people make about the severity and probability of a risk, and may vary person to person. Any human endeavor carries some risk, but some are much riskier than others.

## Definitions

The Oxford English Dictionary cites the earliest use of the word in English (in the spelling of *risque* from its from French original, 'risque' ) as of 1621, and the spelling as *risk* from 1655. It defines *risk* as:

(Exposure to) the possibility of loss, injury, or other adverse or unwelcome circumstance; a chance or situation involving such a possibility.

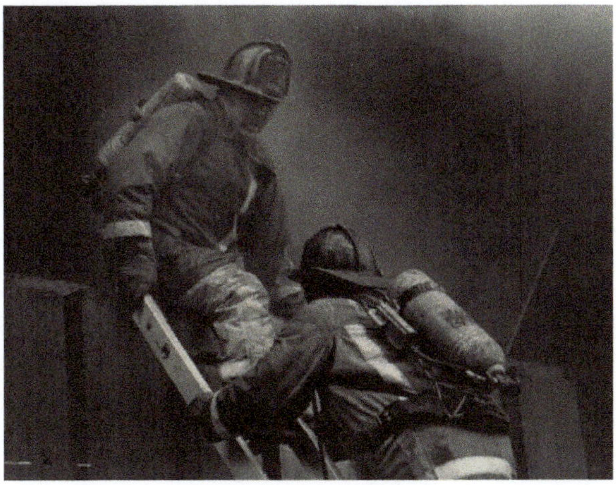

Firefighters at work

1. Risk is an uncertain event or condition that, if it occurs, has an effect on at least one [project] objective. (This definition, using project terminology, is easily made universal by removing references to projects).

2. The probability of something happening multiplied by the resulting cost or benefit if it does. (This concept is more properly known as the 'Expectation Value' or 'Risk Factor' and is used to compare levels of risk)

3. The probability or threat of quantifiable damage, injury, liability, loss, or any other negative occurrence that is caused by external or internal vulnerabilities, and that may be avoided through preemptive action.

4. Finance: The possibility that an actual return on an investment will be lower than the expected return.

5. Insurance: A situation where the probability of a variable (such as burning down of a building) is known but when a mode of occurrence or the actual value of the occurrence (whether the fire will occur at a particular property) is not. A risk is not an uncertainty (where neither the probability nor the mode of occurrence is known), a peril (cause of loss), or a hazard (something that makes the occurrence of a peril more likely or more severe).

6. Securities trading: The probability of a loss or drop in value. Trading risk is divided into two general categories: (1) Systematic risk affects all securities in the same class and is linked to the overall capital-market system and therefore cannot be eliminated by diversification. Also called market risk. (2) Non-systematic risk is any risk that isn't market-related. Also called non-market risk, extra-market risk or diversifiable risk.

7. Workplace: Product of the consequence and probability of a hazardous event or phenomenon. For example, the risk of developing cancer is estimated as the incremental probability of developing cancer over a lifetime as a result of exposure to potential carcinogens (cancer-causing substances).

## International Organization for Standardization

The ISO 31000 (2009) / ISO Guide 73:2002 definition of risk is the 'effect of uncertainty on objectives'. In this definition, uncertainties include events (which may or may not happen) and uncertainties caused by ambiguity or a lack of information. It also includes both negative and positive impacts on objectives. Many definitions of risk exist in common usage, however this definition was developed by an international committee representing over 30 countries and is based on the input of several thousand subject matter experts.

## Other

Very different approaches to risk management are taken in different fields, e.g. "Risk is the unwanted subset of a set of uncertain outcomes" (Cornelius Keating).

> Risk can be seen as relating to the probability of uncertain future events. For example, according to factor analysis of information risk, risk is: the probable frequency and probable magnitude of future loss. In computer science this definition is used by The Open Group.
>
> OHSAS (Occupational Health & Safety Advisory Services) defines risk as the combination of the probability of a hazard resulting in an adverse event, and the severity of the event.
>
> In information security risk is defined as "the potential that a given threat will exploit vulnerabilities of an asset or group of assets and thereby cause harm to the organization".
>
> Financial risk is often defined as the unpredictable variability or volatility of returns, and this would include both potential better-than-expected and worse-than-expected returns. References to negative risk below should be read as also applying to positive impacts or opportunity (e.g. for "loss" read "loss or gain") unless the context precludes this interpretation.
>
> The related terms "threat" and "hazard" are often used to mean something that could cause harm.

## Practice Areas

Risk is ubiquitous in all areas of life and risk management is something that we all must do, whether we are managing a major organization or simply crossing the road. When describing risk however, it is convenient to consider that risk practitioners operate in some specific practice areas.

## Economic Risk

Economic risks can be manifested in lower incomes or higher expenditures than expected. The causes can be many, for instance, the hike in the price for raw materials, the lapsing of deadlines for construction of a new operating facility, disruptions in a production process, emergence of a serious competitor on the market, the loss of key personnel, the change of a political regime, or natural disasters.

## Health

Risks in personal health may be reduced by primary prevention actions that decrease early causes of illness or by secondary prevention actions after a person has clearly measured clinical signs or symptoms recognized as risk factors. Tertiary prevention reduces the negative impact of an already established disease by restoring function and reducing disease-related complications. Ethical medical practice requires careful discussion of risk factors with individual patients to obtain informed consent for secondary and tertiary prevention efforts, whereas public health efforts in primary prevention require education of the entire population at risk. In each case, careful communication about risk factors, likely outcomes and certainty must distinguish between causal events that must be decreased and associated events that may be merely consequences rather than causes.

In epidemiology, the lifetime risk of an effect is the *cumulative incidence*, also called *incidence proportion* over an entire lifetime.

## Health, Safety, and Environment

Health, safety, and environment (HSE) are separate practice areas; however, they are often linked. The reason for this is typically to do with organizational management structures; however, there are strong links among these disciplines. One of the strongest links between these is that a single risk event may have impacts in all three areas, albeit over differing timescales. For example, the uncontrolled release of radiation or a toxic chemical may have immediate short-term safety consequences, more protracted health impacts, and much longer-term environmental impacts. Events such as Chernobyl, for example, caused immediate deaths, and in the longer term, deaths from cancers, and left a lasting environmental impact leading to birth defects, impacts on wildlife, etc.

Over time, a form of risk analysis called environmental risk analysis has developed. Environmental risk analysis is a field of study that attempts to understand events and activities that bring risk to human health or the environment.

Human health and environmental risk is the likelihood of an adverse outcome. As such, risk is a function of hazard and exposure. Hazard is the intrinsic danger or harm that is posed, e.g. the toxicity of a chemical compound. Exposure is the likely contact with that hazard. Therefore, the risk of even a very hazardous substance approaches zero as the exposure nears zero, given a person's (or other organism's) biological makeup, activities and location.

## Information Technology and Information Security

Information technology risk, or IT risk, IT-related risk, is a risk related to information technology. This relatively new term was developed as a result of an increasing awareness that information security is simply one facet of a multitude of risks that are relevant to IT and the real world processes it supports.

The increasing dependencies of modern society on information and computers networks (both in private and public sectors, including military) has led to new terms like IT risk and Cyberwarfare.

Information security means protecting information and information systems from unauthorized access, use, disclosure, disruption, modification, perusal, inspection, recording or destruction. Information security grew out of practices and procedures of computer security.Information security has grown to information assurance (IA) i.e. is the practice of managing risks related to the use, processing, storage, and transmission of information or data and the systems and processes used for those purposes.While focused dominantly on information in digital form, the full range of IA encompasses not only digital but also analog or physical form.Information assurance is interdisciplinary and draws from multiple fields, including accounting, fraud examination, forensic science, management science, systems engineering, security engineering, and criminology, in addition to computer science.

So, *IT risk* is narrowly focused on computer security, while *information security* extends to risks related to other forms of information (paper, microfilm). *Information assurance* risks include the ones related to the consistency of the business information stored in IT systems and the information stored by other means and the relevant business consequences.

## Insurance

Insurance is a risk treatment option which involves risk sharing. It can be considered as a form of contingent capital and is akin to purchasing an option in which the buyer pays a small premium to be protected from a potential large loss.

Insurance risk is often taken by insurance companies, who then bear a pool of risks including market risk, credit risk, operational risk, interest rate risk, mortality risk, longevity risks, etc.

## Business and Management

Means of assessing risk vary widely between professions. Indeed, they may define these professions; for example, a doctor manages medical risk, while a civil engineer manages risk of structural failure. A professional code of ethics is usually focused on risk assessment and mitigation (by the professional on behalf of client, public, society or life in general).

In the workplace, incidental and inherent risks exist. Incidental risks are those that occur naturally in the business but are not part of the core of the business. Inherent risks have a negative effect on the operating profit of the business.

## In Human Services

The experience of many people who rely on human services for support is that 'risk' is often used as a reason to prevent them from gaining further independence or fully accessing the community, and that these services are often unnecessarily risk averse. "People's autonomy used to be compromised by institution walls, now it's too often our risk management practices", according to John O'Brien. Michael Fischer and Ewan Ferlie (2013) find that contradictions between formal risk controls and the role of subjective factors in human services (such as the role of emotions and ideology) can undermine service values, so producing tensions and even intractable and 'heated' conflict.

## High Reliability Organizations (HROs)

A high reliability organization (HRO) is an organization that has succeeded in avoiding catastrophes in an environment where normal accidents can be expected due to risk factors and complexity. Most studies of HROs involve areas such as nuclear aircraft carriers, air traffic control, aerospace and nuclear power stations. Organizations such as these share in common the ability to consistently operate safely in complex, interconnected environments where a single failure in one component could lead to catastrophe. Essentially, they are organizations which appear to operate 'in spite' of an enormous range of risks.

Some of these industries manage risk in a highly quantified and enumerated way. These include the nuclear power and aircraft industries, where the possible failure of a complex series of engineered systems could result in highly undesirable outcomes. The usual measure of risk for a class of events is then: $R$ = probability of the event × the severity of the consequence.

The total risk is then the sum of the individual class-risks.

In the nuclear industry, consequence is often measured in terms of off-site radiological release, and this is often banded into five or six decade-wide bands.

The risks are evaluated using fault tree/event tree techniques. Where these risks are low, they are normally considered to be "broadly acceptable". A higher level of risk (typically up to 10 to 100 times what is considered broadly acceptable) has to be justified against the costs of reducing it further and the possible benefits that make it tolerable—these risks are described as "Tolerable if ALARP". Risks beyond this level are classified as "intolerable".

The level of risk deemed broadly acceptable has been considered by regulatory bodies in various countries—an early attempt by UK government regulator and academic F. R. Farmer used the example of hill-walking and similar activities, which have definable risks that people appear to find acceptable. This resulted in the so-called Farmer Curve of acceptable probability of an event versus its consequence.

The technique as a whole is usually referred to as probabilistic risk assessment (PRA) (or probabilistic safety assessment, PSA).

## Finance

In finance, risk is the chance that the return achieved on an investment will be different from that expected, and also takes into account the size of the difference. This includes the possibility of losing some or all of the original investment. In a view advocated by Damodaran, risk includes not only "downside risk" but also "upside risk" (returns that exceed expectations). Some regard the standard deviation of the historical returns or average returns of a specific investment as providing some historical measure of risk; see modern portfolio theory. Financial risk may be market-dependent, determined by numerous market factors, or operational, resulting from fraudulent behavior (e.g. Bernard Madoff). Recent studies suggest that endocrine levels may play a role in risk-taking in financial decision-making.

A fundamental idea in finance is the relationship between risk and return. The greater the potential return one might seek, the greater the risk that one generally assumes. A free market reflects this principle in the pricing of an instrument: strong demand for a safer instrument drives its price higher (and its return correspondingly lower) while weak demand for a riskier instrument drives its price lower (and its potential return thereby higher). For example, a US Treasury bond is considered to be one of the safest investments. In comparison to an investment or speculative grade corporate bond, US Treasury notes and bonds yield lower rates of return. The reason for this is that a corporation is more likely to default on debt than the U.S. government. Because the risk of investing in a corporate bond is higher, investors are offered a correspondingly higher rate of return.

A popular risk measure is value-at-risk (VaR).

There are different types of VaR: long term VaR, marginal VaR, factor VaR and shock VaR. The latter is used in measuring risk during the extreme market stress conditions.

In finance, *risk* has no single definition.

Artzner et al. write "we call risk the investor's future net worth". In Novak "risk is a possibility of an undesirable event".

In financial markets, one may need to measure credit risk, information timing and source risk, probability model risk, and legal risk if there are regulatory or civil actions taken as a result of "investor's regret".

It is not always obvious if financial instruments are "hedging" (purchasing/selling a financial instrument specifically to reduce or cancel out the risk in another investment) or "speculation" (increasing measurable risk and exposing the investor to catastrophic loss in pursuit of very high windfalls that increase expected value).

Some people may be "risk seeking", i.e. their utility function's second derivative is positive. Such an individual willingly pays a premium to assume risk (e.g. buys a lottery ticket). Knowing one's risk appetite in conjunction with one's financial well-being are important.

## Security

Popular labeling

Security risk management involves protection of assets from harm caused by deliberate acts. A more detailed definition is: "A security risk is any event that could result in the compromise of organizational assets i.e. the unauthorized use, loss, damage, disclosure or modification of organizational assets for the profit, personal interest or political interests of individuals, groups or other entities constitutes a compromise of the asset, and includes the risk of harm to people. Compromise of organizational assets may adversely affect the enterprise, its business units and their clients. As such, consideration of security risk is a vital component of risk management."

## Human Factors

One of the growing areas of focus in risk management is the field of human factors where behavioral and organizational psychology underpin our understanding of risk based decision making. This field considers questions such as "how do we make risk based decisions?", "why are we irrationally more scared of sharks and terrorists than we are of motor vehicles and medications?"

In decision theory, regret (and anticipation of regret) can play a significant part in decision-making, distinct from risk aversion (preferring the status quo in case one becomes worse off).

Framing is a fundamental problem with all forms of risk assessment. In particular, because of bounded rationality (our brains get overloaded, so we take mental shortcuts), the risk of extreme events is discounted because the probability is too low to evaluate intuitively. As an example, one of the leading causes of death is road accidents caused by drunk driving – partly because any given driver frames the problem by largely or totally ignoring the risk of a serious or fatal accident.

For instance, an extremely disturbing event (an attack by hijacking, or moral hazards) may be ignored in analysis despite the fact it has occurred and has a nonzero probability. Or, an event that everyone agrees is inevitable may be ruled out of analysis due to greed or an unwillingness to admit that it is believed to be inevitable. These human tendencies for error and wishful thinking often affect even the most rigorous applications of the scientific method and are a major concern of the philosophy of science.

All decision-making under uncertainty must consider cognitive bias, cultural bias, and notational bias: No group of people assessing risk is immune to “groupthink”: acceptance of obviously wrong answers simply because it is socially painful to disagree, where there are conflicts of interest.

Framing involves other information that affects the outcome of a risky decision. The right prefrontal cortex has been shown to take a more global perspective while greater left prefrontal activity relates to local or focal processing.

From the Theory of Leaky Modules McElroy and Seta proposed that they could predictably alter the framing effect by the selective manipulation of regional prefrontal activity with finger tapping or monaural listening. The result was as expected. Rightward tapping or listening had the effect of narrowing attention such that the frame was ignored. This is a practical way of manipulating regional cortical activation to affect risky decisions, especially because directed tapping or listening is easily done.

## Psychology of Risk Taking

A growing area of research has been to examine various psychological aspects of risk taking. Researchers typically run randomized experiments with a treatment and control group to ascertain the effect of different psychological factors that may be associated with risk taking. Thus, positive and negative feedback about past risk taking can affect future risk taking. In an experiment, people who were led to believe they are very competent at decision making saw more opportunities in a risky choice and took more risks, while those led to believe they were not very competent saw more threats and took fewer risks.

## Maintenance

The concept of risk-based maintenance is an advanced form of Reliability centered maintenance. In case of chemical industries, apart from probability of failure, consequences of failure is also very important. Therefore, the selection of maintenance policies should be based on risk, instead of reliability. Risk-based maintenance methodology acts as a tool for maintenance planning and decision making to reduce the probability of failure and its consequences. In risk-based maintenance decision making, the maintenance resources can be utilized optimally based on the risk class (high, medium, or low) of equipment or machines, to achieve tolerable risk criteria.

## Risk Assessment and Analysis

Since risk assessment and management is essential in security management, both are tightly related. Security assessment methodologies like CRAMM contain risk assessment modules as an important part of the first steps of the methodology. On the other hand, risk assessment methodologies like Mehari evolved to become security assessment methodologies. An ISO standard on risk management (Principles and guidelines on implementation) was published under code ISO 31000 on 13 November 2009.

## Quantitative Analysis

There are many formal methods used to "measure" risk.

Often the probability of a negative event is estimated by using the frequency of past similar events. Probabilities for rare failures may be difficult to estimate. This makes risk assessment difficult in hazardous industries, for example nuclear energy, where the frequency of failures is rare, while harmful consequences of failure are severe.

Statistical methods may also require the use of a cost function, which in turn may require the calculation of the cost of loss of a human life. This is a difficult problem. One approach is to ask what people are willing to pay to insure against death or radiological release (e.g. GBq of radio-iodine), but as the answers depend very strongly on the circumstances it is not clear that this approach is effective.

Risk is often measured as the expected value of an undesirable outcome. This combines the probabilities of various possible events and some assessment of the corresponding harm into a single value. The simplest case is a binary possibility of *Accident* or *No accident*. The associated formula for calculating risk is then:

$$R = (\text{probability of the accident occurring}) \times (\text{expected loss in case of the accident})$$

For example, if performing activity $X$ has a probability of 0.01 of suffering an accident of $A$, with a loss of 1000, then total risk is a loss of 10, the product of 0.01 and 1000.

Situations are sometimes more complex than the simple binary possibility case. In a situation with several possible accidents, total risk is the sum of the risks for each different accident, provided that the outcomes are comparable:

$$R = \sum_{\text{For all accidents}} (\text{probability of the accident occurring}) \times (\text{expected loss in case of the accident})$$

For example, if performing activity $X$ has a probability of 0.01 of suffering an accident of $A$, with a loss of 1000, and a probability of 0.000001 of suffering an accident of type $B$, with a loss of 2,000,000, then total loss expectancy is 12, which is equal to a loss of 10 from an accident of type $A$ and 2 from an accident of type $B$.

One of the first major uses of this concept was for the planning of the Delta Works in 1953, a flood protection program in the Netherlands, with the aid of the mathematician David van Dantzig. The kind of risk analysis pioneered there has become common today in fields like nuclear power, aerospace and the chemical industry.

In statistical decision theory, the risk function is defined as the expected value of a given loss function as a function of the decision rule used to make decisions in the face of uncertainty.

## Fear as Intuitive Risk Assessment

People may rely on their fear and hesitation to keep them out of the most profoundly unknown circumstances. Fear is a response to perceived danger. Risk could be said to be the way we collectively measure and share this "true fear"—a fusion of rational doubt, irrational fear, and a set of unquantified biases from our own experience.

The field of behavioral finance focuses on human risk-aversion, asymmetric regret, and other ways that human financial behavior varies from what analysts call "rational". Risk in that case is the degree of uncertainty associated with a return on an asset. Recognizing and respecting the irrational influences on human decision making may do much to reduce disasters caused by naive risk assessments that presume rationality but in fact merely fuse many shared biases.

## Anxiety, Risk and Decision Making

### Fear, Anxiety and Risk

According to one set of definitions, fear is a fleeting emotion ascribed to a particular object, while anxiety is a trait of fear (this is referring to "trait anxiety", as distinct from how the term "anxiety" is generally used) that lasts longer and is not attributed to a specific stimulus (these particular definitions are not used by all authors cited on this page). Some studies show a link between anxious behavior and risk (the chance that an outcome will have an unfavorable result). Joseph Forgas introduced valence based research where emotions are grouped as either positive or negative (Lerner and Keltner, 2000). Positive emotions, such as happiness, are believed to have more optimistic risk assessments and negative emotions, such as anger, have pessimistic risk assessments. As an emotion with a negative valence, fear, and therefore anxiety, has long been associated with negative risk perceptions. Under the more recent appraisal tendency framework of Jennifer Lerner et al., which refutes Forgas' notion of valence and promotes the idea that specific emotions have distinctive influences on judgments, fear is still related to pessimistic expectations.

Psychologists have demonstrated that increases in anxiety and increases in risk perception are related and people who are habituated to anxiety experience this awareness of risk more intensely than normal individuals. In decision-making, anxiety promotes the use of biases and quick thinking to evaluate risk. This is referred to as affect-as-information according to Clore, 1983. However, the accuracy of these risk perceptions when making choices is not known.

## Consequences of Anxiety

Experimental studies show that brief surges in anxiety are correlated with surges in general risk perception. Anxiety exists when the presence of threat is perceived (Maner and Schmidt, 2006). As risk perception increases, it stays related to the particular source impacting the mood change as opposed to spreading to unrelated risk factors. This increased awareness of a threat is significantly more emphasized in people who are conditioned to anxiety. For example, anxious individuals who are predisposed to generating reasons for negative results tend to exhibit pessimism. Also, findings suggest that the perception of a lack of control and a lower inclination to participate in risky decision-making (across various behavioral circumstances) is associated with individuals experiencing relatively high levels of trait anxiety. In the previous instance, there is supporting clinical research that links emotional evaluation (of control), the anxiety that is felt and the option of risk avoidance.

There are various views presented that anxious/fearful emotions cause people to access involuntary responses and judgments when making decisions that involve risk. Joshua A. Hemmerich et al. probes deeper into anxiety and its impact on choices by exploring "risk-as-feelings" which are quick, automatic, and natural reactions to danger that are based on emotions. This notion is supported by an experiment that engages physicians in a simulated perilous surgical procedure. It was demonstrated that a measurable amount of the participants' anxiety about patient outcomes was related to previous (experimentally created) regret and worry and ultimately caused the physicians to be led by their feelings over any information or guidelines provided during the mock surgery. Additionally, their emotional levels, adjusted along with the simulated patient status, suggest that anxiety level and the respective decision made are correlated with the type of bad outcome that was experienced in the earlier part of the experiment. Similarly, another view of anxiety and decision-making is dispositional anxiety where emotional states, or moods, are cognitive and provide information about future pitfalls and rewards (Maner and Schmidt, 2006). When experiencing anxiety, individuals draw from personal judgments referred to as pessimistic outcome appraisals. These emotions promote biases for risk avoidance and promote risk tolerance in decision-making.

## Dread Risk

It is common for people to dread some risks but not others: They tend to be very afraid of epidemic diseases, nuclear power plant failures, and plane accidents but are relatively unconcerned about some highly frequent and deadly events, such as traffic crashes, household accidents, and medical errors. One key distinction of dreadful risks seems to be their potential for catastrophic consequences, threatening to kill a large number of people within a short period of time. For example, immediately after the September 11 attacks, many Americans were afraid to fly and took their car instead, a decision that led to a significant increase in the number of fatal crashes in the time period following the 9/11 event compared with the same time period before the attacks.

Different hypotheses have been proposed to explain why people fear dread risks. First, the psychometric paradigm suggests that high lack of control, high catastrophic potential, and severe consequences account for the increased risk perception and anxiety associated with dread risks. Second, because people estimate the frequency of a risk by recalling instances of its occurrence from their social circle or the media, they may overvalue relatively rare but dramatic risks because of their overpresence and undervalue frequent, less dramatic risks. Third, according to the preparedness hypothesis, people are prone to fear events that have been particularly threatening to survival in human evolutionary history. Given that in most of human evolutionary history people lived in relatively small groups, rarely exceeding 100 people, a dread risk, which kills many people at once, could potentially wipe out one's whole group. Indeed, research found that people's fear peaks for risks killing around 100 people but does not increase if larger groups are killed. Fourth, fearing dread risks can be an ecologically rational strategy. Besides killing a large number of people at a single point in time, dread risks reduce the number of children and young adults who would have potentially produced offspring. Accordingly, people are more concerned about risks killing younger, and hence more fertile, groups.

## Anxiety and Judgmental Accuracy

The relationship between higher levels of risk perception and "judgmental accuracy" in anxious individuals remains unclear (Joseph I. Constans, 2001). There is a chance that "judgmental accuracy" is correlated with heightened anxiety. Constans conducted a study to examine how worry propensity (and current mood and trait anxiety) might influence college student's estimation of their performance on an upcoming exam, and the study found that worry propensity predicted subjective risk bias (errors in their risk assessments), even after variance attributable to current mood and trait anxiety had been removed. Another experiment suggests that trait anxiety is associated with pessimistic risk appraisals (heightened perceptions of the probability and degree of suffering associated with a negative experience), while controlling for depression.

## Risk in Auditing

The audit risk model expresses the risk of an auditor providing an inappropriate opinion of a commercial entity's financial statements. It can be analytically expressed as:

$$AR = IR \times CR \times DR$$

Where AR is *audit risk*, IR is *inherent risk*, CR is *control risk* and DR is *detection risk*.

## Risk and Uncertainty

In his seminal work *Risk, Uncertainty, and Profit*, Frank Knight (1921) established the distinction between risk and uncertainty.

... Uncertainty must be taken in a sense radically distinct from the familiar notion of Risk, from which it has never been properly separated. The term "risk," as loosely used in everyday speech and in economic discussion, really covers two things which, functionally at least, in their causal relations to the phenomena of economic organization, are categorically different. ... The essential fact is that "risk" means in some cases a quantity susceptible of measurement, while at other times it is something distinctly not of this character; and there are far-reaching and crucial differences in the bearings of the phenomenon depending on which of the two is really present and operating. ... It will appear that a measurable uncertainty, or "risk" proper, as we shall use the term, is so far different from an unmeasurable one that it is not in effect an uncertainty at all. We ... accordingly restrict the term "uncertainty" to cases of the non-quantitive type.:

Thus, Knightian uncertainty is immeasurable, not possible to calculate, while in the Knightian sense risk is measurable.

Another distinction between risk and uncertainty is proposed by Douglas Hubbard:

> Uncertainty: The lack of complete certainty, that is, the existence of more than one possibility. The "true" outcome/state/result/value is not known.
>
> Measurement of uncertainty: A set of probabilities assigned to a set of possibilities. Example: "There is a 60% chance this market will double in five years"
>
> Risk: A state of uncertainty where some of the possibilities involve a loss, catastrophe, or other undesirable outcome.
>
> Measurement of risk: A set of possibilities each with quantified probabilities and quantified losses. Example: "There is a 40% chance the proposed oil well will be dry with a loss of $12 million in exploratory drilling costs".

In this sense, one may have uncertainty without risk but not risk without uncertainty. We can be uncertain about the winner of a contest, but unless we have some personal stake in it, we have no risk. If we bet money on the outcome of the contest, then we have a risk. In both cases there are more than one outcome. The measure of uncertainty refers only to the probabilities assigned to outcomes, while the measure of risk requires both probabilities for outcomes and losses quantified for outcomes.

## Risk Attitude, Appetite and Tolerance

The terms attitude, appetite and tolerance are often used similarly to describe an organization's or individual's attitude towards risk taking. Risk averse, risk neutral and risk seeking are examples of the terms that may be used to describe a risk attitude. Risk tolerance looks at acceptable/unacceptable deviations from what is expected. Risk appetite looks at how much risk one is willing to accept. There can still be deviations that are within a risk appetite. For example, recent research finds that insured individuals are significantly likely to divest from risky asset holdings in response to a decline in health, controlling for variables such as income, age, and out-of-pocket medical expenses.

Gambling is a risk-increasing investment, wherein money on hand is risked for a possible large return, but with the possibility of losing it all. Purchasing a lottery ticket is a very risky investment with a high chance of no return and a small chance of a very high return. In contrast, putting money in a bank at a defined rate of interest is a risk-averse action that gives a guaranteed return of a small gain and precludes other investments with possibly higher gain. The possibility of getting no return on an investment is also known as the rate of ruin.

## Risk as a Vector Quantity

Hubbard also argues that defining risk as the product of impact and probability presumes (probably incorrectly) that the decision makers are risk neutral. Only for a risk neutral person is the "certain monetary equivalent" exactly equal to the probability of the loss times the amount of the loss. For example, a risk neutral person would consider 20% chance of winning $1 million exactly equal to $200,000 (or a 20% chance of losing $1 million to be exactly equal to losing $200,000). However, most decision makers are not actually risk neutral and would not consider these equivalent choices. This gave rise to Prospect theory and Cumulative prospect theory. Hubbard proposes instead that risk is a kind of "vector quantity" that does not collapse the probability and magnitude of a risk by presuming anything about the risk tolerance of the decision maker. Risks are simply described as a set or function of possible loss amounts each associated with specific probabilities. How this array is collapsed into a single value cannot be done until the risk tolerance of the decision maker is quantified.

Risk can be both negative and positive, but it tends to be the negative side that people focus on. This is because some things can be dangerous, such as putting their own or someone else's life at risk. Risks concern people as they think that they will have a negative effect on their future.

## Areas of Risk

## Business Risks

The term business risk refers to the possibility of inadequate profits or even losses due to uncertainties e.g., changes in tastes, preferences of consumers, strikes, increased competition, change in government policy, obsolescence etc .Every business organization contains various risk elements while doing the business. Business risks implies uncertainty in profits or danger of loss and the events that could pose a risk due to some unforeseen events in future, which causes business to fail.

For example, an owner of a business may face different risks like in production,risks due to irregular supply of raw materials, machinery breakdown, labor unrest, etc. In marketing, risks may arise due to different market price fluctuations, changing trends and fashions, error in sales forecasting, etc. In addition, there may be loss of assets of the firm due to fire, flood, earthquakes, riots or war and political unrest which may cause unwanted interruptions in the business operations. Thus business risks may take place in different forms depending upon the nature and size of the business.

Business risks can major by the influence by two major risks: internal risks (risks arising from the events taking place within the organization) and external risks (risks arising from the events taking place outside the organization).

Internal risks arise from factors (endogenous variables, which can be controlled) such as human factors (talent management, strikes), technological factors (emerging technologies), physical factors (failure of machines, fire or theft), operational factors (access to credit, cost cutting, advertisement). External risks arise from factors (exogenous variables, which cannot be controlled) such as economic factors (market risks, pricing pressure), natural factors (floods, earthquakes), political factors (compliance and regulations of government).

## Classification

The Business risk is classified into different 5 main types

1. Strategic Risk: They are the risks associated with the operations of that particular industry.These kind of risks arise from

    1. Business Environment: Buyers and sellers interacting to buy and sell goods and services, changes in supply and demand, competitive structures and introduction of new technologies.

    2. Transaction: Assets relocation of mergers and acquisitions, spin-offs, alliances and joint ventures.

    3. Investor Relations: Strategy for communicating with individuals who have invested in the business.

2. Financial Risk: These are the risks associated with the financial structure and transactions of the particular industry.

3. Operational Risk: These are the risks associated with the operational and administrative procedures of the particular industry.

4. Compliance Risk(Legal Risk): These are risks associated with the need to comply with the rules and regulations of the government.
5. Other risks: There would be different risks like natural disaster(floods) and others depend upon the nature and scale of the industry.

## Sampling Risk

Sampling risk is one of the many types of risks an auditor may face when performing the necessary procedure of audit sampling. Audit sampling exists because of the impractical and costly effects of examining all or 100% of a client's records or books. As a result, a "sample" of a client's accounts are examined. Due to the negative effects produced by sampling risk, an auditor may have to perform additional procedures which in turn can impact the overall efficiency of the audit.

Sampling risk represents the possibility that an auditor's conclusion based on a sample is different from that reached if the entire population were subject to audit procedure. The auditor may conclude that material misstatements exist, when in fact they do not; or material misstatements do not exist but in fact they do exist. Auditors can lower the sampling risk by increasing the sampling size.

Although there are many types of risks associated with the audit process, each type primarily has an effect on the overall audit engagement. The effects produced by sampling risk generally can increase audit risk, the risk that an entity's financial statements will contain a material misstatement, though given an unqualified ('clean') audit report. Sampling risk can also increase detection risk which suggests the possibility that an auditor will not find material misstatements relating to the financial statements through substantive tests and analysis.

## Types of Sampling Risk

## Typical Scenarios

Auditors must often make professional judgments in assessing sampling risk. When testing samples the auditor is primarily concerned with two aspects of sampling risk:

Risk of accepting incorrect data: the sample supports the conclusion that the recorded account balance is not materially misstated when it is materially misstated.

Risk of incorrect rejection: the risk that the sample supports the conclusion that the recorded amount balance is materially misstated when it is not materially misstated.

In addition, the auditor is concerned with sampling risk and its relationship with controls. Two types of sample risk/control risks are:

Assessing too low: the risk that the assessed level of control risk based on the sample is less than the true operating effectiveness of the control.

Assessing too high: the risk that the assessed level of control risk based on the sample is greater than the true operating effectiveness of the control.

## Sample Selection

When selecting a sampling approach there are two approaches to audit sampling: non-statistical and statistical approach. Three ways that statistical sampling can assist the auditor are: to maximize the productivity with minimum wasted effort in designing the sample, to measure the sufficiency of the evidence taken during the audit, and to analyze the results. The statistical approach allows the auditor to measure the risk that is being sampled to help in reducing it to an acceptable level. With respect to performing samples, statistical sampling involves different kinds of costs such as training the auditors, designing individual samples to meet the requirements, and choosing the items to be examined. If there is insufficient audit evidence it is the responsibility of the auditor to choose between non statistical or the statistical sampling approaches considering their effectiveness and related costs.

Although exercising careful judgment is crucial during every step of the sampling process, it is extremely necessary when choosing the non-statistical approach. This method does not include the use of tables or statistical percentages, but rather it relies upon professional judgment on the part of the auditor as well as the policy implemented by the firm. Under this approach, it is common practice for most CPA firms to create universal guidelines for auditors in order to determine a proper sample size. For example, if a given client's control risk is high, a firm would typically require a high sample size when selecting records.

In order to successfully gather a sample, it is important to consider the collection as a whole and the relevance of the particular items. The most common successful method is to select an even amount of items which accurately represents the list as a whole. Selecting only large or small amounts could distort the sample which creates risk.

## Financial Risk

Financial risk is an umbrella term for multiple types of risk associated with financing, including financial transactions that include company loans in risk of default. Risk is a term often used to imply downside risk, meaning the uncertainty of a return and the potential for financial loss.

A science has evolved around managing market and financial risk under the general title of modern portfolio theory initiated by Dr. Harry Markowitz in 1952 with his article, "Portfolio Selection". In modern portfolio theory, the variance (or standard deviation) of a portfolio is used as the definition of risk.

# Types of Risk

## Asset-backed Risk

Risk that the changes in one or more assets that support an asset-backed security will significantly impact the value of the supported security. Risks include interest rate, term modification, and prepayment risk.

## Credit Risk

Credit risk, also called *default risk*, is the risk associated with a borrower going into default (not making payments as promised). Investor losses include lost principal and interest, decreased cash flow, and increased collection costs. An investor can also assume credit risk through direct or indirect use of leverage. For example, an investor may purchase an investment using margin. Or an investment may directly or indirectly use or rely on repo, forward commitment, or derivative instruments.

## Foreign Investment Risk

Risk of rapid and extreme changes in value due to: smaller markets; differing accounting, reporting, or auditing standards; nationalization, expropriation or confiscatory taxation; economic conflict; or political or diplomatic changes. Valuation, liquidity, and regulatory issues may also add to foreign investment risk.

## Liquidity Risk

This is the risk that a given security or asset cannot be traded quickly enough in the market to prevent a loss (or make the required profit). There are two types of liquidity risk:

- *Asset liquidity* - An asset cannot be sold due to lack of liquidity in the market - essentially a sub-set of market risk. This can be accounted for by:
    - Widening bid-offer spread
    - Making explicit liquidity reserves
    - Lengthening holding period for VaR calculations
- *Funding liquidity* - Risk that liabilities:
    - Cannot be met when they fall due
    - Can only be met at an uneconomic price
    - Can be name-specific or systemic

## Market Risk

The four standard market risk factors are equity risk, interest rate risk, currency risk, and commodity risk:

- Equity risk is the risk that stock prices in general (not related to a particular company or industry) or the implied volatility will change.
- Interest rate risk is the risk that interest rates or the implied volatility will change.
- Currency risk is the risk that foreign exchange rates or the implied volatility will change, which affects, for example, the value of an asset held in that currency.
- Commodity risk is the risk that commodity prices (e.g. corn, copper, crude oil) or implied volatility will change.

## Operational Risk

## Other Risks

- Reputational risk
- Legal risk
- IT risk

## Model Risk

## Diversification

Financial risk, market risk, and even inflation risk, can at least partially be moderated by forms of diversification.

The returns from different assets are highly unlikely to be perfectly correlated and the correlation may sometimes be negative. For instance, an increase in the price of oil will often favour a company that produces it, but negatively impact the business of a firm such an airline whose variable costs are heavily based upon fuel. However, share prices are driven by many factors, such as the general health of the economy which will increase the correlation and reduce the benefit of diversification. If one constructs a portfolio by including a wide variety of equities, it will tend to exhibit the same risk and return characteristics as the market as a whole, which many investors see as an attractive prospect, so that index funds have been developed that invest in equities in proportion to the weighting they have in some well known index such as the FTSE.

However, history shows that even over substantial periods of time there is a wide range of returns that an index fund may experience; so an index fund by itself is not "fully diversified". Greater diversification can be obtained by diversifying across asset classes; for instance a portfolio of many bonds and many equities can be constructed in order to further narrow the dispersion of possible portfolio outcomes.

A key issue in diversification is the correlation between assets, the benefits increasing with lower correlation. However this is not an observable quantity, since the future return on any asset can never be known with complete certainty. This was a serious issue in the Late-2000s recession when assets that had previously had small or even negative correlations suddenly starting moving in the same direction causing severe financial stress to market participants who had believed that their diversification would protect them against any plausible market conditions, including funds that had been explicitly set up to avoid being affected in this way

Diversification has costs. Correlations must be identified and understood, and since they are not constant it may be necessary to rebalance the portfolio which incurs transaction costs due to buying and selling assets. There is also the risk that as an investor or fund manager diversifies their ability to monitor and understand the assets may decline leading to the possibility of losses due to poor decisions or unforeseen correlations.

## Hedging

Hedging is a method for reducing risk where a combination of assets are selected to offset the movements of each other. For instance when investing in a stock it is possible to buy an option to sell that stock at a defined price at some point in the future. The combined portfolio of stock and option is now much less likely to move below a given value. As in diversification there is a cost, this time in buying the option for which there is a premium. Derivatives are used extensively to mitigate many types of risk.

## Financial / Credit Risk Related Acronyms

ACPM Active credit portfolio management

EAD Exposure at default

EL Expected loss

LGD Loss given default

PD Probability of default

KMV quantitative credit analysis solution developed by credit rating agency Moody's

VaR value at risk, a common methodology for measuring risk due to market movements

## Operational Risk

Operational risk is "the risk of a change in value caused by the fact that actual losses, incurred for inadequate or failed internal processes, people and systems, or from external events (including legal risk), differ from the expected losses". This definition, adopted by the European union Solvency II Directive for insurers, is a variation from that adopted in the Basel II regulations for banks. In October 2014, the Basel Committee on Banking Supervision proposed a revision to its operational risk capital framework that sets out a new standardized approach to replace the basic indicator approach and the standardized approach for calculating operational risk capital.

It can also include other classes of risk, such as fraud, security, privacy protection, legal risks, physical (e.g. infrastructure shutdown) or environmental risks.

Operational risk is a broad discipline, close to good management and quality management.

In similar fashion, operational risks affect client satisfaction, reputation and shareholder value, all while increasing business volatility.

Contrary to other risks (e.g. credit risk, market risk, insurance risk) operational risks are usually not willingly incurred nor are they revenue driven. Moreover, they are not diversifiable and cannot be laid off, meaning that, as long as people, systems and processes remain imperfect, operational risk cannot be fully eliminated.

Operational risk is, nonetheless, manageable as to keep losses within some level of risk tolerance (i.e. the amount of risk one is prepared to accept in pursuit of his objectives), determined by balancing the costs of improvement against the expected benefits.

Wider trends such as globalization, the expansion of the internet and the rise of social media, as well as the increasing demands for greater corporate accountability worldwide, reinforce the need for proper operational risk management.

## Background

Until Basel II reforms to banking supervision, operational risk was a residual category reserved for risks and uncertainties which were difficult to quantify and manage in traditional ways - the "other risks" basket.

Such regulations institutionalized operational risk as a category of regulatory and managerial attention and connected operational risk management with good corporate governance.

Of course, businesses in general, and other institutions such as the military, have been aware, for many years, of hazards arising from operational factors, internal or external. The primary goal of the military is to fight and win wars in quick and decisive fashion, and with minimal losses. For the military, and the businesses of the world alike, operational risk management is an effective process for preserving resources by anticipation.

Two decades (from 1980 to the early 2000s) of globalization and deregulation (e.g. Big Bang (financial markets)), combined with the increased sophistication of financial services around the world, have introduced additional complexities into the activities of banks, insurers and firms in general and therefore their risk profiles.

Since the mid-1990s, the topics of market risk and credit risk have been the subject of much debate and research, with the result that financial institutions have made significant progress in the identification, measurement and management of both these forms of risk.

However, the near collapse of the U.S. financial system in September 2008 is an indication that our ability to measure market and credit risk is far from perfect and eventually led to introduction of new regulatory requirements worldwide, including Basel III regulations for banks and Solvency II regulations for insurers.

Events such as the September 11 terrorist attacks, rogue trading losses at Société Générale, Barings, AIB, UBS and National Australia Bank serve to highlight the fact that the scope of risk management extends beyond merely market and credit risk.

These reasons underscore banks' and supervisors' growing focus upon the identification and measurement of operational risk.

The list of risks (and, more importantly, the scale of these risks) faced by banks today includes fraud, system failures, terrorism and employee compensation claims. These types of risk are generally classified under the term 'operational risk'.

The identification and measurement of operational risk is a real and live issue for modern-day banks, particularly since the decision by the Basel Committee on Banking Supervision (BCBS) to introduce a capital charge for this risk as part of the new capital adequacy framework (Basel II).

## Definition

The Basel II Committee defines operational risk as:

"The risk of loss resulting from inadequate or failed internal processes, people and systems or from external events."

However, the Basel Committee recognizes that operational risk is a term that has a variety of meanings and therefore, for internal purposes, banks are permitted to adopt their own definitions of operational risk, provided that the minimum elements in the Committee's definition are included.

## Scope Exclusions

The Basel II definition of operational risk excludes, for example, strategic risk - the risk of a loss arising from a poor strategic business decision.

Other risk terms are seen as potential consequences of operational risk events. For example, reputational risk (damage to an organization through loss of its reputation or standing) can arise as a consequence (or impact) of operational failures - as well as from other events.

## Basel II Seven Event Type Categories

The following lists the official Basel II defines the seven event types with some examples for each category:

1. Internal Fraud - misappropriation of assets, tax evasion, intentional mismarking of positions, bribery
2. External Fraud - theft of information, hacking damage, third-party theft and forgery
3. Employment Practices and Workplace Safety - discrimination, workers compensation, employee health and safety
4. Clients, Products, and Business Practice - market manipulation, antitrust, improper trade, product defects, fiduciary breaches, account churning
5. Damage to Physical Assets - natural disasters, terrorism, vandalism
6. Business Disruption and Systems Failures - utility disruptions, software failures, hardware failures
7. Execution, Delivery, and Process Management - data entry errors, accounting errors, failed mandatory reporting, negligent loss of client assets

## Difficulties

It is relatively straightforward for an organization to set and observe specific, measurable levels of market risk and credit risk because models exist which attempt to predict the potential impact of market movements, or changes in the cost of credit. It should be noted however that these models are only as good as the underlying assumptions, and a large part of the recent financial crisis arose because the valuations generated by these models for particular types of investments were based on incorrect assumptions.

By contrast it is relatively difficult to identify or assess levels of operational risk and its many sources. Historically organizations have accepted operational risk as an unavoidable cost of doing business. Many now though collect data on operational losses - for example through system failure or fraud - and are using this data to model operational risk and to calculate a capital reserve against future operational losses. In addition to the Basel II requirement for banks, this is now a requirement for European insurance firms who are in the process of implementing Solvency II, the equivalent of Basel II for the banking sector.

## Methods of Operational Risk Management

Basel II and various Supervisory bodies of the countries have prescribed various soundness standards for Operational Risk Management for Banks and similar Financial Institutions. To complement these standards, Basel II has given guidance to 3 broad methods of Capital calculation for Operational Risk

- Basic Indicator Approach - based on annual revenue of the Financial Institution
- Standardized Approach - based on annual revenue of each of the broad business lines of the Financial Institution
- Advanced Measurement Approaches - based on the internally developed risk measurement framework of the bank adhering to the standards prescribed (methods include IMA, LDA, Scenario-based, Scorecard etc.)

The Operational Risk Management framework should include identification, measurement, monitoring, reporting, control and mitigation frameworks for Operational Risk.

## IT Risk

Information technology risk, or IT risk, IT-related risk, is any risk related to information technology. While information has long been appreciated as a valuable and important asset, the rise of the knowledge economy has led to organizations becoming increasingly dependent on information, information processing and especially IT. Various events or incidents that compromise IT in some way can therefore cause adverse impacts on the organization's business processes or mission, ranging from inconsequential to catastrophic in scale.

Assessing the probability of likelihood of various types of event/incident with their predicted impacts or consequences should they occur is a common way to assess and measure IT risks. Alternative methods of measuring IT risk typically involve assessing other contributory factors such as the threats, vulnerabilities, exposures, and asset values.

## Definitions of IT Risk

### ISO

IT risk: *the potential that a given threat will exploit vulnerabilities of an asset or group of assets and thereby cause harm to the organization. It is measured in terms of a combination of the probability of occurrence of an event and its consequence.*

## Committee on National Security Systems

The Committee on National Security Systems of United States of America defined risk in different documents:

- From CNSS Instruction No. 4009 dated 26 April 2010 the basic and more technical focused definition:

  *Risk - Possibility that a particular threat will adversely impact an IS by exploiting a particular vulnerability.*

- National Security Telecommunications and Information Systems Security Instruction (NSTISSI) No. 1000, introduces a probability aspect, quite similar to NIST SP 800-30 one:

  *Risk - A combination of the likelihood that a threat will occur, the likelihood that a threat occurrence will result in an adverse impact, and the severity of the resulting impact*

National Information Assurance Training and Education Center defines risk in the IT field as:

1. The loss potential that exists as the result of threat-vulnerability pairs. Reducing either the threat or the vulnerability reduces the risk.
2. The uncertainty of loss expressed in terms of probability of such loss.
3. The probability that a hostile entity will successfully exploit a particular telecommunications or COMSEC system for intelligence purposes; its factors are threat and vulnerability.
4. A combination of the likelihood that a threat shall occur, the likelihood that a threat occurrence shall result in an adverse impact, and the severity of the resulting adverse impact.
5. the probability that a particular threat will exploit a particular vulnerability of the system.

## NIST

Many NIST publications define risk in IT context in different publications: FISMApedia term provide a list. Between them:

- According to NIST SP 800-30:

*Risk is a function of the likelihood of a given threat-source's exercising a particular potential vulnerability, and the resulting impact of that adverse event on the organization.*

- From NIST FIPS 200

  Risk - The level of impact on organizational operations (including mission, functions, image, or reputation), organizational assets, or individuals resulting from the operation of an information system given the potential impact of a threat and the likelihood of that threat occurring.

NIST SP 800-30 defines:

IT-related risk

*The net mission impact considering:*

1. *the probability that a particular threat-source will exercise (accidentally trigger or intentionally exploit) a particular information system vulnerability and*
2. *the resulting impact if this should occur. IT-related risks arise from legal liability or mission loss due to:*
    1. *Unauthorized (malicious or accidental) disclosure, modification, or destruction of information*
    2. *Unintentional errors and omissions*
    3. *IT disruptions due to natural or man-made disasters*
    4. *Failure to exercise due care and diligence in the implementation and operation of the IT system.*

## Risk Management Insight

IT risk is the probable frequency and probable magnitude of future loss.

## ISACA

ISACA published the Risk IT Framework in order to provides an end-to-end, comprehensive view of all risks related to the use of IT. There, IT risk is defined as:

*The business risk associated with the use, ownership, operation, involvement, influence and adoption of IT within an enterprise*

According to Risk IT, IT risk has a broader meaning: it encompasses not just only the negative impact of operations and service delivery which can bring destruction or reduction of the value of the organization, but also the benefit\value enabling risk associated to missing opportunities to use technology to enable or enhance business or the IT project management for aspects like overspending or late delivery with adverse business impact

## Measuring IT Risk

It is useful to introduce related terms, to properly measure IT risk.

Information security event

> *An identified occurrence of a system, service or network state indicating a possible breach of information security policy or failure of safeguards, or a previously unknown situation that may be security relevant.*
>
> *Occurrence of a particular set of circumstances*
>
> - *The event can be certain or uncertain.*
> - *The event can be a single occurrence or a series of occurrences. :(ISO/IEC Guide 73)*

Information security incident

> *is indicated by a single or a series of unwanted information security events that have a significant probability of compromising business operations and threatening information security*
>
> *An event [G.11] that has been assessed as having an actual or potentially adverse effect on the security or performance of a system.*

Impact

> The result of an unwanted incident [G.17].(ISO/IEC PDTR 13335-1)

Consequence

> *Outcome of an event [G.11]*
>
> - *There can be more than one consequence from one event.*
> - *Consequences can range from positive to negative.*
> - *Consequences can be expressed qualitatively or quantitatively (ISO/IEC Guide 73)*

The risk R is the product of the likelihood L of a security incident occurring times the impact I that will be incurred to the organization due to the incident, that is:

$R = L \times I$

The likelihood of a security incident occurrence is a function of the likelihood that a threat appears and the likelihood that the threat can successfully exploit the relevant system vulnerabilities.

The consequence of the occurrence of a security incident are a function of likely impact that the incident will have on the organization as a result of the harm the organization assets will sustain. Harm is related to the value of the assets to the organization; the same asset can have different values to different organizations.

So R can be function of four factors:

- A = Value of the assets
- T = the likelihood of the threat
- V = the nature of vulnerability i.e. the likelihood that can be exploited (proportional to the potential benefit for the attacker and inversely proportional to the cost of exploitation)
- I = the likely impact, the extent of the harm

If numerical values (money for impact and probabilities for the other factors), the risk can be expressed in monetary terms and compared to the cost of countermeasures and the residual risk after applying the security control. It is not always practical to express this values, so in the first step of risk evaluation, risk are graded dimensionless in three or five steps scales.

OWASP proposes a practical risk measurement guideline based on:

- Estimation of Likelihood as a mean between different factors in a 0 to 9 scale:
    - Threat agent factors
        - Skill level: How technically skilled is this group of threat agents? No technical skills (1), some technical skills (3), advanced computer user (4), network and programming skills (6), security penetration skills (9)
        - Motive: How motivated is this group of threat agents to find and exploit this vulnerability? Low or no reward (1), possible reward (4), high reward (9)
        - Opportunity: What resources and opportunity are required for this group of threat agents to find and exploit this vulnerability? full access or expensive resources required (0), special access or resources required (4), some access or resources required (7), no

access or resources required (9)

- Size: How large is this group of threat agents? Developers (2), system administrators (2), intranet users (4), partners (5), authenticated users (6), anonymous Internet users (9)

- Vulnerability Factors: the next set of factors are related to the vulnerability involved. The goal here is to estimate the likelihood of the particular vulnerability involved being discovered and exploited. Assume the threat agent selected above.

  - Ease of discovery: How easy is it for this group of threat agents to discover this vulnerability? Practically impossible (1), difficult (3), easy (7), automated tools available (9)

  - Ease of exploit: How easy is it for this group of threat agents to actually exploit this vulnerability? Theoretical (1), difficult (3), easy (5), automated tools available (9)

  - Awareness: How well known is this vulnerability to this group of threat agents? Unknown (1), hidden (4), obvious (6), public knowledge (9)

  - Intrusion detection: How likely is an exploit to be detected? Active detection in application (1), logged and reviewed (3), logged without review (8), not logged (9)

- Estimation of Impact as a mean between different factors in a 0 to 9 scale

  - Technical Impact Factors; technical impact can be broken down into factors aligned with the traditional security areas of concern: confidentiality, integrity, availability, and accountability. The goal is to estimate the magnitude of the impact on the system if the vulnerability were to be exploited.

    - Loss of confidentiality: How much data could be disclosed and how sensitive is it? Minimal non-sensitive data disclosed (2), minimal critical data disclosed (6), extensive non-sensitive data disclosed (6), extensive critical data disclosed (7), all data disclosed (9)

    - Loss of integrity: How much data could be corrupted and how damaged is it? Minimal slightly corrupt data (1), minimal seriously corrupt data (3), extensive slightly corrupt data (5), extensive seriously corrupt data (7), all data totally corrupt (9)

        - Loss of availability How much service could be lost and how vital is it? Minimal secondary services interrupted (1), minimal primary services interrupted (5), extensive secondary services interrupted (5), extensive primary services interrupted (7), all services completely lost (9)

        - Loss of accountability: Are the threat agents' actions traceable to an individual? Fully traceable (1), possibly traceable (7), completely anonymous (9)

    - Business Impact Factors: The business impact stems from the technical impact, but requires a deep understanding of what is important to the company running the application. In general, you should be aiming to support your risks with business impact, particularly if your audience is executive level. The business risk is what justifies investment in fixing security problems.

        - Financial damage: How much financial damage will result from an exploit? Less than the cost to fix the vulnerability (1), minor effect on annual profit (3), significant effect on annual profit (7), bankruptcy (9)

        - Reputation damage: Would an exploit result in reputation damage that would harm the business? Minimal damage (1), Loss of major accounts (4), loss of goodwill (5), brand damage (9)

        - Non-compliance: How much exposure does non-compliance introduce? Minor violation (2), clear violation (5), high-profile violation (7)

        - Privacy violation: How much personally identifiable information could be disclosed? One individual (3), hundreds of people (5), thousands of people (7), millions of people (9)

    - If the business impact is calculated accurately use it in the following otherwise use the Technical impact

- Rate likelihood and impact in a LOW, MEDIUM, HIGH scale assuming that less than 3 is LOW, 3 to less than 6 is MEDIUM, and 6 to 9 is HIGH.

- Calculate the risk using the following table

| Overall Risk Severity | | | | |
|---|---|---|---|---|
| Impact | HIGH | Medium | High | Critical |
| | MEDIUM | Low | Medium | High |
| | LOW | None | Low | Medium |
| | | LOW | MEDIUM | HIGH |
| | Likelihood | | | |

## IT Risk Management

Risk Management Elements

IT risk management can be considered a component of a wider enterprise risk management system.(faisal)

The establishment, maintenance and continuous update of an ISMS provide a strong indication that a company is using a systematic approach for the identification, assessment and management of information security risks.

Different methodologies have been proposed to manage IT risks, each of them divided in processes and steps.

The Certified Information Systems Auditor Review Manual 2006 produced by ISACA, an international professional association focused on IT Governance, provides the following definition of risk management: *"Risk management is the process of identifying vulnerabilities and threats to the information resources used by an organization in achieving business objectives, and deciding what countermeasures, if any, to take in reducing risk to an acceptable level, based on the value of the information resource to the organization."*

## IT Risk Laws and Regulations

In the following a brief description of applicable rules organized by source.

## United Nations

United Nations issued the following:

- UN Guidelines concerning computerized personal data files of 14 December 1990 Generic data processing activities using digital processing methods. Nonbinding guideline to UN nations calling for national regulation in this field

## OECD

OECD issued the following:

- Organisation for Economic Co-operation and Development (OECD) Recommendation of the Council concerning guidelines governing the protection of privacy and trans-border flows of personal data (23 September 1980)
- OECD Guidelines for the Security of Information Systems and Networks: Towards a Culture of Security (25 July 2002). Topic: General information security. Scope: Non binding guidelines to any OECD entities (governments, businesses, other organisations and individual users who develop, own, provide, manage, service, and use information systems and networks). The OECD Guidelines state the basic principles underpinning risk management and information security practices. While no part of the text is binding as such, non-compliance with any of the principles is indicative of a serious breach of RM/RA good practices that can potentially incur liability.

## European Union

The European Union issued the following, divided by topic:

- Privacy
    - Regulation (EC) No 45/2001 on the protection of individuals with regard to the processing of personal data by the Community institutions and bodies and on the free movement of such data provide an internal regulation which is a practical application of the principles of the Privacy Directive described below. Furthermore, article 35 of the Regulation requires the Community institutions and bodies to take similar precautions with regard to their telecommunications infrastructure, and to properly inform the users of any specific risks of security breaches.
    - Directive 95/46/EC on the protection of individuals with regard to the processing of personal data and on the free movement of such data require that any personal data processing activity undergoes a prior risk analysis in order to determine the privacy implications of the activity, and to determine the appropriate legal, technical and organisation measures to protect such activities;is effectively protected by such measures, which must be state of the art keeping into account the sensitivity

and privacy implications of the activity (including when a third party is charged with the processing task) is notified to a national data protection authority, including the measures taken to ensure the security of the activity. Furthermore, article 25 and following of the Directive requires Member States to ban the transfer of personal data to non-Member States, unless such countries have provided adequate legal protection for such personal data, or barring certain other exceptions.

- Commission Decision 2001/497/EC of 15 June 2001 on standard contractual clauses for the transfer of personal data to third countries, under Directive 95/46/EC; and Commission Decision 2004/915/EC of 27 December 2004 amending Decision 2001/497/EC as regards the introduction of an alternative set of standard contractual clauses for the transfer of personal data to third countries. Topic: Export of personal data to third countries, specifically non-E.U. countries which have not been recognised as having a data protection level that is adequate (i.e. equivalent to that of the E.U.). Both Commission Decisions provide a set of voluntary model clauses which can be used to export personal data from a data controller (who is subject to E.U. data protection rules) to a data processor outside the E.U. who is not subject to these rules or to a similar set of adequate rules.
- International Safe Harbor Privacy Principles
- Directive 2002/58/EC of 12 July 2002 concerning the processing of personal data and the protection of privacy in the electronic communications sector

- National Security
  - Directive 2006/24/EC of 15 March 2006 on the retention of data generated or processed in connection with the provision of publicly available electronic communications services or of public communications networks and amending Directive 2002/58/EC ('Data Retention Directive'). Topic: Requirement for the providers of public electronic telecommunications service providers to retain certain information for the purposes of the investigation, detection and prosecution of serious crime
  - Council Directive 2008/114/EC of 8 December 2008 on the identification and designation of European critical infrastructures and the assessment of the need to improve their protection. Topic: Identification and protection of European Critical Infrastructures. Scope: Applicable to Member States and to the operators of European Critical Infrastructure (defined by the draft directive as 'critical infrastructures the disruption or destruction of which would significantly affect two or more Member States, or a single Member State if the critical infrastructure is located

in another Member State. This includes effects resulting from cross-sector dependencies on other types of infrastructure'). Requires Member States to identify critical infrastructures on their territories, and to designate them as ECIs. Following this designation, the owners/operators of ECIs are required to create Operator Security Plans (OSPs), which should establish relevant security solutions for their protection

- Civil and Penal law
  - Council Framework Decision 2005/222/JHA of 24 February 2005 on attacks against information systems. Topic: General decision aiming to harmonise national provisions in the field of cyber crime, encompassing material criminal law (i.e. definitions of specific crimes), procedural criminal law (including investigative measures and international cooperation) and liability issues. Scope: Requires Member States to implement the provisions of the Framework Decision in their national legal frameworks. Framework decision is relevant to RM/RA because it contains the conditions under which legal liability can be imposed on legal entities for conduct of certain natural persons of authority within the legal entity. Thus, the Framework decision requires that the conduct of such figures within an organisation is adequately monitored, also because the Decision states that a legal entity can be held liable for acts of omission in this regard.

## Council of Europe

- Council of Europe Convention on Cybercrime, Budapest, 23.XI.2001, European Treaty Series-No. 185. Topic: General treaty aiming to harmonise national provisions in the field of cyber crime, encompassing material criminal law (i.e. definitions of specific crimes), procedural criminal law (including investigative measures and international cooperation), liability issues and data retention. Apart from the definitions of a series of criminal offences in articles 2 to 10, the Convention is relevant to RM/RA because it states the conditions under which legal liability can be imposed on legal entities for conduct of certain natural persons of authority within the legal entity. Thus, the Convention requires that the conduct of such figures within an organisation is adequately monitored, also because the Convention states that a legal entity can be held liable for acts of omission in this regard.

## USA

United States issued the following, divided by topic:

- Civil and Penal law

  - Amendments to the Federal Rules of Civil Procedure with regard to electronic discovery. Topic: U.S. Federal rules with regard to the production of electronic documents in civil proceedings. The discovery rules allow a party in civil proceedings to demand that the opposing party produce all relevant documentation (to be defined by the requesting party) in its possession, so as to allow the parties and the court to correctly assess the matter. Through the e-discovery amendment, which entered into force on 1 December 2006, such information may now include electronic information. This implies that any party being brought before a U.S. court in civil proceedings can be asked to produce such documents, which includes finalised reports, working documents, internal memos and e-mails with regard to a specific subject, which may or may not be specifically delineated. Any party whose activities imply a risk of being involved in such proceedings must therefore take adequate precautions for the management of such information, including the secure storage. Specifically: The party must be capable of initiating a 'litigation hold', a technical/organisational measure which must ensure that no relevant information can be modified any longer in any way. Storage policies must be responsible: while deletion of specific information of course remains allowed when this is a part of general information management policies ('routine, good-faith operation of the information system', Rule 37 (f)), the wilful destruction of potentially relevant information can be punished by extremely high fines (in one specific case of 1.6 billion US$). Thus, in practice, any businesses who risk civil litigation before U.S. courts must implement adequate information management policies, and must implement the necessary measures to initiate a litigation hold.

- Privacy

  - Gramm–Leach–Bliley Act (GLBA)

  - USA PATRIOT Act, Title III

  - Health Insurance Portability and Accountability Act (HIPAA) From an RM/RA perspective, the Act is particularly known for its provisions with regard to Administrative Simplification (Title II of HIPAA). This title required the U.S. Department of Health and Human Services (HHS) to draft specific rule sets, each of which would provide specific standards which would improve the efficiency of the health care system and prevent abuse. As a result, the HHS has adopted five principal rules: the Privacy Rule, the Transactions and Code Sets Rule, the Unique Identifiers Rule, the Enforcement Rule, and the Security Rule. The latter, published in the Federal Register on 20 February 2003 (see: http://www.cms.hhs.gov/SecurityStandard/Downloads/securityfinalrule.pdf), is specifically relevant, as it specifies a series of administrative, technical, and physical security procedures to assure the confidentiality of electronic protected health information. These aspects have been further outlined in a set of Security Standards on Administrative, Physical, Organisational and Technical Safeguards, all of which have been published, along with a guidance document on the basics of HIPAA risk management and risk assessment <http://www.cms.hhs.gov/EducationMaterials/04_SecurityMaterials.asp>. European or other countries health care service providers will generally not be affected by HIPAA obligations if they are not active on the U.S. market. However, since their data processing activities are subject to similar obligations under general European law (including the Privacy Directive), and since the underlying trends of modernisation and evolution towards electronic health files are the same, the HHS safeguards can be useful as an initial yardstick for measuring RM/RA strategies put in place by European health care service providers, specifically with regard to the processing of electronic health information. HIPAA security standards include the following:

- Administrative safeguards:
    - Security Management Process
    - Assigned Security Responsibility
    - Workforce Security
    - Information Access Management
    - Security Awareness and Training
    - Security Incident Procedures
    - Contingency Plan
    - Evaluation
    - Business Associate Contracts and Other Arrangements
- Physical safeguards
    - Facility Access Controls
    - Workstation Use
    - Workstation Security
    - Device and Media Controls

            - Technical safeguards
                - Access Control
                - Audit Controls
                - Integrity
                - Person or Entity Authentication
                - Transmission Security
            - Organisational requirements
                - Business Associate Contracts & Other Arrangements
                - Requirements for Group Health Plans
    - International Safe Harbor Privacy Principles issued by the US Department of Commerce on July 21, 2000 Export of personal data from a data controller who is subject to E.U. privacy regulations to a U.S. based destination; before personal data may be exported from an entity subject to E.U. privacy regulations to a destination subject to U.S. law, the European entity must ensure that the receiving entity provides adequate safeguards to protect such data against a number of mishaps. One way of complying with this obligation is to require the receiving entity to join the Safe Harbor, by requiring that the entity self-certifies its compliance with the so-called Safe Harbor Principles. If this road is chosen, the data controller exporting the data must verify that the U.S. destination is indeed on the Safe Harbor list
- Sarbanes–Oxley Act
- FISMA

## Standards Organizations and Standards

- International standard bodies:
    - International Organization for Standardization - ISO
    - Payment Card Industry Security Standards Council
    - Information Security Forum
    - The Open Group
- United States standard bodies:

  - National Institute of Standards and Technology - NIST
  - Federal Information Processing Standards - FIPS by NIST devoted to Federal Government and Agencies
- UK standard bodies
  - British Standard Institute

## Short Description of Standards

The list is chiefly based on:

## ISO

- ISO/IEC 13335-1:2004 - Information technology—Security techniques—Management of information and communications technology security—Part 1: Concepts and models for information and communications technology security management Standard containing generally accepted descriptions of concepts and models for information and communications technology security management. The standard is a commonly used code of practice, and serves as a resource for the implementation of security management practices and as a yardstick for auditing such practices.
- ISO/IEC TR 15443-1:2005 – Information technology—Security techniques—A framework for IT security assurance. Topic: Security assurance – the Technical Report (TR) contains generally accepted guidelines which can be used to determine an appropriate assurance method for assessing a security service, product or environmental factor
- ISO/IEC 15816:2002 - Information technology—Security techniques—Security information objects for access control. Topic: Security management – Access control. The standard allows security professionals to rely on a specific set of syntactic definitions and explanations with regard to SIOs, thus avoiding duplication or divergence in other standardisation efforts.
- ISO/IEC TR 15947:2002 - Information technology—Security techniques—IT intrusion detection framework. Topic: Security management – Intrusion detection in IT systems. The standard allows security professionals to rely on a specific set of concepts and methodologies for describing and assessing security risks with regard to potential intrusions in IT systems. It does not contain any RM/RA obligations as such, but it is rather a tool for facilitating RM/RA activities in the affected field.
- ISO/IEC 15408-1/2/3:2005 - Information technology — Security techniques — Evaluation criteria for IT security — Part 1: Introduction and general model

(15408-1) Part 2: Security functional requirements (15408-2) Part 3: Security assurance requirements (15408-3). Standard containing a common set of requirements for the security functions of IT products and systems and for assurance measures applied to them during a security evaluation. Scope: Publicly available ISO standard, which can be voluntarily implemented. The text is a resource for the evaluation of the security of IT products and systems, and can thus be used as a tool for RM/RA. The standard is commonly used as a resource for the evaluation of the security of IT products and systems; including (if not specifically) for procurement decisions with regard to such products. The standard can thus be used as an RM/RA tool to determine the security of an IT product or system during its design, manufacturing or marketing, or before procuring it.

- ISO/IEC 17799:2005 - Information technology—Security techniques—Code of practice for information security management. Topic: Standard containing generally accepted guidelines and general principles for initiating, implementing, maintaining, and improving information security management in an organization, including business continuity management. The standard is a commonly used code of practice, and serves as a resource for the implementation of information security management practices and as a yardstick for auditing such practices.
- ISO/IEC TR 15446:2004 – Information technology—Security techniques—Guide for the production of Protection Profiles and Security Targets. Technical Report (TR) containing guidelines for the construction of Protection Profiles (PPs) and Security Targets (STs) that are intended to be compliant with ISO/IEC 15408 (the "Common Criteria"). The standard is predominantly used as a tool for security professionals to develop PPs and STs, but can also be used to assess the validity of the same (by using the TR as a yardstick to determine if its standards have been obeyed). Thus, it is a (nonbinding) normative tool for the creation and assessment of RM/RA practices.
- ISO/IEC 18028:2006 - Information technology—Security techniques—IT network security. However, the standard is not free of charge, and its provisions are not publicly available. For this reason, specific provisions cannot be quoted). Topic: Five part standard (ISO/IEC 18028-1 to 18028-5) containing generally accepted guidelines on the security aspects of the management, operation and use of information technology networks. The standard is considered an extension of the guidelines provided in ISO/IEC 13335 and ISO/IEC 17799 focusing specifically on network security risks. The standard is a commonly used code of practice, and serves as a resource for the implementation of security management practices and as a yardstick for auditing such practices.

- ISO/IEC 27001:2005 - Information technology—Security techniques—Information security management systems—Requirements Topic: Standard containing generally accepted guidelines for the implementation of an Information Security Management System within any given organisation. Scope: Not publicly available ISO standard, which can be voluntarily implemented. While not legally binding, the text contains direct guidelines for the creation of sound information security practices The standard is a very commonly used code of practice, and serves as a resource for the implementation of information security management systems and as a yardstick for auditing such systems and/or the surrounding practices. Its application in practice is often combined with related standards.

- ISO/IEC 27001:2013, the updated standard for information security management systems.

- ISO/IEC TR 18044:2004 – Information technology—Security techniques—Information security incident management. Topic: Technical Report (TR) containing generally accepted guidelines and general principles for information security incident management in an organization.Scope: Not publicly available ISO TR, which can be voluntarily used.While not legally binding, the text contains direct guidelines for incident management. The standard is a high level resource introducing basic concepts and considerations in the field of incident response. As such, it is mostly useful as a catalyst to awareness raising initiatives in this regard.

- ISO/IEC 18045:2005 - Information technology—Security techniques—Methodology for IT security evaluation. Standard containing auditing guidelines for assessment of compliance with ISO/IEC 15408 (Information technology—Security techniques—Evaluation criteria for IT security) Scope Publicly available ISO standard, to be followed when evaluating compliance with ISO/IEC 15408 (Information technology—Security techniques—Evaluation criteria for IT security). The standard is a 'companion document', which is thus primarily of used for security professionals involved in evaluating compliance with ISO/IEC 15408 (Information technology—Security techniques—Evaluation criteria for IT security). Since it describes minimum actions to be performed by such auditors, compliance with ISO/IEC 15408 is impossible if ISO/IEC 18045 has been disregarded.

- ISO/TR 13569:2005 - Financial services—Information security guidelines. Topic: Standard containing guidelines for the implementation and assessment of information security policies in financial services institutions. The standard is a commonly referenced guideline, and serves as a resource for the implementation of information security management programmes in institutions of the financial sector, and as a yardstick for auditing such programmes.

- ISO/IEC 21827:2008 - Information technology—Security techniques—Systems Security Engineering—Capability Maturity Model (SSE-CMM): ISO/IEC 21827:2008 specifies the Systems Security Engineering - Capability Maturity Model (SSE-CMM), which describes the essential characteristics of an organization's security engineering process that must exist to ensure good security engineering. ISO/IEC 21827:2008 does not prescribe a particular process or sequence, but captures practices generally observed in industry. The model is a standard metric for security engineering practices.

## BSI

- BS 25999-1:2006 - Business continuity management Part 1: Code of practice Note: this is only part one of BS 25999, which was published in November 2006. Part two (which should contain more specific criteria with a view of possible accreditation) is yet to appear. Standard containing a business continuity code of practice. The standard is intended as a code of practice for business continuity management, and will be extended by a second part that should permit accreditation for adherence with the standard. Given its relative newness, the potential impact of the standard is difficult to assess, although it could be very influential to RM/RA practices, given the general lack of universally applicable standards in this regard and the increasing attention to business continuity and contingency planning in regulatory initiatives. Application of this standard can be complemented by other norms, in particular PAS 77:2006 - IT Service Continuity Management Code of Practice. The TR allows security professionals to determine a suitable methodology for assessing a security service, product or environmental factor (a deliverable). Following this TR, it can be determined which level of security assurance a deliverable is intended to meet, and if this threshold is actually met by the deliverable.

- BS 7799-3:2006 - Information security management systems—Guidelines for information security risk management. Topic: Standard containing general guidelines for information security risk management.Scope: Not publicly available BSI standard, which can be voluntarily implemented. While not legally binding, the text contains direct guidelines for the creation of sound information security practices. The standard is mostly intended as a guiding complementary document to the application of the aforementioned ISO 27001:2005, and is therefore typically applied in conjunction with this standard in risk assessment practices

## Information Security Forum

- Standard of Good Practice

## Audit Risk

Audit risk (also referred to as residual risk) refers to the risk that an auditor may issue unqualified report due to the auditor's failure to detect material misstatement either due to error or fraud. This risk is composed of inherent risk (IR), control risk (CR) and detection risk (DR), and can be calculated thus:

$$AR = IR \times CR \times DR$$

IR refers to the risk involved in the nature of business or transaction. Example, transactions involving exchange of cash may have higher IR than transactions involving settlement by cheques.

CR refers to the risk that a misstatement could occur but may not be detected and corrected or prevented by entity's internal control mechanism. Example,control risk assessment may be higher in an entity where separation of duties is not well defined.

DR is the probability that the audit procedures may fail to detect existence of a material error or fraud. While CR depends on the strength or weakness of the internal control procedures, DR is either due to sampling error or human factors.

## References


- Trevisani, Daniele (2007). Regie di Cambiamento (Translated Title: The Directions of Change), Franco Angeli Publisher, Milan, ISBN 9788846483775
- Crockford, Neil (1986). An Introduction to Risk Management (2 ed.). Cambridge, UK: Woodhead-Faulkner. p. 18. ISBN 0-85941-332-2.
- Dorfman, Mark S. (2007). Introduction to Risk Management and Insurance (9 ed.). Englewood Cliffs, N.J: Prentice Hall. ISBN 0-13-224227-3.
- Lev Virine and Michael Trumper. ProjectThink: Why Good Managers Make Poor Project Choices. Gower Pub Co. ISBN 978-1409454984
- Peter Simon and David Hillson, Practical Risk Management: The ATOM Methodology (2012). Management Concepts. Vienna, VA. ISBN 978-1567263664
- Flyvbjerg, Bent (2003). Megaprojects and Risk: An Anatomy of Ambition. Cambridge University Press. ISBN 0521804205.
- Craig Taylor; Erik VanMarcke, eds. (2002). Acceptable Risk Processes: Lifelines and Natural Hazards. Reston, VA: ASCE, TCLEE. ISBN 9780784406236.
- Cortada, James W. (2007-11-06). The Digital Hand, Vol 3: How Computers Changed the Work of American Public Sector Industries. USA: Oxford University Press. p. 496. ISBN 978-0-19-516586-9.
- Saghee M, Sandle T, Tidswell E (editors) (2011). Microbiology and Sterility Assurance in Pharmaceuticals and Medical Devices (1st ed.). Business Horizons. ISBN 978-8190646741.
- Alan B. Bernstein and Cindy Rakowitz (2012). Emergency Public Relations: Crisis Management In a 3.0 World. p. 5. ISBN 978-1469159546
- Fischer, Robert. P., Halibozek, Edward., & Green, Gion, (2008) "Introduction to Security". 8th Edition, p. 256 ISBN 978-0-7506-8432-3.

2

# Different Types of Risk Management

Enterprise risk management includes methods and processes that are used by companies to manage risks. It helps in providing frameworks for risk management. The other types of risk management included in this chapter are project risk management, social risk management, operational risk management, financial risk management, IT risk management etc. The topics discussed in the section are of great importance to broaden the existing knowledge on risk management.

## Enterprise Risk Management

Enterprise risk management (ERM or E.R.M.) in business includes the methods and processes used by organizations to manage risks and seize opportunities related to the achievement of their objectives. ERM provides a framework for risk management, which typically involves identifying particular events or circumstances relevant to the organization's objectives (risks and opportunities), assessing them in terms of likelihood and magnitude of impact, determining a response strategy, and monitoring progress. By identifying and proactively addressing risks and opportunities, business enterprises protect and create value for their stakeholders, including owners, employees, customers, regulators, and society overall.

ERM can also be described as a risk-based approach to managing an enterprise, integrating concepts of internal control, the Sarbanes–Oxley Act, and strategic planning. ERM is evolving to address the needs of various stakeholders, who want to understand the broad spectrum of risks facing complex organizations to ensure they are appropriately managed. Regulators and debt rating agencies have increased their scrutiny on the risk management processes of companies.

### ERM Frameworks Defined

There are various important ERM frameworks, each of which describes an approach for identifying, analyzing, responding to, and monitoring risks and opportunities, within the internal and external environment facing the enterprise. Management selects a *risk response strategy* for specific risks identified and analyzed, which may include:

1. Avoidance: exiting the activities giving rise to risk

2. Reduction: taking action to reduce the likelihood or impact related to the risk

3. Alternative Actions: deciding and considering other feasible steps to minimize risks.
4. Share or Insure: transferring or sharing a portion of the risk, to finance it
5. Accept: no action is taken, due to a cost/benefit decision

Monitoring is typically performed by management as part of its internal control activities, such as review of analytical reports or management committee meetings with relevant experts, to understand how the risk response strategy is working and whether the objectives are being achieved.

## Casualty Actuarial Society framework

In 2003, the Casualty Actuarial Society (CAS) defined ERM as the discipline by which an organization in any industry assesses, controls, exploits, finances, and monitors risks from all sources for the purpose of increasing the organization's short- and long-term value to its stakeholders." The CAS conceptualized ERM as proceeding across the two dimensions of *risk type* and *risk management processes*. The risk types and examples include:

Hazard risk

Liability torts, Property damage, Natural catastrophe

Financial risk

Pricing risk, Asset risk, Currency risk, Liquidity risk

Operational risk

Customer satisfaction, Product failure, Integrity, Reputational risk; Internal Poaching; Knowledge drain

Strategic risks

Competition, Social trend, Capital availability

The risk management process involves:

1. Establishing Context: This includes an understanding of the current conditions in which the organization operates on an internal, external and risk management context.
2. Identifying Risks: This includes the documentation of the material threats to the organization's achievement of its objectives and the representation of areas that the organization may exploit for competitive advantage.
3. Analyzing/Quantifying Risks: This includes the calibration and, if possible, cre-

ation of probability distributions of outcomes for each material risk.

4. Integrating Risks: This includes the aggregation of all risk distributions, reflecting correlations and portfolio effects, and the formulation of the results in terms of impact on the organization's key performance metrics.

5. Assessing/Prioritizing Risks: This includes the determination of the contribution of each risk to the aggregate risk profile, and appropriate prioritization.

6. Treating/Exploiting Risks: This includes the development of strategies for controlling and exploiting the various risks.

7. Monitoring and Reviewing: This includes the continual measurement and monitoring of the risk environment and the performance of the risk management strategies.

## COSO ERm Framework

The COSO "Enterprise Risk Management-Integrated Framework" published in 2004 defines ERM as a "...process, effected by an entity's board of directors, management, and other personnel, applied in strategy setting and across the enterprise, designed to identify potential events that may affect the entity, and manage risk to be within its risk appetite, to provide reasonable assurance regarding the achievement of entity objectives."

The COSO ERM Framework has eight Components and four objectives categories. It is an expansion of the COSO Internal Control-Integrated Framework published in 1992 and amended in 1994. The eight components - additional components highlighted - are:

- Authority and pledge to the ERM
- RISK Management policy
- Mixer of ERM in the institution
- Risk Assessment
- Risk Response
- communication and reporting
- Information and Communication
- Monitoring

The four objectives categories - additional components highlighted - are:

- Strategy - high-level goals, aligned with and supporting the organization's mission

- Operations - effective and efficient use of resources
- Financial Reporting - reliability of operational and financial reporting
- Compliance - compliance with applicable laws and regulations

## RIMS Risk Maturity Model

The RIMS Risk Maturity Model (RMM) for Enterprise Risk Management, published in 2006, is an umbrella framework of content and methodology that detail the requirements for sustainable and effective enterprise risk management. The RMM model consists of twenty-five competency drivers for seven attributes that create ERM's value and utility in an organization. The 7 attributes are:

- ERM-based approach
- ERM process management
- Risk appetite management
- Root cause discipline
- Uncovering risks
- Performance management
- Business resiliency and sustainability

The model was developed by Steven Minsky, CEO of LogicManager, and published by the Risk and Insurance Management Society in collaboration with the RIMS ERM Committee. The Risk Maturity Model is based on the Capability Maturity Model, a methodology founded by the Carnegie Mellon University Software Engineering Institute (SEI) in the 1980s.

## Implementing an ERM Program

## Goals of an ERM Program

Organizations by nature manage risks and have a variety of existing departments or functions ("risk functions") that identify and manage particular risks. However, each risk function varies in capability and how it coordinates with other risk functions. A central goal and challenge of ERM is improving this capability and coordination, while integrating the output to provide a unified picture of risk for stakeholders and improving the organization's ability to manage the risks effectively.

## Typical Risk Functions

The primary risk functions in large corporations that may participate in an ERM program typically include:

- Strategic planning - identifies external threats and competitive opportunities, along with strategic initiatives to address them
- Marketing - understands the target customer to ensure product/service alignment with customer requirements
- Compliance & Ethics - monitors compliance with code of conduct and directs fraud investigations
- Accounting / Financial compliance - directs the Sarbanes-Oxley Section 302 and 404 assessment, which identifies financial reporting risks
- Law Department - manages litigation and analyzes emerging legal trends that may impact the organization
- Insurance - ensures the proper insurance coverage for the organization
- Treasury - ensures cash is sufficient to meet business needs, while managing risk related to commodity pricing or foreign exchange
- Operational Quality Assurance - verifies operational output is within tolerances
- Operations management - ensures the business runs day-to-day and that related barriers are surfaced for resolution
- Credit - ensures any credit provided to customers is appropriate to their ability to pay
- Customer service - ensures customer complaints are handled promptly and root causes are reported to operations for resolution
- Internal audit - evaluates the effectiveness of each of the above risk functions and recommends improvements

## Common Challenges in ERM Implementation

Various consulting firms offer suggestions for how to implement an ERM program. Common topics and challenges include:

- Identifying executive sponsors for ERM.
- Establishing a common risk language or glossary.
- Describing the entity's risk appetite (i.e., risks it will and will not take)
- Identifying and describing the risks in a "risk inventory".
- Implementing a risk-ranking methodology to prioritize risks within and across functions.
- Establishing a risk committee and or Chief Risk Officer (CRO) to coordinate

certain activities of the risk functions.

- Establishing ownership for particular risks and responses.
- Demonstrating the cost-benefit of the risk management effort.
- Developing action plans to ensure the risks are appropriately managed.
- Developing consolidated reporting for various stakeholders.
- Monitoring the results of actions taken to mitigate risk.
- Ensuring efficient risk coverage by internal auditors, consulting teams, and other evaluating entities.
- Developing a technical ERM framework that enables secure participation by 3rd parties and remote employees.

## Internal Audit Role

In addition to information technology audit, internal auditors play an important role in evaluating the risk management processes of an organization and advocating their continued improvement. However, to preserve its organizational independence and objective judgment, Internal Audit professional standards indicate the function should not take any direct responsibility for making risk management decisions for the enterprise or managing the risk management function.

Internal auditors typically perform an annual risk assessment of the enterprise, to develop a plan of audit engagements for the upcoming year. This plan is updated at various frequencies in practice. This typically involves review of the various risk assessments performed by the enterprise (e.g., strategic plans, competitive benchmarking, and SOX top-down risk assessment), consideration of prior audits, and interviews with a variety of senior management. It is designed for identifying audit projects, not to identify, prioritize, and manage risks directly for the enterprise.

## Current Issues in ERM

The risk management processes of U.S. corporations are under increasing regulatory and private scrutiny. Risk is an essential part of any business. Properly managed, it drives growth and opportunity. Executives struggle with business pressures that may be partly or completely beyond their immediate control, such as distressed financial markets; mergers, acquisitions and restructurings; disruptive technology change; geopolitical instabilities; and the rising price of energy.

## Sarbanes-Oxley Act Requirements

Section 404 of the Sarbanes-Oxley Act of 2002 required U.S. publicly traded corporations to utilize a control framework in their internal control assessments. Many opted for the COSO Internal Control Framework, which includes a risk assessment element. In addition, new guidance issued by the Securities and Exchange Commission (SEC) and PCAOB in 2007 placed increasing scrutiny on top-down risk assessment and included a specific requirement to perform a fraud risk assessment. Fraud risk assessments typically involve identifying scenarios of potential (or experienced) fraud, related exposure to the organization, related controls, and any action taken as a result.

## NYSE Corporate Governance rules

The New York Stock Exchange requires the Audit Committees of its listed companies to "discuss policies with respect to risk assessment and risk management." The related commentary continues: "While it is the job of the CEO and senior management to assess and manage the company's exposure to risk, the audit committee must discuss guidelines and policies to govern the process by which this is handled. The audit committee should discuss the company's major financial risk exposures and the steps management has taken to monitor and control such exposures. The audit committee is not required to be the sole body responsible for risk assessment and management, but, as stated above, the committee must discuss guidelines and policies to govern the process by which risk assessment and management is undertaken. Many companies, particularly financial companies, manage and assess their risk through mechanisms other than the audit committee. The processes these companies have in place should be reviewed in a general manner by the audit committee, but they need not be replaced by the audit committee."

## ERM and Corporate Debt Ratings

Standard & Poor's (S&P), the debt rating agency, plans to include a series of questions about risk management in its company evaluation process. This will rollout to financial companies in 2007. The results of this inquiry is one of the many factors considered in debt rating, which has a corresponding impact on the interest rates lenders charge companies for loans or bonds. On May 7, 2008, S&P also announced that it would begin including an ERM assessment in its ratings for non-financial companies starting in 2009, with initial comments in its reports during Q4 2008.

## ISO 31000 : the new International Risk Management Standard

ISO 31000 is an International Standard for Risk Management which was published on 13 November 2009. An accompanying standard, ISO 31010 - Risk Assessment Techniques, soon followed publication (December 1, 2009) together with the updated Risk Management vocabulary ISO Guide 73.

## Actuarial Response

### Casualty Actuarial Society

In 2003, the Enterprise Risk Management Committee of the Casualty Actuarial Society (CAS) issued its overview of ERM. This paper laid out the evolution, rationale, definitions, and frameworks for ERM from the casualty actuarial perspective, and also included a vocabulary, conceptual and technical foundations, actual practice and applications, and case studies.

The CAS has specific stated ERM goals, including being "a leading supplier internationally of educational materials relating to Enterprise Risk Management (ERM) in the property casualty insurance arena," and has sponsored research, development, and training of casualty actuaries in that regard. The CAS has refrained from issuing its own credential; instead, in 2007, the CAS Board decided that the CAS should participate in the initiative to develop a global ERM designation, and make a final decision at some later date.

### Society of Actuaries

In 2007, the Society of Actuaries developed the Chartered Enterprise Risk Analyst (CERA) credential in response to the growing field of enterprise risk management. This is the first new professional credential to be introduced by the SOA since 1949. A CERA studies to focus on how various risks, including operational, investment, strategic, and reputational combine to affect organizations. CERAs work in environments beyond insurance, reinsurance and the consulting markets, including broader financial services, energy, transportation, media, technology, manufacturing and healthcare.

It takes approximately three to four years to complete the CERA curriculum which combines basic actuarial science, ERM principles and a course on professionalism. To earn the CERA credential, candidates must take five exams, fulfill an educational experience requirement, complete one online course, and attend one in-person course on professionalism.

### CERA Global

Initially all CERAs were members of the Society of Actuaries but in 2009 the CERA designation became a global specialized professional credential, awarded and regulated by multiple actuarial bodies.

### Institute and Faculty of Actuaries

The Institute and Faculty of Actuaries (the merged body formed in 2010 from the Institute of Actuaries and the Faculty of Actuaries) is the professional body representing actuaries in the United Kingdom. In March 2008, Enterprise Risk Management was adopted as one of the six actuarial practice areas, reflecting the increased involvement of actuaries in the ERM field.

A regular newsletter communicates the ongoing work that the profession performs in respect of ERM.

Some of the key areas that the profession works on are summarised below (together with some of the recent outcomes in each area):

- Education, CPD, Career Support and Development

From April 2010 actuaries were able to study ERM as one of the Specialist Technical Stage exams (ST9 course information), which (with other exam passes) gives candidates the Chartered Enterprise Risk Actuary (CERA) qualification. In July 2010 the first nine actuaries to obtain the CERA qualification were announced.

Various events (e.g. networking evenings and webinars) are available to actuaries and other interested parties. The main event is the Risk and Investment Conference, which is often held during the summer months (e.g. 2011 Risk & Investment Conference). There is also some regularly reviewed material available from the profession which may be of use in developing knowledge of ERM.

- Research & Thought Leadership

A committee has been established to consider research and thought leadership in the ERM field (including what the "elevator speech" on ERM issues might be, definition of the scope of ERM and demonstration of the value of ERM).

Some areas in which work has been completed include:

- ERM - A guide to Implementation- A survey on actuaries in risk management- A suggested common risk classification system for the actuarial profession

Research topics will be categorised and subject to a number of tests before proceeding with the research.

- enterprise-wide test (not just topic-specific / silo-based)- risk management test (management = taking actions, not just modelling)- director test (important enough for the Board, not just line managers)

- Communications & Marketing

Actuaries continue to look to demonstrate and promote the value of actuaries and the CERA qualification in the field of ERM - including through publication of articles in the Actuary.

The Actuarial Profession also liaises with other professions where appropriate- e.g. the Institution of Civil Engineers on considering ERM in the context of Risk Analysis and Management for Projects (RAMP).

## Companies Increasingly Focusing on ERM

It is clear that companies recognize ERM as a critical management issue. This is demonstrated through the prominence assigned to ERM within organizations and the resources devoted to building ERM capabilities. In a 2008 survey by Towers Perrin, at most life insurance companies, responsibility for ERM resides within the C-suite. Most often, the chief risk officer (CRO) or the chief financial officer (CFO) is in charge of ERM, and these individuals typically report directly to the chief executive officer. From their vantage point, the CRO and CFO are able to look across the organization and develop a perspective on the risk profile of the firm and how that profile matches its risk appetite. They act as drivers to improve skills, tools and processes for evaluating risks and to weigh various actions to manage those exposures. Companies are also actively enhancing their ERM tools and capabilities. Three quarters of responding companies said they have tools for specifically monitoring and managing enterprise-wide risk. These tools are used primarily for identifying and measuring risk and for management decision making. Respondents also reported that they have made good progress in building their ERM capabilities in certain areas.

In this study, more than 80% of respondents reported that they currently have adequate or better controls in place for most major risks. In addition, about 60% currently have a coordinated process for risk governance and include risk management in decision making to optimize risk adjusted returns.

In another survey conducted in May and June 2008, against the backdrop of the developing financial crisis, six major findings came to light regarding risk and capital management among insurers worldwide:

- Embedding ERM is proving to be a significant challenge
- Company size matters
- European insurers are better positioned
- ERM is influencing important strategic decisions
- Economic capital standards are gaining ground
- Operational risk remains a weak spot

## ERM Examples

## Nedbank Group

Nedbank in South Africa approaches ERM as a strategic enable to help them “optimise risk versus return on a sustainable basis, and risk management is therefore approached across three integrated core dimensions: Managing risk as a THREAT...as an UNCERTAINTY and as an OPPORTUNITY”.

### The Reserve Bank of Australia

The Reserve Bank of Australia - The Bank has established a risk appetite statement regarding its key risks, including risk appetite statements, a supporting risk management framework, and implementation guidelines.

## Project Risk Management

Project risk management is an important aspect of project management. According to the Project Management Institute's PMBOK, Risk management is one of the ten knowledge areas in which a project manager must be competent. Project risk is defined by PMI as, "an uncertain event or condition that, if it occurs, has a positive or negative effect on a project's objectives."

Project risk management remains a relatively undeveloped discipline, distinct from the risk management used by Operational, Financial and Underwriters' risk management. This gulf is due to several factors: Risk Aversion, especially public understanding and risk in social activities, confusion in the application of risk management to projects, and the additional sophistication of probability mechanics above those of accounting, finance and engineering.[1]

With the above disciplines of Operational, Financial and Underwriting risk management, the concepts of risk, risk management and individual risks are nearly interchangeable; being either personnel or monetary impacts respectively. Impacts in project risk management are more diverse, overlapping monetary, schedule, capability, quality and engineering disciplines. For this reason, in project risk management, it is necessary to specify the differences (paraphrased from the "Department of Defense Risk, Issue, and Opportunity Management Guide for Defense Acquisition Programs"):

- Risk Management: Organizational policy for optimizing investments and (individual) risks to minimize the possibility of failure.
- Risk: The likelihood that a project will fail to meet its objectives.
- A risk: A single action, event or hardware component that contributes to an effort's "Risk."

An improvement on the PMBOK definition of risk management is to add a future date to the definition of a risk. Mathematically, this is expressed as a probability multiplied by an impact, with the inclusion of a future impact date and critical dates. This addition of future dates allows predictive approaches.

Good Project Risk Management depends on supporting organizational factors, having clear roles and responsibilities, and technical analysis.

Chronologically, Project Risk Management may begin in recognizing a threat, or by examining an opportunity. For example, these may be competitor developments or novel products. Due to lack of definition, this is frequently performed qualitatively, or semi-quantitatively, using product or averaging models. This approach is used to prioritize possible solutions, where necessary.

In some instances it is possible to begin an analysis of alternatives, generating cost and development estimates for potential solutions. With this data, the program, RiskAoA, allows quantitative discrimination of risk and the display of the trade-space between estimated costs, development times and the reasonableness of approach. Aggressive application of RiskAoA may also analyze threats from rival company's internal developments and reveal their most probable decisions.

Once an approach is selected, more familiar risk management tools and a general project risk management process may be used for the new projects:

- A Planning risk management
- Risk identification and monetary identification
- Performing qualitative risk analysis
- Communicating the risk to stakeholders and the funders of the project
- Refining or iterating the risk based on research and new information
- Monitoring and controlling risks

Project risk tolerance comes from two sources, corporate culture and the type of project. Risk tolerance is accounted for if the project began with RiskAoA. However, if the project begins without its normalization, the type of project necessitates an understanding and possibly metrics for risk tolerance. For example, a research and development project has more risk than a software project, which has different risk then a new product launch.

The general risk process above accounts for managing the line elements, or the individual risks of a project as if they were actions items. This approach manages individual risks well, however, it is akin to treating each piece of a puzzle, without regard for the larger picture. This results in only a fraction of risk management capability being used, and is especially limiting to its intrinsic predictive character.

A poorly understood complication in project risk management is scheduling. Schedules are ubiquitous to every planning phase of a project, for every kind of project. However, using risk management tools invariably produces incorrect results for predicting completion dates and other milestones. This is a result of the mechanics of probability impact models, which are generalizations designed to predict individual events. At this time there are no noteworthy non-experientially-based approaches to schedule risk management; Master Schedulers and logistics-based (negligible risk) systems are the accepted state of the art. Unfortunately, many risk-scheduling tools blindly apply the probability impact model without interrelation and mathematic considerations.

Finally, risks must be integrated to provide a complete picture, so projects should be integrated into enterprise wide risk management, to seize opportunities related to the achievement of their objectives.

[1] Complementing this difficulty is the novelty requirement for academic study: With the exception of RiskAoA, it is unlikely that future novel approaches applying probability to the discipline of risk management are possible.

## Social Risk Management

Social risk management (SRM) is a conceptual framework developed by the World Bank, specifically its Social Protection and Labor Sector under the leadership of Robert Holzmann, since the end 1990s. The objective of SRM is to extend the traditional framework of social protection to include prevention, mitigation, and coping strategies to protect basic livelihoods and promote risk taking. SRM focuses specifically on the poor, who are the most vulnerable to risk and more likely to suffer in the face of economic shocks. Through its strategies SRM aims to reduce the vulnerability of the poor and encourage them to participate in riskier but higher-return activities in order to transition out of chronic poverty.

### Motivations

Social Protection has been a part of OECD economies for a long time but it has not played much of a role in development work because the imitation of these measures in developing countries is criticized based on equity and efficiency trade-off arguments. This view changed as a result of the following policy, conceptual and institutional triggers that led to the creation of SRM as a new Social Protection framework:

- The East Asian economic crisis in 1997 revealed the volatility of high growth rates in the face of negative economic shocks. Moreover, informal social safety net arrangements and public support programs were shown to be inadequate under those circumstances.
- Globalization has led to higher income variability, which together with marginalization and social exclusion leaves major groups like women and ethnic minorities highly vulnerable. Also, higher mobility of factors of production has reduced government ability to raise revenue, pursue independent economic policies, and to have national policies to help the poor when they need them the most.
- Fulfillment of World Bank's mission to reduce poverty requires a deeper "un-

derstanding of the nature and characteristics of poverty" itself. Research in this area exposed the long-term negative consequences of seemingly transitory shocks and suggested the need for a preventative view of poverty based on vulnerability.

- World Development Report 2000/01 presented social protection as a key element in attacking global poverty.
- World Bank's Social Protection and Labor Sector is one of its youngest units established in 1996. Analysis of past experiences in this area for a future policy proposal in the sector's strategy paper revealed the need for a new framework of social protection that shifted its focus from instruments to objectives

## Source of Social Risks

There are three important categories that aid in the classification of sources of risks:

1. Catastrophic vs. non-catastrophic shocks: Some events occur with low frequency, but have severe income effects like old-age, death in the family, and disabling accidents or illnesses, permanent unemployment, and the technological redundancy of skills. These catastrophic events can hit households hard and may require a continuing flow of transfers to the affected household if it cannot acquire sufficient assets. On the other end of the scale are high frequency events with non-severe income effects like transient illness, crop loss, and temporary unemployment. Protection against these non-catastrophic events need not require long-term net transfers to the afflicted household. If appropriate mechanisms are available, households may use savings or loans with no net transfers from others over time.

2. Idiosyncratic shocks vs. covariant shocks: Some sources lead to losses in only some households in a community like noncommunicative illness or frictional unemployment whereas others hit all households at the same time like drought, inflation or financial crisis. The former are known as idiosyncratic (or micro) shocks while the latter are referred to as covariant (or macro) shocks. Many more mechanisms are available for coping with idiosyncratic shocks than covariant shocks. The latter can be particularly devastating, leaving households with nowhere in the community to turn for relief. For poor and isolated households even idiosyncratic shocks might be difficult to cope with.

3. Single vs. Repeated shocks: A third distinction concerns shocks following one another like drought followed by sickness and death versus shocks that occur as single events. The former are known as repeated shocks and are typically difficult to handle through informal means.

The following table lists social risks and their degree of variance varying from idiosyncratic (micro), regional covariant (meso), to nationwide covariant (macro).

| Main Sources of Risks *(adapted from Holzmann and Jorgensen, 2000)* | | | |
|---|---|---|---|
| | **Micro (idiosyncratic)** | **Meso < -------->** | **Macro (covariate)** |
| **Natural** | | Rainfall<br>Landslides<br>Volcanic eruption | Earthquakes<br>Floods<br>Drought<br>Tornadoes<br>Asteroid impacts |
| **Health** | Illness<br>Injury<br>Disability<br>Food poisoning | Pandemics<br>Food poisoning | Pandemics |
| **Life-cycle** | Birth<br>Old age<br>Death | | |
| **Social** | Crimes<br>Domestic violences<br>Drug addiction | Terrorism<br>Gangs | Civil strife<br>War<br>Social upheaval<br>Drug addiction<br>Child abuses |
| **Economic** | Unemployment<br>Harvest failure | Unemployment<br>Harvest failure<br>Resettlement | Blue chip company collapsing<br>Financial or currency crisis<br>Market trading shocks |
| **Administrative & Political** | Ethnic discrimination | Ethnic conflict<br>Riots<br>Chemical & biological mass destruction<br>Administrative induced accidents & disasters | Political induced malfunction on social programs<br>Coup |
| **Environmental** | | Pollution<br>Deforestation<br>Nuclear disasters<br>Soil salinities<br>Acid rains | Global warming |

## Strategies

Risk management strategies fall in three broad categories.:

## Prevention Strategies

These are introduced before a risk occurs to reduce the probability of a down-side risk. Reducing the probability of an adverse risk increases people's expected income and reduces income variance. Both effects increase welfare. Strategies to prevent or reduce the occurrence of income risks have a very broad range varying from small-scale informal arrangements to national economic policies. Examples include:

- Avoiding risky crop production
- Migration when current residence region is exposed to high vulnerability
- Engaging in hygiene and other disease prevention activities
- Skill training to reduce the risk of unemployment and underemployment
- Increasing financial market literacy
- Optimizing macroeconomic policies to reduce the shocks of financial crisis, such as oil price surges or unpredictable market moves on currencies, indices and blue chip stocks.
- Improving labor standards to meet international standards including child labor reduction interventions
- Putting disability policies in place to prevent further disadvantaging the disabled population
- Prevention of pandemic illnesses by implementing vaccination and educational public health programs
- Establishing community-based insurance schemes to compensate pensioners
- Building nursing homes for the elderly and setting up public housing for the homeless and orphans.

## Mitigation Strategies

Mitigation strategies are also employed before the risk occurs to decrease the potential impact of a future down-side risk. Whereas preventive strategies reduce the probability of the risk occurring, mitigation strategies reduce the potential impact if the risk were to occur. Risk mitigation can take several forms:

- Portfolio diversification to reduce the variability of income by relying on a variety of assets that are not correlated strongly enough to have the same returns.
- Formal as well as informal insurance policies. While formal insurance benefits from a large pool of participants, informal insurance has the advantage of low information asymmetry. The characteristics of formal insurance are straightforward while informal insurance arrangements are more difficult to describe as they come in different and often disguised forms.
- Hedging losses using financial instruments like stocks, exchange-traded funds, insurance, forward contracts, swaps, options, many types of over-the-counter and derivative products, and futures contracts.

- Microfinance
- Pension systems
- Access to financial markets for the poor
- Community arrangements that allow for shared tenancy and small-scale pension plans
- Mandatory insurance for unemployment, old age, disability, sickness, etc.

## Coping Strategies

Coping strategies are designed to relieve the impact of the risk once it has occurred. The government has an important role in assisting people in coping, for example, in the case where individual households have not saved enough to handle repeated or catastrophic risks. Individuals may have been poor for their entire lifetime with no possibility to accumulate assets at all, being rendered destitute by the smallest income loss and running the risk of being faced with irreversible damages. The main forms of coping consist of:

- Individual borrowing from community members and banks
- Seasonal or temporary migration
- Selling labor including sending children to work
- Reduction of food intake
- Reliance on public, private and intra-community transfers.
- Dissaving of human capital
- Seasonal/temporary migration
- Selling of financial assets
- Disaster relief
- Social assistance in the form of asset and cash transfers
- Subsidies
- Public work projects
- Government relief fund or publicly raised money.
- Setting up unemployment benefit schemes.

## Feasibility Study: Togo

In coordination with national governments of Togo and Yemen, World Bank conducted two feasibility studies of the social risk management framework.

Within the Africa Region, Togo was selected as a pilot country to test this approach. The process of application was launched with a workshop in Lomé for key stakeholders from the government and civil society in November 1998. During the workshop, available data was analyzed to determine sources of risks, available arrangements of social protection and vulnerable groups in Togo.

Since Togo's independence in 1960, the government has provided social security for the privileged minority working in the formal sector and social assistance to a few people or groups conventionally identified as vulnerable (widows, orphans, handicapped). This leaves 95% of the Togolese to rely mostly on informal arrangements through both internal arrangements, which are organized by the prospective beneficiaries and external arrangements, which are organized by agents generally not belonging to the community.

In order to improve social protection, the government rethought its social protection policy in the framework of SRM and the following prevention, mitigation and coping strategies were proposed:

- Conducting information and education campaigns focused on key preventive measures, especially for health and environment.
- Revising family laws and land tenure laws.
- Improving the collaboration between government and communities for better access to basic social services.
- Supporting risk pooling and creative initiatives for economic shocks and chronic risks.
- Discouraging widowhood rituals, harmful traditional practices and conspicuous consumption.
- Filling the gaps of informal arrangements.
- Reforming social security in the formal sector.
- Discouraging the exploitation of child labor and trafficking.
- Organizing a more efficient mechanism to provide assistance for disaster relief

## Criticisms

There is a lack of empirical evidence of SRM's practical application. Besides Yemen and Togo, SRM has not been experimentally studied within the development field. This raises skepticism regarding the framework's feasibility in the arena of international development.

SRM is sometimes also viewed as a neo-liberal framework that limits the government's role to coping strategies that spring into action only in the case of market failure.

Its aim to encourage riskier activities that reap higher returns has also come under fire in light of individual risk-taking behaviors that are determined by a multitude of factors and not just decreased risk vulnerability. Also, riskier behaviors not only hold the potential for higher returns but also for bigger losses making World Bank's encouragement of such activities inappropriate.

Lack of risk monitoring and reviewing to maintain an updated inventory of contextually appropriate risks and strategies is another serious deficit of the SRM framework.

### Future Implications

World Bank's Social Protection and Labor Sector is under the process of formulating its Social Protection and Labor Strategy 2012 – 2022. Conceptual note for the strategy outlines four indicative strategic directions:

- Expanding from improving individual programs to building social protection systems
- Strengthening the focus on low income and fragile states
- Emphasizing promotion of opportunities and livelihoods as a core element of the practice
- Continuing to build on core strengths in knowledge, innovation and results.

The upcoming Strategy is also aimed at dealing with SRM's operational issues exhibited by lack of sufficient guidance to design and implement effective social protection systems.

## Operational Risk Management

The term Operational Risk Management (ORM) is defined as a continual cyclic process which includes risk assessment, risk decision making, and implementation of risk controls, which results in acceptance, mitigation, or avoidance of risk. ORM is the oversight of operational risk, including the risk of loss resulting from inadequate or failed internal processes and systems; human factors; or external events.

## Four Principles of ORM

The U.S. Department of Defense summarizes the principles of ORM as follows:

- Accept risk when benefits outweigh the cost.
- Accept no unnecessary risk.
- Anticipate and manage risk by planning.
- Make risk decisions at the right level.

## Three Levels of ORM

In Depth

> In depth risk management is used before a project is implemented, when there is plenty of time to plan and prepare. Examples of in depth methods include training, drafting instructions and requirements, and acquiring personal protective equipment.

Deliberate

> Deliberate risk management is used at routine periods through the implementation of a project or process. Examples include quality assurance, on-the-job training, safety briefs, performance reviews, and safety checks.

Time Critical

> Time critical risk management is used during operational exercises or execution of tasks. It is defined as the effective use of all available resources by individuals, crews, and teams to safely and effectively accomplish the mission or task using risk management concepts when time and resources are limited. Examples of tools used includes execution check-lists and change management. This requires a high degree of situational awareness.

## ORM Process

## In depth

The International Organization for Standardization defines the risk management process in a four-step model:

1. Establish context
2. Risk assessment
    - Risk identification

- Risk analysis
- Risk evaluation

3. Risk treatment
4. Monitor and review

This process is cyclic as any changes to the situation (such as operating environment or needs of the unit) requires re-evaluation per step one.

## Deliberate

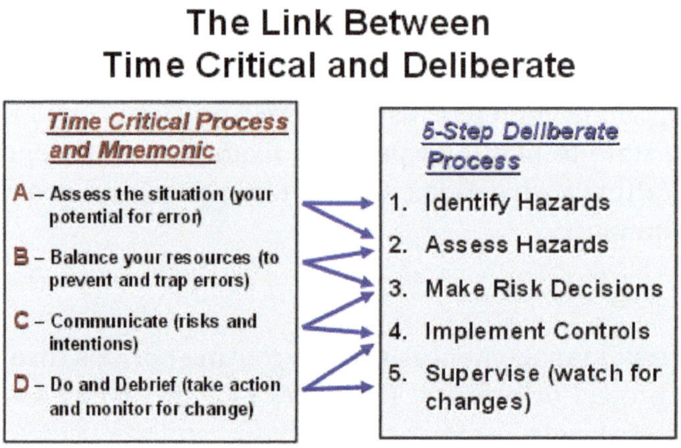


The U.S. Department of Defense summarizes the deliberate level of ORM process in a five-step model:

1. Identify hazards
2. Assess hazards
3. Make risk decisions
4. Implement controls
5. Supervise (and watch for changes)

## Time Critical

The U.S. Navy summarizes the time-critical risk management process in a four-step model:

1. Assess the situation.

The three conditions of the Assess step are task loading, additive conditions, and human factors.

- Task loading refers to the negative effect of increased tasking on performance of the tasks.
- Additive factors refers to having a situational awareness of the cumulative effect of variables (conditions, etc.).
- Human factors refers to the limitations of the ability of the human body and mind to adapt to the work environment (e.g. stress, fatigue, impairment, lapses of attention, confusion, and willful violations of regulations).

2. Balance your resources.

This refers to balancing resources in three different ways:

- Balancing resources and options available. This means evaluating and leveraging all the informational, labor, equipment, and material resources available.
- Balancing Resources verses hazards. This means estimating how well prepared you are to safely accomplish a task and making a judgement call.
- Balancing individual verses team effort. This means observing individual risk warning signs. It also means observing how well the team is communicating, knows the roles that each member is supposed to play, and the stress level and participation level of each team member.

3. Communicate risks and intentions.

- Communicate hazards and intentions.
- Communicate to the right people.
- Use the right communication style. Asking questions is a technique to opening the lines of communication. A direct and forceful style of communication gets a specific result from a specific situation.

4. Do and debrief. (Take action and monitor for change.)

This is accomplished in three different phases:

- Mission Completion is a point where the exercise can be evaluated and reviewed in full.
- Execute and Gauge Risk involves managing change and risk while an exercise is in progress.
- Future Performance Improvements refers to preparing a "lessons learned" for the next team that plans or executes a task.

## Benefits of ORM

1. Reduction of operational loss.
2. Lower compliance/auditing costs.
3. Early detection of unlawful activities.
4. Reduced exposure to future risks.

## Chief Operational Risk Officer

The role of the Chief Operational Risk Officer (CORO) continues to evolve and gain importance. In addition to being responsible for setting up a robust Operational Risk Management function at companies, the role also plays an important part in increasing awareness of the benefits of sound operational risk management.

Most complex financial institutions have a Chief Operational Risk Officer. The position is also required for Banks that fall into the Basel II Advanced Measurement Approach "mandatory" category.

## ORM Software

The impact of the Enron failure and the implementation of the Sarbanes–Oxley Act has caused several software development companies to create enterprise-wide software packages to manage risk. These software systems allow the financial audit to be executed at lower cost.

Forrester Research has identified 115 Governance, Risk and Compliance vendors that cover operational risk management projects. Active Agenda is an open source project dedicated to operational risk management.

# Financial Risk Management

Financial risk management is the practice of economic value in a firm by using financial instruments to manage exposure to risk, particularly credit risk and market risk. Other types include Foreign exchange risk, Shape risk, Volatility risk, Sector risk, Liquidity risk, Inflation risk, etc. Similar to general risk management, financial risk management requires identifying its sources, measuring it, and plans to address them.

Financial risk management can be qualitative and quantitative. As a specialization of risk management, financial risk management focuses on when and how to hedge using financial instruments to manage costly exposures to risk.

In the banking sector worldwide, the Basel Accords are generally adopted by internationally active banks for tracking, reporting and exposing operational, credit and market risks.

### When to use Financial Risk Management

Finance theory (i.e., financial economics) prescribes that a firm should take on a project when it increases shareholder value. Finance theory also shows that firm managers cannot create value for shareholders, also called its investors, by taking on projects that shareholders could do for themselves at the same cost.

When applied to financial risk management, this implies that firm managers should not hedge risks that investors can hedge for themselves at the same cost. This notion was captured by the so-called "hedging irrelevance proposition": *In a perfect market, the firm cannot create value by hedging a risk when the price of bearing that risk within the firm is the same as the price of bearing it outside of the firm.* In practice, financial markets are not likely to be perfect markets.

This suggests that firm managers likely have many opportunities to create value for shareholders using financial risk management, wherein they have to determine which risks are cheaper for the firm to manage than the shareholders. Market risks that result in unique risks for the firm are commonly the best candidates for financial risk management.

The concepts of financial risk management change dramatically in the international realm. Multinational Corporations are faced with many different obstacles in overcoming these challenges. There has been some research on the risks firms must consider when operating in many countries, such as the three kinds of foreign exchange exposure for various future time horizons: transactions exposure, accounting exposure, and economic exposure.

## Fuel Price Risk Management

A specialization of both financial risk management and oil price analysis – and similar to conventional risk management practice – fuel price risk management is a continual cyclic process that includes risk assessment, risk decision making, and the implementation of risk controls. Fuel price risk management focuses primarily on when and how an organization can best hedge against exposure to fuel price volatility. Fuel price risk management is generally referred to as *bunker hedging* in marine and shipping contexts and *fuel hedging* in aviation and trucking contexts.

### Providers of Fuel Price Risk Management Services

Fuel price risk management services are predominantly provided by specialist teams within fuel management companies, oil companies, financial institutions, utilities and trading companies. Examples include:

1. Fuel Management companies - Mercatus Energy Advisors, INTL FCStone, World Fuel Services
2. Oil companies - Total S.A., Royal Dutch Shell, ExxonMobil, Koch Industries, BP
3. Financial institutions - BNP Paribas, Goldman Sachs, Nomura, Barclays plc, Macquarie Bank, Citigroup, Morgan Stanley, Wells Fargo
4. Utilities - RWE Supply and Trading GmbH, EdF
5. Independent Trading Companies - DRW, Optiver

## The Fuel Price Risk Management Process

Similar to conventional risk management practice, fuel price risk management is considered a continual cyclic process that includes the following:

1. Establishing the context
    - current and future business environment
    - financial position and budgets
    - objectives and needs
    - required fuel consumption, etc.
2. Risk assessment
    - fuel cost calculations
    - risk identification
    - the organization's attitude to risk
    - exposure analysis to fuel price fluctuations
    - scenarios of various hedging strategies
3. Risk treatment
    - implementation of a fuel price risk strategy
4. Monitor and review

An alternative to the above described process is the following:

1. Identify, analyze and quantify the fuel related risks
2. Determine tolerance for risk and develop a fuel price risk management policy

3. Develop fuel price risk management implementation strategies
4. Establish controls and procedures
5. Initial implementation of fuel price risk management strategies
6. Monitor, analyze and reporting
7. Repeat the process on as needed basis

## IT Risk Management

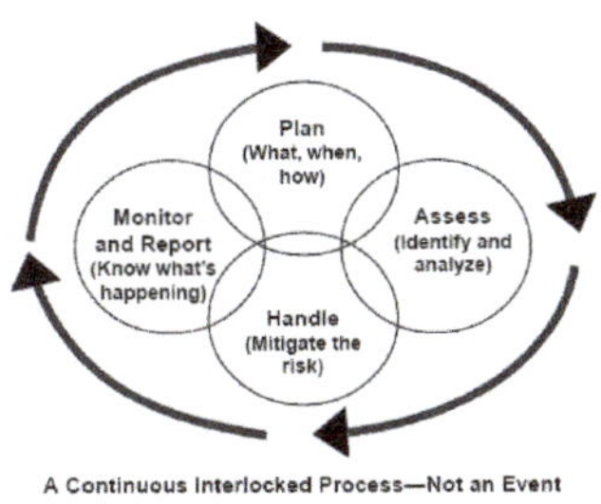


Risk Management Elements

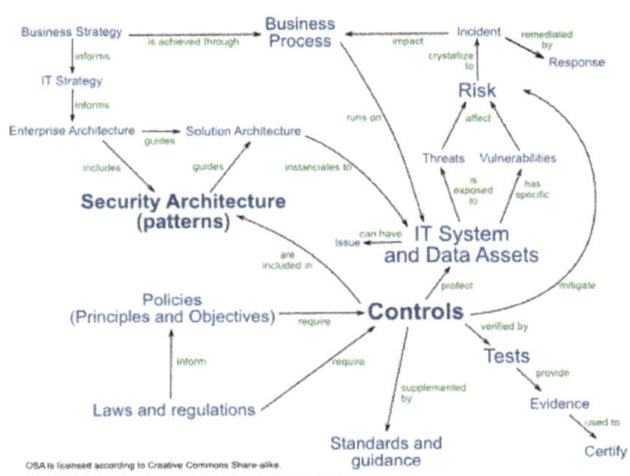


Relationships between IT security entity

IT risk management is the application of risk management methods to Information technology in order to manage IT risk, i.e.:

> *The business risk associated with the use, ownership, operation, involvement, influence and adoption of IT within an enterprise or organization*

IT risk management can be considered a component of a wider enterprise risk management system.(faisal)

The establishment, maintenance and continuous update of an ISMS provide a strong indication that a company is using a systematic approach for the identification, assessment and management of information security risks.

Different methodologies have been proposed to manage IT risks, each of them divided in processes and steps.

According to Risk IT, it encompasses not just only the negative impact of operations and service delivery which can bring destruction or reduction of the value of the organization, but also the benefit\value enabling risk associated to missing opportunities to use technology to enable or enhance business or the IT project management for aspects like overspending or late delivery with adverse business impact.

Because risk is strictly tied to uncertainty, Decision theory should be applied to manage risk as a science, i.e. rationally making choices under uncertainty.

Generally speaking, risk is the product of likelihood times impact (Risk = Likelihood * Impact).

The measure of an IT risk can be determined as a product of threat, vulnerability and asset values:

Risk = Threat * Vulnerability * Asset

A more current Risk management framework for IT Risk would be the TIK framework: Risk = ((Vulnerability * Threat) / Counter Measure) * Asset Value at Risk IT Risk

## Definitions

The Certified Information Systems Auditor Review Manual 2006 produced by ISACA, an international professional association focused on IT Governance, provides the following definition of risk management: *"Risk management is the process of identifying vulnerabilities and threats to the information resources used by an organization in achieving business objectives, and deciding what countermeasures, if any, to take in reducing risk to an acceptable level, based on the value of the information resource to the organization."*

There are two things in this definition that may need some clarification. First, the *process* of risk management is an ongoing iterative process. It must be repeated indefinitely. The business environment is constantly changing and new threats and vulnerabilities emerge every day. Second, the choice of countermeasures (controls) used to manage risks must strike a balance between productivity, cost, effectiveness of the countermeasure, and the value of the informational asset being protected.

*Risk management is the process that allows IT managers to balance the operational and economic costs of protective measures and achieve gains in mission capability by protecting the IT systems and data that support their organizations' missions. This*

*process is not unique to the IT environment; indeed it pervades decision-making in all areas of our daily lives.*

The head of an organizational unit must ensure that the organization has the capabilities needed to accomplish its mission. These mission owners must determine the security capabilities that their IT systems must have to provide the desired level of mission support in the face of real world threats. Most organizations have tight budgets for IT security; therefore, IT security spending must be reviewed as thoroughly as other management decisions. A well-structured risk management methodology, when used effectively, can help management identify appropriate controls for providing the mission-essential security capabilities.

Risk management in the IT world is quite a complex, multi faced activity, with a lot of relations with other complex activities. The picture show the relationships between different related terms.

The American National Information Assurance Training and Education Center defines risk management in the IT field as:

1. *The total process to identify, control, and minimize the impact of uncertain events. The objective of the risk management program is to reduce risk and obtain and maintain DAA approval. The process facilitates the management of security risks by each level of management throughout the system life cycle. The approval process consists of three elements: risk analysis, certification, and approval.*
2. *An element of managerial science concerned with the identification, measurement, control, and minimization of uncertain events. An effective risk management program encompasses the following four phases:*
    1. a *Risk assessment, as derived from an evaluation of threats and vulnerabilities.*
    2. *Management decision.*
    3. *Control implementation.*
    4. *Effectiveness review.*
3. *The total process of identifying, measuring, and minimizing uncertain events affecting AIS resources. It includes risk analysis, cost benefit analysis, safeguard selection, security test and evaluation, safeguard implementation, and systems review.*
4. *The total process of identifying, controlling, and eliminating or minimizing uncertain events that may affect system resources. lt includes risk analysis, cost benefit analysis, selection, implementation and test, security evaluation of safeguards, and overall security review.*

## Risk Management as Part of Enterprise Risk Management

Some organizations have, and many others should have, a comprehensive Enterprise risk management (ERM) in place. The four objectives categories addressed, according to Committee of Sponsoring Organizations of the Treadway Commission (COSO) are:

- Strategy - high-level goals, aligned with and supporting the organization's mission
- Operations - effective and efficient use of resources
- Financial Reporting - reliability of operational and financial reporting
- Compliance - compliance with applicable laws and regulations

According to Risk It framework by ISACA, IT risk is transversal to all four categories. The IT risk should be managed in the framework of Enterprise risk management: Risk appetite and Risk sensitivity of the whole enterprise should guide the IT risk management process. ERM should provide the context and business objectives to IT risk management

## Risk Management Methodology

**The Risk Management Process**

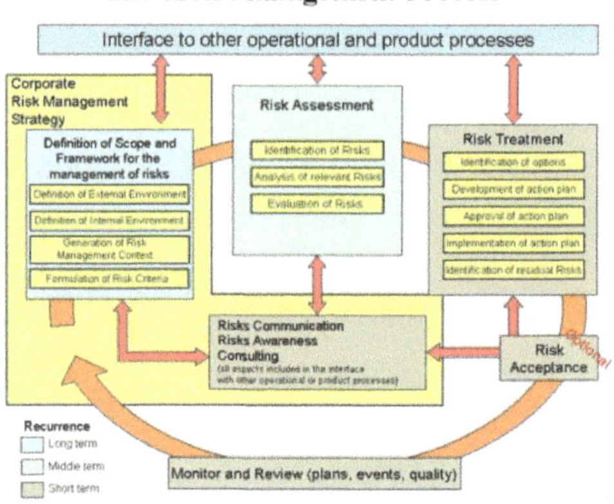


ENISA: The Risk Management Process, according to ISO Standard 13335

The term methodology means an organized set of principles and rules that drive action in a particular field of knowledge. A methodology does not describe specific methods; nevertheless it does specify several processes that need to be followed. These processes constitute a generic framework. They may be broken down in sub-processes, they may be combined, or their sequence may change. However, any risk management exercise must carry out these processes in one form or another, The following table compare the processes foreseen by three leading standards. ISACA Risk IT framework is more recent. The Risk IT Practitioner-Guide compares Risk IT and ISO 27005. The overall comparison is illustrated in the following table.

<table>
<tr><th colspan="4">Risk management constituent processes</th></tr>
<tr><th>ISO/IEC 27005:2008</th><th>BS 7799-3:2006</th><th>SP 800-30</th><th>Risk IT</th></tr>
<tr><td>Context establishment</td><td>Organizational context</td><td></td><td>RG and RE Domains more precisely<ul><li>RG1.2 Propose IT risk tolerance,</li><li>RG2.1 Establish and maintain accountability for IT risk management</li><li>RG2.3 Adapt IT risk practices to enterprise risk practices,</li><li>RG2.4 Provide adequate resources for IT risk management,</li><li>RE2.1 Define IT risk analysis scope.</li></ul></td></tr>
<tr><td>Risk assessment</td><td>Risk assessment</td><td>Risk assessment</td><td>RE2 process includes:<ul><li>RE2.1 Define IT risk analysis scope.</li><li>RE2.2 Estimate IT risk.</li><li>RE2.3 Identify risk response options.</li><li>RE2.4 Perform a peer review of IT risk analysis.</li></ul>In general, the elements as described in the ISO 27005 process are all included in Risk IT; however, some are structured and named differently.</td></tr>
<tr><td>Risk treatment</td><td>Risk treatment and management decision making</td><td>Risk mitigation</td><td><ul><li>RE 2.3 Identify risk response options</li><li>RR2.3 Respond to discovered risk exposure and opportunity</li></ul></td></tr>
<tr><td>Risk acceptance</td><td></td><td></td><td>RG3.4 Accept IT risk</td></tr>
<tr><td>Risk communication</td><td>Ongoing risk management activities</td><td></td><td><ul><li>RG1.5 Promote IT risk-aware culture</li><li>RG1.6 Encourage effective communication of IT risk</li><li>RE3.6 Develop IT risk indicators.</li></ul></td></tr>
</table>

| | | | |
|---|---|---|---|
| Risk monitoring and review | | Evaluation and assessment | • RG2 Integrate with ERM.<br>• RE2.4 Perform a peer review of IT risk analysis.<br>• RG2.5 Provide independent assurance over IT risk management |

Due to the probabilistic nature and the need of cost benefit analysis, the IT risks are managed following a process that accordingly to NIST SP 800-30 can be divided in the following steps:

1. risk assessment,
2. risk mitigation, and
3. evaluation and assessment.

Effective risk management must be totally integrated into the Systems Development Life Cycle.

Information risk analysis conducted on applications, computer installations, networks and systems under development should be undertaken using structured methodologies.

## Context Establishment

This step is the first step in ISO ISO/IEC 27005 framework. Most of the elementary activities are foreseen as the first sub process of Risk assessment according to NIST SP 800-30. This step implies the acquisition of all relevant information about the organization and the determination of the basic criteria, purpose, scope and boundaries of risk management activities and the organization in charge of risk management activities. The purpose is usually the compliance with legal requirements and provide evidence of due diligence supporting an ISMS that can be certified. The scope can be an incident reporting plan, a business continuity plan.

Another area of application can be the certification of a product.

Criteria include the risk evaluation, risk acceptance and impact evaluation criteria. These are conditioned by:

- legal and regulatory requirements
- the strategic value for the business of information processes
- stakeholder expectations
- negative consequences for the reputation of the organization

Establishing the scope and boundaries, the organization should be studied: its mission, its values, its structure; its strategy, its locations and cultural environment. The constraints (budgetary, cultural, political, technical) of the organization are to be collected and documented as guide for next steps.

## Organization for Security Management

The set up of the organization in charge of risk management is foreseen as partially fulfilling the requirement to provide the resources needed to establish, implement, operate, monitor, review, maintain and improve an ISMS. The main roles inside this organization are:

- Senior Management
- Chief information officer (CIO)
- System and Information owners
- the business and functional managers
- the Information System Security Officer (ISSO) or Chief information security officer (CISO)
- IT Security Practitioners
- Security Awareness Trainers

## Risk Assessment

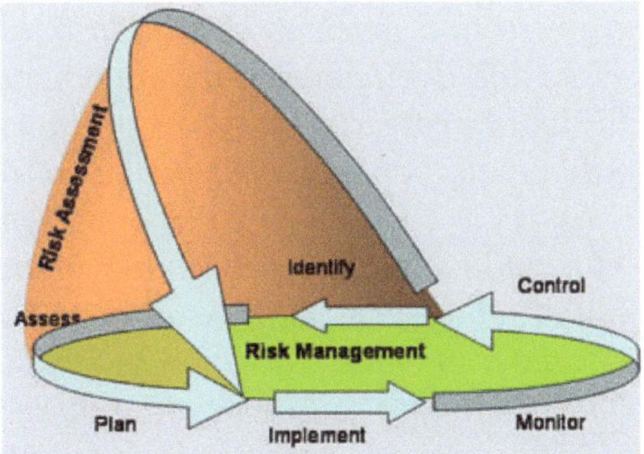


ENISA: Risk assessment inside risk management

Risk Management is a recurrent activity that deals with the analysis, planning, implementation, control and monitoring of implemented measurements and the enforced security policy. On the contrary, Risk Assessment is executed at discrete time points (e.g. once a year, on demand, etc.) and – until the performance of the next assessment - provides a temporary view of assessed risks and while parameterizing the entire Risk Management process. This view of the relationship of Risk Management to Risk Assessment is depicted in figure as adopted from OCTAVE.

Risk assessment is often conducted in more than one iteration, the first being a high-level assessment to identify high risks, while the other iterations detailed the analysis of the major risks and other risks.

According to National Information Assurance Training and Education Center risk assessment in the IT field is:

1. *A study of the vulnerabilities, threats, likelihood, loss or impact, and theoretical effectiveness of security measures. Managers use the results of a risk assessment to develop security requirements and specifications.*
2. *The process of evaluating threats and vulnerabilities, known and postulated, to determine expected loss and establish the degree of acceptability to system operations.*
3. *An identification of a specific ADP facility's assets, the threats to these assets, and the ADP facility's vulnerability to those threats.*
4. An analysis of system assets and vulnerabilities to establish an expected loss from certain events based on estimated probabilities of the occurrence of those events. The purpose of a risk assessment is to determine if countermeasures are adequate to reduce the probability of loss or the impact of loss to an acceptable level.
5. *A management tool which provides a systematic approach for determining the relative value and sensitivity of computer installation assets, assessing vulnerabilities, assessing loss expectancy or perceived risk exposure levels, assessing existing protection features and additional protection alternatives or acceptance of risks and documenting management decisions. Decisions for implementing additional protection features are normally based on the existence of a reasonable ratio between cost/benefit of the safeguard and sensitivity/value of the assets to be protected. Risk assessments may vary from an informal review of a small scale microcomputer installation to a more formal and fully documented analysis (i. e., risk analysis) of a large scale computer installation. Risk assessment methodologies may vary from qualitative or quantitative approaches to any combination of these two approaches.*

## ISO 27005 Framework

Risk assessment receives as input the output of the previous step Context establishment; the output is the list of assessed risks prioritized according to risk evaluation criteria. The process can be divided into the following steps:

- Risk analysis, further divided in:
    - Risk identification

  - Risk estimation
- Risk evaluation

The following table compares these ISO 27005 processes with Risk IT framework processes:

| Risk assessment constituent processes | |
|---|---|
| **ISO 27005** | **Risk IT** |
| Risk analysis | • RE2 Analyse risk comprises more than what is described by the ISO 27005 process step. RE2 has as its objective developing useful information to support risk decisions that take into account the business relevance of risk factors.<br>• RE1 Collect data serves as input to the analysis of risk (e.g., identifying risk factors, collecting data on the external environment). |
| Risk identification | This process is included in RE2.2 Estimate IT risk. The identification of risk comprises the following elements:<br>• Risk scenarios<br>• Risk factors |
| Risk estimation | RE2.2 Estimate IT risk |
| Risk evaluation | RE2.2 Estimate IT risk |

The ISO/IEC 27002:2005 Code of practice for information security management recommends the following be examined during a risk assessment:

- security policy,
- organization of information security,
- asset management,
- human resources security,
- physical and environmental security,
- communications and operations management,
- access control,
- information systems acquisition, development and maintenance,
- information security incident management,
- business continuity management, and
- regulatory compliance.

## Risk Identification

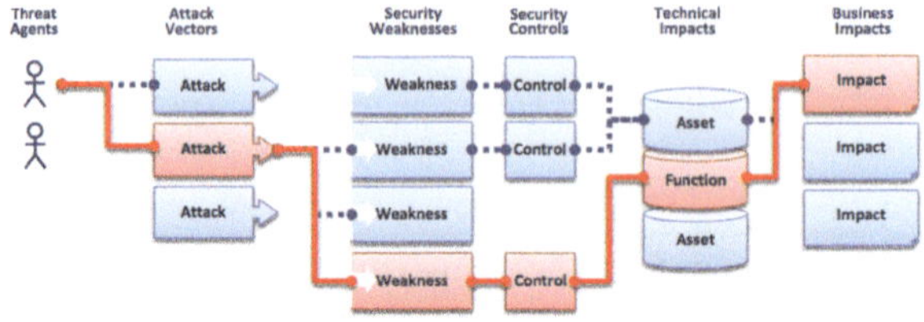


OWASP: relationship between threat agent and business impact

Risk identification states what could cause a potential loss; the following are to be identified:

- assets, primary (i.e. Business processes and related information) and supporting (i.e. hardware, software, personnel, site, organization structure)
- threats
- existing and planned security measures
- vulnerabilities
- consequences
- related business processes

The output of sub process is made up of:

- list of asset and related business processes to be risk managed with associated list of threats, existing and planned security measures
- list of vulnerabilities unrelated to any identified threats
- list of incident scenarios with their consequences.

## Risk Estimation

There are two methods of risk assessment in information security field, quantitative and qualitative.

Purely quantitative risk assessment is a mathematical calculation based on security metrics on the asset (system or application). For each risk scenario, taking into consideration the different risk factors a Single loss expectancy (SLE) is determined. Then, considering the probability of occurrence on a given period basis, for example the annual rate of occurrence (ARO), the Annualized Loss Expectancy is determined as the product of ARO X SLE. It is important to point out that the values of assets to be considered are those of all involved assets, not only the value of the directly affected resource.

For example, if you consider the risk scenario of a Laptop theft threat, you should consider the value of the data (a related asset) contained in the computer and the reputation and liability of the company (other assets) deriving from the lost of availability and confidentiality of the data that could be involved. It is easy to understand that intangible assets (data, reputation, liability) can be worth much more than physical resources at risk (the laptop hardware in the example). Intangible asset value can be huge, but is not easy to evaluate: this can be a consideration against a pure quantitative approach.

Qualitative risk assessment (three to five steps evaluation, from Very High to Low) is performed when the organization requires a risk assessment be performed in a relatively short time or to meet a small budget, a significant quantity of relevant data is not available, or the persons performing the assessment don't have the sophisticated mathematical, financial, and risk assessment expertise required. Qualitative risk assessment can be performed in a shorter period of time and with less data. Qualitative risk assessments are typically performed through interviews of a sample of personnel from all relevant groups within an organization charged with the security of the asset being assessed. Qualitative risk assessments are descriptive versus measurable. Usually a qualitative classification is done followed by a quantitative evaluation of the highest risks to be compared to the costs of security measures.

Risk estimation has as input the output of risk analysis and can be split in the following steps:

- assessment of the consequences through the valuation of assets
- assessment of the likelihood of the incident (through threat and vulnerability valuation)
- assign values to the likelihood and consequence of the risks

The output is the list of risks with value levels assigned. It can be documented in a risk register.

Risks arising from security threats and adversary attacks may be particularly difficult to estimate. This difficulty is made worse because, at least for any IT system connected to the Internet, any adversary with intent and capability may attack because physical closeness or access is not necessary. Some initial models have been proposed for this problem.

During risk estimation there are generally three values of a given asset, one for the loss of one of the CIA properties: Confidentiality, Integrity, Availability.

## Risk Evaluation

The risk evaluation process receives as input the output of risk analysis process. It compares each risk level against the risk acceptance criteria and prioritise the risk list with risk treatment indications.

## NIST SP 800 30 Framework

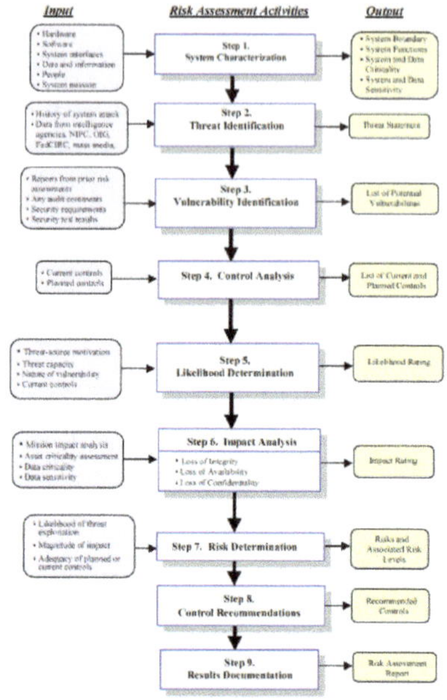


Figure 3-1. Risk Assessment Methodology Flowchart

Risk assessment according NIST SP 800-30 Figure 3-1

To determine the likelihood of a future adverse event, threats to an IT system must be in conjunction with the potential vulnerabilities and the controls in place for the IT system. Impact refers to the magnitude of harm that could be caused by a threat's exercise of vulnerability. The level of impact is governed by the potential mission impacts and produces a relative value for the IT assets and resources affected (e.g., the criticality sensitivity of the IT system components and data). The risk assessment methodology encompasses nine primary steps:

- Step 1 System Characterization
- Step 2 Threat Identification
- Step 3 Vulnerability Identification
- Step 4 Control Analysis
- Step 5 Likelihood Determination
- Step 6 Impact Analysis
- Step 7 Risk Determination
- Step 8 Control Recommendations
- Step 9 Results Documentation

## Risk Mitigation

Risk mitigation, the second process according to SP 800-30, the third according to ISO 27005 of risk management, involves prioritizing, evaluating, and implementing the appropriate risk-reducing controls recommended from the risk assessment process. Because the elimination of all risk is usually impractical or close to impossible, it is the responsibility of senior management and functional and business managers to use the least-cost approach and implement the most appropriate controls to decrease mission risk to an acceptable level, with minimal adverse impact on the organization's resources and mission.

## ISO 27005 Framework

The risk treatment process aim at selecting security measures to:

- reduce
- retain
- avoid
- transfer

risk and produce a risk treatment plan, that is the output of the process with the residual risks subject to the acceptance of management.

There are some list to select appropriate security measures, but is up to the single organization to choose the most appropriate one according to its business strategy, constraints of the environment and circumstances. The choice should be rational and documented. The importance of accepting a risk that is too costly to reduce is very high and led to the fact that risk acceptance is considered a separate process.

Risk transfer apply were the risk has a very high impact but is not easy to reduce significantly the likelihood by means of security controls: the insurance premium should be compared against the mitigation costs, eventually evaluating some mixed strategy to partially treat the risk. Another option is to outsource the risk to somebody more efficient to manage the risk.

Risk avoidance describe any action where ways of conducting business are changed to avoid any risk occurrence. For example, the choice of not storing sensitive information about customers can be an avoidance for the risk that customer data can be stolen.

The *residual risks*, i.e. the risk reaming after risk treatment decision have been taken, should be estimated to ensure that sufficient protection is achieved. If the residual risk is unacceptable, the risk treatment process should be iterated.

## NIST SP 800 30 Framework

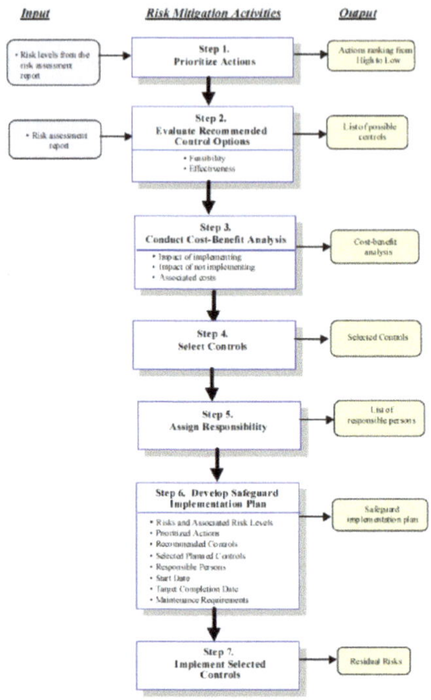


Figure 4-2. Risk Mitigation Methodology Flowchart

Risk mitigation methodology flow chart from NIST SP 800-30 Figure 4-2

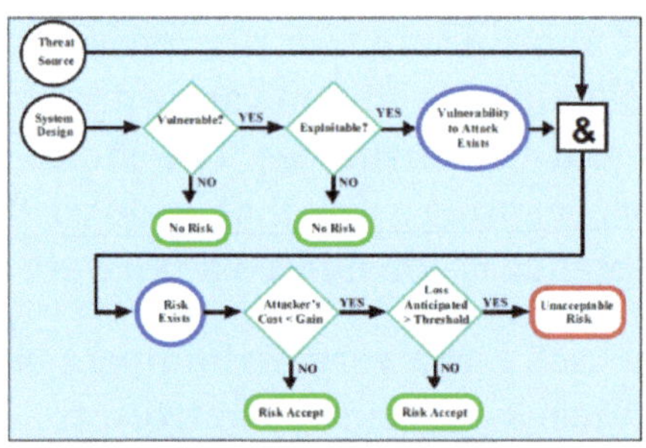


Figure 4-1. Risk Mitigation Action Points

Risk mitigation action point according to NIST SP 800-30 Figure 4-1

Risk mitigation is a systematic methodology used by senior management to reduce mission risk.Risk mitigation can be achieved through any of the following risk mitigation options:

- Risk Assumption. To accept the potential risk and continue operating the IT system or to implement controls to lower the risk to an acceptable level
- Risk Avoidance. To avoid the risk by eliminating the risk cause and/or consequence (e.g., forgo certain functions of the system or shut down the system when risks are identified)

- Risk Limitation. To limit the risk by implementing controls that minimize the adverse impact of a threat's exercising a vulnerability (e.g., use of supporting, preventive, detective controls)
- Risk Planning. To manage risk by developing a risk mitigation plan that prioritizes, implements, and maintains controls
- Research and Acknowledgement. To lower the risk of loss by acknowledging the vulnerability or flaw and researching controls to correct the vulnerability
- Risk Transference. To transfer the risk by using other options to compensate for the loss, such as purchasing insurance.

Address the greatest risks and strive for sufficient risk mitigation at the lowest cost, with minimal impact on other mission capabilities: this is the suggestion contained in

## Risk Communication

Risk communication is a horizontal process that interacts bidirectionally with all other processes of risk management. Its purpose is to establish a common understanding of all aspect of risk among all the organization's stakeholder. Establishing a common understanding is important, since it influences decisions to be taken. The Risk Reduction Overview method is specifically designed for this process. It presents a comprehensible overview of the coherence of risks, measures and residual risks to achieve this common understanding.

## Risk Monitoring and Review

Risk management is an ongoing, never ending process. Within this process implemented security measures are regularly monitored and reviewed to ensure that they work as planned and that changes in the environment rendered them ineffective. Business requirements, vulnerabilities and threats can change over the time.

Regular audits should be scheduled and should be conducted by an independent party, i.e. somebody not under the control of whom is responsible for the implementations or daily management of ISMS.

## IT Evaluation and Assessment

Security controls should be validated. Technical controls are possible complex systems that are to tested and verified. The hardest part to validate is people knowledge of procedural controls and the effectiveness of the real application in daily business of the security procedures.

Vulnerability assessment, both internal and external, and Penetration test are instruments for verifying the status of security controls.

Information technology security audit is an organizational and procedural control with the aim of evaluating security. The IT systems of most organization are evolving quite rapidly. Risk management should cope with these changes through change authorization after risk re evaluation of the affected systems and processes and periodically review the risks and mitigation actions.

Monitoring system events according to a security monitoring strategy, an incident response plan and security validation and metrics are fundamental activities to assure that an optimal level of security is obtained. It is important to monitor the new vulnerabilities, apply procedural and technical security controls like regularly updating software, and evaluate other kinds of controls to deal with zero-day attacks.

The attitude of involved people to benchmark against best practice and follow the seminars of professional associations in the sector are factors to assure the state of art of an organization IT risk management practice.

## Integrating Risk Management into System Development Life Cycle

Effective risk management must be totally integrated into the SDLC. An IT system's SDLC has five phases: initiation, development or acquisition, implementation, operation or maintenance, and disposal. The risk management methodology is the same regardless of the SDLC phase for which the assessment is being conducted. Risk management is an iterative process that can be performed during each major phase of the SDLC.

**Table 2-1 Integration of Risk Management into the SDLC**

| SDLC Phases | Phase Characteristics | Support from Risk Management Activities |
|---|---|---|
| Phase 1: Initiation | The need for an IT system is expressed and the purpose and scope of the IT system is documented | Identified risks are used to support the development of the system requirements, including security requirements, and a security concept of operations (strategy) |
| Phase 2: Development or Acquisition | The IT system is designed, purchased, programmed, developed, or otherwise constructed | The risks identified during this phase can be used to support the security analyses of the IT system that may lead to architecture and design tradeoffs during system development |
| Phase 3: Implementation | The system security features should be configured, enabled, tested, and verified | The risk management process supports the assessment of the system implementation against its requirements and within its modeled operational environment. Decisions regarding risks identified must be made prior to system operation |

| | | |
|---|---|---|
| Phase 4: Operation or Maintenance | The system performs its functions. Typically the system is being modified on an ongoing basis through the addition of hardware and software and by changes to organizational processes, policies, and procedures | Risk management activities are performed for periodic system reauthorization (or reaccreditation) or whenever major changes are made to an IT system in its operational, production environment (e.g., new system interfaces) |
| Phase 5: Disposal | This phase may involve the disposition of information, hardware, and software. Activities may include moving, archiving, discarding, or destroying information and sanitizing the hardware and software | Risk management activities are performed for system components that will be disposed of or replaced to ensure that the hardware and software are properly disposed of, that residual data is appropriately handled, and that system migration is conducted in a secure and systematic manner |

NIST SP 800-64 is devoted to this topic.

Early integration of security in the SDLC enables agencies to maximize return on investment in their security programs, through:

- Early identification and mitigation of security vulnerabilities and misconfigurations, resulting in lower cost of security control implementation and vulnerability mitigation;
- Awareness of potential engineering challenges caused by mandatory security controls;
- Identification of shared security services and reuse of security strategies and tools to reduce development cost and schedule while improving security posture through proven methods and techniques; and
- Facilitation of informed executive decision making through comprehensive risk management in a timely manner.

This guide focuses on the information security components of the SDLC. First, descriptions of the key security roles and responsibilities that are needed in most information system developments are provided. Second, sufficient information about the SDLC is provided to allow a person who is unfamiliar with the SDLC process to understand the relationship between information security and the SDLC. The document integrates the security steps into the linear, sequential (a.k.a. waterfall) SDLC. The five-step SDLC cited in the document is an example of one method of development and is not intended to mandate this methodology. Lastly, SP 800-64 provides insight into IT projects and initiatives that are not as clearly defined as SDLC-based developments, such as service-oriented architectures, cross-organization projects, and IT facility developments.

Security can be incorporated into information systems acquisition, development and maintenance by implementing effective security practices in the following areas.

- Security requirements for information systems
- Correct processing in applications
- Cryptographic controls
- Security of system files
- Security in development and support processes
- Technical vulnerability management

Information systems security begins with incorporating security into the requirements process for any new application or system enhancement. Security should be designed into the system from the beginning. Security requirements are presented to the vendor during the requirements phase of a product purchase. Formal testing should be done to determine whether the product meets the required security specifications prior to purchasing the product.

Correct processing in applications is essential in order to prevent errors and to mitigate loss, unauthorized modification or misuse of information. Effective coding techniques include validating input and output data, protecting message integrity using encryption, checking for processing errors, and creating activity logs.

Applied properly, cryptographic controls provide effective mechanisms for protecting the confidentiality, authenticity and integrity of information. An institution should develop policies on the use of encryption, including proper key management. Disk Encryption is one way to protect data at rest. Data in transit can be protected from alteration and unauthorized viewing using SSL certificates issued through a Certificate Authority that has implemented a Public Key Infrastructure.

System files used by applications must be protected in order to ensure the integrity and stability of the application. Using source code repositories with version control, extensive testing, production back-off plans, and appropriate access to program code are some effective measures that can be used to protect an application's files.

Security in development and support processes is an essential part of a comprehensive quality assurance and production control process, and would usually involve training and continuous oversight by the most experienced staff.

Applications need to be monitored and patched for technical vulnerabilities. Procedures for applying patches should include evaluating the patches to determine their appropriateness, and whether or not they can be successfully removed in case of a negative impact.

## Critique of Risk Management as a Methodology

Risk management as a scientific methodology has been criticized as being shallow. Major programs that implies risk management applied to IT systems of large organizations as FISMA has been criticized.

The risk management methodology is based on scientific foundations of statistical decision making: indeed, by avoiding the complexity that accompanies the formal probabilistic model of risks and uncertainty, risk management looks more like a process that attempts to guess rather than formally predict the future on the basis of statistical evidence. It is highly subjective in assessing the value of assets, the likelihood of threats occurrence and the significance of the impact.

Having considered this criticisms the risk management is a very important instrument in designing, implementing and operating secure information systems because it systematically classifies and drives the process of deciding how to treat risks. Its usage is foreseen by legislative rules in many countries. A better way to deal with the subject has not emerged.

## Risk Managements Methods

It is quite hard to list most of the methods that at least partially support the IT risk management process. Efforts in this direction were done by:

- NIST Description of Automated Risk Management Packages That NIST/NCSC Risk Management Research Laboratory Has Examined, updated 1991
- ENISA in 2006; a list of methods and tools is available on line with a comparison engine. Among them the most widely used are:
    - CRAMM Developed by British government is compliant to ISO/IEC 17799, Gramm–Leach–Bliley Act (GLBA) and Health Insurance Portability and Accountability Act (HIPAA)
    - EBIOS developed by the French government it is compliant with major security standards: ISO/IEC 27001, ISO/IEC 13335, ISO/IEC 15408, ISO/IEC 17799 and ISO/IEC 21287
    - Standard of Good Practice developed by Information Security Forum (ISF)
    - Mehari developed by Clusif Club de la Sécurité de l'Information Français
    - TIK IT Risk Framework developed by IT Risk Institute
    - Octave developed by Carnegie Mellon University, SEI (Software Engineering Institute) The Operationally Critical Threat, Asset, and Vulnerability EvaluationSM (OCTAVE) approach defines a risk-based strategic assessment and planning technique for security.

  - IT-Grundschutz (IT Baseline Protection Manual) developed by Federal Office for Information Security (BSI) (Germany); IT-Grundschutz provides a method for an organization to establish an Information Security Management System (ISMS). It comprises both generic IT security recommendations for establishing an applicable IT security process and detailed technical recommendations to achieve the necessary IT security level for a specific domain

Enisa report classified the different methods regarding completeness, free availability, tool support; the result is that:

- EBIOS, ISF methods, IT-Grundschutz cover deeply all the aspects (Risk Identification, Risk analysis, Risk evaluation, Risk assessment, Risk treatment, Risk acceptance, Risk communication),
- EBIOS and IT-Grundschutz are the only ones freely available and
- only EBIOS has an open source tool to support it.

The Factor Analysis of Information Risk (FAIR) main document, "An Introduction to Factor Analysis of Information Risk (FAIR)", Risk Management Insight LLC, November 2006; outline that most of the methods above lack of rigorous definition of risk and its factors. FAIR is not another methodology to deal with risk management, but it complements existing methodologies.

FAIR has had a good acceptance, mainly by The Open Group and ISACA.

ISACA developed a methodology, called Risk IT, to address various kind of IT related risks, chiefly security related risks. It is integrated with COBIT, a general framework to manage IT. Risk IT has a broader concept of IT risk than other methodologies, it encompasses not just only the negative impact of operations and service delivery which can bring destruction or reduction of the value of the organization, but also the benefit\ value enabling risk associated to missing opportunities to use technology to enable or enhance business or the IT project management for aspects like overspending or late delivery with adverse business impact.

The "*Build Security In*" initiative of Homeland Security Department of United States, cites FAIR. The initiative Build Security In is a collaborative effort that provides practices, tools, guidelines, rules, principles, and other resources that software developers, architects, and security practitioners can use to build security into software in every phase of its development. So it chiefly address Secure coding.

## Standards

There are a number of standards about IT risk and IT risk management.

## References


- Hopkin, Paul "Fundamentals of Risk Management 2nd Edition" Kogan-Page (2012) ISBN 978-0-7494-6539-1
- Peter F. Christoffersen (22 November 2011). Elements of Financial Risk Management. Academic Press. ISBN 978-0-12-374448-7.
- Allan M. Malz (13 September 2011). Financial Risk Management: Models, History, and Institutions. John Wiley & Sons. ISBN 978-1-118-02291-7.
- John J. Hampton (1982). Modern Financial Theory: Perfect and Imperfect Markets. Reston Publishing Company. ISBN 978-0-8359-4553-0.
- Zahirul Hoque (2005). Handbook of Cost and Management Accounting. Spiramus Press Ltd. pp. 201–. ISBN 978-1-904905-01-1.
- Kirt C. Butler (28 August 2012). Multinational Finance: Evaluating Opportunities, Costs, and Risks of Operations. John Wiley & Sons. pp. 37–. ISBN 978-1-118-28276-2.
- Dietmar Franzen (6 December 2012). Design of Master Agreements for OTC Derivatives. Springer Science & Business Media. pp. 7–. ISBN 978-3-642-56932-6.
- Crockford, Neil (1986). An Introduction to Risk Management (2nd ed.). Woodhead-Faulkner. ISBN 0-85941-332-2.
- Technical Standard Risk Taxonomy ISBN 1-931624-77-1 Document Number: C081 Published by The Open Group, January 2009.

3

# Theory Related to Risk Management

The basic theory that is related to risk management is the dragon king theory. It is used as a metaphor to refer to an event that is extremely large and has developed from a rare and unique situation. The topic discussed in this chapter is of vital importance, and provides the readers with a better understanding of risk management.

## Dragon King Theory

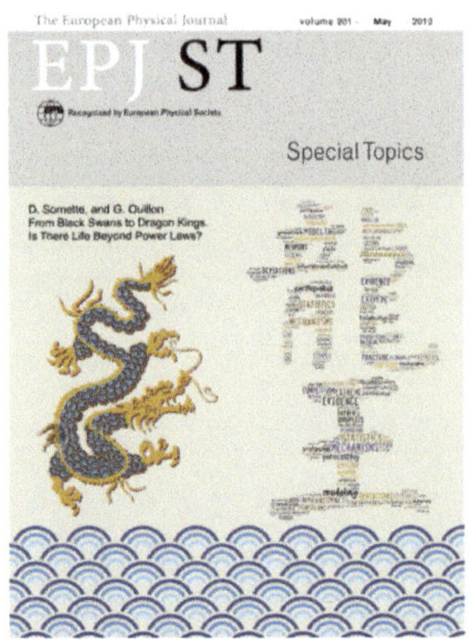


The cover of a collection of articles about Dragon Kings

Dragon king (DK) is double metaphor for an event that is both extremely large in size or impact (a "king") and born of unique origins (a "dragon") relative to its peers (other events from the same system). DK events are generated by / correspond to mechanisms such as positive feedback, tipping points, bifurcations, and phase transitions, that tend to occur in nonlinear and complex systems, and serve to amplify DK events to extreme levels. By understanding and monitoring these dynamics, some predictability of such events may be obtained.

The theory has been developed by Prof. Didier Sornette, who hypothesizes that many of the crises that we face are in fact DK rather than black swans—i.e., they may be predictable to some degree. Given the importance of crises to the long-term organization of a variety of systems, the DK theory urges that special attention be given to the study and monitoring of extremes, and that a dynamic view be taken. From a scientific viewpoint, such extremes are interesting because they may reveal underlying, often hidden, organizing principles. Practically speaking, one should ambitiously study extreme risks, but not forget that significant uncertainty will almost always be present, and should be rigorously considered in decisions regarding risk management and design.

The theory of DK is related to concepts such as: black swan theory, outliers, complex systems, nonlinear dynamics, power laws, extreme value theory, prediction, extreme risks, risk management, etc.

## Black Swans and Dragon Kings

The Black Swan: The Impact of the Highly Improbable.

Black swan can be considered a metaphor for an event that is surprising (to the observer), has a major effect, and, after being observed, is rationalized in hindsight. The theory of black swans is epistemological, relating to the limited knowledge and understanding of the observer. The term was introduced and popularized by Nassim Taleb and has been associated with concepts such as heavy tails, non-linear payoffs, model error, and even Knightian uncertainty, whose "unknowable unknown" event terminology was popularized by former United States Secretary of Defence Donald Rumsfeld. Taleb claims that black swan events are not predictable, and in practice, the theory encourages one to "prepare rather than predict", and limit one's exposure to extreme fluctuations.

The black swan concept is important and poses a valid criticism of people, firms, and societies that are irresponsible in the sense that they are overly confident in their ability to anticipate and manage risk. However, claiming that extreme events are – in general – unpredictable may also lead to a lack of accountability in risk management roles. In fact, it is known that in a wide range of physical systems that extreme events are predictable to some degree. One simply needs to have a sufficiently deep understanding of the structure and dynamics of the focal system, and the ability to monitor it. This is the domain of the dragon kings. Such events have been referred to as Grey Swans by

Taleb. A more rigorous distinction between black swans, grey swans, and dragon kings is difficult as black swans are not precisely defined in physical and mathematical terms. However technical elaboration of concepts in the Black Swan book are elaborated in the Silent Risk document. An analysis of the precise definition of a black swan in a risk management context was written by Prof. Terje Aven

## Dragon Kings Live Beyond Power Laws

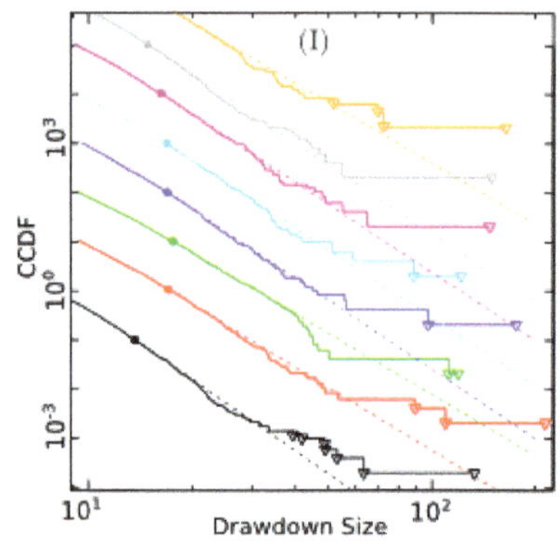


The 5000 largest drawdowns for 8 different futures contracts plotted according to their empirical CCDF, shifted by factors of 10 for visibility. The dashed lines are power law fits.

It is well known that many phenomena in both the natural and social sciences have power law statistics (Pareto distribution). Furthermore, from extreme value theory, it is known that a broad range of distributions (the Frechet class) have tails that are asymptotically power law. The result of this is that, when dealing with crises and extremes, power law tails are the "normal" case. The unique property of power laws is that they are scale-invariant / self-similar / fractal. This property implies that all events – both large and small – are generated by the same mechanism, and thus there will be no distinct precursors by which the largest events may be predicted. A well known conceptual framework for events of this type is self-organized criticality. Such concepts are compatible with the theory of the black swan. However Taleb has also stated that considering the power law as a model instead of a model with lighter tails (e.g., a Gaussian) "converts black swans into gray ones", in the sense that the power law model gives non-negligible probability to large events.

In a variety of studies it has been found that, despite the fact that a power law models the tail of the empirical distribution well, the largest events are significantly outlying (i.e., much larger than what would be expected under the model) . Such events are interpreted as dragon kings as they indicate a departure from the generic process underlying the power law. Examples of this include the largest radiation release events occurring in nuclear power plant accidents, the largest city (agglomeration) within the sample of cities in a country, the largest crashes in financial markets, and intraday wholesale electricity prices.

## Mechanisms for Dragon Kings

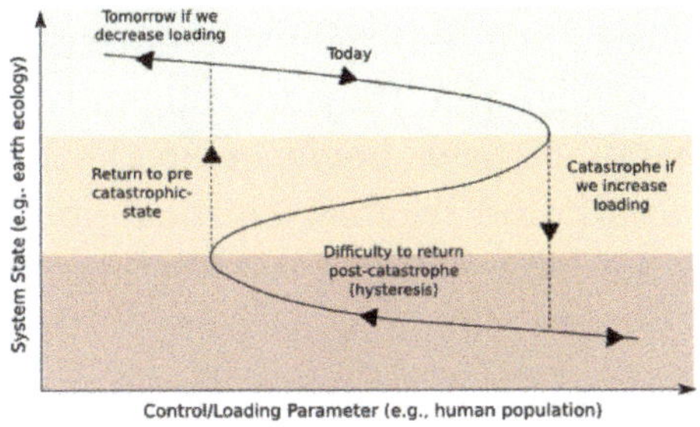


Fold bifurcation in ecology

Physically speaking, dragon kings may be associated with the regime changes, bifurcations, and tipping points of complex out-of-equilibrium systems. For instance, the catastrophe (fold bifurcation) of the global ecology illustrated in the figure could be considered to be a dragon king: Many observers would be surprised by such a dramatic change of state. However, it is well known that in dynamic systems, there are many precursors as the system approaches the catastrophe.

Positive feedback is also a mechanism that can spawn dragon kings. For instance, in a stampede the number of cattle running increases the level of panic which causes more cattle to run, and so on. In human dynamics such herding and mob behavior has also been observed in crowds, stock markets, and so on.

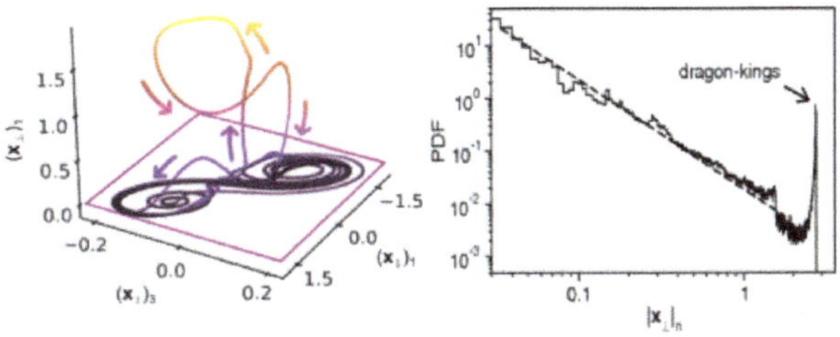


Left: Illustration of the system trajectory in the vicinity of a bubbling event. Right: empirical pdf (histogram) of peak heights in trajectories in double logarithmic scale

Dragon kings are also caused by attractor bubbling in coupled oscillator systems. Attractor bubbling is a generic behavior appearing in networks of coupled oscillators where the system typically orbits in an invariant manifold with a chaotic attractor (where the peak trajectories are low), but is intermittently pushed (by noise) into a region where orbits are locally repelled from the invariant manifold (where the peak trajectories are large). These excursions form the dragon kings, as illustrated in the figure. It is claimed that such models can describe many real phenomena such as earthquakes, brain activity, etc. A block and spring mechanical model, considered as a model of geological faults and their earthquake dynamics, produced a similar distribution.

It could also be the case that dragon kings are created as a result of system control or intervention. That is, trying to suppress the release of stress or death in dynamic complex systems may lead to an accumulation of stress or a maturation towards instability. For instance, brush/forest fires are a natural occurrence in many areas. Such fires are inconvenient and thus we may wish that they are diligently extinguished. This leads to long periods without inconvenient fires, however, in the absence of fires, dead wood accumulates. Once this accumulation reaches a critical point, and a fire starts, the fire becomes so large that it cannot be controlled – a singular event that could be considered to be a dragon king. Other policies, such as doing nothing (allowing for small fires to occur naturally), or performing strategic controlled burning, would avoid enormous fires by allowing for frequent small ones. Another example is monetary policy. Quantitative easing programs and low interest rate policies are common, with the intention of avoiding recessions, promoting growth, etc. However, such programs build instability by increasing income inequality, keeping weak firms alive, and inflating asset bubbles. Ultimately such policies, aimed at smoothing out economic fluctuations, will enable an enormous correction – a dragon king.

## Detecting DK as Statistical Outliers

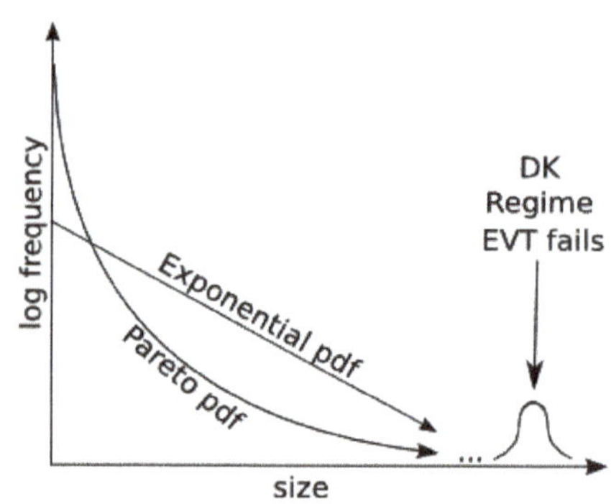


Probability density function schematic where the dragon king regime is represented by a lump of mass deep in the tail.

DK are outliers by definition. However, when calling DK outliers there is an important proviso: In standard statistics outliers are typically erroneous values and are discarded, or statistical methods are chosen that are somehow insensitive to outliers. Contrarily, DK are outliers that are highly informative, and should be the focus of much statistical attention. Thus a first step is identifying DK in historical data. Existing tests are either based on the asymptotic properties of the empirical distribution function (EDF) or on an assumption about the underlying cumulative distribution function (CDF) of the data.

It turns out that testing for outliers relative to an exponential distribution is very general. The latter follows from the Pickands–Balkema–de Haan theorem theorem of Extreme value theory which states that a wide range of distributions asymptotically (above high thresholds) have exponential or power law tails. As an aside, this is one explanation why power law tails are so common when studying extremes. To finish the point, since the natural logarithm of a power law tail is exponential, one can take the logarithm of power law data and then test for outliers relative to an exponential tail. There are many test statistics and techniques for testing for outliers in an exponential sample. An inward test sequentially tests the largest point, then the second largest, and so on, until the first test that is not rejected (i.e., the null hypothesis that the point is not an outlier is not rejected). The number of rejected tests identifies the number of outliers. For instance, where $x_{(1)} > x_{(2)} > \cdots > x_{(n)}$ is the sorted sample, the inward robust test uses the test statistic $T_{r,m} = x_{(r)} / (x_{(m)} + \ldots + x_{(n)})$ where r is the point being tested $(r = 1, 2, 3\ldots)$, and $r < m < n$ where m is the pre-specified maximum number of outliers. At each step the p-value for the test statistic must be computed and, if lower than some level, the test rejected. This test has many desirable properties: It does not require that the number of outliers be specified, it is not prone to under (masking) and over (swamping) estimation of the number outliers, it is easy to implement, and the test is independent of the value of the parameter of the exponential tail.

## Examples

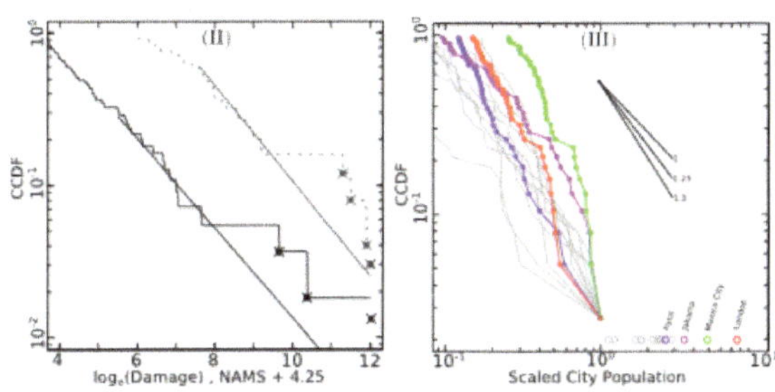


(II) Empirical CCDF of the log of radiation released (grey dashed) and damage (black) caused by accidents at nuclear power plants, with solid lines giving the fitted power law tail. (III) Empirical CCDF of populations in urban agglomerations within a country, scaled so that the second largest has size 1. Outliers are labeled.

Some examples of where dragon kings have been detected as outliers include:

(I) financial crashes as measured by drawdowns, where the outliers correspond to terrorist attacks (e.g., the 2005 London bombing), and the Flash crash of 2010;

(II) the radiation released and loss ($) caused by accidents at nuclear power plants, where outliers correspond to runaway disasters where safety mechanisms were overwhelmed;

(III) the largest city (measured by the population in its agglomeration) in the population of cities within a country, where the largest city plays a disproportionately important role in the dynamics of the country, and benefits from unique growth; and,

(IV) intraday wholesale electricity prices.

## Modeling and Prediction

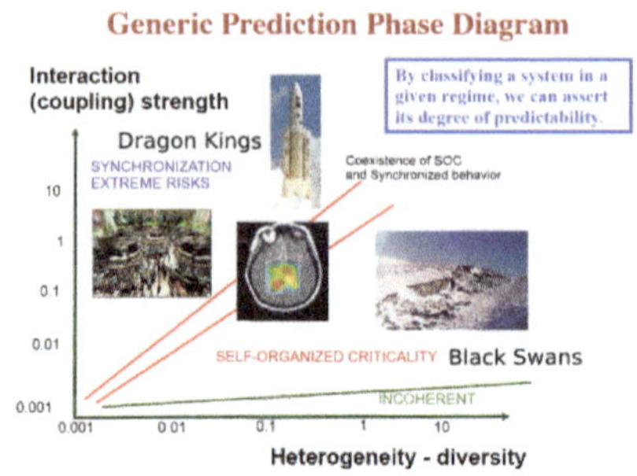


Predictability based on interaction and diversity in a system

How one models and predicts dragon kings depends on the underlying mechanism. However, the common approach will require continuous monitoring of the focal system and comparing measurements with a (non-linear or complex) dynamic model. It has been proposed that the more homogeneous the system, and the stronger its interactions, the more predictable it will be.

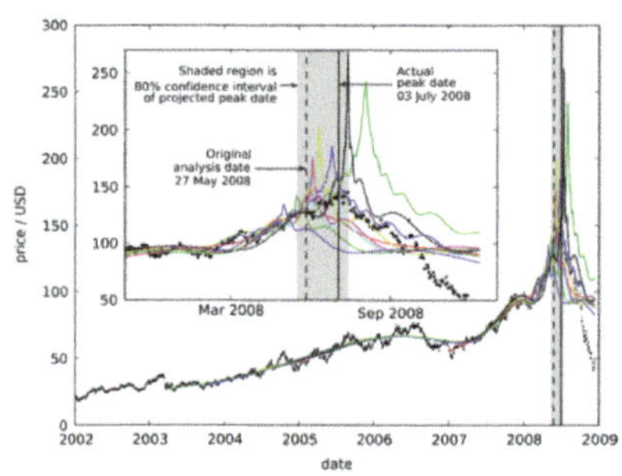


Modeling and prediction of a bubble (super-exponential growth) with the log-periodic power law

For instance, in non-linear systems with phase transitions at a critical point, it is well known that a window of predictability occurs in the neighborhood of the critical point due to precursory signs: the system recovers more slowly from perturbations, autocorrelation changes, variance increases, spatial coherence increases, etc. These properties have been used for prediction in many applications ranging from changes in the biosphere to rupture of pressure tanks on the Ariane rocket.

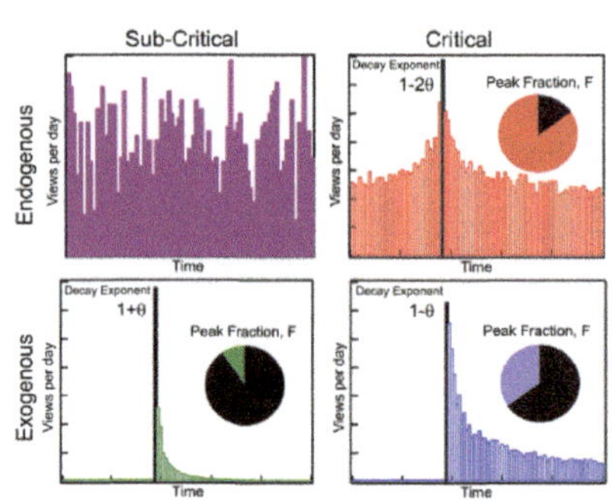


Four regimes of views per day of YouTube videos.

For the phenomena of unsustainable growth (e.g., of populations or stock prices), one can consider a growth model that features a finite time singularity, which is a critical point where the growth regime changes. In systems that are discrete scale invariant such a model is power law growth, decorated with a log-periodic function. Fitting this model on the growth data (non-linear regression) allows for the prediction of the singularity, i.e., the end of unsustainable growth. This has been applied to many problems, for instance: rupture in materials, earthquakes, and the growth and burst of bubbles in financial markets.

An interesting dynamic to consider, that may reveal the development of a block-buster success, is Epidemic phenomena: e.g., the spread of plague, viral phenomena in media, the spread of panic and volatility in stock markets, etc. In such a case, a powerful approach is to decompose activity/fluctuations into exogeneous and endogeneous parts, and learn about the endogenous dynamics that may lead to high impact bursts in activity.

## Prediction and Decision-Making

Given a model and data, one can obtain a statistical model estimate. This model estimate can then be used to compute interesting quantities such as the conditional probability of the occurrence of a dragon king event in a future time interval, and the most probable occurrence time. When doing statistical modeling of extremes, and using complex or nonlinear dynamic models, there is bound to be substantial uncertainty. Thus, one should be diligent in uncertainty quantification: not only considering the randomness present in the fitted stochastic model, but also the uncertainty of its' estimated parameters (e.g., with Bayesian techniques or by first simulating parameters and then simulating from the model with those parameters), and the uncertainty in model selection (e.g., by considering an ensemble of different models).

One can then use the estimated probabilities and their associated uncertainties to inform decisions. In the simplest case, one performs a binary classification: predicting that a dragon king will occur in a future interval if its probability of occurrence is high enough, with sufficient certainty. For instance, one may take a specific action if a dragon king is predicted to occur. An optimal decision will then balance the cost of false negatives/false positives and misses/false alarms according to a specified loss function. For instance, if the cost of a miss is very large relative to the cost of a false alarm, the optimal decision will detect dragon kings more frequently than they occur. One should also study the true positive rate of the prediction. The smaller this value is, the weaker the test, and the closer one is to black swan territory. In practice the selection of the optimal decision, and the computation of its properties must be done by cross validation with historical data (if available), or on simulated data (if one knows how to simulate the dragon kings).

In a dynamic setting the dataset will grow over time, and the model estimate, and its estimated probabilities will evolve. One may then consider combining the sequence of estimates/probabilities when performing prediction. In this dynamic setting, the test will likely be weak most of the time (e.g., when the system is around equilibrium), but as one approaches a dragon king, and precursors become visible, the true positive rate should increase.

## The Importance of Extreme Risks

Dragon kings form special kinds of events leading to extreme risks (which can also be opportunities). That extreme risks are important should be self-evident. Natural disasters provide many examples (e.g., asteroid impacts leading to extinction). Some statistical examples of the impact of extremes are that: the largest nuclear power plant accident (2011 Fukushima disaster) caused more damage than all (>200) other historical accidents together, the largest 10 percent of private data breaches from organizations accounts for 99 percent of the total breached private information, the largest 5 epidemics since 1900 caused 20 times the fatalities of the remaining 1363, etc. In general such statistics arrive in the presence of heavy tailed distributions, and the presence of dragon kings will augment the already over-sized impact of extreme events.

Despite the importance of extreme events, due to ignorance, misaligned incentives, and cognitive biases, we often fail to adequately anticipate them. Technically speaking, this leads to poorly specified models where distributions that are not heavy tailed enough, and under-appreciating both serial and multivariate dependence of extreme events. Some examples of such failures in risk assessment include the use of Gaussian models in finance (Black-Scholes, the Gaussian copula, LTCM), the use of Gaussian processes and linear wave theory failing to predict the occurrence of rogue waves, the failure of economic models in general to predict the 2007 financial crisis, and the under-appreciation of external events, cascades, and nonlinear effects in probabilistic risk assessment, leading to not anticipating the 2011 Fukushima disaster. Such high impact failures emphasize the importance of the study of extremes.

## Risk Management

The dragon king concept raises many questions about how one can deal with risk. Of course, if possible, one should avoid exposure to large risks (often referred to as the black swan approach). However, in many developments, exposure to risk is a necessity, and a trade-off between risk and return needs to be navigated. This nontrivial case is the one that must be considered.

In an adaptive system, where prediction of dragon kings is successful, one can act to defend the system or even profit. How to design such resilient systems, as well as their real time risk monitoring systems , is an important and interdisciplinary problem where dragon kings must be considered.

On another note, when it comes to the quantification of risk in a given system (whether it be a bank, an insurance company, a dike, a bridge, or a socio-economic system), risk needs to be accounted for over a period, such as annually. Typically one is interested in statistics such as the annual probability of loss or damage in excess of some value (Value at risk), other tail risk measures, and return periods. To provide such risk characterizations, the dynamic dragon kings must be reasoned about in terms of annual frequency and severity statistics. These frequency and severity statistics can then be brought together in a model such as a Compound Poisson Process.

Provided that the statistical properties of the system are consistent over time (stationary), frequency and severity statistics may be constructed based on past observations, simulations, and/or assumptions. If not, one may only construct scenarios. However, in any case, given the uncertainty present, a range of scenarios should be considered. Due to the shortage of data for extreme events, the principle of parsimony, and theoretical results from extreme value theory about universal tail models, one typically relies on a GPD tail model. However such a model excludes DK. Thus, when one has sufficient reason to believe that DK are present, or if one simply wants to consider a scenario, one may e.g., consider a density mixture of a GPD and a density for the DK regime.

## References


- Sornette, Didier, and Peter Cauwels. "Managing risk in a creepy world." Journal of Risk Management in Financial Institutions 8.1 (2015): 83-108.
- Wheatley, Spencer, Thomas Maillart, and Didier Sornette. "The Extreme Risk of Personal Data Breaches & The Erosion of Privacy." arXiv preprint arXiv:1505.07684 (2015).
- Sornette, Didier, and Peter Cauwels. "1980–2008: The illusion of the perpetual money machine and what it bodes for the future." Risks 2.2 (2014): 103-131.
- Strogatz, Steven H. Nonlinear dynamics and chaos: with applications to physics, biology, chemistry, and engineering. Westview press, 2014
- Guha-Sapir, D., R. Below, and Ph Hoyois. "EM-DAT: International disaster database." Univ. Cathol. Louvain, Brussels: Belgium. www. em-dat. net. (2014).
- Sornette, Didier, and Tatyana Kovalenko. "Dynamical Diagnosis and Solutions for Resilient Natural and Social Systems." Planet@ Risk 1 (1) (2013) 7-33.
- Cavalcante, Hugo LD de S., et al. "Predictability and suppression of extreme events in a chaotic system." Physical review letters 111.19 (2013): 198701.
- Barnosky, Anthony D., et al. "Approaching a state shift in Earth's biosphere."Nature 486.7401 (2012): 52-58.
- Filimonov, Vladimir, and Didier Sornette. "Quantifying reflexivity in financial markets: Toward a prediction of flash crashes." Physical Review E 85.5 (2012): 056108.

4

# Analysis and Assessment of Risk Management

Risk analysis is defined in a number of ways; the definitions usually depend on how risk analysis relates to other concepts. Risk management can be divided into two components, risk assessment and risk management. This section on analysis and assessment of risk management is an overview of the subject matter incorporating all the major aspects of the topic.

## Risk Analysis

Risk analysis can be defined in many different ways, and much of the definition depends on how risk analysis relates to other concepts. Risk analysis can be "broadly defined to include risk assessment, risk characterization, risk communication, risk management, and policy relating to risk, in the context of risks of concern to individuals, to public- and private-sector organizations, and to society at a local, regional, national, or global level." A useful construct is to divide risk analysis into two components: (1) risk assessment (identifying, evaluating, and measuring the probability and severity of risks) and (2) risk management (deciding what to do about risks). Some books take a slightly different approach and define risk management as the overarching concept, where risk analysis is the component that seeks to identify and measure the risks and risk mitigation is determining what to do about the risks.

Risk analysis can be qualitative or quantitative. Qualitative risk analysis uses words or colors to identify and evaluate risks or presents a written description of the risk, and quantitative risk analysis (QRA) calculates numerical probabilities over the possible consequences.

### Quantitative Risk Analysis

QRA seeks to numerically assess probabilities for the potential consequences of risk, and is often called probabilistic risk analysis or probabilistic risk assessment (PRA). The analysis often seeks to describe the consequences in numerical units such as dollars, time, or lives lost. PRA often seeks to answer three questions:

1. What can happen? (i.e., what can go wrong?)
2. How likely is it that it will happen?

3. If it does happen, what are the consequences?

Thus, risk $R$ can be described as a set of triplets, $R=\{<s_i,p_i,c_i>\}$, $i=1,2,...,N$ where $s_i$ is scenario $i$, $p_i$ is the probability of scenario $i$, $c_i$ are the consequences if scenario $i$ occurs, and $N$ is the total number of scenarios. This type of analysis typically results in a probability distribution over the consequences.

Although actuarial science has used probabilities to measure risk for more than a hundred years, PRA as a specific mode of inquiry was initially developed to analyze engineering risks such as nuclear power plants and the space shuttle. More recently, it has also been applied to other areas, such as business, climate change, health risks, food safety and security. Especially with the increasing importance of terrorism, game theory has become a quantitative tool to analyze the risks of intelligent adversaries who seek to do harm against a system or people. These game-theoretic techniques may be probabilistic or deterministic.

### Pseudo-quantitative Risk Assessment

Pseudo-quantitative risk assessments generally assign numbers to the likelihood and consequences for a risk but do not build a mathematical model of the risk as suggested by PRA. The most popular pseudo-quantitative method is probably the risk matrix, which classifies the likelihood of a risk in one category and the consequences in another category. The combination of the likelihood and consequence categories corresponds to a risk level, usually a color such as red, orange, yellow, and green. A risk matrix is sometimes called a pseudo-quantitative method because the categories may be determined from numbers. For example, the likelihood category *Unlikely* may correspond to a probability of occurrence between 0.1 and 0.3.

These pseudo-quantitative or scoring methods have been heavily criticized because they do not obey mathematical rules and may not correctly rank risks. They have the appearance of being rigorous but provide a false sense of security to those organizations that rely on them to manage risks. Undertaking a full QRA provides a more rigorous analysis and a better foundation for making good risk management decisions than relying on pseudo-quantitative methods.

## Hazard Analysis

A hazard analysis is used as the first step in a process used to assess risk. The result of a hazard analysis is the identification of different type of hazards. A hazard is a potential condition and exists or not (probability is 1 or 0). It may in single existence or in combination with other hazards (sometimes called events) and conditions become an actual Functional Failure or Accident (Mishap). The way this exactly happens in one particular sequence is called a scenario. This scenario has a probability (between 1 and 0) of occurrence. Often a system has many potential failure scenarios. It also is assigned a classification, based on the worst case severity of the end condition. Risk is the combination of probability and severity. Preliminary risk levels can be provided in the hazard analysis. The validation, more precise prediction (verification) and acceptance of risk is determined in the Risk assessment (analysis). The main goal of both is to provide the best selection of means of controlling or eliminating the risk. The term is used in several engineering specialties, including avionics, chemical process safety, safety engineering, reliability engineering and food safety.

## Hazards and Risk

A hazard is defined as a "Condition, event, or circumstance that could lead to or contribute to an unplanned or undesirable event." Seldom does a single hazard cause an accident or a functional failure. More often an accident or operational failure occurs as the result of a sequence of causes. A hazard analysis will consider system state, for example operating environment, as well as failures or malfunctions.

While in some cases, safety or reliability risk can be eliminated, in most cases a certain degree of risk must be accepted. In order to quantify expected costs before the fact, the potential consequences and the probability of occurrence must be considered. Assessment of risk is made by combining the severity of consequence with the likelihood of occurrence in a matrix. Risks that fall into the "unacceptable" category (e.g., high severity and high probability) must be mitigated by some means to reduce the level of safety risk.

IEEE STD-1228-1994 Software Safety Plans prescribes industry best practices for conducting software safety hazard analyses to help ensure safety requirements and attributes are defined and specified for inclusion in software that commands, controls or monitors critical functions. When software is involved in a system, the development and design assurance of that software is often governed by DO-178B. The severity of consequence identified by the hazard analysis establishes the criticality level of the software. Software criticality levels range from A to E, corresponding to the severity of Catastrophic to No Safety Effect. Higher levels of rigor are required for level A and B software and corresponding functional tasks and work products is the system safety domain are used as objective evidence of meeting safety criteria and requirements.

Recently a leading edge commercial standard was promulgated based on decades of proven system safety processes in DoD and NASA. ANSI/GEIA-STD-0010-2009 (Standard Best Practices for System Safety Program Development and Execution) is a demilitarized commercial best practice that uses proven holistic, comprehensive and tailored approaches for hazard prevention, elimination and control. It is centered around the hazard analysis and functional based safety process.

## Severity Definitions - Safety Related

| Severity | Definition |
|---|---|
| Catastrophic | Results in multiple fatalities and/or loss of the system |
| Hazardous | Reduces the capability of the system or the operator ability to cope with adverse conditions to the extent that there would be:<br>• Large reduction in safety margin or functional capability<br>• Crew physical distress/excessive workload such that operators cannot be relied upon to perform required tasks accurately or completely<br>• Serious or fatal injury to small number of occupants of aircraft (except operators)<br>• Fatal injury to ground personnel and/or general public |
| Major | Reduces the capability of the system or the operators to cope with adverse operating conditions to the extent that there would be:<br>• Significant reduction in safety margin or functional capability<br>• Significant increase in operator workload<br>• Conditions impairing operator efficiency or creating significant discomfort<br>• Physical distress to occupants of aircraft (except operator) including injuries<br>• Major occupational illness and/or major environmental damage, and/or major property damage |
| Minor | Does not significantly reduce system safety. Actions required by operators are well within their capabilities. Include:<br>• Slight reduction in safety margin or functional capabilities<br>• Slight increase in workload such as routine flight plan changes<br>• Some physical discomfort to occupants or aircraft (except operators)<br>• Minor occupational illness and/or minor environmental damage, and/or minor property damage |
| No Safety Effect | Has no effect on safety |

## Likelihood of Occurrence

| Likelihood | Definition |
|---|---|
| Probable | • Qualitative: Anticipated to occur one or more times during the entire system/operational life of an item.<br>• Quantitative: Probability of occurrence per operational hour is greater than |
| Remote | • Qualitative: Unlikely to occur to each item during its total life. May occur several times in the life of an entire system or fleet.<br>• Quantitative: Probability of occurrence per operational hour is less than , but greater than |
| Extremely Remote | • Qualitative: Not anticipated to occur to each item during its total life. May occur a few times in the life of an entire system or fleet.<br>• Quantitative: Probability of occurrence per operational hour is less than but greater than |
| Extremely Improbable | • Qualitative: So unlikely that it is not anticipated to occur during the entire operational life of an entire system or fleet.<br>• Quantitative: Probability of occurrence per operational hour is less than |

# Fault Tree Analysis

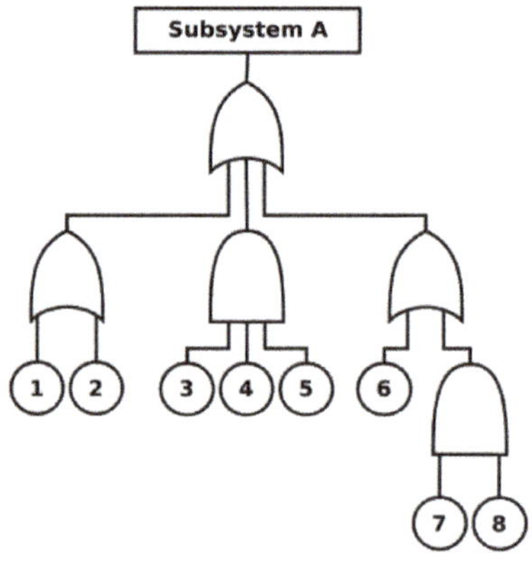


A fault tree diagram

Fault tree analysis (FTA) is a top down, deductive failure analysis in which an undesired state of a system is analyzed using Boolean logic to combine a series of lower-level events. This analysis method is mainly used in the fields of safety engineering and reliability engineering to understand how systems can fail, to identify the best ways to reduce risk or to determine (or get a feeling for) event rates of a safety accident or a particular system level (functional) failure. FTA is used in the aerospace, nuclear power, chemical and process, pharmaceutical, petrochemical and other high-hazard industries; but is also used in fields as diverse as risk factor identification relating to social service system failure. FTA is also used in software engineering for debugging purposes and is closely related to cause-elimination technique used to detect bugs.

In aerospace, the more general term "system Failure Condition" is used for the "undesired state" / Top event of the fault tree. These conditions are classified by the severity of their effects. The most severe conditions require the most extensive fault tree analysis. These "system Failure Conditions" and their classification are often previously determined in the functional Hazard analysis.

## Usage

Fault Tree Analysis can be used to:

- understand the logic leading to the top event / undesired state.
- show compliance with the (input) system safety / reliability requirements.
- prioritize the contributors leading to the top event - Creating the Critical Equipment/Parts/Events lists for different importance measures.
- monitor and control the safety performance of the complex system (e.g., is a particular aircraft safe to fly when fuel valve *x* malfunctions? For how long is it allowed to fly with the valve malfunction?).
- minimize and optimize resources.
- assist in designing a system. The FTA can be used as a design tool that helps to create (output / lower level) requirements.
- function as a diagnostic tool to identify and correct causes of the top event. It can help with the creation of diagnostic manuals / processes.

## History

Fault Tree Analysis (FTA) was originally developed in 1962 at Bell Laboratories by H.A. Watson, under a U.S. Air Force Ballistics Systems Division contract to evaluate the Minuteman I Intercontinental Ballistic Missile (ICBM) Launch Control System. The use of fault trees has since gained widespread support and is often used as a failure analysis tool by reliability experts. Following the first published use of FTA in the 1962 Minuteman I Launch Control Safety Study, Boeing and AVCO expanded use of FTA to the entire Minuteman II system in 1963-1964. FTA received extensive coverage at a 1965 System Safety Symposium in Seattle sponsored by Boeing and the University of Washington. Boeing began using FTA for civil aircraft design around 1966.

Subsequently, within the U.S. military, application of FTA for use with fuzes was explored by Picatinny Arsenal in the 1960s and 1970s. In 1976 the U.S. Army Materiel Command incorporated FTA into an Engineering Design Handbook on Design for Reliability. The Reliability Analysis Center at Rome Laboratory and its successor organizations now with the Defense Technical Information Center (Reliability Information Analysis Center and now Defense Systems Information Analysis Center, https://www.dsiac.org/) has published documents on FTA and reliability block diagrams since the 1960s. MIL-HDBK-338B provides a more recent reference.

In 1970, the U.S. Federal Aviation Administration (FAA) published a change to 14 CFR 25.1309 airworthiness regulations for transport category aircraft in the Federal Register at 35 FR 5665 (1970-04-08). This change adopted failure probability criteria for aircraft systems and equipment and led to widespread use of FTA in civil aviation. In 1998, the FAA published Order 8040.4, establishing risk management policy including hazard analysis in a range of critical activities beyond aircraft certification, including air traffic control and modernization of the U.S. National Airspace System. This led to the publication of the FAA System Safety Handbook, which describes the use of FTA in various types of formal hazard analysis.

Early in the Apollo project the question was asked about the probability of successfully sending astronauts to the moon and returning them safely to Earth. A risk, or reliability, calculation of some sort was performed and the result was a mission success probability that was unacceptably low. This result discouraged NASA from further quantitative risk or reliability analysis until after the Challenger accident in 1986. Instead, NASA decided to rely on the use of failure modes and effects analysis (FMEA) and other qualitative methods for system safety assessments. After the Challenger accident, the importance of PRA and FTA in systems risk and reliability analysis was realized and its use at NASA has begun to grow and now FTA is considered as one of the most important system reliability and safety analysis techniques.

Within the nuclear power industry, the U.S. Nuclear Regulatory Commission began using probabilistic risk assessment (PRA) methods including FTA in 1975, and significantly expanded PRA research following the 1979 incident at Three Mile Island. This eventually led to the 1981 publication of the NRC Fault Tree Handbook NUREG–0492, and mandatory use of PRA under the NRC's regulatory authority.

Following process industry disasters such as the 1984 Bhopal disaster and 1988 Piper Alpha explosion, in 1992 the United States Department of Labor Occupational Safety and Health Administration (OSHA) published in the Federal Register at 57 FR 6356 (1992-02-24) its Process Safety Management (PSM) standard in 19 CFR 1910.119. OSHA PSM recognizes FTA as an acceptable method for process hazard analysis (PHA).

Today FTA is widely used in system safety and reliability engineering, and in all major fields of engineering.

## Methodology

FTA methodology is described in several industry and government standards, including NRC NUREG–0492 for the nuclear power industry, an aerospace-oriented revision to NUREG–0492 for use by NASA, SAE ARP4761 for civil aerospace, MIL–HDBK–338 for military systems, IEC standard IEC 61025 is intended for cross-industry use and has been adopted as European Norm EN 61025.

Any sufficiently complex system is subject to failure as a result of one or more subsystems failing. The likelihood of failure, however, can often be reduced through improved system design. Fault tree analysis maps the relationship between faults, subsystems, and redundant safety design elements by creating a logic diagram of the overall system.

The undesired outcome is taken as the root ('top event') of a tree of logic. For instance the undesired outcome of a metal stamping press operation is a human appendage being stamped. Working backward from this top event we might determine there are two ways this could happen: during normal operation or during maintenance operation. This condition is a logical OR. Considering the branch of occurring during normal operation perhaps we determine there are two ways this could happen: the press cycles and harms the operator or the press cycles and harms another person. This is another logical OR. We can make a design improvement by requiring the operator to press two buttons to cycle the machine—this is a safety feature in the form of a logical AND. The button may have an intrinsic failure rate—this becomes a fault stimulus we can analyze. When fault trees are labeled with actual numbers for failure probabilities, computer programs can calculate failure probabilities from fault trees. When a specific event is found to have more than one effect event, i.e. it has impact on several subsystems, it is called a common cause or common mode. Graphically speaking, it means this event will appear at several locations in the tree. Common causes introduce dependency relations between events. The probability computations of a tree which contains some common causes are much more complicated than regular trees where all events are considered as independent. Not all software tools available on the market provide such capability.

The Tree is usually written out using conventional logic gate symbols. The route through a tree between an event and an initiator in the tree is called a Cut Set. The shortest credible way through the tree from fault to initiating event is called a Minimal Cut Set.

Some industries use both fault trees and event trees. An Event Tree starts from an undesired initiator (loss of critical supply, component failure etc.) and follows possible further system events through to a series of final consequences. As each new event is considered, a new node on the tree is added with a split of probabilities of taking either branch. The probabilities of a range of 'top events' arising from the initial event can then be seen.

Classic programs include the Electric Power Research Institute's (EPRI) CAFTA software, which is used by many of the US nuclear power plants and by a majority of US and international aerospace manufacturers, and the Idaho National Laboratory's SAPHIRE, which is used by the U.S. Government to evaluate the safety and reliability of nuclear reactors, the Space Shuttle, and the International Space Station. Outside the US, the software RiskSpectrum is a popular tool for Fault Tree and Event Tree analysis and is licensed for use at almost half of the world's nuclear power plants for Probabilistic Safety Assessment.

## Graphic Symbols

The basic symbols used in FTA are grouped as events, gates, and transfer symbols. Minor variations may be used in FTA software.

## Event Symbols

Event symbols are used for *primary events* and *intermediate events*. Primary events are not further developed on the fault tree. Intermediate events are found at the output of a gate. The event symbols are shown below:

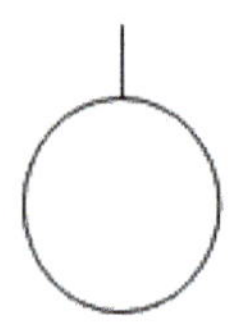

Basic event

External event

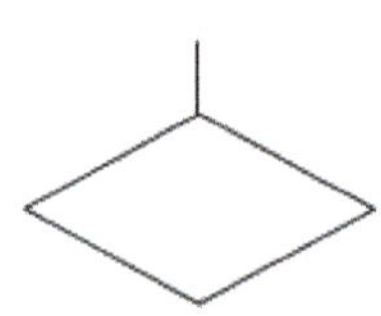

Undeveloped event

- Basic event - failure or error in a system component or element (example: switch stuck in open position)
- External event - normally expected to occur (not of itself a fault)
- Undeveloped event - an event about which insufficient information is available, or which is of no consequence

- Conditioning event - conditions that restrict or affect logic gates (example: mode of operation in effect)

An intermediate event gate can be used immediately above a primary event to provide more room to type the event description. FTA is top to bottom approach.

## Gate Symbols

Gate symbols describe the relationship between input and output events. The symbols are derived from Boolean logic symbols:

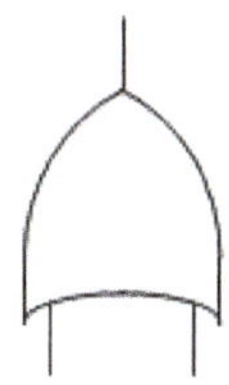

OR gate

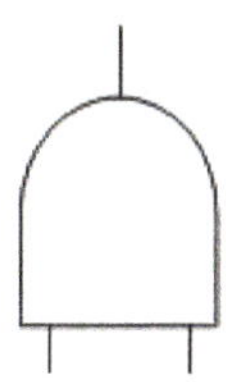

AND gate

Exclusive OR gate

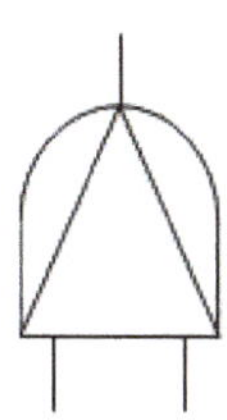

Priority AND gate

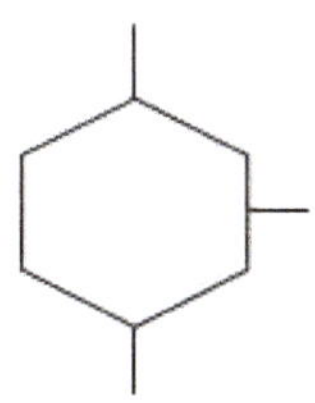

Inhibit gate

The gates work as follows:

- OR gate - the output occurs if any input occurs
- AND gate - the output occurs only if all inputs occur (inputs are independent)
- Exclusive OR gate - the output occurs if exactly one input occurs
- Priority AND gate - the output occurs if the inputs occur in a specific sequence specified by a conditioning event
- Inhibit gate - the output occurs if the input occurs under an enabling condition specified by a conditioning event

## Transfer Symbols

Transfer symbols are used to connect the inputs and outputs of related fault trees, such as the fault tree of a subsystem to its system. NASA prepared a complete document about FTA through practical incidents.

Transfer in

Transfer out

## Basic Mathematical Foundation

Events in a fault tree are associated with statistical probabilities. For example, component failures may typically occur at some constant failure rate λ (a constant hazard function). In this simplest case, failure probability depends on the rate λ and the exposure time t:

$$P = 1 - \exp(-\lambda t)$$

$$P \approx \lambda t, \lambda t < 0.1$$

A fault tree is often normalized to a given time interval, such as a flight hour or an average mission time. Event probabilities depend on the relationship of the event hazard function to this interval.

Unlike conventional logic gate diagrams in which inputs and outputs hold the binary values of TRUE (1) or FALSE (0), the gates in a fault tree output probabilities related to the set operations of Boolean logic. The probability of a gate's output event depends on the input event probabilities.

An AND gate represents a combination of independent events. That is, the probability of any input event to an AND gate is unaffected by any other input event to the same gate. In set theoretic terms, this is equivalent to the intersection of the input event sets, and the probability of the AND gate output is given by:

$$P\,(A \text{ and } B) = P\,(A \cap B) = P(A)\,P(B)$$

An OR gate, on the other hand, corresponds to set union:

$$P\,(A \text{ or } B) = P\,(A \cup B) = P(A) + P(B) - P\,(A \cap B)$$

Since failure probabilities on fault trees tend to be small (less than .01), $P\,(A \cap B)$ usually becomes a very small error term, and the output of an OR gate may be conservatively approximated by using an assumption that the inputs are mutually exclusive events:

$$P\,(A \text{ or } B) \approx P(A) + P(B),\ P\,(A \cap B) \approx 0$$

An exclusive OR gate with two inputs represents the probability that one or the other input, but not both, occurs:

$$P\,(A \text{ xor } B) = P(A) + P(B) - 2P\,(A \cap B)$$

Again, since $P\,(A \cap B)$ usually becomes a very small error term, the exclusive OR gate has limited value in a fault tree.

## Analysis

Many different approaches can be used to model a FTA, but the most common and popular way can be summarized in a few steps. A single fault tree is used to analyze one and only one undesired event or top event, which may be subsequently fed into another fault tree as a basic event. Though the nature of the undesired event may vary dramatically, a FTA follows the same procedure for any undesired event; be it a delay of 0.25 ms for the generation of electrical power, an undetected cargo bay fire, or the random, unintended launch of an ICBM. Due to labor cost, FTA is normally only performed for more serious undesired events.

FTA analysis involves five steps:

1. Define the undesired event to study
    - Definition of the undesired event can be very hard to catch, although some of the events are very easy and obvious to observe. An engineer

with a wide knowledge of the design of the system or a system analyst with an engineering background is the best person who can help define and number the undesired events. Undesired events are used then to make the FTA, one event for one FTA; no two events will be used to make one FTA.

2. Obtain an understanding of the system

    - Once the undesired event is selected, all causes with probabilities of affecting the undesired event of 0 or more are studied and analyzed. Getting exact numbers for the probabilities leading to the event is usually impossible for the reason that it may be very costly and time consuming to do so. Computer software is used to study probabilities; this may lead to less costly system analysis. System analysts can help with understanding the overall system. System designers have full knowledge of the system and this knowledge is very important for not missing any cause affecting the undesired event. For the selected event all causes are then numbered and sequenced in the order of occurrence and then are used for the next step which is drawing or constructing the fault tree.

3. Construct the fault tree

    - After selecting the undesired event and having analyzed the system so that we know all the causing effects (and if possible their probabilities) we can now construct the fault tree. Fault tree is based on AND and OR gates which define the major characteristics of the fault tree.

4. Evaluate the fault tree

    - After the fault tree has been assembled for a specific undesired event, it is evaluated and analyzed for any possible improvement or in other words study the risk management and find ways for system improvement. This step is as an introduction for the final step which will be to control the hazards identified. In short, in this step we identify all possible hazards affecting in a direct or indirect way the system.

5. Control the hazards identified

    - This step is very specific and differs largely from one system to another, but the main point will always be that after identifying the hazards all possible methods are pursued to decrease the probability of occurrence.

### Comparison with Other Analytical Methods

FTA is a deductive, top-down method aimed at analyzing the effects of initiating faults and events on a complex system. This contrasts with failure mode and effects analysis (FMEA), which is an inductive, bottom-up analysis method aimed at analyzing the effects of single component or function failures on equipment or subsystems. FTA is very good at showing how resistant a system is to single or multiple initiating faults. It is not good at finding all possible initiating faults. FMEA is good at exhaustively cataloging initiating faults, and identifying their local effects. It is not good at examining multiple failures or their effects at a system level. FTA considers external events, FMEA does not. In civil aerospace the usual practice is to perform both FTA and FMEA, with a failure mode effects summary (FMES) as the interface between FMEA and FTA.

Alternatives to FTA include dependence diagram (DD), also known as reliability block diagram (RBD) and Markov analysis. A dependence diagram is equivalent to a success tree analysis (STA), the logical inverse of an FTA, and depicts the system using paths instead of gates. DD and STA produce probability of success (i.e., avoiding a top event) rather than probability of a top event.

## Society for Risk Analysis

The Society for Risk Analysis (SRA) is a learned society providing an open forum for anyone interested in risk analysis. It seeks to: provide an avenue for individuals (from different disciplines from various corners of the globe) to discuss ideas and information as well as methodologies for analyzing risk and solving related issues and problems; promote understanding and encourage collaboration among professionals and organisations relevant to analyzing risk and providing solutions; disseminate and promote risk (methods) knowledge and their applications in research and education; and serve its members in developing and furthering their careers in risk analysis.

### SRA's interests: Risk Analysis Among Others

SRA broadly defines risk analysis to include risk assessment, risk characterization, risk communication, risk management, and policy relating to risk. The society's interests include: risk perception, risks to human health and the environment, both built and natural; threats from physical, chemical, and biological agents and from a variety of human activities as well as natural events; and risks of concern to individuals, to public and private sector organizations, and to society at various geographic scales.

### Awards

Since the first awards were given in 1984, SRA continues to value outstanding contributions to the society and to the field of risk analysis. The following are its most-sought annual awards:

Distinguished Achievement Award. This award is given to any individual for his or her extraordinary achievement in science or public policy relevant to the field of risk analysis.

Richard J Burk Outstanding Service Award. A recognition to the society's member for extraordinary service to SRA.

Outstanding Practitioner Award. Award alternately given to a member in public and private practice for an outstanding practice in the field of risk analysis.

Chauncey Starr Distinguished Young Risk Analyst Award. For an outstanding risk-analysis-related achievement in science or public policy by SRA's member (of 40 years of age or below) and exceptional promise for continued contributions to risk analysis.

Distinguished Educator Award. Awarded to an outstanding teacher, author or mentor for substantial training of new experts in risk analysis.

## Risk Assessment

Risk assessment is the determination of quantitative or qualitative estimate of risk related to a well-defined situation and a recognized threat (also called hazard). *Quantitative risk assessment* requires calculations of two components of risk *(R)*: the magnitude of the potential loss *(L)*, and the probability *(p)* that the loss will occur. An acceptable risk is a risk that is understood and tolerated usually because the cost or difficulty of implementing an effective countermeasure for the associated vulnerability exceeds the expectation of loss. "Health risk assessment" includes variations, such as risk as the type and severity of response, with or without a probabilistic context.

In all types of engineering of complex systems sophisticated risk assessments are often made within safety engineering and reliability engineering when it concerns threats to life, environment or machine functioning. The nuclear, aerospace, oil, rail and military industries have a long history of dealing with risk assessment. Also, medical, hospital, social service and food industries control risks and perform risk assessments on a continual basis. Methods for assessment of risk may differ between industries and whether it pertains to general financial decisions or environmental, ecological, or public health risk assessment.

## Explanation

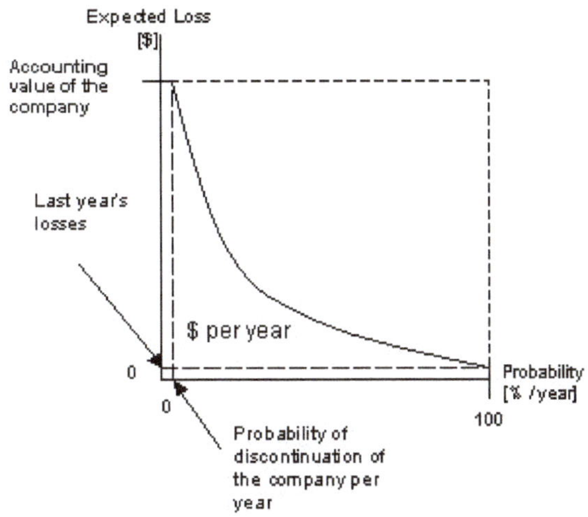


Risk assessment from a financial point of view.

Risk assessment consists of an objective evaluation of risk in which assumptions and uncertainties are clearly considered and presented. Part of the difficulty in risk management is that both the quantities by which risk assessment is concerned – potential loss and probability of occurrence – can be very difficult to measure. The chance of error in measuring these two concepts is high. Risk with a large potential loss and a low probability of occurrence, is often treated differently from one with a low potential loss and a high likelihood of occurrence. In theory, both are of near equal priority, but in practice it can be very difficult to manage when faced with the scarcity of resources, especially time, in which to conduct the risk management process. To see this expressed mathematically, one can define total risk as the sum over individual risks, $R_i$, which can be computed as the product of potential losses, $L_i$, and their probabilities, $p(L_i)$ :

$$R_i = L_i p(L_i)$$

$$R_{total} = \sum_i L_i p(L_i)$$

Even though for some risks $R_i, R_j$, we might have $R_i = R_j$, if the probability $p(L_j)$ is small compared to $p(L_i)$, , its estimation might be based only on a smaller number of prior events, and hence, more uncertain. On the other hand, since $R_i = R_j$, $L_j$ must be larger than $L_i$, so decisions based on this uncertainty would be more consequential, and hence, warrant a different approach.

Financial decisions, such as insurance, express loss in terms of dollar amounts. When risk assessment is used for public health or environmental decisions, loss can be quantified in a common metric such as a country's currency or some numerical measure of a location's quality of life. For public health and environmental decisions, loss is simply a verbal description of the outcome, such as increased cancer incidence or incidence of birth defects. In that case, the "risk" is expressed as

$$R_i = p(L_i)$$

If the risk estimate takes into account information on the number of individuals exposed, it is termed a "population risk" and is in units of expected increased cases per a time period. If the risk estimate does not take into account the number of individuals exposed, it is termed an "individual risk" and is in units of incidence rate per a time period. Population risks are of more use for cost/benefit analysis; individual risks are of more use for evaluating whether risks to individuals are "acceptable".

## Five-step Process In Risk Assessment and Management

| Risk assessment and management process | |
|---|---|
| Establish the context | understand the operating context and environment |
| Identify the risks / hazards | identify the internal and external risks / hazards that poses threat |
| Analyze the risks | systemic analysis of various contributing and leading factors (e.g. extend of the exposure, multiple exposures) |
| Evaluate and prioritize the risks | characterize and prioritize the list of risks for further action |
| Tackle the risks | Identify the range of options to tackle the risk & implement the best choice using available resources |

## In General Health

There are many resources that provide health risk information.

The National Library of Medicine provides risk assessment and regulation information tools for a varied audience. These include:

- TOXNET (databases on hazardous chemicals, environmental health, and toxic releases),
- the Household Products Database (potential health effects of chemicals in over 10,000 common household products),
- TOXMAP (maps of the U.S. Environmental Protection Agency Superfund and Toxics Release Inventory data).

The United States Environmental Protection Agency provides basic information about environmental risk assessments for the public for a wide variety of possible environmental exposures.

Considering the increase in junk food and toxicity FDA required in 1973 that cancer-causing compounds must not be present in meat at concentrations that would cause a cancer risk greater than 1 in a million over a lifetime. The US Environmental Protection Agency provides extensive information about ecological and environmental risk assessments for the public via its risk assessment portal. The Stockholm Convention on persistent organic pollutants (POPs) supports a qualitative risk framework for public health protection from chemicals that display environmental and biological persistence, bioaccumulation, toxicity (PBT) and long range transport; most global chemicals that meet this criteria have been previously assessed quantitatively by national and international health agencies.

## How Risk is Appraised

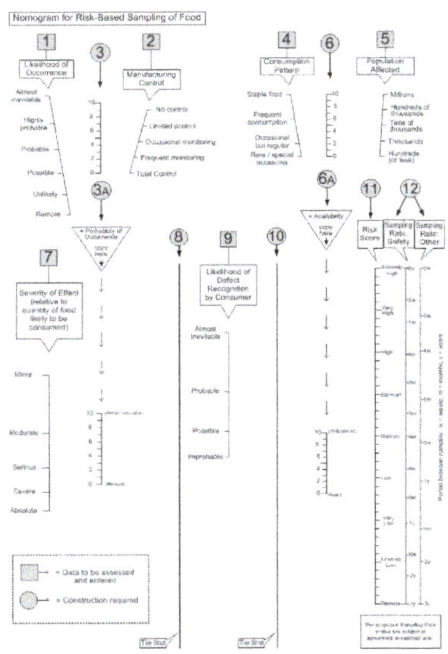


Food risk assessment nomogram

In the estimation of risks, three or more steps are involved that require the inputs of different disciplines:

1. *Hazard Identification*, aims to determine the qualitative nature of the potential adverse consequences of the contaminant (chemical, radiation, noise, etc.) and the strength of the evidence it can have that effect. This is done, for chemical hazards, by drawing from the results of the sciences of toxicology and epidemiology. For other kinds of hazard, engineering or other disciplines are involved.

2. *Dose-Response Analysis*, is determining the relationship between dose and the type of adverse response and/or probability or the incidence of effect (dose-response assessment). The complexity of this step in many contexts derives mainly from the need to extrapolate results from experimental animals (e.g. mouse, rat) to humans, and/or from high to lower doses, including from high acute occupational levels to low chronic environmental levels. In addi-

tion, the differences between individuals due to genetics or other factors mean that the hazard may be higher for particular groups, called susceptible populations. An alternative to dose-response estimation is to determine a concentration unlikely to yield observable effects, that is, a no effect concentration. In developing such a dose, to account for the largely unknown effects of animal to human extrapolations, increased variability in humans, or missing data, a prudent approach is often adopted by including safety or uncertainty factors in the estimate of the "safe" dose, typically a factor of 10 for each unknown step.

3. *Exposure Quantification*, aims to determine the amount of a contaminant (dose) that individuals and populations will receive, either as a contact level (e.g., concentration in ambient air) or as intake (e.g., daily dose ingested from drinking water). This is done by examining the results of the discipline of exposure assessment. As different location, lifestyles and other factors likely influence the amount of contaminant that is received, a range or distribution of possible values is generated in this step. Particular care is taken to determine the exposure of the susceptible population(s).

Finally, the results of the three steps above are then combined to produce an estimate of risk. Because of the different susceptibilities and exposures, this risk will vary within a population. An uncertainty analysis is nearly always included in a health risk assessment.

## Small Subpopulations

When risks apply mainly to small sub-populations, there is uncertainty at which point intervention is necessary. For example, there may be a risk that is very low for everyone, other than 0.1% of the population. It is necessary to determine whether this 0.1% is represented by:

- all infants younger than *X* days or
- recreational users of a particular product.

If the risk is higher for a particular sub-population because of abnormal exposure rather than susceptibility, strategies to further reduce the exposure of that subgroup are considered. If an identifiable sub-population is more susceptible due to inherent genetic or other factors, public policy choices must be made. The choices are:

- to set policies for protecting the general population that are protective of such groups, e.g. for children when data exists, the Clean Air Act for populations such as asthmatics or
- not to set policies, because the group is too small, or the costs too high.

## Acceptable Risk Criteria

The idea of not increasing lifetime risk by more than one in a million has become commonplace in public health discourse and policy. It is a heuristic measure. It provides a numerical basis for establishing a negligible increase in risk.

Environmental decision making allows some discretion for deeming individual risks potentially "acceptable" if less than one in ten thousand chance of increased lifetime risk. Low risk criteria such as these provide some protection for a case where individuals may be exposed to multiple chemicals e.g. pollutants, food additives or other chemicals.

In practice, a true zero-risk is possible only with the suppression of the risk-causing activity.

Stringent requirements of 1 in a million may not be technologically feasible or may be so prohibitively expensive as to render the risk-causing activity unsustainable, resulting in the optimal degree of intervention being a balance between risks vs. benefit. For example, emissions from hospital incinerators result in a certain number of deaths per year. However, this risk must be balanced against the alternatives. There are public health risks, as well as economic costs, associated with all options. The risk associated with no incineration is potential spread of infectious diseases, or even no hospitals. Further investigation identifies options such as separating noninfectious from infectious wastes, or air pollution controls on a medical incinerator.

Intelligent thought about a reasonably full set of options is essential. Thus, it is not unusual for there to be an iterative process between analysis, consideration of options, and follow up analysis.

## In Auditing

For audits performed by an outside audit firm, risk assessment is a crucial stage before accepting an audit engagement. According to ISA315 *Understanding the Entity and its Environment and Assessing the Risks of Material Misstatement*, "the auditor should perform risk assessment procedures to obtain an understanding of the entity and its environment, including its internal control."<evidence relating to the auditor's risk assessment of a material misstatement in the client's financial statements. Then, the auditor obtains initial evidence regarding the classes of transactions at the client and the operating effectiveness of the client's internal controls.In auditing, audit risk is defined as the risk that the auditor will issue a clean unmodified opinion regarding the financial statements, when in fact the financial statements are materially misstated, and therefore do not qualify for a clean unmodified opinion. As a formula, audit risk is the product of two other risks: Risk of Material Misstatement and Detection risk. This formula can be further broken down as follows: inherent risk X control risk X detection risk.

## In Public Health

In the context of public health, risk assessment is the process of characterizing the nature and likelihood of a harmful effect to individuals or populations from certain human activities. Health risk assessment can be mostly qualitative or can include statistical estimates of probabilities for specific populations. In most countries the use of specific chemicals or the operations of specific facilities (e.g. power plants, manufacturing plants) is not allowed unless it can be shown that they do not increase the risk of death or illness above a specific threshold. For example, the American Food and Drug Administration (FDA) regulates food safety through risk assessment.

## In Project Management

In project management, risk assessment is an integral part of the risk management plan, studying the probability, the impact, and the effect of every known risk on the project, as well as the corrective action to take should that risk occur. Of special consideration in this area are the relevant codes of practice that are enforced in the specific jurisdiction. Understanding the regime of regulations that risk management must abide by is integral to formulating safe and compliant risk assessment practices.

## In Information Security

IT risk assessment can be performed by a qualitative or quantitative approach, following different methodologies. One important difference in risk assessments in information security is modifying the threat model to account for the fact that any adversarial system connected to the Internet has access to threaten any other connected system. Risk assessments may therefore need to be modified to account for the threats from all adversaries, instead of just those with reasonable access as is done in other fields.

## For Megaprojects

Megaprojects (sometimes also called "major programs") are extremely large-scale investment projects, typically costing more than US$1 billion per project. Megaprojects include bridges, tunnels, highways, railways, airports, seaports, power plants, dams, wastewater projects, coastal flood protection, oil and natural gas extraction projects, public buildings, information technology systems, aerospace projects, and defence systems. Megaprojects have been shown to be particularly risky in terms of finance, safety, and social and environmental impacts.

## Quantitative Risk Assessment

Quantitative risk assessments include a calculation of the single loss expectancy (SLE) of an asset. The single loss expectancy can be defined as the loss of value to asset based on a single security incident. The team then calculates the Annualized Rate of Occurrence (ARO) of the threat to the asset. The ARO is an estimate based on the data of how often a threat would be successful in exploiting a vulnerability. From this information, the Annualized Loss Expectancy (ALE) can be calculated. The annualized loss expectancy is a calculation of the single loss expectancy multiplied by the annual rate of occurrence, or how much an organization could estimate to lose from an asset based on the risks, threats, and vulnerabilities. It then becomes possible from a financial perspective to justify expenditures to implement countermeasures to protect the asset.

### In Software Evolution

Studies have shown that early parts of the system development cycle such as requirements and design specifications are especially prone to error. This effect is particularly notorious in projects involving multiple stakeholders with different points of view. Evolutionary software processes offer an iterative approach to requirement engineering to alleviate the problems of uncertainty, ambiguity and inconsistency inherent in software developments.

### Criticisms of Quantitative Risk Assessment

Barry Commoner, Brian Wynne and other critics have expressed concerns that risk assessment tends to be overly quantitative and reductive. For example, they argue that risk assessments ignore qualitative differences among risks. Some charge that assessments may drop out important non-quantifiable or inaccessible information, such as variations among the classes of people exposed to hazards. Furthermore, Commoner and O'Brien claim that quantitative approaches divert attention from precautionary or preventative measures. Others, like Nassim Nicholas Taleb consider risk managers little more than "blind users" of statistical tools and methods.

### In shipping Industry

In July 2010, shipping companies agreed to use standardized procedures in order to assess risk in key shipboard operations. These procedures were implemented as part of the amended ISM Code.

## Flood Risk Assessment

A flood risk assessment (FRA) is an assessment of the risk of flooding from all flooding mechanisms, the identification of flood mitigation measures and should provide advice on actions to be taken before and during a flood.

The sources of water which produce floods include:

- Groundwater (saturated groundwater)
- Vadose (water flowing the ground in an unsaturated state)
- Surface water
- Artificial water (burst water mains, canals or reservoirs)
- Rivers, streams or watercourses
- Sewers and drains

For each of the sources of water, different hydraulic intensities occur. Floods can occur because of a combination of sources of flooding, such as high groundwater and an inadequate surface water drainage system. The topography, hydrogeology and physical attributes of the existing or proposed development need to be considered. A flood risk assessment should be an evaluation of the flood risk and the consequences and impact and vulnerability.

*Non-professiona*l flood risk assessments can be produced by members of the public, Architects, environment assessors, or others who are not specifically professionally qualified in this field. However, it is a complex evaluation and such assessments they can be rejected by Authorities as inadequate, or could be considered as negligent in the event of a flooding event, damage and a claim to insurers being made.

In the UK, the writing of *professional* flood risk assessments is undertaken by Civil Engineering Consultants. They will have membership of the Institution of Civil Engineers and are bound by their rules of professional conduct. A key requirement is to ensure such professional flood risk assessments are independent to all parties by carrying out their professional duties with complete objectivity and impartiality. Their professional advice should be supported by professional indemnity insurance for such specific professional advice ultimately held with a Lloyd's of London underwriter.

Professional flood risk assessments can cover single buildings, or whole regions. They can part of a due-diligence process for existing householders or businesses, or can be required in England and Wales to provide independent evidence to a planning application on the flood risk.

## England and Wales

In England and Wales, the Environment Agency requires a professional Flood Risk Assessment (FRA) to be submitted alongside planning applications in areas that are known to be at risk of flooding (within flood zones 2 or 3) and/ or are greater than 1ha in area, planning permission is not usually granted until the FRA has been accepted by the Environment Agency.

## PPS 25 - England Only

Flood Risk Assessments are required to be completed according to the National Planning Policy Framework, which replaces Planning Policy Statement PPS 25: Development and Flood Risk. The initial legislation (PPG25) was introduced in 2001 and subsequently revised.

PPS 25 was designed to "strengthen and clarify the key role of the planning system in managing flood risk and contributing to adapting to the impacts of climate change." and sets out policies for local authorities to ensure flood risk is taken into account during the planning process to prevent inappropriate development in high risk areas and to direct development away from areas at highest risk.

In its introduction, PPS25 states "flooding threatens life and causes substantial damage to property [and that] although [it] cannot be wholly prevented, its impacts can be avoided and reduced through good planning and management".

## Composition of an FRA

For a flood risk assessment to be written, information is needed concerning the existing and proposed developments, the Environment Agency modeled flood levels and topographic levels on site. At its most simple (and cheapest) level an FRA can provide an indication of whether a development will be allowed to take place at a site.

An initial idea of the risk of fluvial flooding to a local area can be found on the Environment Agency flood map website.

FRAs consist of a detailed analysis of available data to inform the Environment Agency of flood risk at an individual site and also recommend to the developer any mitigation measures. More costly analysis of flood risk can be achieved through detailed flood modelling to challenge the agency's modelled levels and corresponding flood zones.

The FRA takes into account the risk and impact of flooding on the site, and takes into consideration how the development may affect flooding in the local area. It also includes provides recommendations as to how the risk of flooding to the development can be mitigated.

FRAs should also consider flooding from all sources including fluvial, groundwater, surface water runoff and sewer flooding.

### Northern Ireland

In 2006, the Planning Service, part of The Department of the Environment, published Planning Policy Statement 15 (PPS15): Planning and flood risk. The guidelines are precautionary and advise against development in flood plains and areas subject to historical flooding. In exceptional cases a FRA can be completed to justify development in flood risk areas. Advice on flood risk assessment is provided to the Planning Service by the Rivers Agency, which is the statutory drainage and flood defence authority for Northern Ireland.

### Republic of Ireland

In 2009, the Department of the Environment, Heritage and Local Government and Office of Public Works published planning guidelines requiring local authorities to apply a sequential approach to flood risk management. The guidelines require that proposed development in flood risk areas must undergo a justification test, consisting of a flood risk assessment.

## Own Risk and Solvency Assessment

At the heart of the prudential Solvency II directive, the Own Risk and Solvency Assessment (ORSA) is defined as a set of processes constituting a tool for decision-making and strategic analysis. It aims to assess, in a continuous and prospective way, the overall solvency needs related to the specific risk profile of the insurance company. Risk Management and Own Risk and Solvency Assessment is a similar regulation that has been enacted in the USA by the NAIC. Other jurisdictions are enacting similar regulations to comply with the Insurance Core Principle 16 enacted by the IAIS.

### Context

The second pillar of Solvency II plans to complete the quantitative capital requirements with quality requirements and a global and appropriate risk management system. The reform provides measures on governance, internal control and internal audit in order to ensure sound and prudent management practices from insurers. Impacts in terms of risk and solvency should supply into upstream strategic decisions. The internal assessment process of risks and solvency, known as the ORSA, is the centerpiece of this plan.

In an operational way, the ORSA is part of global process of Enterprise Risk Management (ERM).

It is part of a cyclical and iterative system involving the board of directors, senior management, internal audit, internal control and all employees of the company. It aims to provide a reasonable insurance on compliance with the strategy of the company against risks.

The ORSA is voluntarily defined broadly by the regulation to encourage insurers to question themselves on the framework of an internal system dedicated to control and risk management. It must in all cases be succinct, easy to update and respect the principles of materiality and proportionality.

## Regulatory References

Since 2003, Solvency II regulation follows the Lamfalussy process, which distinguishes 3 levels of measures, starting from the big principles to the enforcement measures necessary for the operational implementation. The ORSA regulatory update from the NAIC follows the Solvency Modernization Initiative aimed at updating the US regulatory system.

## Solvency II

### Level 1 Measures

Level 1 text is the regulatory basis of the reform. It was adopted in 2009 on the same text by the European Parliament and European Council.

The ORSA is defined in Article 45 of the Directive.

As part of its risk-management system every insurance undertaking and reinsurance undertaking shall conduct its own risk and solvency assessment.

That assessment shall include at least the following:

(a) the overall solvency needs taking into account the specific risk profile, approved risk tolerance limits and the business strategy of the undertaking ;

(b) the compliance, on a continuous basis, with the capital requirements, and with the requirements regarding technical provisions;

(c) the significance with which the risk profile of the undertaking concerned deviates from the assumptions underlying the Solvency Capital Requirement.

### Level 2 Measures

Level 2 measures are technical implementing measures to complement the principles defined in the level 1 text, in view of the operational implementation requirements. Level 2 measures should be adopted by the European Commission on a proposal from EIOPA (European Insurance and Occupational Pensions Authority). In order to advance the development of the reform, EIOPA consults the market, including through Consultation Papers.

The ORSA does not fall within Level 2 measures and as such in 2009, during the broad consultation on Level 2 measures, there were no Consultation Papers devoted exclusively to the ORSA. However, a significant number of them refer to it, for example:

Consultation paper No. 17 on the calculation of capital add-on

Consultation paper No. 24 on the principle of proportionality

Consultation paper No. 33 on the governance system

Consultation paper No. 56 on the validation of internal models

... etc.

Thus, if Level 2 measures do not specify the requirements for the ORSA, they will better understand the interactions of the ORSA with other requirements and clarify the role of the ORSA within the Solvency II system of insurers.

## Level 3 Measures

Level 3 measures will be directly adopted by EIOPA. They generally correspond to non-binding recommendations. Since the creation of EIOPA in January 2011, its responsibilities were, however, extended to the production of Level 3 binding measures.

The ORSA comes under level 3 texts. To this end, a Consultation Paper was published in November 7, 2011.

This Consultation Paper presents a set of instructions for the ORSA:

- General considerations: the importance of the principle of proportionality, the key role played by the administrative, management and supervisory body, the documentation for the ORSA and the principles supervising the governance of the ORSA ;
- Justification and communication for the ORSA processes;
- Specific features regarding the implementation of the ORSA:
    - Assessment of the overall solvency needs: the approach retained must be justified, must be both quantitative and qualitative, must include a sufficient number of stress test and scenarios and must include a prospective dimension;
    - The ORSA should incorporate the information provided by the actuarial function on the validation of technical provisions;
    - The results of the ORSA should be integrated into all strategic management processes;

  - Frequency of the ORSA: at least annually, and must be adapted to the volatility of the risk profile of insurer

- Group specificities of the ORSA

This text is still under consultation, but can anticipate the content of Level 3 measures on the ORSA.

## NAIC ORSA Regulation

While the high level Risk Management and Own Risk and Solvency Assessment Model Act (#505) has been adopted by the NAIC in September 2012, the NAIC ORSA Guidance Manual is being revised in early 2013.

The State legislative process is still ongoing, but can anticipate the regulation to be fully in place in 2015.

South Africa: Solvency Assessment and Management (SAM) ORSA regulation

Similar to Solvency II, Insurers and Reinsurers registered in South Africa will be required from 1 April 2017 to perform regular ORSAs. ORSA requirements in South Africa will meet the IAIS standards. Regular reporting will also be required to the Registrar of Insurers.

## Operational Implementation

Insurance companies are in the process of setting up their Solvency II plans and generally, the setting up of the pillar 1 has been prioritized. Therefore the ORSA plans are still not mature on the market.

However, it appears that four key steps can be identified in the operational implementation of the ORSA:

- The definition of the risk profile
- The implementation of a strategy for risk management
- The evolution of strategic processes
- The production of the ORSA report

In the USA, companies are at various stages of ORSA readiness.

## Definition of The Risk Profile

The risk profile includes all of the risks that the company is exposed, the quantification of these exposures and all protective measures to those risks.

The risk profile is different from the regulatory capital determined under Pillar 1. It takes into account the specificities of each insurance company, it integrates all material risks, in a prospective view, and the ORSA do not surround the definition of solvency or the risk aggregation methodologies.

In practice, the definition of the risk profile will be increased by the realization of an all-risks mapping, including both the risks identified as part of pillar 1 of the reform Solvency II - underwriting risk, market risk, counterparty default risk, operational risk, intangible asset risk - but also other specific risks to each insurer - illiquidity risk, business risk, strategic risk, reputation risk, etc..

Once the mapping is done, a metric must be defined to quantify the risks. The company can use what is done on the pillar 1 such as a measure of risk, a time horizon and/or a different security level most suitable to its strategy for controlling the risks.

## Implementation of a Risk Management Strategy

Once the risk profile is established, the administrative, management and supervisory body must set up the risk management strategy of the company through the following elements:

- The risk appetite
- The risk tolerances

The risk appetite is the maximum aggregated level of risk that a company wishes to take. The risk tolerances represent the risk appetite variation on the different risk factors.

One of the major roles of the risk management function is to support the administrative, management and supervisory body in order to get him to comment on this strategy. The risk management function must not only pass the information necessary to operate, but also give the keys to an appropriation of the culture of risk and a critical analysis of these elements by the leaders.

Finally, the risk limits are the operational implementation of the risk tolerances. The risk management function shall coordinate the trades in order to define:

- How these risk limits should be expressed;
- The methodology for the translation of appetite and tolerances into limits of operational risks.

## Evolution of Strategic Processes

All decisions made in the daily management of the company must then respect the strategy defined. In order to maintain the risk profile to a level consistent with the risk appetite, the leaders have four main strategies:

- Abandonment of risk ;
- Reduction of risk ;
- Transfer of risk ;
- Acceptance of risk.

Major strategic processes of the insurance company, as the definition of trade policies, reinsurance and asset liability management, should be revised to integrate the dimension risk and solvency in the decision-making.

Moreover, the ORSA should enable continued compliance with regulatory requirements in terms of own funds. For that the insurer must establish a set of systematic processes to monitor and control continuous compliance with the risk limits and identify major events - internal or external – which have a significant impact on the risk profile and lead to the update of the ORSA.

## ORSA Report

The ORSA is the subject of several reporting requirements:

- The ORSA is integrated into the narrative of new reports required in Pillar 3 of the reform, both destined for the supervisor and the public;
- The ORSA should be a set of internal reporting, particularly during the strategic processes that it must supply;
- As part of Level 3 measures being drafted by EIOPA, the ORSA should be a specific reporting, the ORSA report, bound for the administrative, management and supervisory body.

Generally, a reporting on the ORSA will contain two parts:

- A qualitative report: Description of the risk profile and risk management processes in place;
- A quantitative report: Description of the quantitative methodologies used in the context of the ORSA, results, defined strategy, and conclusions.

The US ORSA report will contain three sections, as described in the ORSA Guidance Manual:

- Description of the insurer's enterprise risk management framework
- Insurer assessment of risk exposures
- Group risk capital and prospective solvency assessment

## References


- Center for Chemical Process Safety (April 2008). Guidelines for Hazard Evaluation Procedures (3rd ed.). Wiley. ISBN 978-0-471-97815-2.
- Fault Tree Analysis. Edition 2.0. International Electrotechnical Commission. 2006. ISBN 2-8318-8918-9. IEC 61025.
- HMSO (2006, Revised 2010) Planning Policy Statement 25: Development and Flood Risk, TSO, London. ISBN 978-0-11-754099-6
- Government of Ireland (2009) The Planning System and Flood Risk Management, The Stationery Office, Dublin ISBN 978-1-4064-2467-6
- "Fault Tree Handbook with Aerospace Applications" (PDF). NASA. August 2002. Retrieved 8 January 2016. This article incorporates text from this source, which is in the public domain.
- Spring, J.; Kern, S.; Summers, A. (2015-05-01). "Global adversarial capability modeling". 2015 APWG Symposium on Electronic Crime Research (eCrime): 1–21. doi:10.1109/ECRIME.2015.7120797.
- DeLong, Thomas (1970). "A Fault Tree Manual" (pdf). Master's Thesis. Texas A&M University. AD739001. Retrieved 2014-05-18.
- Eckberg, C. R. (1964). WS-133B Fault Tree Analysis Program Plan. Seattle, WA: The Boeing Company. D2-30207-1. Retrieved 2014-05-18.
- Hixenbaugh, A. F. (1968). Fault Tree for Safety. Seattle, WA: The Boeing Company. D6-53604. Retrieved 2014-05-18.

5

# Preventive Measures for Risk Management

The preventive measures for risk management are ISO/TC 223, contingency plan, common alerting protocol, currency analytics and social responsibility. ISO/TC 223 is a committee of international organization for standardization; the purpose of this was the protection of society from emergencies and disasters caused by intentional human activity. This section elucidates the crucial theories of risk management.

## ISO/TC 223

ISO/TC 223 Societal security was a technical committee of the International Organization for Standardization formed in 2001 to develop standards in the area of societal security: i.e. protection of society from and response to incidents, emergencies, and disasters caused by intentional and unintentional human acts, natural hazards, and technical failures.

The sinking of the Russian submarine Kursk to the bottom of the Barents Sea in 2000 can be cited as a major impetus for the formation of ISO/TC 223. The international salvage operation that followed the accident provided painful evidence that the international community lacked the tools necessary to cooperate effectively in emergency situations, resulting in an initiative from the Russian standards organization, GOST, to establish ISO/TC 223. Originally titled Civil defence, the committee was created to standardize international emergency procedures.

The initiative lay dormant for some time. However, terrorist actions, including the 9/11 attacks on New York and Washington, as well as a surge in natural disasters in recent years, led ISO to conduct a large-scale assessment of the role of standardization in the security field. One important decision was to put ISO/TC 223 into action. In 2005 the chairmanship of the committee was taken over by SIS, the Swedish Standards Institute. To better reflect its ambition to take a broader approach toward disruptive incidents that threaten the civil society, the committee was renamed Societal security.

ISO/TC 223 was actively developing a series of international standards for more than 8 years. In 2014, the Technical Management Board of ISO decided to merge ISO/TC 223 with other committees in the area of security for better coordination. The new committee started on the 1st of January 2015 and is called ISO/TC 292 Security

## Scope

ISO/TC 223 worked under the following scope:

*ISO/TC 223 develops International standards that aim to increase societal security, i.e. protection of society from and response to incidents, emergencies, and disasters caused by intentional and unintentional human acts, natural hazards, and technical failures. An all-hazards perspective is used covering adaptive, proactive and reactive strategies in all phases before, during and after a disruptive incident. The area of societal security is multi-disciplinary and involves actors from both the public and private sectors, including not-for-profit organizations.*

## Leadership and Organisation

*Chair* 2006-2012 Mr Krister Kumlin 2013-2014 Mrs Åsa Kyrk Gere *Secretary* 2006 Mr Per Forsgren 2006-2013 Dr Stefan Tangen 2013 Mrs Sanna Edlund 2014 Mr Bengt Rydstedt

ISO/TC 223 established the following Working Groups: WG 1, WG 2, WG 3, WG 4, WG 5 and WG 6.

ISO/TC 223 became one of the larger committees in ISO with around 70 member countries.

## Introduction to Societal Security

The term Societal security was introduced as a political science concept developed by Nicholas Cringall in 1984. The definition of Societal Security for ISO/TC 223 is broader than just TO DEAL what might challenge the group's identity.

In recent years there have been many highly consequential natural disasters, terrorist attacks and severe crises, which have propelled the issue of crisis management to the top of the national agenda in many countries. As functions in society are shared there is a need to engage individuals, organizations, the private sector and the government in an inclusive discussion on how to better prepare, respond to and recover from crises.

Now and in the future, survival of nations and citizens concerns the security of critical functions of society, rather than only the classical focus on the security of the territory. This shift entails the ability of the government and civil society to function, critical infrastructures to be maintained, the democratic ability to govern, and to manifest certain basic values. Such abilities are put under pressure during severe crises. In societal security several elements that traditionally have been kept apart are becoming fused: procedures for peace and war merge, internal and external security are interlocked, and the ambitions of enhancing state security and providing citizen safety become blurred.

These are new and more complex challenges. These challenges have implications for what (concepts and) tools we need to enhance security, citizens safety and crisis management capacity in an increasingly interdependent and borderless world. Such trans-boundary challenges are not covered by the traditional concept of national civil defence.

Thus, the proposed "umbrella"-concept of societal security is aimed at countering the threats and vulnerabilities in society that require comprehensive crisis management and business continuity systems which are multi-sector, multi-national and multi-continental.

Increased societal security requires a capacity for holistic crisis management emphasizing interoperability and including all key phases of crises. This capacity should have an overall flexibility in order to be able to manage crises that include un-predicted and un-expected elements and events. The purpose is to build a greater overall resilience in the face of a broad range of societal vulnerabilities and disruptive challenges.

### The ISO 22300 series

The following international standards and other publications have been developed by ISO/TC 223

*ISO standards* ISO 22300:2012 Societal security – Terminology, ISO 22301:2012 Societal security – Business continuity management systems – Requirements, ISO 22311:2012 Societal security – Video-surveillance – Export interoperability, ISO 22313:2012 Societal security – Business continuity management systems – Guidance, ISO 22315:2014 Societal security – Mass evacuation – Guidelines for planning, ISO 22320:2011 Societal security – Emergency management – Requirements for incident response, ISO 22322:2015 Societal security – Emergency management – Guidelines for public warning, ISO 22324:2015 Societal security – Emergency management – Guidelines for colour-coded alert, ISO 22397:2014 Societal security – Guidelines for establishing partnering arrangements, ISO 22398:2013 Societal security – Guidelines for exercises,

*Others forms of publications* ISO/TR 22312:2011 Societal security – Technological capabilities, ISO/TR 22351:2015 Societal security – Emergency management – Message structure for interoperability, ISO/PAS 22399:2007 Societal security – Guideline for incident preparedness and operational continuity management, ISO/TS 17021-6:2014 Conformity assessment - Requirements for bodies providing audit and certification of management systems - Part 6: Competence requirements for auditing and certification of business continuity management systems *(Joint project with ISO/CASCO)*,

## Contingency Plan

A contingency plan is a plan devised for an outcome other than in the usual (expected) plan.

It is often used for risk management when an exceptional risk that, though unlikely, would have catastrophic consequences. Contingency plans are often devised by governments or businesses. For example, suppose many employees of a company are traveling together on an aircraft which crashes, killing all aboard. The company could be severely strained or even ruined by such a loss. Accordingly, many companies have procedures to follow in the event of such a disaster. The plan may also include standing policies to mitigate a disaster's potential impact, such as requiring employees to travel separately or limiting the number of employees on any one aircraft.

During times of crisis, contingency plans are often developed to explore and prepare for any eventuality. During the Cold War, many governments made contingency plans to protect themselves and their citizens from nuclear attack. Examples of contingency plans designed to inform citizens of how to survive a nuclear attack are the booklets *Survival Under Atomic Attack*, *Protect and Survive*, and *Fallout Protection*, which were issued by the British and American governments. Today there are still contingency plans in place to deal with terrorist attacks or other catastrophes.

The National Institute of Standards and Technology has published a contingency planning guide for Information Technology Systems (2002).

### In the United States

Cantor Fitzgerald, a financial services company, is a prominent example of a successful implementation of a business contingency plan. In the space of two hours, the firm lost 658 of its 960 New York employees in the September 11 Attacks, as well as much of its office space and trading facilities. Despite these significant losses, the firm was able to resume business within a week. It remains a successful company today.

In the United States, all HAZMAT operations require Contingency Plans.

The United States Environmental Protection Agency through RCRA and EPCRA has defined specific formats for Local Emergency Planning and the National Contingency Plan.

## Common Alerting Protocol

The Common Alerting Protocol (CAP) is an XML-based data format for exchanging public warnings and emergencies between alerting technologies. CAP allows a warning message to be consistently disseminated simultaneously over many warning systems to many applications. CAP increases warning effectiveness and simplifies the task of activating a warning for responsible officials.

Standardized alerts can be received from many sources and configure their applications to process and respond to the alerts as desired. Alerts from the Department of Homeland Security, the Department of the Interior's United States Geological Survey, and the United States Department of Commerce's National Oceanic and Atmospheric Administration (NOAA), and state and local government agencies can all be received in the same format, by the same application. That application can, for example, sound different alarms based on the information received.

By normalizing alert data across threats, jurisdictions, and warning systems, CAP also can be used to detect trends and patterns in warning activity, such as trends that might indicate an undetected hazard or hostile act. From a procedural perspective, CAP reinforces a research-based template for effective warning message content and structure.

The CAP data structure is backward-compatible with existing alert formats including the Specific Area Message Encoding (SAME) used in Weatheradio and the broadcast Emergency Alert System as well as new technology such as the Wireless Emergency Alerts (WEA), while adding capabilities including:

- Flexible geographic targeting using latitude/longitude "boxes" and other geospatial representations in three dimensions;
- Multilingual and multi-audience messaging;
- Phased and delayed effective times and expirations;
- Enhanced message update and cancellation features;
- Template support for framing complete and effective warning messages;
- Digital encryption and signature capability;
- Facility for digital images, audio, and video.

## Background

The U.S. National Science and Technology Council (NSTC) November 2000 report on "Effective Disaster Warnings" recommended that "a standard method should be developed to collect and relay instantaneously and automatically all types of hazard warnings and reports locally, regionally and nationally for input into a wide variety of dissemination systems".

In 2001 an international, independent group of over 120 emergency managers convened online by California emergency telecommunications expert Art Botterell began specifying and prototyping the Common Alerting Protocol data structure based on the recommendations of the NSTC report. The project was embraced by the non-profit Partnership for Public Warning and a number of international warning system vendors. A series of field trials and long-term demonstration projects during 2002-03 led to the submission of a draft CAP specification to the OASIS standards process for formalization.

The CAP 1.0 specification was approved by OASIS in April 2004. Based on experience with CAP 1.0, the OASIS Emergency Management Technical Committee adopted an updated CAP 1.1 specification in October 2005. At a meeting in Geneva in October 2006 the CAP 1.1 specification was taken under consideration by the International Telecommunications Union for adoption as an ITU recommendation.

The latest CAP specification version 1.2 is available since July 2010 at the OASIS Web site.

## Implementations

### Worldwide

In 2007, the International Telecommunication Union, Telecommunication Standardization Sector (ITU-T) adopted the Common Alerting Protocol as Recommendation X.1303. The recommendation annex contains an authoritative ASN.1 module translation of the CAP XML schema that may be useful for some implementations. Rec. X.1303 is within the remit of ITUT Study Group 17 (Security), Rapporteur Group on Cybersecurity (Q.4/17) for purposes of further evolution of the standard.

### Australia

The Australian Government Standard for Common Alerting Protocol (CAP-AU-STD, 2012) was developed by a CAP-AU-STD stakeholder group comprising federal agencies Emergency Management Australia, the Bureau of Meteorology, GeoScience Australia, Department of Agriculture, Fisheries and Forestry and the Department of Health, as well as a number of State Government authorities and emergency services agencies. The project was co-ordinated by the Australian Government Attorney-General's Department (Australian Emergency Management).

### Canada

In Canada, a working group composed of public alerting practitioners and government agencies has developed a CAP Canadian Profile (CAP-CP) based on CAP but specialized to address the needs of Canadian public alerting stakeholders, such as bilingualism, geocoding for Canada, managed lists of locations and events, etc. The Canadian government has adopted CAP-CP for its National Public Alerting System (NPAS) project. The CAPCP working group, along with stakeholders and projects such as the Canadian Public Safety Operations Organization (CanOps) and Netalerts' Sarnia Lambton trial, are now working with and refining CAPCP for national application in Canada.

CAP has been implemented for a small-scale, grassroots hazard information system in Sri Lanka following the 2004 Indian Ocean Tsunami. This implementation was part of the "HazInfo Project", funded by Canada's International Development Research Centre.

The province of Alberta adopted CAP as part of its Alberta Emergency Alert system. In March 2015, Alert Ready, a national public warning system based upon CAP-CP, was officially launched. Participation in the system by broadcasters is mandated by the Canadian Radio-television and Telecommunications Commission.

## Germany

The Federal Office for Citizen Protection and Disaster Support (Bundesamt für Bevölkerungsschutz und Katastrophenhilfe, BBK) is working on an implementation based on CAP 1.2, which will allow for Internet-based access to data provided by the nations modular warning system MoWaS. The development of MoWaS is based on the satellite-based warning system SatWaS from 2001, which only provides information to less than 150 state and media entities. In case no broadcast receiver, like a radio or television, is running nearby, the resulting warning effect of SatWaS would be severely limited, because many state-run emergency sirens have been left unmaintained or were dismantled altogether. This is one of the issues, CAP support in MoWaS is hoped to alleviate.

## United States

According to a CAP 1.0 Fact Sheet, CAP implementations have been demonstrated by agencies and companies including: United States Department of Homeland Security; National Weather Service; United States Geological Survey; California Office of Emergency Services; Virginia Department of Transportation; NDS, Ltd.; GeoDecisions, Inc.; Blue292; Warning Systems, Inc.; Comlabs, Inc.; mobileFoundations; Ship Analytics; AlertSense (formerly MyStateUSA); IEM, Inc.; Hormann America, Inc.; Oregon RAINS; Alerting Solutions, Inc. and others.

It is also mentioned by the Internet Society in its 2005 "Public Warning Network Challenge".

In early 2005, the U.S. Department of Homeland Security (DHS), in partnership with the Association of Public Television Stations, demonstrated CAP-based "digital EAS" broadcasts over public television digital TV transmitters and satellite links in the Washington, D.C. area and nationwide.

CAP is the foundation technology for the planned "Integrated Public Alert and Warning System", an all-hazard, all-media national warning architecture being developed by DHS, the National Weather Service within NOAA, and the Federal Communications Commission.

# Currency Analytics

Companies that do business in more than one currency are exposed to exchange rate risk – that is, changes in the value of one currency versus another. Exchange rate risk (also known as foreign exchange risk, FX risk, or currency risk) is especially high in periods of high currency volatility.

Currency analytics are technology tools that enable global companies to manage the risk associated with currency volatility. Currency analytics often involve automation that helps companies access and validate currency exposure data and make decisions that mitigate currency risk.

## How Global Companies Use Currency Analytics to Manage Risk

Currency volatility can impact a company's balance sheet and/or cash flow. Corporate currency analytics help companies manage currency risk in both areas.

## Balance Sheet Risk

In the process of remeasuring transaction currency monetary assets and liability account balances, the difference between the exchange rate when the transaction was posted and exchange rate when the transaction was cleared goes to the functional entity's income statement as an FX gain or loss. Then in the process of translating the functional entity's income statement for the reporting entity's consolidated income statement, that FX gain/loss gets translated at current income statement rate to reporting currency and appears on the consolidated income statement.

Managing balance sheet risk can involve organic (natural) hedging such as using cash positions or intercompany loans to create exposure offsets. It can also involve external hedging such as buying a forward contract to offset FX exposure.

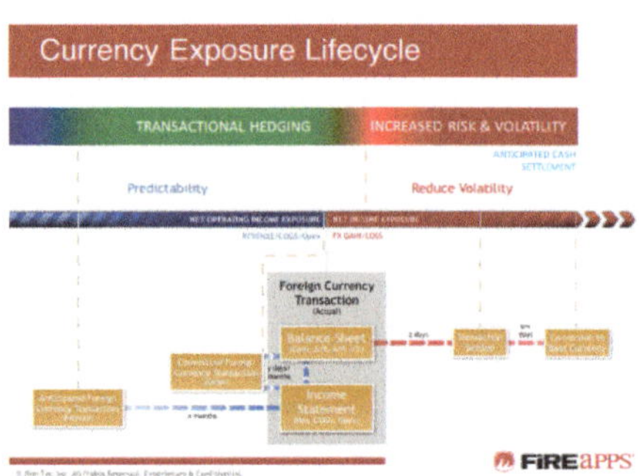


Currency Exposure Lifecycle

In both cases, efficient hedging depends on being able to drill down into the balance sheet to see the currencies of the transactions sitting on the company's books around the world. Currency analytics automates that drill-down process and presents balance sheet exposure data in an easy-to-use dashboard that allows companies to efficiently manage balance sheet risk and minimize FX gain/loss.

### Cash Flow Risk

In the process of translating the functional entity's income statement, revenue, cost of goods sold (COGS), and operating expenses (OpEx) get translated at the current income statement rate to reporting currency and appear on the consolidated income statement. Currency impact to revenue, COGS, and OpEx arises from differences between the current income statement rate and the forecasted rate.

Managing cash flow risk is fundamentally about protecting the economic value of the company's future flow of cash from being eroded by currency volatility. It can involve organic (natural) hedging such as pricing contracts in a particular currency. It can also involve external hedging, but accounting rules require matching hedges to forecasted cash flows and don't allow hedging economic risk.

Currency analytics allow companies to mitigate cash flow risk by uncovering accounting exposures to match the economic exposures so the company can hedge the accounting exposure as a proxy. Currency analytics enable what/if scenario analysis so companies can model how volatility in particular currencies could impact their revenue and expenses in the future.

## Social Responsibility

Social responsibility is an ethical framework and suggests that an entity, be it an organization or individual, has an obligation to act for the benefit of society at large. Social responsibility is a duty every individual has to perform so as to maintain a balance between the economy and the ecosystems. A trade-off may exist between economic development, in the material sense, and the welfare of the society and environment, though this has been challenged by many reports over the past decade. Social responsibility means sustaining the equilibrium between the two. It pertains not only to business organizations but also to everyone whose any action impacts the environment. This responsibility can be passive, by avoiding engaging in socially harmful acts, or active, by performing activities that directly advance social goals.

Businesses can use ethical decision making to secure their businesses by making decisions that allow for government agencies to minimize their involvement with the corporation. For instance if a company follows the United States Environmental Protection Agency (EPA) guidelines for emissions on dangerous pollutants and even goes an extra step to get involved in the community and address those concerns that the public might have; they would be less likely to have the EPA investigate them for environmental concerns. "A significant element of current thinking about privacy, however, stresses "self-regulation" rather than market or government mechanisms for protecting personal information". According to some experts, most rules and regulations are formed due to public outcry, which threatens profit maximization and therefore the well-being of the shareholder, and that if there is not outcry there often will be limited regulation.

Some critics argue that corporate social responsibility (CSR) distracts from the fundamental economic role of businesses; others argue that it is nothing more than superficial window-dressing, or "greenwashing"; others argue that it is an attempt to pre-empt the role of governments as a watchdog over powerful corporations though there is no systematic evidence to support these criticisms. A significant number of studies have shown no negative influence on shareholder results from CSR but rather a slightly negative correlation with improved shareholder returns.

## Student Social Responsibility

Student social responsibility is the responsibility of every student for his/her actions. It is morally binding, and suggests that each person act in such a way that minimizes the adverse effect on those immediately around them. It is a commitment everyone should have towards society – contributing towards social, cultural and ecological causes. SSR is based on an individual's ethics. Instead of giving importance only to those areas where one has material interests the individual supports issues for philanthropic reasons. It forms the base for CSR or Corporate Social Responsibility because if everyone in a business organization does his/her bit the bigger things automatically fall into place. The trends however show that big charitable organizations recorded high growth due to the SR efforts of individuals and not corporations or the government.

## Corporate Social Responsibility

Corporate social responsibility or CSR has been defined by Lord Holme and Richard Watts in the World Business Council for Sustainable Development's publication "Making Good Business Sense" as "...the continuing commitment by business to behave ethically and contribute to economic development while improving the quality of life of the workforce and their families as well as the local community and society at large." CSR is one of the newest management strategies where companies try to create a positive impact on society while doing business. Evidence suggests that CSR taken on voluntarily by companies will be much more effective than CSR mandated by governments. There is no clear-cut definition of what CSR comprises. Every company has different CSR objectives though the main motive is the same. All companies have a two-point agenda—to improve qualitatively (the management of people and processes) and quantitatively (the impact on society). The second is as important as the first and stake holders of every company are increasingly taking an interest in "the outer circle"-the activities of the company and how these are impacting the environment and society. The other motive behind this is that the companies should not be focused only on maximization of profits.

While many corporations include social responsibility in their operations, it is still important for those procuring the goods and services to ensure the products are socially sustainable. Verification tools are available from a multitude of entities internationally, such as the Underwriters Laboratories environmental standards, BIFMA, BioPreferred, and Green Seal. These resources help corporations and their consumers identify potential risks associated with a product's lifecycle and enable end users to confirm the corporation's practices adhere to social responsibility ideals.

## Social Responsibility of Scientists and Engineers

One common view is that scientists and engineers are morally responsible for the negative consequences which result from the various applications of their knowledge and inventions. After all, if scientists and engineers take personal pride in the many positive achievements of science and technology, why should they be allowed to escape responsibility for the negative consequences related to the use or abuse of scientific knowledge and technological innovations? Furthermore, scientists and engineers have a collective responsibility for the choice and conduct of their work. Committees of scientists and engineers are often involved in the planning of governmental and corporate research programs, including those devoted to the development of military technologies and weaponry. Many professional societies and national organizations, such as the National Academy of Science and the National Academy of Engineering in the United States, have ethical guidelines. Clearly, there is recognition that scientists and engineers, both individually and collectively, have a special and much greater responsibility than average citizens with respect to the generation and use of scientific knowledge.

Unfortunately, it has been pointed out that the situation is not that simple and scientists and engineers should not be blamed for all the evils created by new scientific knowledge and technological innovations. First, there is the common problem of fragmentation and diffusion of responsibility. Because of the intellectual and physical division of labor, the resulting fragmentation of knowledge, the high degree of specialization, and the complex and hierarchical decision-making process within corporations and government research laboratories, it is exceedingly difficult for individual scientists and engineers to control the applications of their innovations. This fragmentation of both work and decision-making results in fragmented moral accountability, often to the point where "everybody involved was responsible but none could be held responsible."

Another problem is ignorance. The scientists and engineers cannot predict how their newly generated knowledge and technological innovations may be abused or misused for destructive purposes in the near or distant future. While the excuse of ignorance is somewhat acceptable for those scientists involved in very basic and fundamental research where potential applications cannot be even envisioned, the excuse of ignorance is much weaker for scientists and engineers involved in applied scientific research and technological innovation since the work objectives are well known. For example, most corporations conduct research on specific products or services that promise to yield the greatest possible profit for share-holders. Similarly, most of the research funded by governments is mission-oriented, such as protecting the environment, developing new drugs, or designing more lethal weapons. In all cases where the application of scientific knowledge and technological innovation is well known *a priori*, it is impossible for a scientist or engineer to escape responsibility for research and technological innovation that is morally dubious. As John Forge writes in *Moral Responsibility and the Ignorant Scientist*: "Ignorance is not an excuse precisely because scientists can be blamed for being ignorant."

Another point of view is that responsibility falls on those who provide the funding for the research and technological developments, which in most cases are corporations and government agencies. Furthermore, because taxpayers provide indirectly the funds for government-sponsored research, they and the politicians that represent them, i.e., society at large, should be held accountable for the uses and abuses of science. Compared to earlier times when scientists could often conduct their own research independently, today's experimental research requires expensive laboratories and instrumentation, making scientists dependent on those who pay for their studies.

, or soft law principle has received some normative status in relation to private and public corporations in the United Nations Educational, Scientific and Cultural Organization (UNESCO) *Universal Declaration on Bioethics and Human Rights* developed by the UNESCO International Bioethics Committee particularly in relation to child and maternal welfare.(Faunce and Nasu 2009) The International Organization for Standardizationrd will "encourage voluntary commitment to social responsibility and will lead to common guidance on concepts, definitions and methods of evaluation."

## Risk Pool

A risk pool is one of the forms of risk management mostly practiced by insurance companies. Under this system, insurance companies come together to form a pool, which can provide protection to insurance companies against catastrophic risks such as floods, earthquakes etc. The term is also used to describe the pooling of similar risks that underlies the concept of insurance. While risk pooling is necessary for insurance to work, not all risks can be effectively pooled. In particular, it is difficult to pool dissimilar risks in a voluntary insurance bracket, unless there is a subsidy available to encourage participation.

Risk pooling is an important concept in supply chain management. Risk pooling suggests that demand variability is reduced if one aggregates demand across locations because as demand is aggregated across different locations, it becomes more likely that high demand from one customer will be offset by low demand from another. This reduction in variability allows a decrease in safety stock and therefore reduces average inventory.

For example: in the centralized distribution system, the warehouse serves all customers, which leads to a reduction in variability measured by either the standard deviation or the coefficient of variation.

The three critical points to risk pooling are:

1. Centralized inventory saves safety stock and average inventory in the system.
2. When demands from markets are negatively correlated, the higher the coefficient of variation, the greater the benefit obtained from centralized systems; that is, the greater the benefit from risk pooling.
3. The benefits from risk pooling depend directly on the relative market behavior. This is explained as follows: If we compare two markets and when demand from both markets are more or less than the average demand, we say that the demands from the market are positively correlated. Thus the benefits derived from risk pooling decreases as the correlation between demands from the two markets becomes more positive.

## In Government

Intergovernmental risk pools (IRPs) operate under the same general principle, except that they are made up of public entities, such as government agencies, school districts, county governments and municipalities. Thus, IRPs provide alternative risk financing and transfer mechanisms to their members through self-funding, where particular types of risk are underwritten with contributions (premiums), with losses and expenses shared in agreed ratios. In other words, Intergovernmental Risk Pools are a cooperative group of governmental entities joining together through written agreement to finance an exposure, liability or risk. Although they are not considered insurance, these pools extend nearly identical coverage through similar underwriting and claim activities, as well as provide other risk management services. Pools have many advantages over insurers for their members. Pools tend to protect their members from cyclic insurance rates, offer loss prevention services, offer savings (as they are non-profit organizations and do not lose funds through broker fees), and have focus and expertise in governmental entities often not found in insurers.

Intergovernmental risk pools may include, but are not limited to, authorities, joint power authorities, associations, agencies, trusts, risk management funds, and other risk pools.

# Risk Management Programme

*Risk Management* is a research programme set up by The Geneva Association, also known as the International Association for the Study of Insurance Economics. The focus of this programme is manifold and address the following issues: fostering the use of the tools of risk assessment and risk management in new fields of application such as policy making; providing a platform between the insurance community, the engineering and academic communities and policy makers to discuss risk issues; promoting the concept of the insurability of risks as the natural borderline between State legislation and the market economy; identifying new opportunities for insurers in the emerging sustainability concept in order to enlarge the field of insurable risks.

## Selected Key Issues

- What are the vulnerabilities in our industrial and services value-added processes?
- Where are the mechanisms for understanding, managing and mitigating these risks?
- How can insurance cope with a more complex and demanding risk scenario?
- What is the new risk environment that has been created in recent years?
- What about technologies being a new source of vulnerability?

6

# Risk Management: Tools, Methods and Techniques

There are mainly three types of risk tool and two of these are identified by their own approach while the third is the basis of project risk management. The types of risk tools are capital asset pricing model and probabilistic risk assessment. Event chain methodology, risk register and the Monte Carlo method are some of the other topics in this section. The chapter discusses the methods and techniques of risk management in a critical manner providing key analysis to the subject matter.

## Risk Management Tools

There are three distinct types of risk tools: Two are identified by their approach, Capital asset pricing model (CAP-M) and RiskAoA, and the third, Probabilistic risk assessment (PRA), is the mainstay of project risk management. These are classified by the quality and fidelity of information required for their calculations. Market-Level tools use market forces to make risk decisions between securities. System-Level tools use project constraints to make risk decisions between projects. Component-Level tools use the functions of probability and impact of individual risks to make decisions between resource allocations.

### Market-Level (CAP-M)

CAP-M uses market or economic statistics and assumptions to determine the appropriate required rate of return of an asset, given that asset's non-diversifiable risk.

### System or Project-Level (RiskAoA)

RiskAoA is a predictive tool used to discriminate between proposals, choices, or alternatives, by expressing risk for each as a single number. It uses Ceteris paribus statistics to develop state equations for each alternative considered. The results are an alternative's culturally adjusted trade-space between cost, scheduled time and risk.

### Component-Level (PRA)

These tools are applications of PRA and allow planners to explicitly address uncertainty by identifying and generating metrics, parameterizing, prioritizing, and developing responses, and tracking risk from components, tasks or costs. PRA, also called

Likelihood-Consequence or Probability-Impact, is based upon single-point estimates of probability of occurrence, initiating event frequency, and recovery success (e.g., human intervention) of a specific consequence (e.g., cost or schedule delay).

## Notable PRA Tools and Techniques

- Event chain methodology - A method of managing risk and uncertainties affecting project schedules
- The RIMS Risk Maturity Model (RMM) for enterprise risk management, was published in 2006. The RMM is an umbrella framework of content and methodology that details the requirements for sustainable and effective enterprise risk management. The RMM model consists of twenty-five competency drivers for seven attributes that create ERM's value and utility in an organization. The 7 attributes are: an ERM-based approach, ERM process management, risk appetite management, root cause discipline, uncovering risks, performance management, and business resiliency and sustainability. The model was published by the Risk and Insurance Management Society and developed by Steven Minsky, CEO of LogicManager in collaboration with the RIMS ERM Committee. The Risk Maturity Model is based on the Capability Maturity Model, a methodology founded by the Carnegie Mellon University Software Engineering Institute (SEI) in the 1980s.
- Risk Radar Enterprise (RRE) - Web based application for enterprise-wide program and/or project level Risk Management. RRE enables effective management and communication of project Cost, Schedule, Technical and Performance risk in one or many projects within a common flexible and scalable enterprise framework.
- Risk register – A project planning and organizational risk assessment tool. It is often referred to as a Risk Log.
- Systems Analysis Programs for Hands-on Integrated Reliability Evaluations (SAPHIRE) – A probabilistic safety and reliability engineering assessment software tool.
- SimpleRisk - a simplified, open-source enterprise risk management system based on NIST 800-30 risk management framework.
- Importantly, ISO/IEC 31010 (Risk assessment techniques) has a detailed but non-exhaustive list of tools and techniques available for assessing risk.

## Types of Risk Tools

## Capital Asset Pricing Model

In finance, the capital asset pricing model (CAPM) is a model used to determine a theoretically appropriate required rate of return of an asset, to make decisions about adding assets to a well-diversified portfolio.

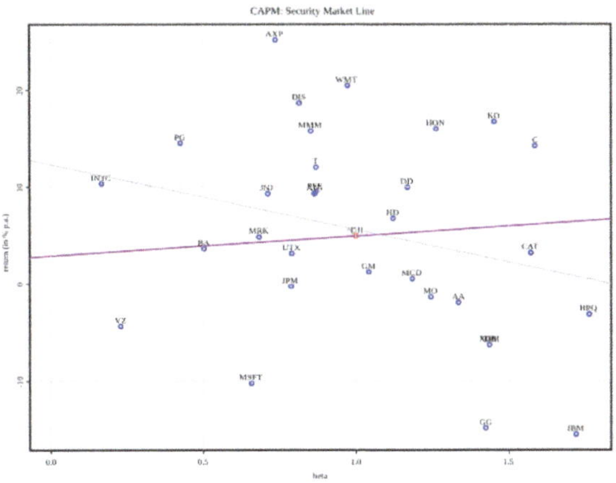


An estimation of the CAPM and the security market line (purple) for the Dow Jones IndustrialAverage over 3 years for monthly data.

## Overview

The model takes into account the asset's sensitivity to non-diversifiable risk (also known as systematic risk or market risk), often represented by the quantity beta (β) in the financial industry, as well as the expected return of the market and the expected return of a theoretical risk-free asset. CAPM assumes a particular form of utility functions (in which only first and second moments matter, that is risk is measured by variance, for example a quadratic utility) or alternatively asset returns whose probability distributions are completely described by the first two moments (for example, the normal distribution) and zero transaction costs (necessary for diversification to get rid of all idiosyncratic risk). Under these conditions, CAPM shows that the cost of equity capital is determined only by beta. Despite it failing numerous empirical tests, and the existence of more modern approaches to asset pricing and portfolio selection (such as arbitrage pricing theory and Merton's portfolio problem), the CAPM still remains popular due to its simplicity and utility in a variety of situations.

## Inventors

The CAPM was introduced by Jack Treynor (1961, 1962), William F. Sharpe (1964), John Lintner (1965a,b) and Jan Mossin (1966) independently, building on the earlier work of Harry Markowitz on diversification and modern portfolio theory. Sharpe, Markowitz and Merton Miller jointly received the 1990 Nobel Memorial Prize in Economics for this contribution to the field of financial economics. Fischer Black (1972) developed another version of CAPM, called Black CAPM or zero-beta CAPM, that does not assume the existence of a riskless asset. This version was more robust against empirical testing and was influential in the widespread adoption of the CAPM.

## Formula

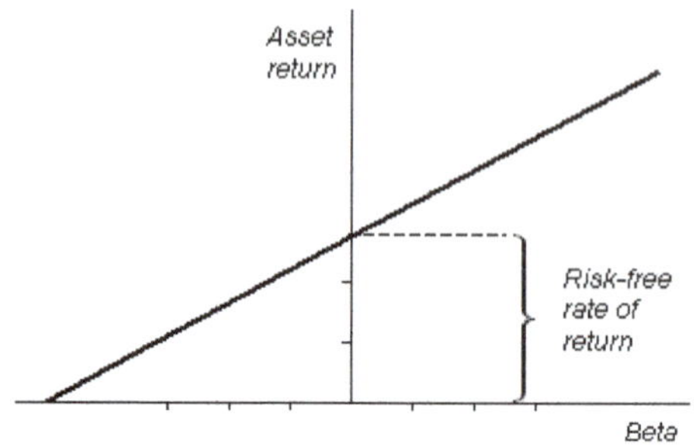


The security market line, seen here in a graph, describes a relation between the beta and the asset's expected rate of return.

The CAPM is a model for pricing an individual security or portfolio. For individual securities, we make use of the security market line (SML) and its relation to expected return and systematic risk (beta) to show how the market must price individual securities in relation to their security risk class. The SML enables us to calculate the reward-to-risk ratio for any security in relation to that of the overall market. Therefore, when the expected rate of return for any security is deflated by its beta coefficient, the reward-to-risk ratio for any individual security in the market is equal to the market reward-to-risk ratio, thus:

$$\frac{E(R_i)-R_f}{\beta_i}=E(R_m)-R_f$$

The market reward-to-risk ratio is effectively the market risk premium and by rearranging the above equation and solving for $E(R_i)$ , we obtain the capital asset pricing model (CAPM).

$$E(R_i)=R_f+\beta_i(E(R_m)-R_f)$$

where:

- $E(R_i)$ is the expected return on the capital asset
- $R_f$ is the risk-free rate of interest such as interest arising from government bonds
- $\beta_i$ (the *beta*) is the sensitivity of the expected excess asset returns to the expected excess market returns, or also $\beta_i=\frac{\mathrm{Cov}(R_i,R_m)}{\mathrm{Var}(R_m)} = \rho_{i,m}\frac{\sigma_i}{\sigma_m}$
- $E(R_m)$ is the expected return of the market
- $E(R_m)-R_f$ is sometimes known as the *market premium* (the difference be-

tween the expected market rate of return and the risk-free rate of return).

- $E(R_i) - R_f$ is also known as the *risk premium*

Restated, in terms of risk premium, we find that:

$$E(R_i) - R_f = \beta_i(E(R_m) - R_f)$$

which states that the *individual risk premium* equals the *market premium* times $\beta$.

Note 1: the expected market rate of return is usually estimated by measuring the arithmetic average of the historical returns on a market portfolio (e.g. S&P 500).

Note 2: the risk free rate of return used for determining the risk premium is usually the arithmetic average of historical risk free rates of return and not the current risk free rate of return.

## Modified Formula

CAPM can be modified to include size premium and specific risk. This is important for investors in privately held companies who often do not hold a well-diversified portfolio. The equation is similar to the traditional CAPM equation "with the market risk premium replaced by the product of beta times the market risk premium:"

$$E(R_i) = R_f + \beta(RP_m) + RP_s + RP_u"$$

"where:

$E(R_i)$ is required return on security i

$R_f$ is risk-free rate

$RP_m$ is general market risk premium

$RP_s$ is risk premium for small size

$RP_u$ is risk premium due to company-specific risk factor"

## Security Market Line

The SML essentially graphs the results from the capital asset pricing model (CAPM) formula. The *x*-axis represents the risk (beta), and the *y*-axis represents the expected return. The market risk premium is determined from the slope of the SML.

The relationship between β and required return is plotted on the *securities market line* (SML), which shows expected return as a function of β. The intercept is the nominal risk-free rate available for the market, while the slope is the market premium, E($R_m$)– $R_f$. The securities market line can be regarded as representing a single-factor model of the asset price, where Beta is exposure to changes in value of the Market. The equation of the SML is thus:

$$\text{SML}: E(R_i) = R_f + \beta_i(E(R_M) - R_f).$$

It is a useful tool in determining if an asset being considered for a portfolio offers a reasonable expected return for risk. Individual securities are plotted on the SML graph. If the security's expected return versus risk is plotted above the SML, it is undervalued since the investor can expect a greater return for the inherent risk. And a security plotted below the SML is overvalued since the investor would be accepting less return for the amount of risk assumed.

## Asset Pricing

Once the expected/required rate of return $E(R_i)$ is calculated using CAPM, we can compare this required rate of return to the asset's estimated rate of return over a specific investment horizon to determine whether it would be an appropriate investment. To make this comparison, you need an independent estimate of the return outlook for the security based on either fundamental or technical analysis techniques, including P/E, M/B etc.

Assuming that the CAPM is correct, an asset is correctly priced when its estimated price is the same as the present value of future cash flows of the asset, discounted at the rate suggested by CAPM. If the estimated price is higher than the CAPM valuation, then the asset is undervalued (and overvalued when the estimated price is below the CAPM valuation). When the asset does not lie on the SML, this could also suggest mis-pricing. Since the expected return of the asset at time $t$ is $E(R_t) = \frac{E(P_{t+1}) - P_t}{P_t}$, a higher expected return than what CAPM suggests indicates that $P_t$ is too low (the asset is currently undervalued), assuming that at time $t+1$ the asset returns to the CAPM suggested price.

The asset price $P_0$ using CAPM, sometimes called the certainty equivalent pricing formula, is a linear relationship given by

$$P_0 = \frac{1}{1+R_f}\left[E(P_T) - \frac{\text{Cov}(P_T, R_M)(E(R_M) - R_f)}{\text{Var}(R_M)}\right]$$

where $P_T$ is the payoff of the asset or portfolio.

## Asset-specific Required Return

The CAPM returns the asset-appropriate required return or discount rate—i.e. the rate at which future cash flows produced by the asset should be discounted given that asset's relative riskiness. Betas exceeding one signify more than average "riskiness"; betas below one indicate lower than average. Thus, a more risky stock will have a higher beta and will be discounted at a higher rate; less sensitive stocks will have lower betas and be discounted at a lower rate. Given the accepted concave utility function, the CAPM is consistent with intuition—investors (should) require a higher return for holding a more risky asset.

Since beta reflects asset-specific sensitivity to non-diversifiable, i.e. market risk, the market as a whole, by definition, has a beta of one. Stock market indices are frequently used as local proxies for the market—and in that case (by definition) have a beta of one. An investor in a large, diversified portfolio (such as a mutual fund), therefore, expects performance in line with the market.

## Risk and Diversification

The risk of a portfolio comprises systematic risk, also known as undiversifiable risk, and unsystematic risk which is also known as idiosyncratic risk or diversifiable risk. Systematic risk refers to the risk common to all securities—i.e. market risk. Unsystematic risk is the risk associated with individual assets. Unsystematic risk can be diversified away to smaller levels by including a greater number of assets in the portfolio (specific risks "average out"). The same is not possible for systematic risk within one market. Depending on the market, a portfolio of approximately 30–40 securities in developed markets such as the UK or US will render the portfolio sufficiently diversified such that risk exposure is limited to systematic risk only. In developing markets a larger number is required, due to the higher asset volatilities.

A rational investor should not take on any diversifiable risk, as only non-diversifiable risks are rewarded within the scope of this model. Therefore, the required return on an asset, that is, the return that compensates for risk taken, must be linked to its riskiness in a portfolio context—i.e. its contribution to overall portfolio riskiness—as opposed to its "stand alone risk." In the CAPM context, portfolio risk is represented by higher variance i.e. less predictability. In other words, the beta of the portfolio is the defining factor in rewarding the systematic exposure taken by an investor.

## Efficient Frontier

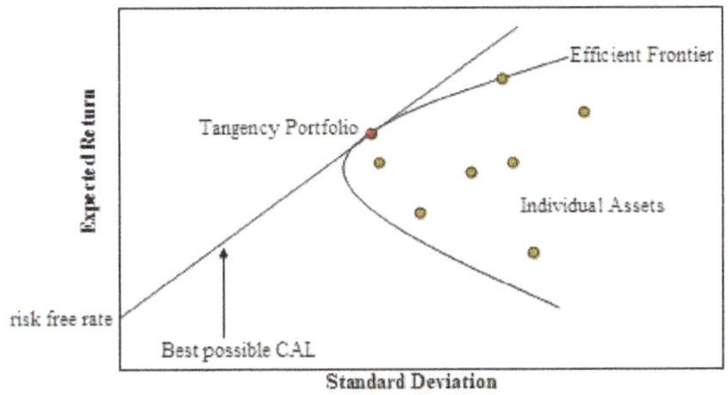


The (Markowitz) efficient frontier. CAL stands for the capital allocation line.

The CAPM assumes that the risk-return profile of a portfolio can be optimized—an optimal portfolio displays the lowest possible level of risk for its level of return. Additionally, since each additional asset introduced into a portfolio further diversifies the portfolio, the optimal portfolio must comprise every asset, (assuming no trading costs) with each asset value-weighted to achieve the above (assuming that any asset is infinitely divisible). All such optimal portfolios, i.e., one for each level of return, comprise the efficient frontier.

Because the unsystematic risk is diversifiable, the total risk of a portfolio can be viewed as beta.

## Assumptions of CAPM

All investors:

1. Aim to maximize economic utilities (Asset quantities are given and fixed).
2. Are rational and risk-averse.
3. Are broadly diversified across a range of investments.
4. Are price takers, i.e., they cannot influence prices.
5. Can lend and borrow unlimited amounts under the risk free rate of interest.
6. Trade without transaction or taxation costs.
7. Deal with securities that are all highly divisible into small parcels (All assets are perfectly divisible and liquid).
8. Have homogeneous expectations.
9. Assume all information is available at the same time to all investors.

## Problems of CAPM

In their 2004 review, Fama and French argue that "the failure of the CAPM in empirical tests implies that most applications of the model are invalid".

- The model assumes that the variance of returns is an adequate measurement of risk. This would be implied by the assumption that returns are normally distributed, or indeed are distributed in any two-parameter way, but for general return distributions other risk measures (like coherent risk measures) will reflect the active and potential shareholders' preferences more adequately. Indeed, risk in financial investments is not variance in itself, rather it is the probability of losing: it is asymmetric in nature. Barclays Wealth have published some research on asset allocation with non-normal returns which shows that investors with very low risk tolerances should hold more cash than CAPM suggests.

- The model assumes that all active and potential shareholders have access to the same information and agree about the risk and expected return of all assets (homogeneous expectations assumption).
- The model assumes that the probability beliefs of active and potential shareholders match the true distribution of returns. A different possibility is that active and potential shareholders' expectations are biased, causing market prices to be informationally inefficient. This possibility is studied in the field of behavioral finance, which uses psychological assumptions to provide alternatives to the CAPM such as the overconfidence-based asset pricing model of Kent Daniel, David Hirshleifer, and Avanidhar Subrahmanyam (2001).
- The model does not appear to adequately explain the variation in stock returns. Empirical studies show that low beta stocks may offer higher returns than the model would predict. Some data to this effect was presented as early as a 1969 conference in Buffalo, New York in a paper by Fischer Black, Michael Jensen, and Myron Scholes. Either that fact is itself rational (which saves the efficient-market hypothesis but makes CAPM wrong), or it is irrational (which saves CAPM, but makes the EMH wrong – indeed, this possibility makes volatility arbitrage a strategy for reliably beating the market).{H deSilva, CFA Institutes Conference Proceedings Quarterly, March 2012:46-55}{Benchmarks as Limits to Arbitrage: Understanding the Low-Volatility Anomaly. Malcolm Baker, Brendan Bradley, and Jeffrey Wurgler. people.stern.nyu.edu/jwurgler/papers/faj-benchmarks.pdf }
- The model assumes that given a certain expected return, active and potential shareholders will prefer lower risk (lower variance) to higher risk and conversely given a certain level of risk will prefer higher returns to lower ones. It does not allow for active and potential shareholders who will accept lower returns for higher risk. Casino gamblers pay to take on more risk, and it is possible that some stock traders will pay for risk as well.
- The model assumes that there are no taxes or transaction costs, although this assumption may be relaxed with more complicated versions of the model.
- The market portfolio consists of all assets in all markets, where each asset is weighted by its market capitalization. This assumes no preference between markets and assets for individual active and potential shareholders, and that active and potential shareholders choose assets solely as a function of their risk-return profile. It also assumes that all assets are infinitely divisible as to the amount which may be held or transacted.
- The market portfolio should in theory include all types of assets that are held by anyone as an investment (including works of art, real estate, human capital...) In practice, such a market portfolio is unobservable and people usually

substitute a stock index as a proxy for the true market portfolio. Unfortunately, it has been shown that this substitution is not innocuous and can lead to false inferences as to the validity of the CAPM, and it has been said that due to the inobservability of the true market portfolio, the CAPM might not be empirically testable. This was presented in greater depth in a paper by Richard Roll in 1977, and is generally referred to as Roll's critique.

- The model assumes economic agents optimise over a short-term horizon, and in fact investors with longer-term outlooks would optimally choose long-term inflation-linked bonds instead of short-term rates as this would be more risk-free asset to such an agent.
- The model assumes just two dates, so that there is no opportunity to consume and rebalance portfolios repeatedly over time. The basic insights of the model are extended and generalized in the intertemporal CAPM (ICAPM) of Robert Merton, and the consumption CAPM (CCAPM) of Douglas Breeden and Mark Rubinstein.
- CAPM assumes that all active and potential shareholders will consider all of their assets and optimize one portfolio. This is in sharp contradiction with portfolios that are held by individual shareholders: humans tend to have fragmented portfolios or, rather, multiple portfolios.
- Empirical tests show market anomalies like the size and value effect that cannot be explained by the CAPM.

## Probabilistic Risk Assessment

Probabilistic risk assessment (PRA) is a systematic and comprehensive methodology to evaluate risks associated with a complex engineered technological entity (such as an airliner or a nuclear power plant).

Risk in a PRA is defined as a feasible detrimental outcome of an activity or action. In a PRA, risk is characterized by two quantities:

1. the magnitude (severity) of the possible adverse consequence(s), and
2. the likelihood (probability) of occurrence of each consequence.

Consequences are expressed numerically (e.g., the number of people potentially hurt or killed) and their likelihoods of occurrence are expressed as probabilities or frequencies (i.e., the number of occurrences or the probability of occurrence per unit time). The total risk is the expected loss: the sum of the products of the consequences multiplied by their probabilities.

The spectrum of risks across classes of events are also of concern, and are usually controlled in licensing processes – it would be of concern if rare but high consequence events were found to dominate the overall risk, particularly as these risk assessments are very sensitive to assumptions (how rare is a high consequence event?).

Probabilistic Risk Assessment usually answers three basic questions:

1. What can go wrong with the studied technological entity, or what are the initiators or initiating events (undesirable starting events) that lead to adverse consequence(s)?
2. What and how severe are the potential detriments, or the adverse consequences that the technological entity may be eventually subjected to as a result of the occurrence of the initiator?
3. How likely to occur are these undesirable consequences, or what are their probabilities or frequencies?

Two common methods of answering this last question are Event Tree Analysis and Fault Tree Analysis.

In addition to the above methods, PRA studies require special but often very important analysis tools like human reliability analysis (HRA) and common-cause-failure analysis (CCF). HRA deals with methods for modeling human error while CCF deals with methods for evaluating the effect of inter-system and intra-system dependencies which tend to cause simultaneous failures and thus significant increases in overall risk.

## RIMS Risk Maturity Model

The RIMS Risk Maturity Model (RMM) is a best practice framework and online assessment tool for enterprise risk management. The RMM enables risk professionals to measure their programs against its methodology and receive a corresponding ERM maturity score.

### History

The RIMS Risk Maturity Model was developed in 2006 by Steven Minsky, CEO of LogicManager, and published in 2008 by the Risk and Insurance Management Society. Today, the RMM serves as a free online resource for planning, implementing and maintaining mature enterprise risk management practices within organizations across industries and geographies.

The Risk Maturity Model's umbrella framework covers ISO 31000, OCEG, Red Book, BS 31100, COSO, FERMA, and Solvency II standards. It was originally based on the

Capability Maturity Model, a methodology founded by the Carnegie Mellon University Software Engineering Institute (SEI) in the 1980s.

## RMM Assessment and Scoring

The RMM's methodology is broken down into 7 attributes, 25 competency drivers, and 68 key readiness indicators. ERM programs are benchmarked against these dimensions to identify their strengths and weaknesses. Maturity scores on the RMM range from 1-5, with scores of 3 and above signifying the presence of a repeatable and above risk-based ERM program.

The 7 attributes of the RIMS Risk Maturity Model are:

- Adoption of an ERM-Based Process
- ERM Process Management
- Risk Appetite Management
- Root Cause Discipline
- Uncovering Risks
- Performance Management
- Business Resiliency and Sustainability.

## Research and Accreditation

Over 2,000 organizations have baselined their ERM maturity with the RIMS Risk Maturity Model for ERM.

In 2008, a research study concluded that at the 95% confidence level, there was a positive correlation between higher RMM assessment scores and higher credit ratings, an accpeted measure of business performance and value.

In 2014, a study of RMM data entitled "The Valuation Impact of Enterprise Risk Management Maturity," was published in The Journal of Risk and Insurance by a research team from Queen's University. The study provides statistical evidence of up to a 25% market valuation premium for firms that reach mature levels of enterprise risk management, as measured by the RIMS Risk Maturity Model for ERM.

## Industry Adoption

The RIMS Risk Maturity Model for ERM has been recognized as a best practice framework by the following organizations:

- Institute of Internal Auditors

- National Association of Insurance Commissioners (NAIC)
- Risk and Insurance Management Society (RIMS)

### Risk Maturity Model Recognition Program

The Risk Maturity Model Recognition Program was launched in 2015 and aims to recognize the leaders in enterprise risk management while enhancing the discipline of ERM. Organizations are nominated for this distinction on an annual basis, based on the scores of their RMM assessment.

## Event Chain Methodology

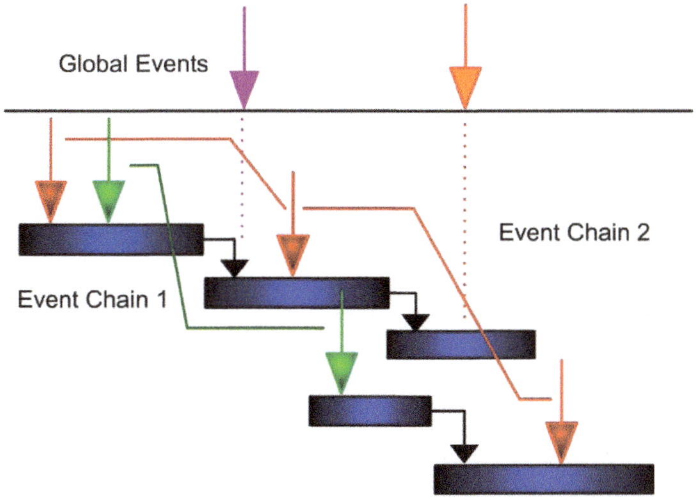


Event chain diagram

Event chain methodology is an uncertainty modeling and schedule network analysis technique that is focused on identifying and managing events and event chains that affect project schedules. Event chain methodology is the next advance beyond critical path method and critical chain project management.

Event chain methodology helps to mitigate the effect of motivational and cognitive biases in estimating and scheduling.

### Event Chain Methodology Principles

### Moment of risk and state of activity

An activity (task) in most real life processes is not a continuous uniform procedure. Tasks are affected by external events, which transform an activity from one state to another.

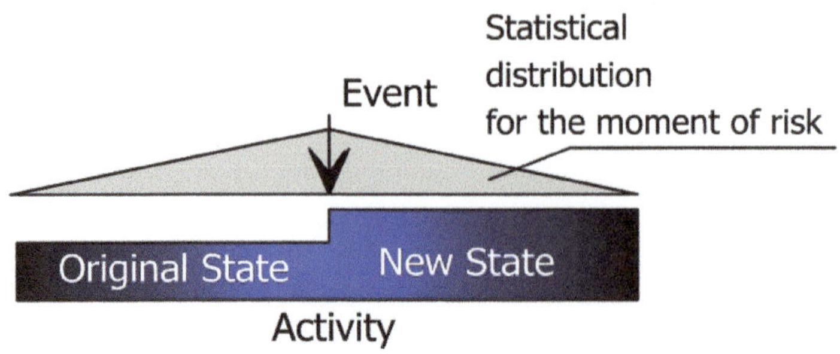


Moment of risk and state of activity

One of the important properties of an event is the moment when an event occurs during the course of an activity. This moment, when an event occurs, in most cases is probabilistic and can be defined using statistical distribution.

## Event Chains

Events can cause other events, which will create event chains. These event chains can significantly affect the course of the project. For example, requirement changes can cause an activity to be delayed. To accelerate the activity, the project manager allocates a resource from another activity, which then leads to a missed deadline. Eventually, this can lead to the failure of the project.

## Monte Carlo Simulations

Once events and event chains are defined, quantitative analysis using Monte Carlo simulation can be performed to quantify the cumulative effect of the events. Probabilities and effects of risks are used as input data for Monte Carlo simulation of the project schedule. In most real life projects, it is necessary to supplement the information regarding the uncertainties expressed as an event, with distributions related to duration, start time, cost, and other parameters.

## Critical Event Chains

The single events or the event chains that have the most potential to affect the projects are the "critical events" or "critical chains of events." By identifying critical events or critical chains of events, we can mitigate their negative effects. These critical chains of events can be identified by analyzing the correlations between the main project parameters, such as project duration or cost, and the event chains.

## Performance Tracking with Event Chains

Monitoring the activity's progress ensures that updated information is used to perform the analysis. During the course of the project, the probability and time of the events can be recalculated based on actual data. The main issue with performance tracking is forecasting an activity's duration and cost if an activity is partially completed and certain events are assigned to the activity. The simple heuristic approach to this problem is to analyze the moment of risk, which is defined as one of the event parameters. Advanced analysis can be performed using a Bayesian approach.

## Event Chain Diagrams

Event Chain Diagrams are visualizations that show the relationships between events and tasks and how the events affect each other. The simplest way to represent these chains is to depict them as arrows associated with certain tasks or time intervals on the Gantt chart. Different events and event chains can be displayed using different colors. Events can be global (for all tasks in the project) and local (for a particular task). By using Event Chain Diagrams to visualize events and event chains, the modeling and analysis of risks and uncertainties can be significantly simplified.

## Event Chain Methodology Phenomena

## Repeated Activities

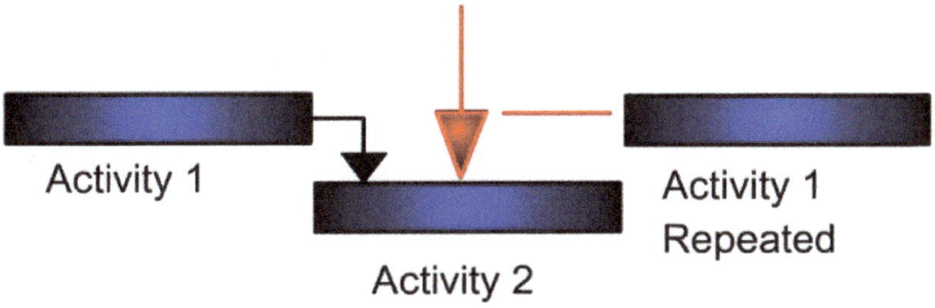


Repeated Activity

Sometimes events can cause the start of an activity that has already been completed. This is a very common scenario for real life projects; sometimes a previous activity must be repeated based on the results of a succeeding activity. Modeling of these scenarios using event chain methodology is simple. The original project schedule does not need to be updated, as all that is required is to define the event and assign it to an activity that points to the previous activity. In addition, a limit to the number of times an activity can be repeated needs to be defined.

## Event Chains and Risk Mitigation

If event or event chain occurs during the course of a project, it may require some mitigation effort. In some cases, mitigation plans can be generated. Mitigation plans are an activity or group of activities (small schedule) that augment the project schedule if a certain event occurs. The solution is to assign the mitigation plan to an event or event chain. These small schedules will be triggered when an event chain occurs. The same mitigation plan can be used for different events.

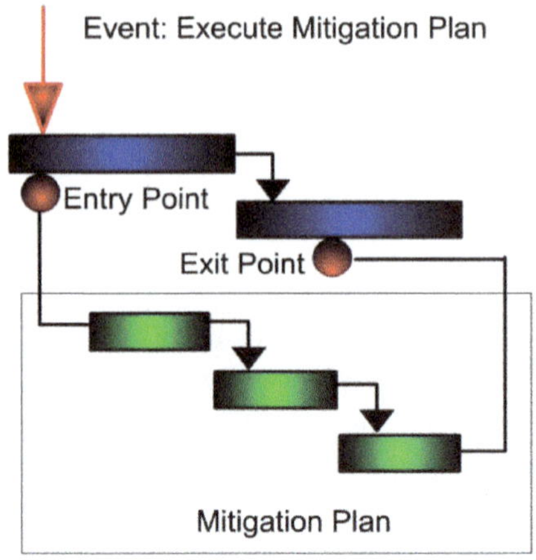


Mitigation plan

## Resource Allocation Based on Events

One potential event is the reassignment of a resource from one activity to another, which can occur under certain conditions. For example, if an activity requires more resources to complete it within a fixed period, this will trigger an event to reallocate the resource from another activity. Reallocation of resources can also occur when activity duration reaches a certain deadline or the cost exceeds a certain value. Events can be used to model different situations with resources, e.g. temporary leave, illness, vacations, etc.

# Risk Register

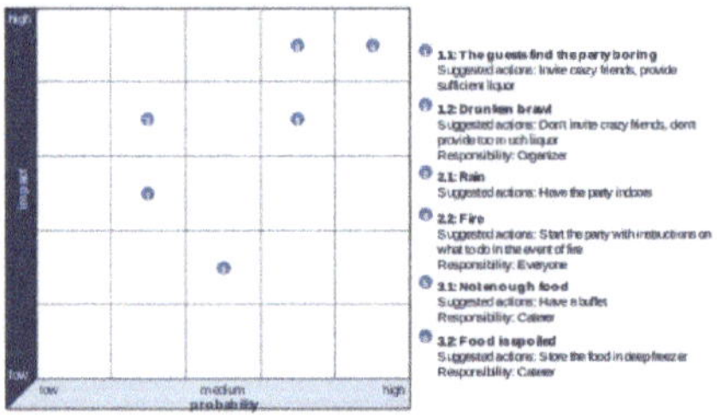


A Risk register plots the impact of a given risk over of its probability. The presented example deals with some issues which can arise on a usual Saturday-night party.

A risk register (or risk log e.g. in PRINCE2) is a scatterplot used as risk management tool and to fulfill regulatory compliance acting as a repository for all risks identified and includes additional information about each risk, e.g. nature of the risk, reference and owner, mitigation measures.

ISO 73:2009 Risk management—Vocabulary defines a risk register to be a "record of information about identified risks".

## Example

Risk register the project "barbecue party" with somebody inexperienced handling the grill, both in table format (below) and as plot (right).

| Category | Name | - | Probability | Impact | Mitigation | Contin-gency | Risk Score after Miti-gation | Action By | Action When |
|---|---|---|---|---|---|---|---|---|---|
| Guests | The guests find the party boring | 1.1. | low | medium | Invite crazy friends, provide suffi-cient liquor | Bring out the karaoke | 2 | | within 2hrs |
| Guests | Drunken brawl | 1.2. | medium | low | Don't invite crazy friends, don't provide too much liquor | Call 911 | x | | Now |
| Nature | Rain | 2.1. | low | high | Have the party indoors | Move the party indoors | 0 | | 10mins |
| Nature | Fire | 2.2. | highest | highest | Start the party with in-structions on what to do in the event of fire | Imple-ment the appro-priate response plan | 1 | Everyone | As per plan |
| Food | Not enough food | 3.1. | high | high | Have a buffet | Order pizza | 1 | | 30mins |
| Food | Food is spoiled | 3.2. | high | highest | Store the food in deep freezer | Order pizza | 1 | | 30mins |

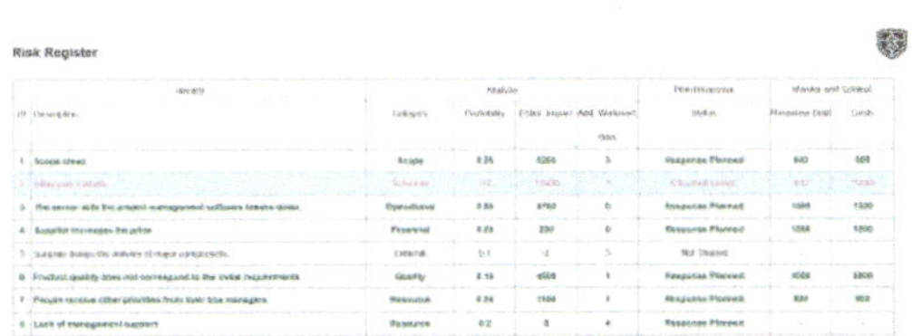

An example of the Risk Register for a project that includes 4 steps: Identify, Analyze, Plan Response, Monitor and Control.

## Terminology

A Risk Register can contain many different items. There are recommendations for Risk Register content made by the Project Management Institute Body of Knowledge (PM-BOK) and PRINCE2. ISO 31000:2009 does not use the term risk register, however it does state that risks need to be documented.

There are many different tools that can act as risk registers from comprehensive soft-ware suites to simple spreadsheets. The effectiveness of these tools depends on their implementation and the organisation's culture.

A typical risk register contains:

- A risk category to group similar risks
- A brief description or name of the risk to make the risk easy to discuss
- The *impact* (or *consequence*) if event actually occurs rated on an integer scale
- The *probability* or likelihood of its occurrence rated on an integer scale
- The *Risk Score* (or *Risk Rating*) is the multiplication of Probability and Impact and is often used to rank the risks.
- Common *mitigation steps* (e.g. within IT projects) are Identify, Analyze, Plan Response, Monitor and Control.

The risk register is called "qualitative if the probabilities are estimated by ranking them, as "high" to "low" impact. It is called "quantitative" both the impact and the probability is put into numbers, e.g. a risk might have a "$1m" impact and a "50%" probability.

Contingent response - the actions to be taken should the risk event actually occur.

Contingency - the budget allocated to the contingent response

Trigger - an event that itself results in the risk event occurring (for example the risk event might be "flooding" and "heavy rainfall" the trigger)

### Criticism

Although risk registers are commonly used tools not only in projects and programs but also in companies, research has found that they can lead to dysfunctions, for instance Toyota's risk register listed reputation risks caused by Prius' malfunctions but the company failed to take action. Risk registers often lead to ritualistic decision-making, illusion of control, and the fallacy of misplaced concreteness: mistaking the map for the territory. However, if used with common sense risk registers are a useful tool to stimulate cross-functional debate and cooperation.

## Predictive Analytics

Predictive analytics encompasses a variety of statistical techniques from predictive modeling, machine learning, and data mining that analyze current and historical facts to make predictions about future or otherwise unknown events.

In business, predictive models exploit patterns found in historical and transactional data to identify risks and opportunities. Models capture relationships among many factors to allow assessment of risk or potential associated with a particular set of conditions, guiding decision making for candidate transactions.

The defining functional effect of these technical approaches is that predictive analytics provides a predictive score (probability) for each individual (customer, employee, healthcare patient, product SKU, vehicle, component, machine, or other organizational unit) in order to determine, inform, or influence organizational processes that pertain across large numbers of individuals, such as in marketing, credit risk assessment, fraud detection, manufacturing, healthcare, and government operations including law enforcement.

Predictive analytics is used in actuarial science, marketing, financial services, insurance, telecommunications, retail, travel, healthcare, child protection, pharmaceuticals, capacity planning and other fields.

One of the most well known applications is credit scoring, which is used throughout financial services. Scoring models process a customer's credit history, loan application, customer data, etc., in order to rank-order individuals by their likelihood of making future credit payments on time.

## Definition

Predictive analytics is an area of data mining that deals with extracting information from data and using it to predict trends and behavior patterns. Often the unknown event of interest is in the future, but predictive analytics can be applied to any type of unknown whether it be in the past, present or future. For example, identifying suspects after a crime has been committed, or credit card fraud as it occurs. The core of predictive analytics relies on capturing relationships between explanatory variables and the predicted variables from past occurrences, and exploiting them to predict the unknown outcome. It is important to note, however, that the accuracy and usability of results will depend greatly on the level of data analysis and the quality of assumptions.

Predictive analytics is often defined as predicting at a more detailed level of granularity, i.e., generating predictive scores (probabilities) for each individual organizational element. This distinguishes it from forecasting. For example, "Predictive analytics—Technology that learns from experience (data) to predict the future behavior of individuals in order to drive better decisions." In future industrial systems, the value of predictive analytics will be to predict and prevent potential issues to achieve near-zero break-down and further be integrated into prescriptive analytics for decision optimization. Furthermore, the converted data can be used for closed-loop product life cycle improvement which is the vision of Industrial Internet Consortium.

## Types

Generally, the term predictive analytics is used to mean predictive modeling, "scoring" data with predictive models, and forecasting. However, people are increasingly using the term to refer to related analytical disciplines, such as descriptive modeling and decision modeling or optimization. These disciplines also involve rigorous data analysis, and are widely used in business for segmentation and decision making, but have different purposes and the statistical techniques underlying them vary.

## Predictive Models

Predictive models are models of the relation between the specific performance of a unit in a sample and one or more known attributes or features of the unit. The objective of the model is to assess the likelihood that a similar unit in a different sample will exhibit the specific performance. This category encompasses models in many areas, such as marketing, where they seek out subtle data patterns to answer questions about customer performance, or fraud detection models. Predictive models often perform calculations during live transactions, for example, to evaluate the risk or opportunity of a given customer or transaction, in order to guide a decision. With advancements in computing speed, individual agent modeling systems have become capable of simulating human behaviour or reactions to given stimuli or scenarios.

The available sample units with known attributes and known performances is referred to as the "training sample". The units in other samples, with known attributes but unknown performances, are referred to as "out of [training] sample" units. The out of sample bear no chronological relation to the training sample units. For example, the training sample may consists of literary attributes of writings by Victorian authors, with known attribution, and the out-of sample unit may be newly found writing with unknown authorship; a predictive model may aid in attributing a work to a known author. Another example is given by analysis of blood splatter in simulated crime scenes in which the out of sample unit is the actual blood splatter pattern from a crime scene. The out of sample unit may be from the same time as the training units, from a previous time, or from a future time.

## Descriptive Models

Descriptive models quantify relationships in data in a way that is often used to classify customers or prospects into groups. Unlike predictive models that focus on predicting a single customer behavior (such as credit risk), descriptive models identify many different relationships between customers or products. Descriptive models do not rank-order customers by their likelihood of taking a particular action the way predictive models do. Instead, descriptive models can be used, for example, to categorize customers by their product preferences and life stage. Descriptive modeling tools can be utilized to develop further models that can simulate large number of individualized agents and make predictions.

## Decision Models

Decision models describe the relationship between all the elements of a decision—the known data (including results of predictive models), the decision, and the forecast results of the decision—in order to predict the results of decisions involving many variables. These models can be used in optimization, maximizing certain outcomes while minimizing others. Decision models are generally used to develop decision logic or a set of business rules that will produce the desired action for every customer or circumstance.

## Applications

Although predictive analytics can be put to use in many applications, we outline a few examples where predictive analytics has shown positive impact in recent years.

## Analytical Customer Relationship Management (CRM)

Analytical customer relationship management (CRM) is a frequent commercial application of predictive analysis. Methods of predictive analysis are applied to customer data to pursue CRM objectives, which involve constructing a holistic view of the customer no matter where their information resides in the company or the department involved. CRM uses predictive analysis in applications for marketing campaigns, sales, and customer services to name a few. These tools are required in order for a company to posture and focus their efforts effectively across the breadth of their customer base. They must analyze and understand the products in demand or have the potential for high demand, predict customers' buying habits in order to promote relevant products at multiple touch points, and proactively identify and mitigate issues that have the potential to lose customers or reduce their ability to gain new ones. Analytical customer relationship management can be applied throughout the customers lifecycle (acquisition, relationship growth, retention, and win-back). Several of the application areas described below (direct marketing, cross-sell, customer retention) are part of customer relationship management.

## Child Protection

Over the last 5 years, some child welfare agencies have started using predictive analytics to flag high risk cases. The approach has been called "innovative" by the Commission to Eliminate Child Abuse and Neglect Fatalities (CECANF), and in Hillsborough County, Florida, where the lead child welfare agency uses a predictive modeling tool, there have been no abuse-related child deaths in the target population as of this writing.

## Clinical Decision Support Systems

Experts use predictive analysis in health care primarily to determine which patients are at risk of developing certain conditions, like diabetes, asthma, heart disease, and other lifetime illnesses. Additionally, sophisticated clinical decision support systems incorporate predictive analytics to support medical decision making at the point of care. A working definition has been proposed by Jerome A. Osheroff and colleagues: *Clinical decision support (CDS) provides clinicians, staff, patients, or other individuals with knowledge and person-specific information, intelligently filtered or presented at appropriate times, to enhance health and health care. It encompasses a variety of tools and interventions such as computerized alerts and reminders, clinical guidelines, order sets, patient data reports and dashboards, documentation templates, diagnostic support, and clinical workflow tools.*

A 2016 study of neurodegenerative disorders provides a powerful example of a CDS platform to diagnose, track, predict and monitor the progression of Parkinson's disease. Using large and multi-source imaging, genetics, clinical and demographic data, these investigators developed a decision support system that can predict the state of the disease with high accuracy, consistency and precision. They employed classical model-based and machine learning model-free methods to discriminate between different patient and control groups. Similar approaches may be used for predictive diagnosis and disease progression forecasting in many neurodegenerative disorders like Alzheimer's, Huntington's, Amyotrophic Lateral Sclerosis, as well as for other clinical and biomedical applications where Big Data is available.

## Collection Analytics

Many portfolios have a set of delinquent customers who do not make their payments on time. The financial institution has to undertake collection activities on these customers to recover the amounts due. A lot of collection resources are wasted on customers who are difficult or impossible to recover. Predictive analytics can help optimize the allocation of collection resources by identifying the most effective collection agencies, contact strategies, legal actions and other strategies to each customer, thus significantly increasing recovery at the same time reducing collection costs.

## Cross-sell

Often corporate organizations collect and maintain abundant data (e.g. customer records, sale transactions) as exploiting hidden relationships in the data can provide a competitive advantage. For an organization that offers multiple products, predictive analytics can help analyze customers' spending, usage and other behavior, leading to efficient cross sales, or selling additional products to current customers. This directly leads to higher profitability per customer and stronger customer relationships.

## Customer Retention

With the number of competing services available, businesses need to focus efforts on maintaining continuous customer satisfaction, rewarding consumer loyalty and minimizing customer attrition. In addition, small increases in customer retention have been shown to increase profits disproportionately. One study concluded that a 5% increase in customer retention rates will increase profits by 25% to 95%. Businesses tend to respond to customer attrition on a reactive basis, acting only after the customer has initiated the process to terminate service. At this stage, the chance of changing the customer's decision is almost zero. Proper application of predictive analytics can lead to a more proactive retention strategy. By a frequent examination of a customer's past service usage, service performance, spending and other behavior patterns, predictive models can determine the likelihood of a customer terminating service sometime soon. An intervention with lucrative offers can increase the chance of retaining the customer. Silent attrition, the behavior of a customer to slowly but steadily reduce usage, is another problem that many companies face. Predictive analytics can also predict this behavior, so that the company can take proper actions to increase customer activity.

## Direct Marketing

When marketing consumer products and services, there is the challenge of keeping up with competing products and consumer behavior. Apart from identifying prospects, predictive analytics can also help to identify the most effective combination of product versions, marketing material, communication channels and timing that should be used to target a given consumer. The goal of predictive analytics is typically to lower the cost per order or cost per action.

## Fraud Detection

Fraud is a big problem for many businesses and can be of various types: inaccurate credit applications, fraudulent transactions (both offline and online), identity thefts and false insurance claims. These problems plague firms of all sizes in many industries. Some examples of likely victims are credit card issuers, insurance companies, retail merchants, manufacturers, business-to-business suppliers and even services providers. A predictive model can help weed out the "bads" and reduce a business's exposure to fraud.

Predictive modeling can also be used to identify high-risk fraud candidates in business or the public sector. Mark Nigrini developed a risk-scoring method to identify audit targets. He describes the use of this approach to detect fraud in the franchisee sales reports of an international fast-food chain. Each location is scored using 10 predictors. The 10 scores are then weighted to give one final overall risk score for each location. The same scoring approach was also used to identify high-risk check kiting accounts, potentially fraudulent travel agents, and questionable vendors. A reasonably complex model was used to identify fraudulent monthly reports submitted by divisional controllers.

The Internal Revenue Service (IRS) of the United States also uses predictive analytics to mine tax returns and identify tax fraud.

Recent advancements in technology have also introduced predictive behavior analysis for web fraud detection. This type of solution utilizes heuristics in order to study normal web user behavior and detect anomalies indicating fraud attempts.

## Portfolio, Product or Economy-level Prediction

Often the focus of analysis is not the consumer but the product, portfolio, firm, industry or even the economy. For example, a retailer might be interested in predicting store-level demand for inventory management purposes. Or the Federal Reserve Board might be interested in predicting the unemployment rate for the next year. These types of problems can be addressed by predictive analytics using time series techniques. They can also be addressed via machine learning approaches which transform the original time series into a feature vector space, where the learning algorithm finds patterns that have predictive power.

## Project Risk Management

When employing risk management techniques, the results are always to predict and benefit from a future scenario. The capital asset pricing model (CAP-M) "predicts" the best portfolio to maximize return. Probabilistic risk assessment (PRA) when combined with mini-Delphi techniques and statistical approaches yields accurate forecasts. These are examples of approaches that can extend from project to market, and from near to long term. Underwriting and other business approaches identify risk management as a predictive method.

## Underwriting

Many businesses have to account for risk exposure due to their different services and determine the cost needed to cover the risk. For example, auto insurance providers need to accurately determine the amount of premium to charge to cover each automobile and driver. A financial company needs to assess a borrower's potential and ability to pay before granting a loan. For a health insurance provider, predictive analytics can analyze a few years of past medical claims data, as well as lab, pharmacy and other records where available, to predict how expensive an enrollee is likely to be in the future. Predictive analytics can help underwrite these quantities by predicting the chances of illness, default, bankruptcy, etc. Predictive analytics can streamline the process of customer acquisition by predicting the future risk behavior of a customer using application level data. Predictive analytics in the form of credit scores have reduced the amount of time it takes for loan approvals, especially in the mortgage market where lending decisions are now made in a matter of hours rather than days or even weeks. Proper predictive analytics can lead to proper pricing decisions, which can help mitigate future risk of default.

## Technology and Big Data Influences

Big data is a collection of data sets that are so large and complex that they become awkward to work with using traditional database management tools. The volume, variety and velocity of big data have introduced challenges across the board for capture, storage, search, sharing, analysis, and visualization. Examples of big data sources include web logs, RFID, sensor data, social networks, Internet search indexing, call detail records, military surveillance, and complex data in astronomic, biogeochemical, genomics, and atmospheric sciences. Big Data is the core of most predictive analytic services offered by IT organizations. Thanks to technological advances in computer hardware—faster CPUs, cheaper memory, and MPP architectures—and new technologies such as Hadoop, MapReduce, and in-database and text analytics for processing big data, it is now feasible to collect, analyze, and mine massive amounts of structured and unstructured data for new insights. It is also possible to run predictive algorithms on streaming data. Today, exploring big data and using predictive analytics is within reach of more organizations than ever before and new methods that are capable for handling such datasets are proposed

## Analytical Techniques

The approaches and techniques used to conduct predictive analytics can broadly be grouped into regression techniques and machine learning techniques.

## Regression Techniques

Regression models are the mainstay of predictive analytics. The focus lies on establishing a mathematical equation as a model to represent the interactions between the different variables in consideration. Depending on the situation, there are a wide variety of models that can be applied while performing predictive analytics. Some of them are briefly discussed below.

## Linear Regression Model

The linear regression model analyzes the relationship between the response or dependent variable and a set of independent or predictor variables. This relationship is expressed as an equation that predicts the response variable as a linear function of the parameters. These parameters are adjusted so that a measure of fit is optimized. Much of the effort in model fitting is focused on minimizing the size of the residual, as well as ensuring that it is randomly distributed with respect to the model predictions.

The goal of regression is to select the parameters of the model so as to minimize the sum of the squared residuals. This is referred to as ordinary least squares (OLS) estimation and results in best linear unbiased estimates (BLUE) of the parameters if and only if the Gauss-Markov assumptions are satisfied.

Once the model has been estimated we would be interested to know if the predictor variables belong in the model—i.e. is the estimate of each variable's contribution reliable? To do this we can check the statistical significance of the model's coefficients which can be measured using the t-statistic. This amounts to testing whether the coefficient is significantly different from zero. How well the model predicts the dependent variable based on the value of the independent variables can be assessed by using the $R^2$ statistic. It measures predictive power of the model i.e. the proportion of the total variation in the dependent variable that is "explained" (accounted for) by variation in the independent variables.

## Discrete Choice Models

Multivariate regression (above) is generally used when the response variable is continuous and has an unbounded range. Often the response variable may not be continuous but rather discrete. While mathematically it is feasible to apply multivariate regression to discrete ordered dependent variables, some of the assumptions behind the theory of multivariate linear regression no longer hold, and there are other techniques such as discrete choice models which are better suited for this type of analysis. If the dependent variable is discrete, some of those superior methods are logistic regression, multinomial logit and probit models. Logistic regression and probit models are used when the dependent variable is binary.

## Logistic Regression

In a classification setting, assigning outcome probabilities to observations can be achieved through the use of a logistic model, which is basically a method which transforms information about the binary dependent variable into an unbounded continuous variable and estimates a regular multivariate model.

The Wald and likelihood-ratio test are used to test the statistical significance of each coefficient *b* in the model. A test assessing the goodness-of-fit of a classification model is the "percentage correctly predicted".

## Multinomial Logistic Regression

An extension of the binary logit model to cases where the dependent variable has more than 2 categories is the multinomial logit model. In such cases collapsing the data into two categories might not make good sense or may lead to loss in the richness of the data. The multinomial logit model is the appropriate technique in these cases, especially when the dependent variable categories are not ordered (for examples colors like red, blue, green). Some authors have extended multinomial regression to include feature selection/importance methods such as random multinomial logit.

## Probit Regression

Probit models offer an alternative to logistic regression for modeling categorical dependent variables. Even though the outcomes tend to be similar, the underlying distributions are different. Probit models are popular in social sciences like economics.

A good way to understand the key difference between probit and logit models is to assume that the dependent variable is driven by a latent variable z, which is a sum of a linear combination of explanatory variables and a random noise term.

We do not observe z but instead observe y which takes the value 0 (when $z < 0$) or 1 (otherwise). In the logit model we assume that the random noise term follows a logistic distribution with mean zero. In the probit model we assume that it follows a normal distribution with mean zero. Note that in social sciences (e.g. economics), probit is often used to model situations where the observed variable y is continuous but takes values between 0 and 1.

## Logit Versus Probit

The probit model has been around longer than the logit model. They behave similarly, except that the logistic distribution tends to be slightly flatter tailed. One of the reasons the logit model was formulated was that the probit model was computationally difficult due to the requirement of numerically calculating integrals. Modern computing however has made this computation fairly simple. The coefficients obtained from the logit and probit model are fairly close. However, the odds ratio is easier to interpret in the logit model.

Practical reasons for choosing the probit model over the logistic model would be:

- There is a strong belief that the underlying distribution is normal
- The actual event is not a binary outcome (*e.g.*, bankruptcy status) but a proportion (*e.g.*, proportion of population at different debt levels).

## Time Series Models

Time series models are used for predicting or forecasting the future behavior of variables. These models account for the fact that data points taken over time may have an internal structure (such as autocorrelation, trend or seasonal variation) that should be accounted for. As a result, standard regression techniques cannot be applied to time series data and methodology has been developed to decompose the trend, seasonal and cyclical component of the series. Modeling the dynamic path of a variable can improve forecasts since the predictable component of the series can be projected into the future.

Time series models estimate difference equations containing stochastic components. Two commonly used forms of these models are autoregressive models (AR) and moving-average (MA) models. The Box–Jenkins methodology (1976) developed by George Box and G.M. Jenkins combines the AR and MA models to produce the ARMA (autoregressive moving average) model which is the cornerstone of stationary time series analysis. ARIMA (autoregressive integrated moving average models) on the other hand are used to describe non-stationary time series. Box and Jenkins suggest differencing a non stationary time series to obtain a stationary series to which an ARMA model can be applied. Non stationary time series have a pronounced trend and do not have a constant long-run mean or variance.

Box and Jenkins proposed a three-stage methodology which includes: model identification, estimation and validation. The identification stage involves identifying if the series is stationary or not and the presence of seasonality by examining plots of the series, autocorrelation and partial autocorrelation functions. In the estimation stage, models are estimated using non-linear time series or maximum likelihood estimation procedures. Finally the validation stage involves diagnostic checking such as plotting the residuals to detect outliers and evidence of model fit.

In recent years time series models have become more sophisticated and attempt to model conditional heteroskedasticity with models such as ARCH (autoregressive conditional heteroskedasticity) and GARCH (generalized autoregressive conditional heteroskedasticity) models frequently used for financial time series. In addition time series models are also used to understand inter-relationships among economic variables represented by systems of equations using VAR (vector autoregression) and structural VAR models.

## Survival or Duration Analysis

Survival analysis is another name for time to event analysis. These techniques were primarily developed in the medical and biological sciences, but they are also widely used in the social sciences like economics, as well as in engineering (reliability and failure time analysis).

Censoring and non-normality, which are characteristic of survival data, generate difficulty when trying to analyze the data using conventional statistical models such as multiple linear regression. The normal distribution, being a symmetric distribution, takes positive as well as negative values, but duration by its very nature cannot be negative and therefore normality cannot be assumed when dealing with duration/survival data. Hence the normality assumption of regression models is violated.

The assumption is that if the data were not censored it would be representative of the population of interest. In survival analysis, censored observations arise whenever the dependent variable of interest represents the time to a terminal event, and the duration of the study is limited in time.

An important concept in survival analysis is the hazard rate, defined as the probability that the event will occur at time t conditional on surviving until time t. Another concept related to the hazard rate is the survival function which can be defined as the probability of surviving to time t.

Most models try to model the hazard rate by choosing the underlying distribution depending on the shape of the hazard function. A distribution whose hazard function slopes upward is said to have positive duration dependence, a decreasing hazard shows negative duration dependence whereas constant hazard is a process with no memory usually characterized by the exponential distribution. Some of the distributional choices in survival models are: F, gamma, Weibull, log normal, inverse normal, exponential etc. All these distributions are for a non-negative random variable.

Duration models can be parametric, non-parametric or semi-parametric. Some of the models commonly used are Kaplan-Meier and Cox proportional hazard model (non parametric).

## Classification and Regression Trees (CART)

Globally-optimal classification tree analysis (GO-CTA) (also called hierarchical optimal discriminant analysis) is a generalization of optimal discriminant analysis that may be used to identify the statistical model that has maximum accuracy for predicting the value of a categorical dependent variable for a dataset consisting of categorical and continuous variables. The output of HODA is a non-orthogonal tree that combines categorical variables and cut points for continuous variables that yields maximum predictive accuracy, an assessment of the exact Type I error rate, and an evaluation of potential cross-generalizability of the statistical model. Hierarchical optimal discriminant analysis may be thought of as a generalization of Fisher's linear discriminant analysis. Optimal discriminant analysis is an alternative to ANOVA (analysis of variance) and regression analysis, which attempt to express one dependent variable as a linear combination of other features or measurements. However, ANOVA and regression analysis give a dependent variable that is a numerical variable, while hierarchical optimal discriminant analysis gives a dependent variable that is a class variable.

Classification and regression trees (CART) are a non-parametric decision tree learning technique that produces either classification or regression trees, depending on whether the dependent variable is categorical or numeric, respectively.

Decision trees are formed by a collection of rules based on variables in the modeling data set:

- Rules based on variables' values are selected to get the best split to differentiate observations based on the dependent variable
- Once a rule is selected and splits a node into two, the same process is applied to each "child" node (i.e. it is a recursive procedure)

- Splitting stops when CART detects no further gain can be made, or some pre-set stopping rules are met. (Alternatively, the data are split as much as possible and then the tree is later pruned.)

Each branch of the tree ends in a terminal node. Each observation falls into one and exactly one terminal node, and each terminal node is uniquely defined by a set of rules.

A very popular method for predictive analytics is Leo Breiman's Random forests.

## Multivariate Adaptive Regression Splines

Multivariate adaptive regression splines (MARS) is a non-parametric technique that builds flexible models by fitting piecewise linear regressions.

An important concept associated with regression splines is that of a knot. Knot is where one local regression model gives way to another and thus is the point of intersection between two splines.

In multivariate and adaptive regression splines, basis functions are the tool used for generalizing the search for knots. Basis functions are a set of functions used to represent the information contained in one or more variables. Multivariate and Adaptive Regression Splines model almost always creates the basis functions in pairs.

Multivariate and adaptive regression spline approach deliberately overfits the model and then prunes to get to the optimal model. The algorithm is computationally very intensive and in practice we are required to specify an upper limit on the number of basis functions.

## Machine Learning Techniques

Machine learning, a branch of artificial intelligence, was originally employed to develop techniques to enable computers to learn. Today, since it includes a number of advanced statistical methods for regression and classification, it finds application in a wide variety of fields including medical diagnostics, credit card fraud detection, face and speech recognition and analysis of the stock market. In certain applications it is sufficient to directly predict the dependent variable without focusing on the underlying relationships between variables. In other cases, the underlying relationships can be very complex and the mathematical form of the dependencies unknown. For such cases, machine learning techniques emulate human cognition and learn from training examples to predict future events.

A brief discussion of some of these methods used commonly for predictive analytics is provided below. A detailed study of machine learning can be found in Mitchell (1997).

## Neural Networks

Neural networks are nonlinear sophisticated modeling techniques that are able to model complex functions. They can be applied to problems of prediction, classification or control in a wide spectrum of fields such as finance, cognitive psychology/neuroscience, medicine, engineering, and physics.

Neural networks are used when the exact nature of the relationship between inputs and output is not known. A key feature of neural networks is that they learn the relationship between inputs and output through training. There are three types of training in neural networks used by different networks, supervised and unsupervised training, reinforcement learning, with supervised being the most common one.

Some examples of neural network training techniques are backpropagation, quick propagation, conjugate gradient descent, projection operator, Delta-Bar-Delta etc. Some unsupervised network architectures are multilayer perceptrons, Kohonen networks, Hopfield networks, etc.

## Multilayer Perceptron (MLP)

The multilayer perceptron (MLP) consists of an input and an output layer with one or more hidden layers of nonlinearly-activating nodes or sigmoid nodes. This is determined by the weight vector and it is necessary to adjust the weights of the network. The backpropagation employs gradient fall to minimize the squared error between the network output values and desired values for those outputs. The weights adjusted by an iterative process of repetitive present of attributes. Small changes in the weight to get the desired values are done by the process called training the net and is done by the training set (learning rule).

## Radial Basis Functions

A radial basis function (RBF) is a function which has built into it a distance criterion with respect to a center. Such functions can be used very efficiently for interpolation and for smoothing of data. Radial basis functions have been applied in the area of neural networks where they are used as a replacement for the sigmoidal transfer function. Such networks have 3 layers, the input layer, the hidden layer with the RBF non-linearity and a linear output layer. The most popular choice for the non-linearity is the Gaussian. RBF networks have the advantage of not being locked into local minima as do the feed-forward networks such as the multilayer perceptron.

## Support Vector Machines

support vector machines (SVM) are used to detect and exploit complex patterns in data by clustering, classifying and ranking the data. They are learning machines that are used to perform binary classifications and regression estimations. They commonly use kernel based methods to apply linear classification techniques to non-linear classification problems. There are a number of types of SVM such as linear, polynomial, sigmoid etc.

## Naïve Bayes

Naïve Bayes based on Bayes conditional probability rule is used for performing classification tasks. Naïve Bayes assumes the predictors are statistically independent which makes it an effective classification tool that is easy to interpret. It is best employed when faced with the problem of 'curse of dimensionality' i.e. when the number of predictors is very high.

## K-nearest Neighbours

The nearest neighbour algorithm (KNN) belongs to the class of pattern recognition statistical methods. The method does not impose a priori any assumptions about the distribution from which the modeling sample is drawn. It involves a training set with both positive and negative values. A new sample is classified by calculating the distance to the nearest neighbouring training case. The sign of that point will determine the classification of the sample. In the k-nearest neighbour classifier, the k nearest points are considered and the sign of the majority is used to classify the sample. The performance of the kNN algorithm is influenced by three main factors: (1) the distance measure used to locate the nearest neighbours; (2) the decision rule used to derive a classification from the k-nearest neighbours; and (3) the number of neighbours used to classify the new sample. It can be proved that, unlike other methods, this method is universally asymptotically convergent, i.e.: as the size of the training set increases, if the observations are independent and identically distributed (i.i.d.), regardless of the distribution from which the sample is drawn, the predicted class will converge to the class assignment that minimizes misclassification error.

## Geospatial Predictive Modeling

Conceptually, geospatial predictive modeling is rooted in the principle that the occurrences of events being modeled are limited in distribution. Occurrences of events are neither uniform nor random in distribution—there are spatial environment factors (infrastructure, sociocultural, topographic, etc.) that constrain and influence where the locations of events occur. Geospatial predictive modeling attempts to describe those constraints and influences by spatially correlating occurrences of historical geospatial locations with environmental factors that represent those constraints and influences. Geospatial predictive modeling is a process for analyzing events through a geographic filter in order to make statements of likelihood for event occurrence or emergence.

## Tools

Historically, using predictive analytics tools—as well as understanding the results they delivered—required advanced skills. However, modern predictive analytics tools are no longer restricted to IT specialists. As more organizations adopt predictive analytics into decision-making processes and integrate it into their operations, they are creating a shift in the market toward business users as the primary consumers of the information. Business users want tools they can use on their own. Vendors are responding by creating new software that removes the mathematical complexity, provides user-friendly graphic interfaces and/or builds in short cuts that can, for example, recognize the kind of data available and suggest an appropriate predictive model. Predictive analytics tools have become sophisticated enough to adequately present and dissect data problems, so that any data-savvy information worker can utilize them to analyze data and retrieve meaningful, useful results. For example, modern tools present findings using simple charts, graphs, and scores that indicate the likelihood of possible outcomes.

There are numerous tools available in the marketplace that help with the execution of predictive analytics. These range from those that need very little user sophistication to those that are designed for the expert practitioner. The difference between these tools is often in the level of customization and heavy data lifting allowed.

Beside these software packages, specific tools have also been developed for industrial applications. For example, Watchdog Agent Toolbox has been developed and optimized for predictive analysis in prognostics and health management applications and is available for MATLAB and LabVIEW.

The most popular commercial predictive analytics software packages according to the Rexer Analytics Survey for 2013 are IBM SPSS Modeler, SAS Enterprise Miner, and Dell Statistica.

## PMML

In an attempt to provide a standard language for expressing predictive models, the Predictive Model Markup Language (PMML) has been proposed. Such an XML-based language provides a way for the different tools to define predictive models and to share these between PMML compliant applications. PMML 4.0 was released in June, 2009.

## Criticism

There are plenty of skeptics when it comes to computers and algorithms abilities to predict the future, including Gary King, a professor from Harvard University and the director of the Institute for Quantitative Social Science. People are influenced by their environment in innumerable ways. Trying to understand what people will do next assumes that all the influential variables can be known and measured accurately. "People's environments change even more quickly than they themselves do. Everything from the weather to their relationship with their mother can change the way people think and act. All of those variables are unpredictable. How they will impact a person is even less predictable. If put in the exact same situation tomorrow, they may make a completely different decision. This means that a statistical prediction is only valid in sterile laboratory conditions, which suddenly isn't as useful as it seemed before."

# Delphi Method

The Delphi method is a structured communication technique or method, originally developed as a systematic, interactive forecasting method which relies on a panel of experts. The experts answer questionnaires in two or more rounds. After each round, a facilitator or change agent provides an anonymous summary of the experts' forecasts from the previous round as well as the reasons they provided for their judgments. Thus, experts are encouraged to revise their earlier answers in light of the replies of other members of their panel. It is believed that during this process the range of the answers will decrease and the group will converge towards the "correct" answer. Finally, the process is stopped after a predefined stop criterion (e.g. number of rounds, achievement of consensus, stability of results) and the mean or median scores of the final rounds determine the results.

Delphi is based on the principle that forecasts (or decisions) from a structured group of individuals are more accurate than those from unstructured groups. The technique can also be adapted for use in face-to-face meetings, and is then called mini-Delphi or Estimate-Talk-Estimate (ETE). Delphi has been widely used for business forecasting and has certain advantages over another structured forecasting approach, prediction markets.

## History

The name "Delphi" derives from the Oracle of Delphi, although the authors of the method were unhappy with the oracular connotation of the name, "smacking a little of the occult". The Delphi method is based on the assumption that group judgments are more valid than individual judgments.

The Delphi method was developed at the beginning of the Cold War to forecast the impact of technology on warfare. In 1944, General Henry H. Arnold ordered the creation of the report for the U.S. Army Air Corps on the future technological capabilities that might be used by the military.

Different approaches were tried, but the shortcomings of traditional forecasting methods, such as theoretical approach, quantitative models or trend extrapolation, quickly became apparent in areas where precise scientific laws have not been established yet. To combat these shortcomings, the Delphi method was developed by Project RAND during the 1950-1960s (1959) by Olaf Helmer, Norman Dalkey, and Nicholas Rescher. It has been used ever since, together with various modifications and reformulations, such as the Imen-Delphi procedure.

Experts were asked to give their opinion on the probability, frequency, and intensity of possible enemy attacks. Other experts could anonymously give feedback. This process was repeated several times until a consensus emerged.

## Key Characteristics

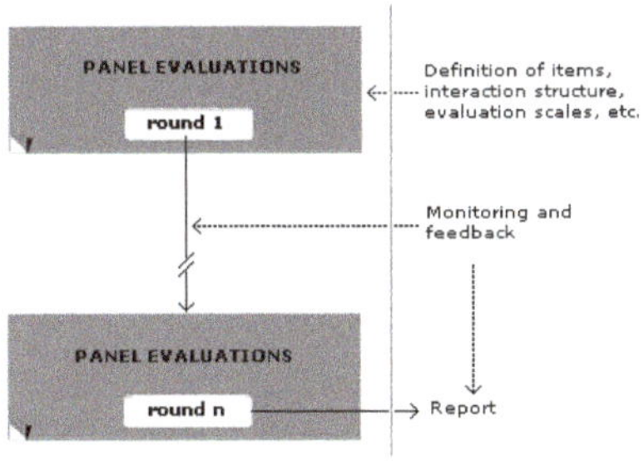


The Delphi Method communication structure

The following key characteristics of the Delphi method help the participants to focus on the issues at hand and separate Delphi from other methodologies: in this technique a panel of experts is drawn from both inside and outside the organisation. The panel consist of experts having knowledge of the area requiring decision making. Each expert is asked to make anonymous predictions.

## Anonymity of the Participants

Usually all participants remain anonymous. Their identity is not revealed, even after the completion of the final report. This prevents the authority, personality, or reputation of some participants from dominating others in the process. Arguably, it also frees participants (to some extent) from their personal biases, minimizes the "bandwagon effect" or "halo effect", allows free expression of opinions, encourages open critique, and facilitates admission of errors when revising earlier judgments.

## Structuring of Information Flow

The initial contributions from the experts are collected in the form of answers to questionnaires and their comments to these answers. The panel director controls the interactions among the participants by processing the information and filtering out irrelevant content. This avoids the negative effects of face-to-face panel discussions and solves the usual problems of group dynamics.

## Regular Feedback

Participants comment on their own forecasts, the responses of others and on the progress of the panel as a whole. At any moment they can revise their earlier statements. While in regular group meetings participants tend to stick to previously stated opinions and often conform too much to the group leader; the Delphi method prevents it.

## Role of the Facilitator

The person coordinating the Delphi method is usually known as a *facilitator* or Leader, and facilitates the responses of their *panel of experts*, who are selected for a reason, usually that they hold knowledge on an opinion or view. The facilitator sends out questionnaires, surveys etc. and if the panel of experts accept, they follow instructions and present their views. Responses are collected and analyzed, then common and conflicting viewpoints are identified. If consensus is not reached, the process continues through thesis and antithesis, to gradually work towards synthesis, and building consensus.

## Applications

## Use in Forecasting

First applications of the Delphi method were in the field of science and technology forecasting. The objective of the method was to combine expert opinions on likelihood and expected development time, of the particular technology, in a single indicator. One of the first such reports, prepared in 1964 by Gordon and Helmer, assessed the direction of long-term trends in science and technology development, covering such topics as scientific breakthroughs, population control, automation, space progress, war prevention and weapon systems. Other forecasts of technology were dealing with vehicle-highway systems, industrial robots, intelligent internet, broadband connections, and technology in education.

Later the Delphi method was applied in other places, especially those related to public policy issues, such as economic trends, health and education. It was also applied successfully and with high accuracy in business forecasting. For example, in one case reported by Basu and Schroeder (1977), the Delphi method predicted the sales of a new product during the first two years with inaccuracy of 3–4% compared with actual sales. Quantitative methods produced errors of 10–15%, and traditional unstructured forecast methods had errors of about 20%.

The Delphi method has also been used as a tool to implement multi-stakeholder approaches for participative policy-making in developing countries. The governments of Latin America and the Caribbean have successfully used the Delphi method as an open-ended public-private sector approach to identify the most urgent challenges for their regional ICT-for-development eLAC Action Plans. As a result, governments have widely acknowledged the value of collective intelligence from civil society, academic and private sector participants of the Delphi, especially in a field of rapid change, such as technology policies.

## Use in Policy-making

From the 1970s, the use of the Delphi technique in public policy-making introduces a number of methodological innovations. In particular:

- the need to examine several types of items (not only *forecasting* items but, typically, *issue* items, *goal* items, and *option* items) leads to introducing different evaluation scales which are not used in the standard Delphi. These often include *desirability*, *feasibility* (technical and political) and *probability*, which the analysts can use to outline different scenarios: the *desired* scenario (from desirability), the *potential* scenario (from feasibility) and the *expected* scenario (from probability);

- the complexity of the issues posed in public policy-making leads to give more importance to the arguments supporting the evaluations of the panelists; so these are often invited to list arguments for and against each option item, and sometimes they are given the possibility to suggest new items to be submitted to the panel;

- for the same reason, the scaling methods, which are used to measure panel evaluations, often include more sophisticated approaches such as multi-dimensional scaling.

Further innovations come from the use of computer-based (and later web-based) Delphi conferences. According to Turoff and Hiltz, in computer-based Delphis:

- the iteration structure used in the paper Delphis, which is divided into three or more discrete rounds, can be replaced by a process of continuous (roundless) interaction, enabling panelists to change their evaluations at any time;

- the statistical group response can be updated in real-time, and shown whenever a panelist provides a new evaluation.

According to Bolognini, web-based Delphis offer two further possibilities, relevant in the context of interactive policy-making and e-democracy. These are:

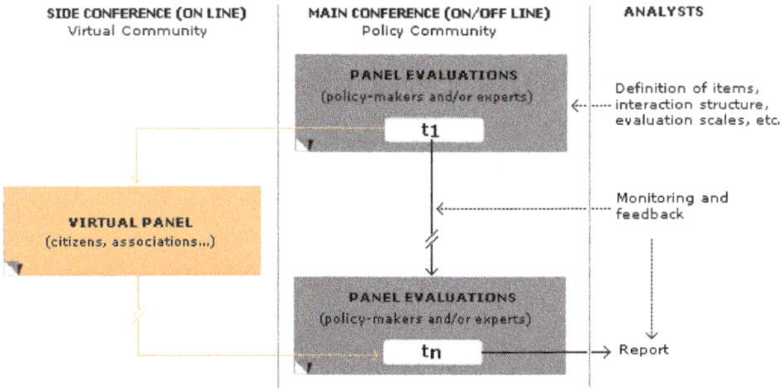


*A web-based communication structure (Hyperdelphi).*

- the involvement of a large number of participants,
- the use of two or more panels representing different groups (such as policy-makers, experts, citizens), which the administrator can give tasks reflecting their diverse roles and expertise, and make them to interact within ad hoc communication structures. For example, the *policy community* members (policy-makers and experts) may interact as part of the *main conference* panel, while they receive inputs from a *virtual community* (citizens, associations etc.) involved in a *side conference*. These web-based variable communication structures, which he calls *Hyperdelphi* (HD), are designed to make Delphi conferences "more fluid and adapted to the hypertextual and interactive nature of digital communication".

One successful example of a (partially) web-based policy Delphi is the five-round Delphi exercise (with 1,454 contributions) for the creation of the eLAC Action Plans in Latin America. It is believed to be the most extensive online participatory policy-making foresight exercise in the history of intergovernmental processes in the developing world at this time. In addition to the specific policy guidance provided, the authors list the following lessons learned include "(1) the potential of Policy Delphi methods to introduce transparency and accountability into public decision-making, especially in developing countries; (2) the utility of foresight exercises to foster multi-agency networking in the development community; (3) the usefulness of embedding foresight exercises into established mechanisms of representative democracy and international multilateralism, such as the United Nations; (4) the potential of online tools to facilitate participation in resource-scarce developing countries; and (5) the resource-efficiency stemming from the scale of international foresight exercises, and therefore its adequacy for resource-scarce regions."

## Online Delphi Systems

A number of Delphi forecasts are conducted using web sites that allow the process to be conducted in real-time. For instance, the TechCast Project uses a panel of 100 experts worldwide to forecast breakthroughs in all fields of science and technology. Another example is the Horizon Project, where educational futurists collaborate online using the Delphi method to come up with the technological advancements to look out for in education for the next few years.

## Variations

Traditionally the Delphi method has aimed at a consensus of the most probable future by iteration. Other versions, such as the Policy Delphi, is instead a decision support method aiming at structuring and discussing the diverse views of the preferred future. In Europe, more recent web-based experiments have used the Delphi method as a communication technique for interactive decision-making and e-democracy. The

Argument Delphi, was developed by Osmo Kuusi, focuses on ongoing discussion and finding relevant arguments rather than focusing on the output. The Disaggregative Policy Delphi, developed by Petri Tapio, uses cluster analysis as a systematic tool to construct various scenarios of the future in the latest Delphi round. The respondent's view on the probable and the preferable future are dealt with as separate cases. The computerization of Argument Delphi is relatively difficult because of several problems like argument resolution, argument aggregation and argument evaluation. The computerization of Argument Delphi, was developed by Sadi Evren Seker, proposes solutions to such problems.

## Discussion

Overall the track record of the Delphi method is mixed. There have been many cases when the method produced poor results. Still, some authors attribute this to poor application of the method and not to the weaknesses of the method itself. It must also be realized that in areas such as science and technology forecasting, the degree of uncertainty is so great that exact and always correct predictions are impossible, so a high degree of error is to be expected.

Another particular weakness of the Delphi method is that future developments are not always predicted correctly by consensus of experts. The issue of ignorance is important. If panelists are misinformed about a topic, the use of Delphi may only add confidence to their ignorance.

One of the initial problems of the method was its inability to make complex forecasts with multiple factors. Potential future outcomes were usually considered as if they had no effect on each other. Later on, several extensions to the Delphi method were developed to address this problem, such as cross impact analysis, that takes into consideration the possibility that the occurrence of one event may change probabilities of other events covered in the survey. Still the Delphi method can be used most successfully in forecasting single scalar indicators.

Despite these shortcomings, today the Delphi method is a widely accepted forecasting tool and has been used successfully for thousands of studies in areas varying from technology forecasting to drug abuse.

## Delphi vs. Prediction Markets

Delphi has characteristics similar to prediction markets as both are structured approaches that aggregate diverse opinions from groups. Yet, there are differences that may be decisive for their relative applicability for different problems.

Some advantages of prediction markets derive from the possibility to provide incentives for participation.

1. They can motivate people to participate over a long period of time and to reveal their true beliefs.
2. They aggregate information automatically and instantly incorporate new information in the forecast.
3. Participants do not have to be selected and recruited manually by a facilitator. They themselves decide whether to participate if they think their private information is not yet incorporated in the forecast.

Delphi seems to have these advantages over prediction markets:

1. Participants reveal their reasoning
2. It is easier to maintain confidentiality
3. Potentially quicker forecasts if experts are readily available.
4. Delphi is applicable in situations where the bets involved might affect the value of the currency used in bets (e.g. a bet on the collapse of the dollar made in dollars might have distorted odds).

## Monte Carlo Method

Monte Carlo methods (or Monte Carlo experiments) are a broad class of computational algorithms that rely on repeated random sampling to obtain numerical results. Their essential idea is using randomness to solve problems that might be deterministic in principle. They are often used in physical and mathematical problems and are most useful when it is difficult or impossible to use other approaches. Monte Carlo methods are mainly used in three distinct problem classes: optimization, numerical integration, and generating draws from a probability distribution.

In physics-related problems, Monte Carlo methods are quite useful for simulating systems with many coupled degrees of freedom, such as fluids, disordered materials, strongly coupled solids, and cellular structures. Other examples include modeling phenomena with significant uncertainty in inputs such as the calculation of risk in business and, in math, evaluation of multidimensional definite integrals with complicated boundary conditions. In application to space and oil exploration problems, Monte Carlo–based predictions of failure, cost overruns and schedule overruns are routinely better than human intuition or alternative "soft" methods.

In principle, Monte Carlo methods can be used to solve any problem having a probabilistic interpretation. By the law of large numbers, integrals described by the expected value of some random variable can be approximated by taking the empirical mean (a.k.a. the sample mean) of independent samples of the variable. When the probability distribution of the variable is parametrized, mathematicians often use a Markov Chain Monte Carlo (MCMC) sampler. The central idea is to design a judicious Markov chain model with a prescribed stationary probability distribution. By the ergodic theorem, the stationary distribution is approximated by the empirical measures of the random states of the MCMC sampler.

In other problems, the objective is generating draws from a sequence of probability distributions satisfying a nonlinear evolution equation. These flows of probability distributions can always be interpreted as the distributions of the random states of a Markov process whose transition probabilities depend on the distributions of the current random states. In other instances we are given a flow of probability distributions with an increasing level of sampling complexity (path spaces models with an increasing time horizon, Boltzmann-Gibbs measures associated with decreasing temperature parameters, and many others). These models can also be seen as the evolution of the law of the random states of a nonlinear Markov chain. A natural way to simulate these sophisticated nonlinear Markov processes is to sample a large number of copies of the process, replacing in the evolution equation the unknown distributions of the random states by the sampled empirical measures. In contrast with traditional Monte Carlo and Markov chain Monte Carlo methodologies these mean field particle techniques rely on sequential interacting samples. The terminology *mean field* reflects the fact that each of the *samples (a.k.a. particles, individuals, walkers, agents, creatures, or phenotypes)* interacts with the empirical measures of the process. When the size of the system tends to infinity, these random empirical measures converge to the deterministic distribution of the random states of the nonlinear Markov chain, so that the statistical interaction between particles vanishes.

## Introduction

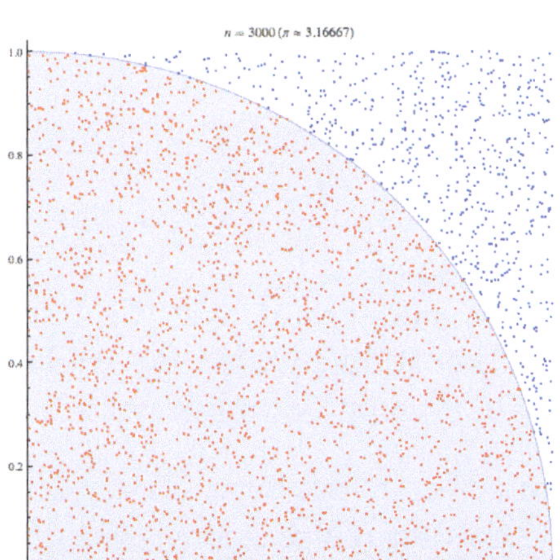


Monte Carlo method applied to approximating the value of π. After placing 30000 random points, the estimate for π is within 0.07% of the actual value.

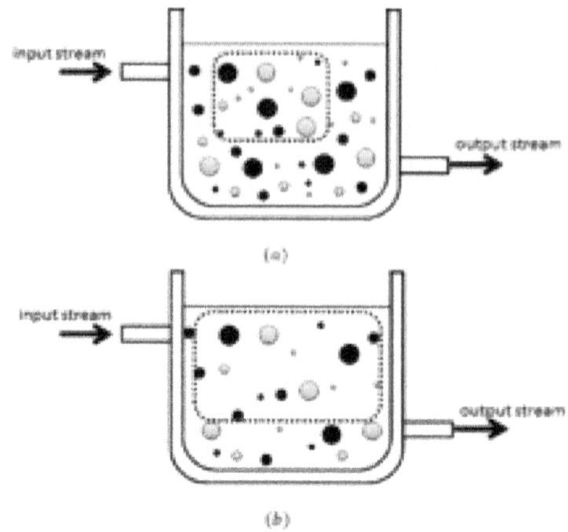


Constant Number Monte Carlo Simulation

Monte Carlo methods vary, but tend to follow a particular pattern:

1. Define a domain of possible inputs.
2. Generate inputs randomly from a probability distribution over the domain.
3. Perform a deterministic computation on the inputs.
4. Aggregate the results.

For example, consider a circle inscribed in a unit square. Given that the circle and the square have a ratio of areas that is $\pi/4$, the value of $\pi$ can be approximated using a Monte Carlo method:

1. Draw a square on the ground, then inscribe a circle within it.
2. Uniformly scatter some objects of uniform size (grains of rice or sand) over the square.
3. Count the number of objects inside the circle and the total number of objects.
4. The ratio of the two counts is an estimate of the ratio of the two areas, which is $\pi/4$. Multiply the result by 4 to estimate $\pi$.

In this procedure the domain of inputs is the square that circumscribes our circle. We generate random inputs by scattering grains over the square then perform a computation on each input (test whether it falls within the circle). Finally, we aggregate the results to obtain our final result, the approximation of $\pi$.

There are two important points to consider here: Firstly, if the grains are not uniformly distributed, then our approximation will be poor. Secondly, there should be a large number of inputs. The approximation is generally poor if only a few grains are randomly dropped into the whole square. On average, the approximation improves as more grains are dropped.

Uses of Monte Carlo methods require large amounts of random numbers, and it was their use that spurred the development of pseudorandom number generators, which were far quicker to use than the tables of random numbers that had been previously used for statistical sampling.

Constant-Number Monte Carlo shows two advantages over the traditional Monte Carlo approaches: First, it is faster; second, the simulation accuracy decays at a much lower rate. Figure schematically shows how this algorithm works. The simulation box always includes a fixed number of particles. As a result, when dilution or thickening occurs, the volume of the box increases or decreases, respectively.

## History

Before the Monte Carlo method was developed, simulations tested a previously understood deterministic problem and statistical sampling was used to estimate uncertainties in the simulations. Monte Carlo simulations invert this approach, solving deterministic problems using a probabilistic analog.

An early variant of the Monte Carlo method can be seen in the Buffon's needle experiment, in which $\pi$ can be estimated by dropping needles on a floor made of parallel and equidistant strips. In the 1930s, Enrico Fermi first experimented with the Monte Carlo method while studying neutron diffusion, but did not publish anything on it.

The modern version of the Markov Chain Monte Carlo method was invented in the late 1940s by Stanislaw Ulam, while he was working on nuclear weapons projects at the Los Alamos National Laboratory. Immediately after Ulam's breakthrough, John von Neumann understood its importance and programmed the ENIAC computer to carry out Monte Carlo calculations. In 1946, physicists at Los Alamos Scientific Laboratory were investigating radiation shielding and the distance that neutrons would likely travel through various materials. Despite having most of the necessary data, such as the average distance a neutron would travel in a substance before it collided with an atomic nucleus, and how much energy the neutron was likely to give off following a collision, the Los Alamos physicists were unable to solve the problem using conventional, deterministic mathematical methods. Stanislaw Ulam had the idea of using random experiments. He recounts his inspiration as follows:

> The first thoughts and attempts I made to practice [the Monte Carlo Method] were suggested by a question which occurred to me in 1946 as I was convalescing from an illness and playing solitaires. The question was what are the chances that a Canfield solitaire laid out with 52 cards will come out successfully? After spending a lot of time trying to estimate them by pure combinatorial calculations, I wondered whether a more practical method than "abstract thinking" might not be to lay it out say one hundred times and simply observe

> and count the number of successful plays. This was already possible to envisage with the beginning of the new era of fast computers, and I immediately thought of problems of neutron diffusion and other questions of mathematical physics, and more generally how to change processes described by certain differential equations into an equivalent form interpretable as a succession of random operations. Later [in 1946], I described the idea to John von Neumann, and we began to plan actual calculations.
>
> –Stanislaw Ulam

Being secret, the work of von Neumann and Ulam required a code name. A colleague of von Neumann and Ulam, Nicholas Metropolis, suggested using the name *Monte Carlo*, which refers to the Monte Carlo Casino in Monaco where Ulam's uncle would borrow money from relatives to gamble. Using lists of "truly random" random numbers was extremely slow, but von Neumann developed a way to calculate pseudorandom numbers, using the middle-square method. Though this method has been criticized as crude, von Neumann was aware of this: he justified it as being faster than any other method at his disposal, and also noted that when it went awry it did so obviously, unlike methods that could be subtly incorrect.

Monte Carlo methods were central to the simulations required for the Manhattan Project, though severely limited by the computational tools at the time. In the 1950s they were used at Los Alamos for early work relating to the development of the hydrogen bomb, and became popularized in the fields of physics, physical chemistry, and operations research. The Rand Corporation and the U.S. Air Force were two of the major organizations responsible for funding and disseminating information on Monte Carlo methods during this time, and they began to find a wide application in many different fields.

The theory of more sophisticated mean field type particle Monte Carlo methods had certainly started by the mid-1960s, with the work of Henry P. McKean Jr. on Markov interpretations of a class of nonlinear parabolic partial differential equations arising in fluid mechanics. We also quote an earlier pioneering article by Theodore E. Harris and Herman Kahn, published in 1951, using mean field genetic-type Monte Carlo methods for estimating particle transmission energies. Mean field genetic type Monte Carlo methodologies are also used as heuristic natural search algorithms (a.k.a. Metaheuristic) in evolutionary computing. The origins of these mean field computational techniques can be traced to 1950 and 1954 with the work of Alan Turing on genetic type mutation-selection learning machines and the articles by Nils Aall Barricelli at the Institute for Advanced Study in Princeton, New Jersey.

Quantum Monte Carlo, and more specifically Diffusion Monte Carlo methods can also be interpreted as a mean field particle Monte Carlo approximation of Feynman-Kac path integrals. The origins of Quantum Monte Carlo methods are often attributed to

Enrico Fermi and Robert Richtmyer who developed in 1948 a mean field particle interpretation of neutron-chain reactions, but the first heuristic-like and genetic type particle algorithm (a.k.a. Resampled or Reconfiguration Monte Carlo methods) for estimating ground state energies of quantum systems (in reduced matrix models) is due to Jack H. Hetherington in 1984 In molecular chemistry, the use of genetic heuristic-like particle methodologies (a.k.a. pruning and enrichment strategies) can be traced back to 1955 with the seminal work of Marshall. N. Rosenbluth and Arianna. W. Rosenbluth.

The use of Sequential Monte Carlo in advanced Signal processing and Bayesian inference is more recent. It was in 1993, that Gordon et al., published in their seminal work the first application of a Monte Carlo resampling algorithm in Bayesian statistical inference. The authors named their algorithm 'the bootstrap filter', and demonstrated that compared to other filtering methods, their bootstrap algorithm does not require any assumption about that state-space or the noise of the system. We also quote another pioneering article in this field of Genshiro Kitagawa on a related "Monte Carlo filter", and the ones by Pierre Del Moral and Himilcon Carvalho, Pierre Del Moral, André Monin and Gérard Salut on particle filters published in the mid-1990s. Particle filters were also developed in signal processing in the early 1989-1992 by P. Del Moral, J.C. Noyer, G. Rigal, and G. Salut in the LAAS-CNRS in a series of restricted and classified research reports with STCAN (Service Technique des Constructions et Armes Navales), the IT company DIGILOG, and the LAAS-CNRS (the Laboratory for Analysis and Architecture of Systems) on RADAR/SONAR and GPS signal processing problems. These Sequential Monte Carlo methodologies can be interpreted as an acceptance-rejection sampler equipped with an interacting recycling mechanism.

From 1950 to 1996, all the publications on Sequential Monte Carlo methodologies including the pruning and resample Monte Carlo methods introduced in computational physics and molecular chemistry, present natural and heuristic-like algorithms applied to different situations without a single proof of their consistency, nor a discussion on the bias of the estimates and on genealogical and ancestral tree based algorithms. The mathematical foundations and the first rigorous analysis of these particle algorithms are due to Pierre Del Moral in 1996. Branching type particle methodologies with varying population sizes were also developed in the end of the 1990s by Dan Crisan, Jessica Gaines and Terry Lyons, and by Dan Crisan, Pierre Del Moral and Terry Lyons. Further developments in this field were developed in 2000 by P. Del Moral, A. Guionnet and L. Miclo.

## Definitions

There is no consensus on how *Monte Carlo* should be defined. For example, Ripley defines most probabilistic modeling as *stochastic simulation*, with *Monte Carlo* being reserved for Monte Carlo integration and Monte Carlo statistical tests. Sawilowsky distinguishes between a simulation, a Monte Carlo method, and a Monte Carlo simulation: a simulation is a fictitious representation of reality, a Monte Carlo method is a technique that can be used to solve a mathematical or statistical problem, and a Monte Carlo simulation uses repeated sampling to determine the properties of some phenomenon (or behavior). Examples:

- Simulation: Drawing one pseudo-random uniform variable from the interval [0,1] can be used to simulate the tossing of a coin: If the value is less than or equal to 0.50 designate the outcome as heads, but if the value is greater than 0.50 designate the outcome as tails. This is a simulation, but not a Monte Carlo simulation.

- Monte Carlo method: Pouring out a box of coins on a table, and then computing the ratio of coins that land heads versus tails is a Monte Carlo method of determining the behavior of repeated coin tosses, but it is not a simulation.

- Monte Carlo simulation: Drawing a large number of pseudo-random uniform variables from the interval [0,1], and assigning values less than or equal to 0.50 as heads and greater than 0.50 as tails, is a *Monte Carlo simulation* of the behavior of repeatedly tossing a coin.

Kalos and Whitlock point out that such distinctions are not always easy to maintain. For example, the emission of radiation from atoms is a natural stochastic process. It can be simulated directly, or its average behavior can be described by stochastic equations that can themselves be solved using Monte Carlo methods. "Indeed, the same computer code can be viewed simultaneously as a 'natural simulation' or as a solution of the equations by natural sampling."

## Monte Carlo and Random Numbers

Monte Carlo simulation methods do not always require truly random numbers to be useful — while for some applications, such as primality testing, unpredictability is vital. Many of the most useful techniques use deterministic, pseudorandom sequences, making it easy to test and re-run simulations. The only quality usually necessary to make good simulations is for the pseudo-random sequence to appear "random enough" in a certain sense.

What this means depends on the application, but typically they should pass a series of statistical tests. Testing that the numbers are uniformly distributed or follow another desired distribution when a large enough number of elements of the sequence are considered is one of the simplest, and most common ones. Weak correlations between successive samples is also often desirable/necessary.

Sawilowsky lists the characteristics of a high quality Monte Carlo simulation:

- the (pseudo-random) number generator has certain characteristics (*e.g.*, a long "period" before the sequence repeats)

- the (pseudo-random) number generator produces values that pass tests for randomness
- there are enough samples to ensure accurate results
- the proper sampling technique is used
- the algorithm used is valid for what is being modeled
- it simulates the phenomenon in question.

Pseudo-random number sampling algorithms are used to transform uniformly distributed pseudo-random numbers into numbers that are distributed according to a given probability distribution.

Low-discrepancy sequences are often used instead of random sampling from a space as they ensure even coverage and normally have a faster order of convergence than Monte Carlo simulations using random or pseudorandom sequences. Methods based on their use are called quasi-Monte Carlo methods.

## Monte Carlo Simulation Versus "What if" Scenarios

There are ways of using probabilities that are definitely not Monte Carlo simulations — for example, deterministic modeling using single-point estimates. Each uncertain variable within a model is assigned a "best guess" estimate. Scenarios (such as best, worst, or most likely case) for each input variable are chosen and the results recorded.

By contrast, Monte Carlo simulations sample from a probability distribution for each variable to produce hundreds or thousands of possible outcomes. The results are analyzed to get probabilities of different outcomes occurring. For example, a comparison of a spreadsheet cost construction model run using traditional "what if" scenarios, and then running the comparison again with Monte Carlo simulation and triangular probability distributions shows that the Monte Carlo analysis has a narrower range than the "what if" analysis. This is because the "what if" analysis gives equal weight to all scenarios, while the Monte Carlo method hardly samples in the very low probability regions. The samples in such regions are called "rare events".

## Applications

Monte Carlo methods are especially useful for simulating phenomena with significant uncertainty in inputs and systems with a large number of coupled degrees of freedom. Areas of application include:

## Physical Sciences

Monte Carlo methods are very important in computational physics, physical chemistry, and related applied fields, and have diverse applications from complicated quantum chromodynamics calculations to designing heat shields and aerodynamic forms as well as in modeling radiation transport for radiation dosimetry calculations. In statistical physics Monte Carlo molecular modeling is an alternative to computational molecular dynamics, and Monte Carlo methods are used to compute statistical field theories of simple particle and polymer systems. Quantum Monte Carlo methods solve the many-body problem for quantum systems. In experimental particle physics, Monte Carlo methods are used for designing detectors, understanding their behavior and comparing experimental data to theory. In astrophysics, they are used in such diverse manners as to model both galaxy evolution and microwave radiation transmission through a rough planetary surface. Monte Carlo methods are also used in the ensemble models that form the basis of modern weather forecasting.

## Engineering

Monte Carlo methods are widely used in engineering for sensitivity analysis and quantitative probabilistic analysis in process design. The need arises from the interactive, co-linear and non-linear behavior of typical process simulations. For example,

- In microelectronics engineering, Monte Carlo methods are applied to analyze correlated and uncorrelated variations in analog and digital integrated circuits.
- In geostatistics and geometallurgy, Monte Carlo methods underpin the design of mineral processing flowsheets and contribute to quantitative risk analysis.
- In wind energy yield analysis, the predicted energy output of a wind farm during its lifetime is calculated giving different levels of uncertainty (P90, P50, etc.)
- impacts of pollution are simulated and diesel compared with petrol.
- In fluid dynamics, in particular rarefied gas dynamics, where the Boltzmann equation is solved for finite Knudsen number fluid flows using the direct simulation Monte Carlo method in combination with highly efficient computational algorithms.
- In autonomous robotics, Monte Carlo localization can determine the position of a robot. It is often applied to stochastic filters such as the Kalman filter or particle filter that forms the heart of the SLAM (simultaneous localization and mapping) algorithm.
- In telecommunications, when planning a wireless network, design must be proved to work for a wide variety of scenarios that depend mainly on the number of users, their locations and the services they want to use. Monte Carlo methods are typically used to generate these users and their states. The network performance is then evaluated and, if results are not satisfactory, the network

design goes through an optimization process.

- In reliability engineering, one can use Monte Carlo simulation to generate mean time between failures and mean time to repair for components.
- In signal processing and Bayesian inference, particle filters and sequential Monte Carlo techniques are a class of mean field particle methods for sampling and computing the posterior distribution of a signal process given some noisy and partial observations using interacting empirical measures.

## Climate Change and Radiative Forcing

The Intergovernmental Panel on Climate Change relies on Monte Carlo methods in probability density function analysis of radiative forcing.

Probability density function (PDF) of ERF due to total GHG, aerosol forcing and total anthropogenic forcing. The GHG consists of WMGHG, ozone and stratospheric water vapour. The PDFs are generated based on uncertainties provided in Table 8.6. The combination of the individual RF agents to derive total forcing over the Industrial Era are done by Monte Carlo simulations and based on the method in Boucher and Haywood (2001). PDF of the ERF from surface albedo changes and combined contrails and contrail-induced cirrus are included in the total anthropogenic forcing, but not shown as a separate PDF. We currently do not have ERF estimates for some forcing mechanisms: ozone, land use, solar, etc.

## Computational Biology

Monte Carlo methods are used in various fields of computational biology, for example for Bayesian inference in phylogeny, or for studying biological systems such as genomes, proteins, or membranes. The systems can be studied in the coarse-grained or *ab initio* frameworks depending on the desired accuracy. Computer simulations allow us to monitor the local environment of a particular molecule to see if some chemical reaction is happening for instance. In cases where it is not feasible to conduct a physical experiment, thought experiments can be conducted (for instance: breaking bonds, introducing impurities at specific sites, changing the local/global structure, or introducing external fields).

## Computer Graphics

Path tracing, occasionally referred to as Monte Carlo ray tracing, renders a 3D scene by randomly tracing samples of possible light paths. Repeated sampling of any given pixel will eventually cause the average of the samples to converge on the correct solution of the rendering equation, making it one of the most physically accurate 3D graphics rendering methods in existence.

## Applied Statistics

The standards for Monte Carlo experiments in statistics were set by Sawilowsky. In applied statistics, Monte Carlo methods are generally used for two purposes:

1. To compare competing statistics for small samples under realistic data conditions. Although type I error and power properties of statistics can be calculated for data drawn from classical theoretical distributions (*e.g.*, normal curve, Cauchy distribution) for asymptotic conditions (*i. e*, infinite sample size and infinitesimally small treatment effect), real data often do not have such distributions.

2. To provide implementations of hypothesis tests that are more efficient than exact tests such as permutation tests (which are often impossible to compute) while being more accurate than critical values for asymptotic distributions.

3. To provide a random sample from the posterior distribution in Bayesian inference. This sample then approximates and summarizes all the essential features of the posterior.

Monte Carlo methods are also a compromise between approximate randomization and permutation tests. An approximate randomization test is based on a specified subset of all permutations (which entails potentially enormous housekeeping of which permutations have been considered). The Monte Carlo approach is based on a specified number of randomly drawn permutations (exchanging a minor loss in precision if a permutation is drawn twice – or more frequently—for the efficiency of not having to track which permutations have already been selected).

## Artificial Intelligence for Games

Monte Carlo methods have been developed into a technique called Monte-Carlo tree search that is useful for searching for the best move in a game. Possible moves are organized in a search tree and a large number of random simulations are used to estimate the long-term potential of each move. A black box simulator represents the opponent's moves.

The Monte Carlo tree search (MCTS) method has four steps:

1. Starting at root node of the tree, select optimal child nodes until a leaf node is reached.

2. Expand the leaf node and choose one of its children.

3. Play a simulated game starting with that node.

4. Use the results of that simulated game to update the node and its ancestors.

The net effect, over the course of many simulated games, is that the value of a node representing a move will go up or down, hopefully corresponding to whether or not that node represents a good move.

Monte Carlo Tree Search has been used successfully to play games such as Go, Tantrix, Battleship, Havannah, and Arimaa.

## Design and Visuals

Monte Carlo methods are also efficient in solving coupled integral differential equations of radiation fields and energy transport, and thus these methods have been used in global illumination computations that produce photo-realistic images of virtual 3D models, with applications in video games, architecture, design, computer generated films, and cinematic special effects.

## Search and Rescue

The US Coast Guard utilizes Monte Carlo methods within its computer modeling software SAROPS in order to calculate the probable locations of vessels during search and rescue operations. Each simulation can generate as many as ten thousand data points which are randomly distributed based upon provided variables. Search patterns are then generated based upon extrapolations of these data in order to optimize the probability of containment (POC) and the probability of detection (POD), which together will equal an overall probability of success (POS). Ultimately this serves as a practical application of probability distribution in order to provide the swiftest and most expedient method of rescue, saving both lives and resources.

## Finance and Business

Monte Carlo methods in finance are often used to evaluate investments in projects at a business unit or corporate level, or to evaluate financial derivatives. They can be used to model project schedules, where simulations aggregate estimates for worst-case, best-case, and most likely durations for each task to determine outcomes for the overall project. Monte Carlo methods are also used in option pricing, default risk analysis.

## Use in Mathematics

In general, Monte Carlo methods are used in mathematics to solve various problems by generating suitable random numbers and observing that fraction of the numbers that obeys some property or properties. The method is useful for obtaining numerical solutions to problems too complicated to solve analytically. The most common application of the Monte Carlo method is Monte Carlo integration.

## Integration

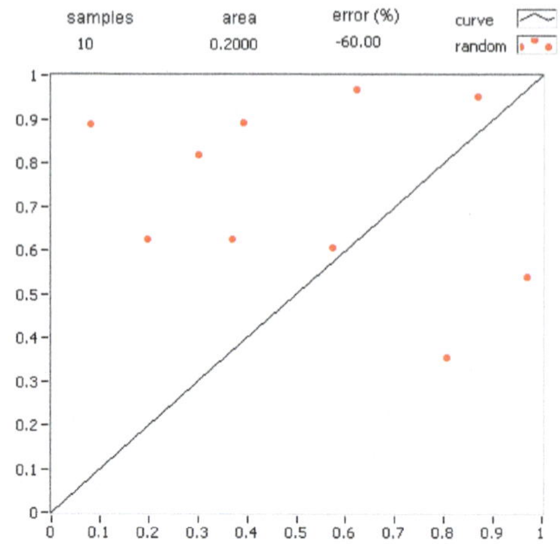


Monte-Carlo integration works by comparing random points with the value of the function

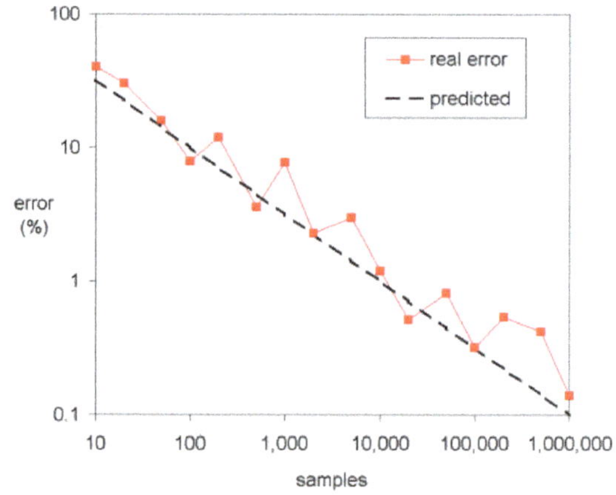


Errors reduce by a factor of

Deterministic numerical integration algorithms work well in a small number of dimensions, but encounter two problems when the functions have many variables. First, the number of function evaluations needed increases rapidly with the number of dimensions. For example, if 10 evaluations provide adequate accuracy in one dimension, then $10^{100}$ points are needed for 100 dimensions—far too many to be computed. This is called the curse of dimensionality. Second, the boundary of a multidimensional region may be very complicated, so it may not be feasible to reduce the problem to an iterated integral. 100 dimensions is by no means unusual, since in many physical problems, a "dimension" is equivalent to a degree of freedom.

Monte Carlo methods provide a way out of this exponential increase in computation time. As long as the function in question is reasonably well-behaved, it can be estimated by randomly selecting points in 100-dimensional space, and taking some kind of average of the function values at these points. By the central limit theorem, this method displays convergence—i.e., quadrupling the number of sampled points halves the error, regardless of the number of dimensions.

A refinement of this method, known as importance sampling in statistics, involves sampling the points randomly, but more frequently where the integrand is large. To do this precisely one would have to already know the integral, but one can approximate the integral by an integral of a similar function or use adaptive routines such as stratified sampling, recursive stratified sampling, adaptive umbrella sampling or the VEGAS algorithm.

A similar approach, the quasi-Monte Carlo method, uses low-discrepancy sequences. These sequences "fill" the area better and sample the most important points more frequently, so quasi-Monte Carlo methods can often converge on the integral more quickly.

Another class of methods for sampling points in a volume is to simulate random walks over it (Markov chain Monte Carlo). Such methods include the Metropolis-Hastings algorithm, Gibbs sampling, Wang and Landau algorithm, and interacting type MCMC methodologies such as the sequential Monte Carlo samplers.

## Simulation and Optimization

Another powerful and very popular application for random numbers in numerical simulation is in numerical optimization. The problem is to minimize (or maximize) functions of some vector that often has a large number of dimensions. Many problems can be phrased in this way: for example, a computer chess program could be seen as trying to find the set of, say, 10 moves that produces the best evaluation function at the end. In the traveling salesman problem the goal is to minimize distance traveled. There are also applications to engineering design, such as multidisciplinary design optimization. It has been applied with quasi-one-dimensional models to solve particle dynamics problems by efficiently exploring large configuration space.

The traveling salesman problem is what is called a conventional optimization problem. That is, all the facts (distances between each destination point) needed to determine the optimal path to follow are known with certainty and the goal is to run through the possible travel choices to come up with the one with the lowest total distance. However, let's assume that instead of wanting to minimize the total distance traveled to visit each desired destination, we wanted to minimize the total time needed to reach each destination. This goes beyond conventional optimization since travel time is inherently uncertain (traffic jams, time of day, etc.). As a result, to determine our optimal path we would want to use simulation - optimization to first understand the range of potential times it could take to go from one point to another (represented by a probability distribution in this case rather than a specific distance) and then optimize our travel decisions to identify the best path to follow taking that uncertainty into account.

## Inverse Problems

Probabilistic formulation of inverse problems leads to the definition of a probability distribution in the model space. This probability distribution combines prior information with new information obtained by measuring some observable parameters (data). As, in the general case, the theory linking data with model parameters is nonlinear, the posterior probability in the model space may not be easy to describe (it may be multimodal, some moments may not be defined, etc.).

When analyzing an inverse problem, obtaining a maximum likelihood model is usually not sufficient, as we normally also wish to have information on the resolution power of the data. In the general case we may have a large number of model parameters, and an inspection of the marginal probability densities of interest may be impractical, or even useless. But it is possible to pseudorandomly generate a large collection of models according to the posterior probability distribution and to analyze and display the models in such a way that information on the relative likelihoods of model properties is conveyed to the spectator. This can be accomplished by means of an efficient Monte Carlo method, even in cases where no explicit formula for the *a priori* distribution is available.

The best-known importance sampling method, the Metropolis algorithm, can be generalized, and this gives a method that allows analysis of (possibly highly nonlinear) inverse problems with complex *a priori* information and data with an arbitrary noise distribution.

## In Popular Culture

- *The Monte Carlo Method*, the 1998 album by the southern California indie rock band Nothing Painted Blue. (Scat. 1998).

# Risk Breakdown Structure

Risk Breakdown Structure (RBS) - A hierarchically organised depiction of the identified project risks arranged by category.

## An Introduction to the Risk Breakdown Structure

When planning a project to meet targets for cost, schedule, or quality, it is useful to identify likely risks to the success of the project. A risk is any possible situation that is not planned for, but that, if it occurs, is likely to divert the project from its planned result. For example, an established project team plans for the work to be done by its staff, but there is the risk that an employee may unexpectedly leave the team.

In Project Management, the *Risk Management Process* has the objectives of identifying, assessing, and managing risks, both positive and negative. All too often, project managers focus only on negative risk, however, good things can happen in a project, "things" that were foreseen, but not expressly planned.

The objective of Risk Management is to predict risks, assess their likelihood and impact, and to actively plan what should be done ahead of time to best deal with situations when they occur.

The risk management process usually occurs in five distinct steps: plan risk management, risk identification, qualitative and quantitative risk analysis, risk response planning, and risk monitoring and control. The central point of risk identification and assessment in risk management is understanding the risk. However, this is also where project managers and risk subject matter experts (SMEs) get the least help from recognized references, best practices, or work standards.

Currently, the Project Management Institute (PMI[r]) has a team of SMEs working on a Practice Standard for Risk Management. This team has identified one very good tool: the Risk Breakdown Structure (RBS). The RBS helps the project manager, the risk manager, and almost any stakeholder to understand, and therefore be able to identify and assess risk.

## What is a "Risk Breakdown Structure?"

The RBS will prove extremely valuable to better grasp when a project needs to receive special scrutiny, in other words, when risk might happen. The RBS can also help the project manager and the risk manager to better understand recurring risks and concentrations of risk that could lead to issues that affect the status of the project.

Following the concept of the Work Breakdown Structure (WBS), the Risk Breakdown Structure provides a means for the project manager and risk manager to structure the risks being addressed or tracked. Just as PMI defines the Work Breakdown Structure as a "deliverable-oriented grouping of project elements that organizes and defines the total work scope of the project..." the RBS could be considered as a "hierarchically organized depiction of the identified project risks arranged by risk category."

In project management language, risks include anything unplanned and unforeseen that can have a negative impact on the project's costs, timing or quality. A good project manager should be able to manage the risks effectively and get the project on track.

Many project managers and risk managers currently use "home-grown" methods for listing, identifying, assessing, and tracking risks in their projects. These methods include: spreadsheets, listing, generic risk taxonomy, based somewhat loosely on various standards and guidelines.

An approach that simply places the risks in a list, a simple table, or even in a database does not provide the strength of using a structured, organized method similar to a Work Breakdown Structure. To fully understand the risks and better identify and assess the risk, a "deep-dive" into each risk, recording as many levels of identification as necessary, may be required. The project value of placing risks in a structure such as this lies in the ability of the project manager and risk manager to then quickly and easily identify and assess the risk, identify the potential risk triggers, and develop a more robust risk response plan . If all risks are placed in a hierarchical structure as they are identified, and the structure is organized by source, the total risk exposure to the project can be more easily understood, and planning for the risk more easily accomplished.

## Templates for Creating a Risk Breakdown Structure

The concept of the RBS is new. The PMBoK (2004), barely references its use; however, the PMI Standards team has incorporated the RBS in the *Practice Standard for Risk Management* (draft for release in 2009). The PMBoK provides an example graphic of the RBS in Chapter 11, Figure 11.4. This reference has as major topics: Technical, External, Organizational, and Project Management. Another source provides the following major topics: Technical, Management, Organizational, External, and Project Management. Dr. David Hillson, in the proceedings of the Project Management Institute Annual Seminars and Symposium, on Oct. 3-10, 2002, provided several different RBS Structure examples, with topics similar to those already shown. Dr. Hillson broke out two different examples, an RBS for Software Development, which had the following major topics: Product Engineering, Development Environment, Program Constraints; and an RBS for Construction Design, which has these major topics: Environment, Industry, Client, Project.

Each RBS is broken into "levels", with each level providing a more in-depth "view" of the identified risk. As an example, in creating a RBS for software development, Level 1 of the RBS might be Technical, followed by Level 2, Requirements, followed by Level 3, Functional Requirements, Informational Requirements, Non-functional Requirements, etc. If desired, Level 3 can be further refined with Level 4, Stability, Completeness, Functionality, Interfaces, Testability, etc., Level 5, etc.

Once the project team has created its RBS, then individual risks can be identified. Several different techniques for defining the individual risks are available, including brain-storming, surveys, workshops, etc. Each identified risk needs to be categorized, and placed in the RBS under a specific topic (or topics if the risk spans two or more topics, such as a risk in gathering requirements might span Technical, organizational and project management.

NOTE: the RBS will be different between projects, even projects within the same project area, e.g., construction, information technology, environmental remediation, etc.

After the RBS has completed its first "pass" in the creation phase, it can then become an input to qualitative risk analysis, where probabilities, priorities, and impacts are determined.

# Creation of Tailor-made Risk Breakdown Structures

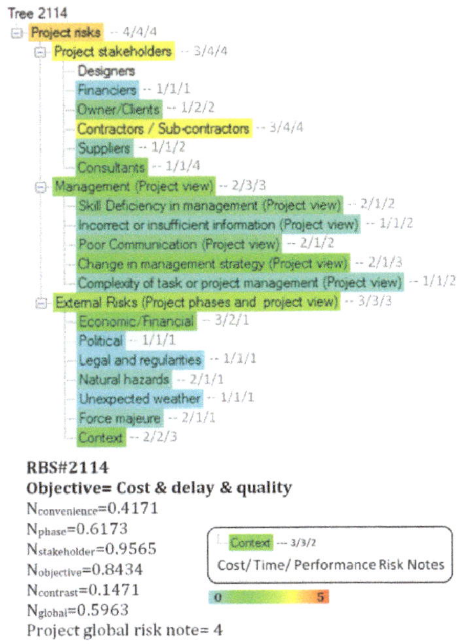


An example of designed tailor-made Risk Breakdown Structure, with results of a multi-objective risk analysis

Construction projects, like all complex activities, involve many partners with different objectives, who are subjected to many risks in an uncertain environment. In practice, different project stakeholders have different understanding and perception of project risks. Each one identifies and analyzes the project risks regarding his objectives, risk attitude and special perspective to project risks without relying on a common and shared methodology. This is why in most of construction projects, discussing the project risks and making risk based decisions are of common difficulties which may also cause to disputes between project parties. Also, the project risk management is a scalable activity and should be commensurate with the size, level of available information and complexity of the project under consideration. Furthermore, this process is iterative, since in each phase of the project, new information is available and some predicted risks events occur while others will not, new unpredicted risk events may occur or may be identified, and the characteristics of those already identified may change. Thus, an iterative risk management should be carried out at all stages of the project life cycle. As consequence, the project risk management process has to be tailored for each particular case and project.

Dr. Rasool Mehdizadeh has developed a methodology for a dynamic, multi-scale and multi-perspective risk management of construction projects. This method is based on the application of tailor-made risk breakdown structures (RBS) which are well adapted to: (1) the stage and degree of development of project, (2) specific requirements and objectives of project stakeholders, and (3) required level of details. Using this method, each of the project stakeholders, at each stage of the project, considering his/her special view to project risks, can build his/her own specific RBS. Moreover, the RBS can also be tailored as a shared support for all the project stakeholders in order to facilitate understanding and discussing project risks. Using these tailored RBSs which are all generated using a unique procedure and knowledge database, each of project stakeholders can identify, analyze and represent the project risks regarding his/her point of view and requirements. The method ensures the consistency of all these perspectives.

## Using the Hierarchical Risk Breakdown Structure

The RBS serves as more than just a "database" for identifying risks to the project. When created, the RBS provides a vehicle for risk analysis and reporting, and risk comparison across projects. Most importantly, the RBS is "the" tool for risk identification.

## Risk Identification and Classification

Risk identification will be the first step in determining which risks may affect a project. Identification also provides documentation of the risk characteristics. The first level (Level 1) of the RBS can be used as a sanity check to make certain that all topics that might include risk are covered during the risk identification process. Using the RBS, an iterative process can be initiated that will persist throughout the project life-cycle. The frequency and applicability of this iterative process will be different in each phase of the life-cycle

Using a risk identification checklist that is focused on the RBS, using Levels 2, 3 and below, assists in identifying specific and generic risks. This checklist can then become a part of the project managers' and risk managers' tool set for future projects.

Risk identification leads to quantitative risk analysis, conducted by the Project Risk Manager. Interestingly, sometimes merely identifying the risk will suggest the proper response, which can be entered into the Risk Response Plan.

## Risk Analysis

## Qualitative Risk Analysis

Risk analysis is more easily achieved if, after identification, the risks are placed in proper perspective within the RBS by categorizing the risks in the various levels. Risk analysis involves the use of techniques for prioritizing the risk, determining the probability of the risk, and calculating the impact of the risk. At no point should the project manager or risk manager decide that the total number of identified risks should cause the cancellation of the project. The total number does not take into account the probability with which the risk will occur, nor the impact to the project, should the risk occur. A few risks, with high probabilities and high impact, are far more critical to the overall success of the project than a large number of risks with low probability and minimal impact. Using the RBS, the project manager and the risk manager should create a "risk score" based on the priority, probability and impact of each risk, and with each "group" of risks (according to the appropriate Level of the RBS).

Using the RBS also offers other valuable understanding into the analysis of the identified risks. Some of these new understandings are:

- Risk exposure type
- Dependencies between risks
- Root causality of risks
- Most significant and least significant risks
- Correlations between risks

Another benefit of the RBS is the ability to focus risk responses to the high probability, high impact, high priority risks using the risk topic groupings.

A specific method was developed by Dr. Mehdizadeh in order to: (1) calculate risk values of risk events regarding different project objectives, (2) aggregate the risk values through the RBS branches and also (3) to calculate global risk score of project. The method combines consistently the quantitative and qualitative approaches, allowing the user to choose the best one for risk assessment at any level, based on the available information and required accuracy. In this method, at the first step, the probability and impact factors of risk events are assessed quantitatively or qualitatively. Two concomitant scales are used: a continuous cardinal scale and a discrete ordinal scale ranging from 1 to 5. Each scale has its own advantage. Continuous scale is closer to physical reality and has a more concrete meaning while discrete scale has a strong symbolic value. The assessments based on each of these scales can be converted to the other one following a defined process. At the second step, the risk values of risk events are calculated and then aggregated through the RBS branches in order to calculate the risk values of risk categories. Finally, application of a multi-criteria decision method allows calculating the global risk score of each category. This method provides a more consistent approach to get more realistic results without suffering from the usual weaknesses of available methods cited in literature.

## Summary

Effective risk management demands that the project manager and risk manager fully understand the risks of a project. A successful risk management process would also require a good knowledge and understanding of the business objectives of the project. During risk identification, a large volume of risks can be identified. Simply listing these risks or putting them in a spreadsheet or database does not provide the in-depth understanding of the identified risks necessary to allow a solid risk response planning task. The RBS provides the tool necessary to assist in identifying risks, analyzing risks, and creating a successful risk response plan, and it provides a vehicle for "deep-dives" into the complexity of the risk. Using a hierarchical RBS, similar in its design to the WBS, allows the project and risk managers the opportunity to carefully align the risks in proper categories, using as deep an analysis as time and resources would permit.

## Control Self-assessment

Control self-assessment is a technique developed in 1987 that is used by a range of organisations including corporations, charities and government departments, to assess the effectiveness of their risk management and control processes.

A "control process" is a check or process performed to reduce or eliminate the risk of error. Since its introduction the technique has been widely adopted in the United States, European Union and other countries. There are a number of ways a control self-assessment can be implemented but its key feature is that, in contrast to a traditional audit, the tests and checks are made by staff whose normal day-to-day responsibilities are within the business unit being assessed. A self-assessment, by identifying the higher risk processes within the organisation, allows internal auditors to plan their work more effectively. A number of governmental organisations require the use of control self-assessment. In the United States it is a requirement of the FFIEC that control self-assessments are performed on IT systems and operational processes on a regular basis. Benefits claimed for control self-assessment include creating a clear line of accountability for controls, reducing the risk of fraud and the creation of an organisation with a lower risk profile.

In certain circumstances control self-assessment is not always effective. For example, it can be difficult to implement in a decentralised environment, in organisations where there is high employee turnover, where the organisation goes through frequent change or where the senior management of the organisation does not foster a culture of open communication.

### Development and Worldwide Adoption

Control self-assessment was developed by Gulf Canada in 1987 when the company's General Auditor, Bruce McCuaig was dissatisfied with the standard auditing techniques in use following the impact of the Watergate affair on the parent company, Gulf Oil Corporation. The decision to fully implement control self-assessment at Gulf Canada was driven by a number of factors. These included the presence of a consent decree requiring the company to report on its internal controls and the difficulties it was facing in estimating its oil and gas reserves using more traditional audit measures.

Over the next ten years Gulf Canada developed a framework to support the analysis and evaluation of control processes by operational staff. This included anonymous voting to ensure there was no impediment to staff expressing their views. The approach was first published in *Internal Auditor* in December 1990. Gulf Canada discontinued this facilitated meeting approach in 1997 although it continued with control self-assessment using different techniques.

Following Gulf Canada's introduction of control self-assessment many private sector organisations implemented similar techniques. In the United States several states made reviews based on control self-assessment practices mandatory as did the Federal Deposit Insurance Corporation and the Canadian Deposit Insurance Corporation.

Initially external auditors ignored the benefits of control self-assessment even though it was effective at providing audit evidence around the "soft" areas (such as staff morale) that are critical to the effectiveness of internal control systems.

After a number of financial scandals, notably the collapse of Robert Maxwell's publishing empire, the United Kingdom government commissioned Adrian Cadbury to chair an investigation into corporate governance. The committee published its report *The Financial Aspects of Corporate Governance* in 1992. In section 4, Reporting and Controls, Cadbury made a number of recommendations that led to the increased adoption of control self-assessment in the UK. In particular section 4.5 of the Code of Practice contained within the report required that the directors of a company should report on the effectiveness of the company's system of internal control in each annual report.

In March 2000 the European Commission approved a white paper on reform that led to a major change in the way the Commission was managed. These changes included recommendations for each department to establish an effective internal control system. To support the implementation of the internal controls the Directorate-General for Budget's Central Financial Service developed a control self-assessment process. This first control self-assessment identified several areas for improvement in internal control across the Commission most notably the need to implement a more systematic approach to risk management. The outcome of this first self-assessment was the implementation of the requirement for every Directorate General to perform a control and risk self-assessment annually.

In 2007 the United States implemented the Sarbanes-Oxley Act. In order to comply with section 404 of the Act the company had to perform a top down risk assessment which necessitated the production of an "internal control report" that affirmed "the responsibility of management for establishing and maintaining an adequate internal control structure and procedures for financial reporting." 15 U.S.C. § 7262(a). This report has to include an evaluation of the effectiveness of the internal controls and procedures that are related to financial reporting. To meet this requirement organisations increasingly began to perform a control self-assessment using a recognised standard methodology. The organisation's external auditors, who are required to sign-off the internal control report, typically became more deeply involved in the control self-assessment process as it facilitated their later review of the internal control report.

In the United Kingdom in 2011 the Financial Services Authority recognised in its recommendations for the improvement of operational risk management that the assessment of risks through a control self-assessment may be an important means of identifying risks. It also noted that for the assessment to be fully effective it had to be fully integrated into the financial organisation's risk-management process.

## Performing the Control Self-Assessment

**Transit Board Self-Assessment Tool Level I**

| Level I Survey Tool: Please rate each measure below, using the rating system of 1 = Strongly Disagree through 5 = Strongly Agree | Strongly Disagree | | | | Strongly Agree |
|---|---|---|---|---|---|
| | 1 | 2 | 3 | 4 | 5 |
| **I. Board Processes** | | | | | |
| 1. The Board sets policy; management implements policy. Board members do not become involved in specific management, personnel, or service issues except in a predetermined oversight role. | | | | | |
| 2. a. Board members devote sufficient time to fulfilling their responsibilities. | | | | | |
| b. Board members attend meetings well prepared and participate fully in all matters. | | | | | |
| 3. Board members work cohesively and cooperatively to try to minimize miscommunication and confusion. | | | | | |
| 4. There is an orientation process for new board members. | | | | | |
| **II. Strategic Planning** | | | | | |
| 5. Board creates and communicates the agency's strategic direction; this is achieved by regularly evaluating core values and strategic mission. | | | | | |
| **III. Fiduciary and Legal Responsibilities** | | | | | |
| 6. Board provides effective monitoring, evaluation, and oversight of the agency's fiscal concerns, including understanding of the funding mechanisms. | | | | | |
| 7. Board supports a code of conduct and ethical practices; each board member is committed to ethical practices and guards against conflicts of interest. | | | | | |
| 8. Board approves annual operating and capital goals and budgets. | | | | | |

Section 1 of the control self-assessment form used by the Federal Transit Administration

The first step in control self-assessment is to document the organisation's control processes with the aim of identifying suitable ways of measuring or testing each control. The actual testing of the controls is performed by staff whose day-to-day role is within the area of the organisation that is being examined as they have the greatest knowledge of how the processes operate. The two common techniques for performing the evaluations are:

- Workshops, that may be but do not have to be independently facilitated, involving some or all staff from the business unit being tested;
- Surveys or questionnaires completed independently by the staff.

Both approaches are the opposite of formal audits where the auditors, not the business unit staff, will perform the assessment.

On completion of the assessment each control may be rated based on the responses received to determine the probability of its failure and the impact if a failure occurred. These ratings can be mapped to produce a heatmap showing potential areas of vulnerability.

## Methodologies

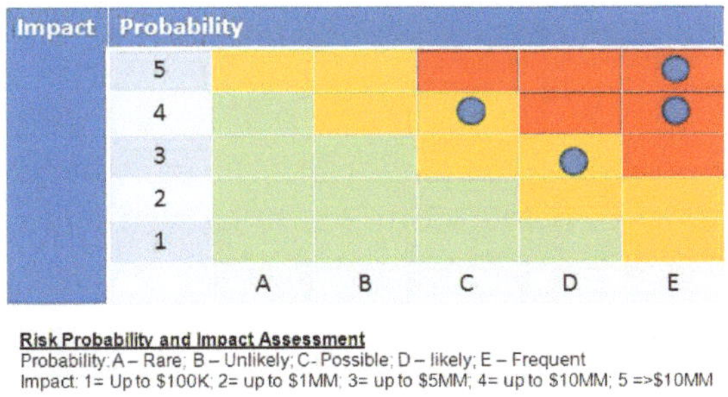


A heatmap produced from the information captured in a control self-assessment. The cluster of issues in the red and amber sections of the heatmap indicate that this is a high risk area and probably in need of new or changed control processes.

Six basic methodologies for control self-assessment have been defined:

- Internal Control Questionnaire (ICQ) self-audit
- Customised questionnaires
- Control guides
- Interview techniques
- Control model workshops
- Interactive workshops

The National Institute of Standards and Technology control self-assessment methodology is based on customised questionnaires. It is an IT focused methodology suitable for assessing system based controls. It provides a cost-effective technique to determine the status of information security controls, identify any weaknesses and, where necessary, define an improvement plan. The methodology uses a questionnaire that contains specific control objectives and techniques against a system or group of systems can be tested and measured. The methodology was designed for United States federal agencies but can also be valuable for private sector organisations.

The COBIT methodology can be used for control self-assessment; like the NIST methodology it was designed for IT focused assessments. COBIT's Process Description component provides a reference model of an organisation's processes and their ownership. Its Control Objectives component provides a set of requirements considered necessary for effective control of each IT process with the organisation. Assessment and evaluation of these components using the Management Guidelines component provides an assessment mechanism that generates a maturity model indicating if the organisation is meeting its control objectives.

The Institute of Internal Auditors based its control self-assessment methodology on the Total Quality Management approaches of the 1990s as well as the COSO's framework. The methodology became part of the *International Standards for Professional Practice of Internal Auditing* and was adopted by a large number of major organisations.

A number of other methodologies to standardise the control self-assessment have been published. The Institute of Internal Auditors offers a certification in control self-assessment practice.

## Software Tools

A number of software packages are available to support the control self-assessment process. These are typically modified versions of software developed originally for internal use by audit and accountancy firms such as Deloitte or by niche vendors specialising in business or financial management tools.

## Benefits

Control self-assessment creates a clear line of accountability for controls, reduces the risk of fraud (by examining data that may flag unusual patterns of transactions) and results in an organisation with a lower risk profile.

A number of other soft benefits have been claimed for organisations performing control self-assessment. These include a better understanding of business operations (by both management and operational staff); stronger awareness of risk practices; a reinforced corporate governance regime and internal audit efficiency improvements.

## Criticism

Some researchers have criticised control self-assessment as a flawed approach as the way risk is defined and measured is unsophisticated. In particular, control self-assessment may understate risk by not identifying extreme downside risk. An extreme downside risk is a highly improbable event that would have catastrophic consequences if it occurred. These risks should have a high overall risk score (generally calculated as a product of the probability of a risk occurring and the impact if it does occur on a scale of 1 to 5). Individuals performing the control self-assessment are consequently unable to significantly differentiate between risks leading to extreme low probability risks either being excluded from the analysis or grouped together with other more probable (but still unlikely) risks that have a less severe impact.

The continual focus on risk elimination that a control self-assessment can lead to has also been criticised. The process of continual evaluation of risks and making plans to mitigate and eliminate them may lead to an unbalanced corporate culture where risks are eliminated ignoring the risk-return ratio of different business choices.

# Scenario Analysis

Scenario analysis is a process of analyzing possible future events by considering alternative possible outcomes (sometimes called "alternative worlds"). Thus, the scenario analysis, which is a main method of projections, does not try to show one exact picture of the future. Instead, it presents consciously several alternative future developments. Consequently, a scope of possible future outcomes is observable. Not only are the outcomes observable, also the development paths leading to the outcomes. In contrast to prognoses, the scenario analysis is not using extrapolation of the past. It does not rely on historical data and does not expect past observations to be still valid in the future. Instead, it tries to consider possible developments and turning points, which may only be connected to the past. In short, several scenarios are demonstrated in a scenario analysis to show possible future outcomes. It is useful to generate a combination of an optimistic, a pessimistic, and a most likely scenario. Although highly discussed, experience has shown that around three scenarios are most appropriate for further discussion and selection. More scenarios could make the analysis unclear.

## Principle

The analysis is designed to allow improved decision-making by allowing consideration of outcomes and their implications.

Scenario analysis can also be used to illuminate "wild cards." For example, analysis of the possibility of the earth being struck by a large celestial object (a meteor) suggests that whilst the probability is low, the damage inflicted is so high that the event is much more important (threatening) than the low probability (in any one year) alone would suggest. However, this possibility is usually disregarded by organizations using scenario analysis to develop a strategic plan since it has such overarching repercussions.

## Applications

## Financial

For example, in economics and finance, a financial institution might attempt to forecast several possible scenarios for the economy (e.g. rapid growth, moderate growth, slow growth) and it might also attempt to forecast financial market returns (for bonds, stocks and cash) in each of those scenarios. It might consider sub-sets of each of the possibilities. It might further seek to determine correlations and assign probabilities to the scenarios (and sub-sets if any). Then it will be in a position to consider how to distribute assets between asset types (i.e. asset allocation); the institution can also calculate the scenario-weighted expected return (which figure will indicate the overall attractiveness of the financial environment). It may also perform stress testing, using adverse scenarios.

Depending on the complexity of the problem scenario analysis can be a demanding exercise. It can be difficult to foresee what the future holds (e.g. the actual future outcome may be entirely unexpected), i.e. to foresee what the scenarios are, and to assign probabilities to them; and this is true of the general forecasts never mind the implied financial market returns. The outcomes can be modeled mathematically/statistically e.g. taking account of possible variability within single scenarios as well as possible relationships between scenarios. In general, one should take care when assigning probabilities to different scenarios as this could invite a tendency to consider only the scenario with the highest probability.

## Geopolitical

In politics or geopolitics, scenario analysis involves modelling the possible alternative paths of a social or political environment and possibly diplomatic and war risks. For example, in the recent Iraq War, the Pentagon certainly had to model alternative possibilities that might arise in the war situation and had to position material and troops accordingly.

## Traditional Critique

While there is utility in weighting hypotheses and branching potential outcomes from them, reliance on scenario analysis without reporting some parameters of measurement accuracy (standard errors, confidence intervals of estimates, metadata, standardization and coding, weighting for non-response, error in reportage, sample design, case counts, etc.) is a poor second to traditional prediction. Especially in "complex" problems, factors and assumptions do not correlate in lockstep fashion. Once a specific sensitivity is undefined, it may call the entire study into question.

It is faulty logic to think, when arbitrating results, that a better hypothesis will render empiricism unnecessary. In this respect, scenario analysis tries to defer statistical laws (e.g., Chebyshev's inequality Law), because the decision rules occur outside a constrained setting. Outcomes are not permitted to "just happen"; rather, they are forced to conform to arbitrary hypotheses ex post, and therefore there is no footing on which to place expected values. In truth, there are no ex ante expected values, only hypotheses, and one is left wondering about the roles of modeling and data decision. In short, comparisons of "scenarios" with outcomes are biased by not deferring to the data; this may be convenient, but it is indefensible.

"Scenario analysis" is no substitute for complete and factual exposure of survey error in economic studies. In traditional prediction, given the data used to model the problem, with a reasoned specification and technique, an analyst can state, within a certain percentage of statistical error, the likelihood of a coefficient being within a certain numerical bound. This exactitude need not come at the expense of very disaggregated statements of hypotheses.

R Software, specifically the module "WhatIf," has been developed for causal inference, and to evaluate counterfactuals. These programs have fairly sophisticated treatments for determining model dependence, in order to state with precision how sensitive the results are to models not based on empirical evidence.

## Black–Scholes Model

The Black–Scholes /ˌblæk ˈʃoʊlz/ or Black–Scholes–Merton model is a mathematical model of a financial market containing derivative investment instruments. From the model, one can deduce the Black–Scholes formula, which gives a theoretical estimate of the price of European-style options. The formula led to a boom in options trading and legitimised scientifically the activities of the Chicago Board Options Exchange and other options markets around the world. lt is widely used, although often with adjustments and corrections, by options market participants. Many empirical tests have shown that the Black–Scholes price is "fairly close" to the observed prices, although there are well-known discrepancies such as the "option smile".

The Black–Scholes model was first published by Fischer Black and Myron Scholes in their 1973 seminal paper, "The Pricing of Options and Corporate Liabilities", published in the *Journal of Political Economy*. They derived a partial differential equation, now called the Black–Scholes equation, which estimates the price of the option over time. The key idea behind the model is to hedge the option by buying and selling the underlying asset in just the right way and, as a consequence, to eliminate risk. This type of hedging is called delta hedging and is the basis of more complicated hedging strategies such as those engaged in by investment banks and hedge funds.

Robert C. Merton was the first to publish a paper expanding the mathematical understanding of the options pricing model, and coined the term "Black–Scholes options pricing model". Merton and Scholes received the 1997 Nobel Memorial Prize in Economic Sciences for their work. Though ineligible for the prize because of his death in 1995, Black was mentioned as a contributor by the Swedish Academy.

The model's assumptions have been relaxed and generalized in many directions, leading to a plethora of models that are currently used in derivative pricing and risk management. It is the insights of the model, as exemplified in the Black–Scholes formula, that are frequently used by market participants, as distinguished from the actual prices. These insights include no-arbitrage bounds and risk-neutral pricing. The Black–Scholes equation, a partial differential equation that governs the price of the option, is also important as it enables pricing when an explicit formula is not possible.

The Black–Scholes formula has only one parameter that cannot be observed in the market: the average future volatility of the underlying asset. Since the formula is increasing in this parameter, it can be inverted to produce a "volatility surface" that is then used to calibrate other models, e.g. for OTC derivatives.

## The Black–Scholes World

The Black–Scholes model assumes that the market consists of at least one risky asset, usually called the stock, and one riskless asset, usually called the money market, cash, or bond.

Now we make assumptions on the assets (which explain their names):

- (riskless rate) The rate of return on the riskless asset is constant and thus called the risk-free interest rate.
- (random walk) The instantaneous log return of stock price is an infinitesimal random walk with drift; more precisely, it is a geometric Brownian motion, and we will assume its drift and volatility is constant (if they are time-varying, we can deduce a suitably modified Black–Scholes formula quite simply, as long as the volatility is not random).
- The stock does not pay a dividend.

Assumptions on the market:

- There is no arbitrage opportunity (i.e., there is no way to make a riskless profit).
- It is possible to borrow and lend any amount, even fractional, of cash at the riskless rate.
- It is possible to buy and sell any amount, even fractional, of the stock (this includes short selling).
- The above transactions do not incur any fees or costs (i.e., frictionless market).

With these assumptions holding, suppose there is a derivative security also trading in this market. We specify that this security will have a certain payoff at a specified date in the future, depending on the value(s) taken by the stock up to that date. It is a surprising fact that the derivative's price is completely determined at the current time, even though we do not know what path the stock price will take in the future. For the special case of a European call or put option, Black and Scholes showed that "it is possible to create a hedged position, consisting of a long position in the stock and a short position in the option, whose value will not depend on the price of the stock". Their dynamic hedging strategy led to a partial differential equation which governed the price of the option. Its solution is given by the Black–Scholes formula.

Several of these assumptions of the original model have been removed in subsequent extensions of the model. Modern versions account for dynamic interest rates (Merton, 1976), transaction costs and taxes (Ingersoll, 1976), and dividend payout.

## Notation

Let

$S$, be the price of the stock, which will sometimes be a random variable and other times a constant (context should make this clear).

$V(S,t)$, the price of a derivative as a function of time and stock price.

$C(S,t)$ the price of a European call option and $P(S,t)$ the price of a European put option.

$K$, the strike price of the option.

$r$, the annualized risk-free interest rate, continuously compounded (the force of interest).

$\mu$, the drift rate of $S$, annualized.

$\sigma$, , the standard deviation of the stock's returns; this is the square root of the quadratic variation of the stock's log price process.

$t$, a time in years; we generally use: now=0, expiry=T.

$\Pi$, , the value of a portfolio.

Finally we will use $N(x)$ to denote the standard normal cumulative distribution function,

$$N(x) = \frac{1}{\sqrt{2\pi}} \int_{-\infty}^{x} e^{-\frac{z^2}{2}} dz.$$

$N'(x)$ will denote the standard normal probability density function,

$$N'(x) = \frac{1}{\sqrt{2\pi}} e^{-\frac{x^2}{2}}$$

## Black–Scholes Equation

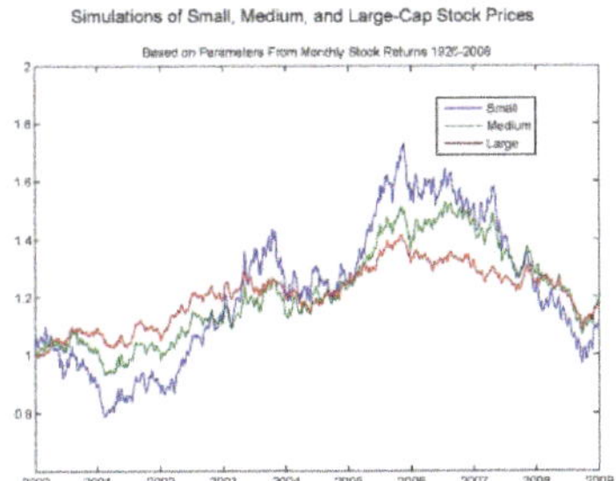


Simulated geometric Brownian motions with parameters from market data

As above, the Black–Scholes equation is a partial differential equation, which describes the price of the option over time. The equation is:

$$\frac{\partial V}{\partial t}+\frac{1}{2}\sigma^2 S^2\frac{\partial^2 V}{\partial S^2}+rS\frac{\partial V}{\partial S}-rV=0$$

The key financial insight behind the equation is that one can perfectly hedge the option by buying and selling the underlying asset in just the right way and consequently "eliminate risk". This hedge, in turn, implies that there is only one right price for the option, as returned by the Black–Scholes formula.

## Black–Scholes Formula

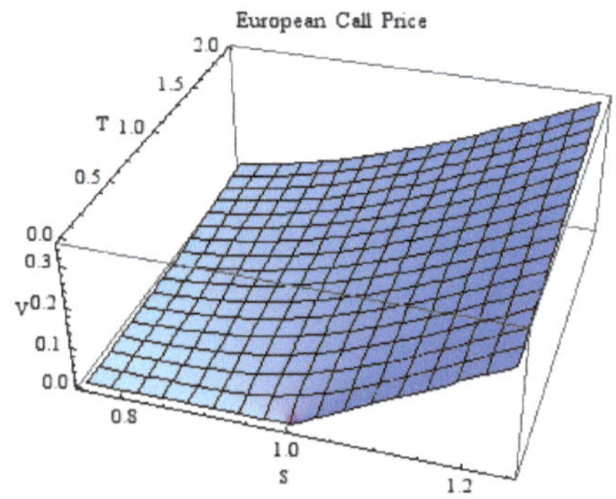


A European call valued using the Black–Scholes pricing equation for varying asset price S and time-to-expiry T. In this particular example, the strike price is set to unity.

The Black–Scholes formula calculates the price of European put and call options. This price is consistent with the Black–Scholes equation as above; this follows since the formula can be obtained by solving the equation for the corresponding terminal and boundary conditions.

The value of a call option for a non-dividend-paying underlying stock in terms of the Black–Scholes parameters is:

$$C(S_t,t)=N(d_1)S_t-N(d_2)Ke^{-r(T-t)}$$

$$d_1=\frac{1}{\sigma\sqrt{T-t}}\left[\ln\left(\frac{S_t}{K}\right)+\left(r+\frac{\sigma^2}{2}\right)(T-t)\right]$$

$$d_2=d_1-\sigma\sqrt{T-t}$$

The price of a corresponding put option based on put-call parity is:

$$P(S_t,t)=Ke^{-r(T-t)}-S_t+C(S_t,t)$$
$$=N(-d_2)Ke^{-r(T-t)}-N(-d_1)S_t$$

For both, as above:

- $N(\cdot)$ is the cumulative distribution function of the standard normal distribution
- $T-t$ is the time to maturity
- $S_t$ is the spot price of the underlying asset
- $K$ is the strike price
- $r$ is the risk free rate (annual rate, expressed in terms of continuous compounding)
- $\sigma$ is the volatility of returns of the underlying asset

## Alternative Formulation

Introducing some auxiliary variables allows the formula to be simplified and reformulated in a form that is often more convenient (this is a special case of the Black '76 formula):

$$C(F,\tau) = D\left(N(d_+)F - N(d_-)K\right)$$
$$d_\pm = \frac{1}{\sigma\sqrt{\tau}}\left[\ln\left(\frac{F}{K}\right) \pm \frac{1}{2}\sigma^2\tau\right]$$
$$d_\pm = d_\mp \pm \sigma\sqrt{\tau}$$

The auxiliary variables are:

- $\tau = T-t$ is the time to expiry (remaining time, backwards time)
- $D = e^{-r\tau}$ is the discount factor
- $F = e^{r\tau}S = \frac{S}{D}$ is the forward price of the underlying asset, and $S = DF$

with $d_+ = d_1$ and $d_- = d_2$ to clarify notation.

Given put-call parity, which is expressed in these terms as:

$$C - P = D(F-K) = S - DK$$

the price of a put option is:

$$P(F,\tau) = D\left[N(-d_-)K - N(-d_+)F\right]$$

## Interpretation

The Black–Scholes formula can be interpreted fairly handily, with the main subtlety the interpretation of the $N(d_\pm)$ (and a fortiori $d_\pm$) terms, particularly $d_+$ and why there are two different terms.

The formula can be interpreted by first decomposing a call option into the difference of two binary options: an asset-or-nothing call minus a cash-or-nothing call (long an asset-or-nothing call, short a cash-or-nothing call). A call option exchanges cash for an asset at expiry, while an asset-or-nothing call just yields the asset (with no cash in exchange) and a cash-or-nothing call just yields cash (with no asset in exchange). The Black–Scholes formula is a difference of two terms, and these two terms equal the value of the binary call options. These binary options are much less frequently traded than vanilla call options, but are easier to analyze.

Thus the formula:

$$C = D\left[N(d_+)F - N(d_-)K\right]$$

breaks up as:

$$C = DN(d_+)F - DN(d_-)K\,,$$

where $DN(d_+)F$ is the present value of an asset-or-nothing call and $DN(d_-)K$ is the present value of a cash-or-nothing call. The *D* factor is for discounting, because the expiration date is in future, and removing it changes *present* value to *future* value (value at expiry). Thus $N(d_+)F$ is the future value of an asset-or-nothing call and $N(d_-)\,K$ is the future value of a cash-or-nothing call. In risk-neutral terms, these are the expected value of the asset and the expected value of the cash in the risk-neutral measure.

The naive, and not quite correct, interpretation of these terms is that $N(d_+)F$ is the probability of the option expiring in the money $N(d_+)$, times the value of the underlying at expiry *F*, while $N(d_-)K$ is the probability of the option expiring in the money $N(d_-)$, times the value of the cash at expiry *K*. This is obviously incorrect, as either both binaries expire in the money or both expire out of the money (either cash is exchanged for asset or it is not), but the probabilities $N(d_+)$ and $N(d_-)$ are not equal. In fact, $d_\pm$ can be interpreted as measures of moneyness (in standard deviations) and $N(d_\pm)$ as probabilities of expiring ITM (*percent moneyness*), in the respective numéraire, as discussed below. Simply-put, the interpretation of the cash option, $N(d_-)K$, is correct, as the value of the cash is independent of movements of the underlying, and thus can be interpreted as a simple product of "probability times value", while the $d_\pm$ is more complicated, as the probability of expiring in the money and the value of the asset at expiry are not independent. More precisely, the value of the asset at expiry is variable in terms of cash, but is constant in terms of the asset itself (a fixed quantity of the asset), and thus these quantities are independent if one changes numéraire to the asset rather than cash.

If one uses spot *S* instead of forward *F*, in $d_\pm$ instead of the $\frac{1}{2}\sigma^2$ term there is $\left(r \pm \frac{1}{2}\sigma^2\right)\tau$, which can be interpreted as a drift factor (in the risk-neutral measure for appropriate numéraire). The use of $d_-$ for moneyness rather than the standardized moneyness $m = \frac{1}{\sigma\sqrt{\tau}}\ln\left(\frac{F}{K}\right)$ – in other words, the reason for the $\frac{1}{2}\sigma^2$ factor – is due to the difference between the median and mean of the log-normal distribution; it is the same factor as in Itō's lemma applied to geometric Brownian motion. In addition, another way to see that the naive interpretation is incorrect is that replacing $N(d_+)$ by $N(d_-)$ in the formula yields a negative value for out-of-the-money call options.

In detail, the terms $N(d_1), N(d_2)$ are the *probabilities of the option expiring in-the-money* under the equivalent exponential martingale probability measure (numéraire=stock) and the equivalent martingale probability measure (numéraire=risk free asset), respectively. The risk neutral probability density for the stock price $S_T \in (0,\infty)$ is

$$p(S,T) = \frac{N'[d_2(S_T)]}{S_T \sigma \sqrt{T}}$$

where $d_2 = d_2(K)$ is defined as above.

Specifically, $N(d_2)$ is the probability that the call will be exercised provided one assumes that the asset drift is the risk-free rate. $N(d_1)$, however, does not lend itself to a simple probability interpretation. $SN(d_1)$ is correctly interpreted as the present value, using the risk-free interest rate, of the expected asset price at expiration, given that the asset price at expiration is above the exercise price. For related discussion – and graphical representation.

The equivalent martingale probability measure is also called the risk-neutral probability measure. Note that both of these are *probabilities* in a measure theoretic sense, and neither of these is the true probability of expiring in-the-money under the real probability measure. To calculate the probability under the real ("physical") probability measure, additional information is required—the drift term in the physical measure, or equivalently, the market price of risk.

## Derivations

A standard derivation for solving the Black–Scholes PDE is given in the article Black–Scholes equation.

The Feynman–Kac formula says that the solution to this type of PDE, when discounted appropriately, is actually a martingale. Thus the option price is the expected value of the discounted payoff of the option. Computing the option price via this expectation is the risk neutrality approach and can be done without knowledge of PDEs. Note the expectation of the option payoff is not done under the real world probability measure, but an artificial risk-neutral measure, which differs from the real world measure.

## The Greeks

"The Greeks" measure the sensitivity of the value of a derivative or a portfolio to changes in parameter value(s) while holding the other parameters fixed. They are partial derivatives of the price with respect to the parameter values. One Greek, "gamma" (as well as others not listed here) is a partial derivative of another Greek, "delta" in this case.

The Greeks are important not only in the mathematical theory of finance, but also for those actively trading. Financial institutions will typically set (risk) limit values for each of the Greeks that their traders must not exceed. Delta is the most important Greek since this usually confers the largest risk. Many traders will zero their delta at the end of the day if they are speculating and following a delta-neutral hedging approach as defined by Black–Scholes.

The Greeks for Black–Scholes are given in closed form below. They can be obtained by differentiation of the Black–Scholes formula.

<table>
<tr><th></th><th></th><th>Calls</th><th>Puts</th></tr>
<tr><td>Delta</td><td>$\frac{\partial C}{\partial S}$</td><td>$N(d_1)$</td><td>$-N(-d_1) = N(d_1) - 1$</td></tr>
<tr><td>Gamma</td><td>$\frac{\partial^2 C}{\partial S^2}$</td><td colspan="2">$\frac{N'(d_1)}{S\sigma\sqrt{T-t}}$</td></tr>
<tr><td>Vega</td><td>$\frac{\partial C}{\partial \sigma}$</td><td colspan="2">$SN'(d_1)\sqrt{T-t}$</td></tr>
<tr><td>Theta</td><td>$\frac{\partial C}{\partial t}$</td><td>$-\frac{SN'(d_1)\sigma}{2\sqrt{T-t}} - rKe^{-r(T-t)}N(d_2)$</td><td>$-\frac{SN'(d_1)\sigma}{2\sqrt{T-t}} + rKe^{-r(T-t)}N(-d_2)$</td></tr>
<tr><td>Rho</td><td>$\frac{\partial C}{\partial r}$</td><td>$K(T-t)e^{-r(T-t)}N(d_2)$</td><td>$-K(T-t)e^{-r(T-t)}N(-d\ )$</td></tr>
</table>

Note that from the formulae, it is clear that the gamma is the same value for calls and puts and so too is the vega the same value for calls and put options. This can be seen directly from put–call parity, since the difference of a put and a call is a forward, which is linear in $S$ and independent of $\sigma$ (so a forward has zero gamma and zero vega). N' is the standard normal probability density function.

In practice, some sensitivities are usually quoted in scaled-down terms, to match the scale of likely changes in the parameters. For example, rho is often reported divided by 10,000 (1 basis point rate change), vega by 100 (1 vol point change), and theta by 365 or 252 (1 day decay based on either calendar days or trading days per year).

(Vega is not a letter in the Greek alphabet; the name arises from reading the Greek letter ν (nu) as a V.)

## Extensions of the Model

The above model can be extended for variable (but deterministic) rates and volatilities. The model may also be used to value European options on instruments paying dividends. In this case, closed-form solutions are available if the dividend is a known proportion of the stock price. American options and options on stocks paying a known cash dividend (in the short term, more realistic than a proportional dividend) are more difficult to value, and a choice of solution techniques is available (for example lattices and grids).

## Instruments Paying Continuous Yield Dividends

For options on indices, it is reasonable to make the simplifying assumption that dividends are paid continuously, and that the dividend amount is proportional to the level of the index.

The dividend payment paid over the time period $[t, t+dt]$ is then modelled as

$$qS_t\,dt$$

for some constant $q$ (the dividend yield).

Under this formulation the arbitrage-free price implied by the Black–Scholes model can be shown to be

$$C(S_t, t) = e^{-r(T-t)}[FN(d_1) - KN(d_2)]$$

and

$$P(S_t, t) = e^{-r(T-t)}[KN(-d_2) - FN(-d_1)]$$

where now

$$F = S_t e^{(r-q)(T-t)}$$

is the modified forward price that occurs in the terms $d_1, d_2$:

$$d_1 = \frac{1}{\sigma\sqrt{T-t}}\left[\ln\left(\frac{S_t}{K}\right) + (r - q + \frac{1}{2}\sigma^2)(T-t)\right]$$

and

$$d_2 = d_1 - \sigma\sqrt{T-t} = \frac{1}{\sigma\sqrt{T-t}}\left[\ln\left(\frac{S_t}{K}\right) + (r - q - \frac{1}{2}\sigma^2)(T-t)\right]$$

Extending the Black Scholes formula Adjusting for payouts of the underlying.

## Instruments Paying Discrete Proportional Dividends

It is also possible to extend the Black–Scholes framework to options on instruments paying discrete proportional dividends. This is useful when the option is struck on a single stock.

A typical model is to assume that a proportion $\delta$ of the stock price is paid out at pre-determined times $t_1, t_2, \ldots$. The price of the stock is then modelled as

$$S_t = S_0(1-\delta)^{n(t)} e^{ut+\sigma W_t}$$

where $n(t)$ is the number of dividends that have been paid by time .

The price of a call option on such a stock is again

$$C(S_0, T) = e^{-rT}[FN(d_1) - KN(d_2)]$$

where now

$$F = S_0(1-\delta)^{n(T)} e^{rT}$$

is the forward price for the dividend paying stock.

## American Options

The problem of finding the price of an American option is related to the optimal stopping problem of finding the time to execute the option. Since the American option can be exercised at any time before the expiration date, the Black–Scholes equation becomes an inequality of the form

$$\frac{\partial V}{\partial t} + \frac{1}{2}\sigma^2 S^2 \frac{\partial^2 V}{\partial S^2} + rS\frac{\partial V}{\partial S} - rV \leq 0$$

with the terminal and (free) boundary conditions: $V(S,T) = H(S)$ and $V(S,t) \geq H(S)$ where $H(S)$ denotes the payoff at stock price $S$.

In general this inequality does not have a closed form solution, though an American call with no dividends is equal to a European call and the Roll-Geske-Whaley method provides a solution for an American call with one dividend.

Barone-Adesi and Whaley is a further approximation formula. Here, the stochastic differential equation (which is valid for the value of any derivative) is split into two components: the European option value and the early exercise premium. With some assumptions, a quadratic equation that approximates the solution for the latter is then obtained. This solution involves finding the critical value, $s*$, such that one is indifferent between early exercise and holding to maturity.

Bjerksund and Stensland provide an approximation based on an exercise strategy corresponding to a trigger price. Here, if the underlying asset price is greater than or equal to the trigger price it is optimal to exercise, and the value must equal $S - X$, otherwise the option "boils down to: (i) a European up-and-out call option... and (ii) a rebate that is received at the knock-out date if the option is knocked out prior to the maturity date." The formula is readily modified for the valuation of a put option, using put call parity. This approximation is computationally inexpensive and the method is fast, with evidence indicating that the approximation may be more accurate in pricing long dated options than Barone-Adesi and Whaley.

## Black–Scholes in Practice

The normality assumption of the Black–Scholes model does not capture extreme movements such as stock market crashes.

The Black–Scholes model disagrees with reality in a number of ways, some significant. It is widely employed as a useful approximation, but proper application requires understanding its limitations – blindly following the model exposes the user to unexpected risk. Among the most significant limitations are:

- the underestimation of extreme moves, yielding tail risk, which can be hedged with out-of-the-money options;
- the assumption of instant, cost-less trading, yielding liquidity risk, which is difficult to hedge;
- the assumption of a stationary process, yielding volatility risk, which can be hedged with volatility hedging;

- the assumption of continuous time and continuous trading, yielding gap risk, which can be hedged with Gamma hedging.

In short, while in the Black–Scholes model one can perfectly hedge options by simply Delta hedging, in practice there are many other sources of risk.

Results using the Black–Scholes model differ from real world prices because of simplifying assumptions of the model. One significant limitation is that in reality security prices do not follow a strict stationary log-normal process, nor is the risk-free interest actually known (and is not constant over time). The variance has been observed to be non-constant leading to models such as GARCH to model volatility changes. Pricing discrepancies between empirical and the Black–Scholes model have long been observed in options that are far out-of-the-money, corresponding to extreme price changes; such events would be very rare if returns were lognormally distributed, but are observed much more often in practice.

Nevertheless, Black–Scholes pricing is widely used in practice, because it is:

- easy to calculate
- a useful approximation, particularly when analyzing the direction in which prices move when crossing critical points
- a robust basis for more refined models
- reversible, as the model's original output, price, can be used as an input and one of the other variables solved for; the implied volatility calculated in this way is often used to quote option prices (that is, as a *quoting convention*).

The first point is self-evidently useful. The others can be further discussed:

Useful approximation: although volatility is not constant, results from the model are often helpful in setting up hedges in the correct proportions to minimize risk. Even when the results are not completely accurate, they serve as a first approximation to which adjustments can be made.

Basis for more refined models: The Black–Scholes model is *robust* in that it can be adjusted to deal with some of its failures. Rather than considering some parameters (such as volatility or interest rates) as *constant,* one considers them as *variables,* and thus added sources of risk. This is reflected in the Greeks (the change in option value for a change in these parameters, or equivalently the partial derivatives with respect to these variables), and hedging these Greeks mitigates the risk caused by the non-constant nature of these parameters. Other defects cannot be mitigated by modifying the model, however, notably tail risk and liquidity risk, and these are instead managed outside the model, chiefly by minimizing these risks and by stress testing.

Explicit modeling: this feature means that, rather than *assuming* a volatility *a priori* and computing prices from it, one can use the model to solve for volatility, which gives the implied volatility of an option at given prices, durations and exercise prices. Solving for volatility over a given set of durations and strike prices one can construct an implied volatility surface. In this application of the Black–Scholes model, a coordinate transformation from the *price domain* to the *volatility domain* is obtained. Rather than quoting option prices in terms of dollars per unit (which are hard to compare across strikes, durations and coupon frequencies), option prices can thus be quoted in terms of implied volatility, which leads to trading of volatility in option markets.

## The Volatility Smile

One of the attractive features of the Black–Scholes model is that the parameters in the model other than the volatility (the time to maturity, the strike, the risk-free interest rate, and the current underlying price) are unequivocally observable. All other things being equal, an option's theoretical value is a monotonic increasing function of implied volatility.

By computing the implied volatility for traded options with different strikes and maturities, the Black–Scholes model can be tested. If the Black–Scholes model held, then the implied volatility for a particular stock would be the same for all strikes and maturities. In practice, the volatility surface (the 3D graph of implied volatility against strike and maturity) is not flat.

The typical shape of the implied volatility curve for a given maturity depends on the underlying instrument. Equities tend to have skewed curves: compared to at-the-money, implied volatility is substantially higher for low strikes, and slightly lower for high strikes. Currencies tend to have more symmetrical curves, with implied volatility lowest at-the-money, and higher volatilities in both wings. Commodities often have the reverse behavior to equities, with higher implied volatility for higher strikes.

Despite the existence of the volatility smile (and the violation of all the other assumptions of the Black–Scholes model), the Black–Scholes PDE and Black–Scholes formula are still used extensively in practice. A typical approach is to regard the volatility surface as a fact about the market, and use an implied volatility from it in a Black–Scholes valuation model. This has been described as using "the wrong number in the wrong formula to get the right price." This approach also gives usable values for the hedge ratios (the Greeks). Even when more advanced models are used, traders prefer to think in terms of Black–Scholes implied volatility as it allows them to evaluate and compare options of different maturities, strikes, and so on.

## Valuing Bond Options

Black–Scholes cannot be applied directly to bond securities because of pull-to-par. As the bond reaches its maturity date, all of the prices involved with the bond become known, thereby decreasing its volatility, and the simple Black–Scholes model does not reflect this process. A large number of extensions to Black–Scholes, beginning with the Black model, have been used to deal with this phenomenon.

## Interest-rate Curve

In practice, interest rates are not constant – they vary by tenor (coupon frequency), giving an interest rate curve which may be interpolated to pick an appropriate rate to use in the Black–Scholes formula. Another consideration is that interest rates vary over time. This volatility may make a significant contribution to the price, especially of long-dated options.This is simply like the interest rate and bond price relationship which is inversely related.

## Short Stock Rate

It is not free to take a short stock position. Similarly, it may be possible to lend out a long stock position for a small fee. In either case, this can be treated as a continuous dividend for the purposes of a Black–Scholes valuation, provided that there is no glaring asymmetry between the short stock borrowing cost and the long stock lending income.

## Criticism and Comments

Espen Gaarder Haug and Nassim Nicholas Taleb argue that the Black–Scholes model merely recasts existing widely used models in terms of practically impossible "dynamic hedging" rather than "risk", to make them more compatible with mainstream neoclassical economic theory. They also assert that Boness in 1964 had already published a formula that is "actually identical" to the Black–Scholes call option pricing equation. Edward Thorp also claims to have guessed the Black–Scholes formula in 1967 but kept it to himself to make money for his investors. Emanuel Derman and Nassim Taleb have also criticized dynamic hedging and state that a number of researchers had put forth similar models prior to Black and Scholes. In response, Paul Wilmott has defended the model.

Living systems need to extract resources to compensate for continuous diffusion. This can be modelled mathematically as lognormal processes. The Black–Scholes equation is a deterministic representation of lognormal processes. The Black–Scholes model can be extended to describe general biological and social systems.

British mathematician Ian Stewart published a criticism in which he suggested that "the equation itself wasn't the real problem" and he stated a possible role as "one ingredient in a rich stew of financial irresponsibility, political ineptitude, perverse incentives and lax regulation" due to its abuse in the financial industry.

In his 2008 letter to the shareholders of Berkshire Hathaway, Warren Buffett wrote: "I believe the Black–Scholes formula, even though it is the standard for establishing the dollar liability for options, produces strange results when the long-term variety are being valued... The Black–Scholes formula has approached the status of holy writ in finance ... If the formula is applied to extended time periods, however, it can produce absurd results. In fairness, Black and Scholes almost certainly understood this point well. But their devoted followers may be ignoring whatever caveats the two men attached when they first unveiled the formula."

## Value at Risk

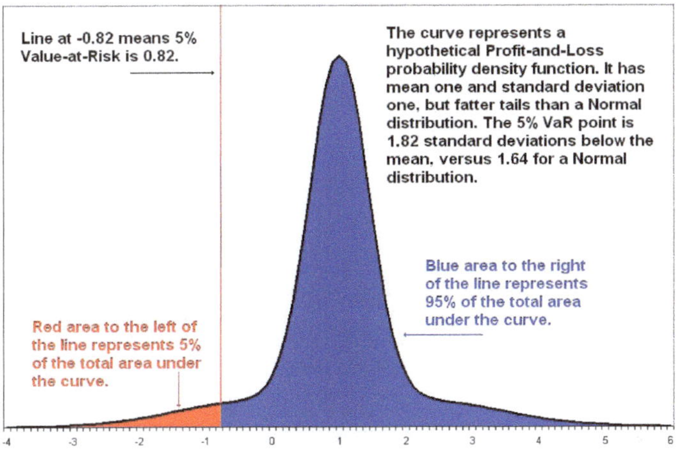


The 5% Value at Risk of a hypothetical profit-and-loss probability density function

Value at Risk (VaR) is a measure of the risk of investments. It estimates how much a set of investments might lose, given normal market conditions, in a set time period such as a day. VaR is typically used by firms and regulators in the financial industry to gauge the amount of assets needed to cover possible losses.

In financial mathematics and financial risk management, VaR is defined as: for a given portfolio, time horizon, and probability $p$, the $p$ VaR is defined as a threshold loss value, such that the probability that the loss on the portfolio over the given time horizon exceeds this value is $p$. This assumes mark-to-market pricing, and no trading in the portfolio.

For example, if a portfolio of stocks has a one-day 5% VaR of $1 million, that means that there is a 0.05 probability that the portfolio will fall in value by more than $1 million over a one-day period if there is no trading. Informally, a loss of $1 million or more on this portfolio is expected on 1 day out of 20 days (because of 5% probability). A loss which exceeds the VaR threshold is termed a "VaR break."

VaR has four main uses in finance: risk management, financial control, financial reporting and computing regulatory capital. VaR is sometimes used in non-financial applications as well.

Important related ideas are economic capital, backtesting, stress testing, expected shortfall, and tail conditional expectation.

## Details

Common parameters for VaR are 1% and 5% probabilities and one day and two week horizons, although other combinations are in use.

The reason for assuming normal markets and no trading, and to restricting loss to things measured in daily accounts, is to make the loss observable. In some extreme financial events it can be impossible to determine losses, either because market prices are unavailable or because the loss-bearing institution breaks up. Some longer-term consequences of disasters, such as lawsuits, loss of market confidence and employee morale and impairment of brand names can take a long time to play out, and may be hard to allocate among specific prior decisions. VaR marks the boundary between normal days and extreme events. Institutions can lose far more than the VaR amount; all that can be said is that they will not do so very often.

The probability level is about equally often specified as one minus the probability of a VaR break, so that the VaR in the example above would be called a one-day 95% VaR instead of one-day 5% VaR. This generally does not lead to confusion because the probability of VaR breaks is almost always small, certainly less than 50%.

Although it virtually always represents a loss, VaR is conventionally reported as a positive number. A negative VaR would imply the portfolio has a high probability of making a profit, for example a one-day 5% VaR of negative $1 million implies the portfolio has a 95% chance of making more than $1 million over the next day.

Another inconsistency is that VaR is sometimes taken to refer to profit-and-loss at the end of the period, and sometimes as the maximum loss at any point during the period. The original definition was the latter, but in the early 1990s when VaR was aggregated across trading desks and time zones, end-of-day valuation was the only reliable number so the former became the *de facto* definition. As people began using multiday VaRs in the second half of the 1990s, they almost always estimated the distribution at the end of the period only. It is also easier theoretically to deal with a point-in-time estimate versus a maximum over an interval. Therefore the end-of-period definition is the most common both in theory and practice today.

## Varieties of VaR

The definition of VaR is nonconstructive; it specifies a property VaR must have, but not how to compute VaR. Moreover, there is wide scope for interpretation in the definition. This has led to two broad types of VaR, one used primarily in risk management and the other primarily for risk measurement. The distinction is not sharp, however, and hybrid versions are typically used in financial control, financial reporting and computing regulatory capital.

To a risk manager, VaR is a system, not a number. The system is run periodically (usually daily) and the published number is compared to the computed price movement in opening positions over the time horizon. There is never any subsequent adjustment to the published VaR, and there is no distinction between VaR breaks caused by input errors (including Information Technology breakdowns, fraud and rogue trading), computation errors (including failure to produce a VaR on time) and market movements.

A frequentist claim is made, that the long-term frequency of VaR breaks will equal the specified probability, within the limits of sampling error, and that the VaR breaks will be independent in time and independent of the level of VaR. This claim is validated by a backtest, a comparison of published VaRs to actual price movements. In this interpretation, many different systems could produce VaRs with equally good backtests, but wide disagreements on daily VaR values.

For risk measurement a number is needed, not a system. A Bayesian probability claim is made, that given the information and beliefs at the time, the subjective probability of a VaR break was the specified level. VaR is adjusted after the fact to correct errors in inputs and computation, but not to incorporate information unavailable at the time of computation. In this context, "backtest" has a different meaning. Rather than comparing published VaRs to actual market movements over the period of time the system has been in operation, VaR is retroactively computed on scrubbed data over as long a period as data are available and deemed relevant. The same position data and pricing models are used for computing the VaR as determining the price movements.

Although some of the sources listed here treat only one kind of VaR as legitimate, most of the recent ones seem to agree that risk management VaR is superior for making short-term and tactical decisions today, while risk measurement VaR should be used for understanding the past, and making medium term and strategic decisions for the future. When VaR is used for financial control or financial reporting it should incorporate elements of both. For example, if a trading desk is held to a VaR limit, that is both a risk-management rule for deciding what risks to allow today, and an input into the risk measurement computation of the desk's risk-adjusted return at the end of the reporting period.

## VaR in Governance

VaR can also be applied to governance of endowments, trusts, and pension plans. Essentially trustees adopt portfolio Values-at-Risk metrics for the entire pooled account and the diversified parts individually managed. Instead of probability estimates they simply define maximum levels of acceptable loss for each. Doing so provides an easy metric for oversight and adds accountability as managers are then directed to manage, but with the additional constraint to avoid losses within a defined risk parameter. VaR utilized in this manner adds relevance as well as an easy way to monitor risk measurement control far more intuitive than Standard Deviation of Return. Use of VaR in this context, as well as a worthwhile critique on board governance practices as it relates to investment management oversight in general can be found in *Best Practices in Governance.*

## Mathematical Definition

Given a confidence level $\alpha \in (0,1)$, VaR of the underlying $X$ at the confidence level $\alpha$ is the smallest number $x$ such that the probability that the underlying $X$ exceeds $-x$ is at least $\alpha$.

Mathematically, if $X$ is the underlying (e.g., the price of a portfolio), then $VaR_\alpha(X)$ is the negative of the $\alpha$-quantile, i.e.,

$$\mathrm{VaR}_\alpha(X) = \inf\{x \in \mathbb{R} : P(X + x < 0) \leq 1 - \alpha\} = \inf\{x \in \mathbb{R} : 1 - F_X(-x) \geq \alpha\}.$$

The left equality is a definition of VaR. The right equality assumes an underlying probability distribution, which makes it true only for parametric VaR. Risk managers typically assume that some fraction of the bad events will have undefined losses, either because markets are closed or illiquid, or because the entity bearing the loss breaks apart or loses the ability to compute accounts. Therefore, they do not accept results based on the assumption of a well-defined probability distribution. Nassim Taleb has labeled this assumption, "charlatanism." On the other hand, many academics prefer to assume a well-defined distribution, albeit usually one with fat tails. This point has probably caused more contention among VaR theorists than any other.

Value of Risks can also be written as a distortion risk measure given by the distortion

function $g(x) = \begin{cases} 0 & \text{if } 0 \leq x < 1 - \alpha \\ 1 & \text{if } 1 - \alpha \leq x \leq 1 \end{cases}.$

## Risk Measure and Risk Metric

The term "VaR" is used both for a risk measure and a risk metric. This sometimes leads to confusion. Sources earlier than 1995 usually emphasize the risk measure, later sources are more likely to emphasize the metric.

The VaR risk measure defines risk as mark-to-market loss on a fixed portfolio over a fixed time horizon. There are many alternative risk measures in finance. Given the inability to use mark-to-market (which uses market prices to define loss) for future performance, loss is often defined (as a substitute) as change in fundamental value. For example, if an institution holds a loan that declines in market price because interest rates go up, but has no change in cash flows or credit quality, some systems do not recognize a loss. Also some try to incorporate the economic cost of harm not measured in daily financial statements, such as loss of market confidence or employee morale, impairment of brand names or lawsuits.

Rather than assuming a static portfolio over a fixed time horizon, some risk measures incorporate the dynamic effect of expected trading (such as a stop loss order) and consider the expected holding period of positions.

The VaR risk metric summarizes the distribution of possible losses by a quantile, a point with a specified probability of greater losses. A common alternative metrics is expected shortfall.

## VaR Risk Management

Supporters of VaR-based risk management claim the first and possibly greatest benefit of VaR is the improvement in systems and modeling it forces on an institution. In 1997, Philippe Jorion wrote:

[T]he greatest benefit of VAR lies in the imposition of a structured methodology for critically thinking about risk. Institutions that go through the process of computing their VAR are forced to confront their exposure to financial risks and to set up a proper risk management function. Thus the process of getting to VAR may be as important as the number itself.

Publishing a daily number, on-time and with specified statistical properties holds every part of a trading organization to a high objective standard. Robust backup systems and default assumptions must be implemented. Positions that are reported, modeled or priced incorrectly stand out, as do data feeds that are inaccurate or late and systems that are too-frequently down. Anything that affects profit and loss that is left out of other reports will show up either in inflated VaR or excessive VaR breaks. "A risk-taking institution that *does not* compute VaR might escape disaster, but an institution that *cannot* compute VaR will not."

The second claimed benefit of VaR is that it separates risk into two regimes. Inside the VaR limit, conventional statistical methods are reliable. Relatively short-term and specific data can be used for analysis. Probability estimates are meaningful, because there are enough data to test them. In a sense, there is no true risk because you have a sum of many independent observations with a left bound on the outcome. A casino doesn't worry about whether red or black will come up on the next roulette spin. Risk managers encourage productive risk-taking in this regime, because there is little true cost. People tend to worry too much about these risks, because they happen frequently, and not enough about what might happen on the worst days.

Outside the VaR limit, all bets are off. Risk should be analyzed with stress testing based on long-term and broad market data. Probability statements are no longer meaningful. Knowing the distribution of losses beyond the VaR point is both impossible and useless. The risk manager should concentrate instead on making sure good plans are in place to limit the loss if possible, and to survive the loss if not.

One specific system uses three regimes.

1. One to three times VaR are normal occurrences. You expect periodic VaR breaks. The loss distribution typically has fat tails, and you might get more than one break in a short period of time. Moreover, markets may be abnormal and trading may exacerbate losses, and you may take losses not measured in daily marks such as lawsuits, loss of employee morale and market confidence and impairment of brand names. So an institution that can't deal with three times VaR losses as routine events probably won't survive long enough to put a VaR system in place.

2. Three to ten times VaR is the range for stress testing. Institutions should be confident they have examined all the foreseeable events that will cause losses in this range, and are prepared to survive them. These events are too rare to estimate probabilities reliably, so risk/return calculations are useless.

3. Foreseeable events should not cause losses beyond ten times VaR. If they do they should be hedged or insured, or the business plan should be changed to avoid them, or VaR should be increased. It's hard to run a business if foreseeable losses are orders of magnitude larger than very large everyday losses. It's hard to plan for these events, because they are out of scale with daily experience. Of course there will be unforeseeable losses more than ten times VaR, but it's pointless to anticipate them, you can't know much about them and it results in needless worrying. Better to hope that the discipline of preparing for all foreseeable three-to-ten times VaR losses will improve chances for surviving the unforeseen and larger losses that inevitably occur.

"A risk manager has two jobs: make people take more risk the 99% of the time it is safe to do so, and survive the other 1% of the time. VaR is the border."

Another reason VaR is useful as a metric is due to its ability to compress the riskiness of a portfolio to a single number, making it comparable across different portfolios (of different assets). Within any portfolio it is also possible to isolate specific position that might better hedge the portfolio to reduce, and minimise, the VaR. An example of market-maker employed strategies for trading linear interest rate derivatives and interest rate swaps portfolios is cited.

## Computation Methods

VaR can be estimated either parametrically (for example, variance-covariance VaR or delta-gamma VaR) or nonparametrically (for examples, historical simulation VaR or resampled VaR). Nonparametric methods of VaR estimation are discussed in Markovich and Novak. A comparison of a number of strategies for VaR prediction is given in Kuester et al.

A McKinsey report published in May 2012 estimated that 85% of large banks were using historical simulation. The other 15% used Monte Carlo methods.

## History of VaR

The problem of risk measurement is an old one in statistics, economics and finance. Financial risk management has been a concern of regulators and financial executives for a long time as well. Retrospective analysis has found some VaR-like concepts in this history. But VaR did not emerge as a distinct concept until the late 1980s. The triggering event was the stock market crash of 1987. This was the first major financial crisis in which a lot of academically-trained quants were in high enough positions to worry about firm-wide survival.

The crash was so unlikely given standard statistical models, that it called the entire basis of quant finance into question. A reconsideration of history led some quants to decide there were recurring crises, about one or two per decade, that overwhelmed the statistical assumptions embedded in models used for trading, investment management and derivative pricing. These affected many markets at once, including ones that were usually not correlated, and seldom had discernible economic cause or warning (although after-the-fact explanations were plentiful). Much later, they were named "Black Swans" by Nassim Taleb and the concept extended far beyond finance.

If these events were included in quantitative analysis they dominated results and led to strategies that did not work day to day. If these events were excluded, the profits made in between "Black Swans" could be much smaller than the losses suffered in the crisis. Institutions could fail as a result.

VaR was developed as a systematic way to segregate extreme events, which are studied qualitatively over long-term history and broad market events, from everyday price movements, which are studied quantitatively using short-term data in specific markets. It was hoped that "Black Swans" would be preceded by increases in estimated VaR or increased frequency of VaR breaks, in at least some markets. The extent to which this has proven to be true is controversial.

Abnormal markets and trading were excluded from the VaR estimate in order to make it observable. It is not always possible to define loss if, for example, markets are closed as after 9/11, or severely illiquid, as happened several times in 2008. Losses can also be hard to define if the risk-bearing institution fails or breaks up. A measure that depends on traders taking certain actions, and avoiding other actions, can lead to self reference.

This is risk management VaR. It was well established in quantitative trading groups at several financial institutions, notably Bankers Trust, before 1990, although neither the name nor the definition had been standardized. There was no effort to aggregate VaRs across trading desks.

The financial events of the early 1990s found many firms in trouble because the same underlying bet had been made at many places in the firm, in non-obvious ways. Since many trading desks already computed risk management VaR, and it was the only common risk measure that could be both defined for all businesses and aggregated without strong assumptions, it was the natural choice for reporting firmwide risk. J. P. Morgan CEO Dennis Weatherstone famously called for a "4:15 report" that combined all firm risk on one page, available within 15 minutes of the market close.

Risk measurement VaR was developed for this purpose. Development was most extensive at J. P. Morgan, which published the methodology and gave free access to estimates of the necessary underlying parameters in 1994. This was the first time VaR had been exposed beyond a relatively small group of quants. Two years later, the methodology was spun off into an independent for-profit business now part of RiskMetrics Group (now part of MSCI).

In 1997, the U.S. Securities and Exchange Commission ruled that public corporations must disclose quantitative information about their derivatives activity. Major banks and dealers chose to implement the rule by including VaR information in the notes to their financial statements.

Worldwide adoption of the Basel II Accord, beginning in 1999 and nearing completion today, gave further impetus to the use of VaR. VaR is the preferred measure of market risk, and concepts similar to VaR are used in other parts of the accord.

## Criticism

VaR has been controversial since it moved from trading desks into the public eye in 1994. A famous 1997 debate between Nassim Taleb and Philippe Jorion set out some of the major points of contention. Taleb claimed VaR:

1. Ignored 2,500 years of experience in favor of untested models built by non-traders
2. Was charlatanism because it claimed to estimate the risks of rare events, which is impossible
3. Gave false confidence
4. Would be exploited by traders

In 2008 David Einhorn and Aaron Brown debated VaR in Global Association of Risk Professionals Review Einhorn compared VaR to "an airbag that works all the time, except when you have a car accident." He further charged that VaR:

1. Led to excessive risk-taking and leverage at financial institutions

2. Focused on the manageable risks near the center of the distribution and ignored the tails
3. Created an incentive to take "excessive but remote risks"
4. Was "potentially catastrophic when its use creates a false sense of security among senior executives and watchdogs."

New York Times reporter Joe Nocera wrote an extensive piece Risk Mismanagement on January 4, 2009 discussing the role VaR played in the Financial crisis of 2007-2008. After interviewing risk managers (including several of the ones cited above) the article suggests that VaR was very useful to risk experts, but nevertheless exacerbated the crisis by giving false security to bank executives and regulators. A powerful tool for professional risk managers, VaR is portrayed as both easy to misunderstand, and dangerous when misunderstood.

Taleb in 2009 testified in Congress asking for the banning of VaR on two arguments. The first that "tail risks are non-measurable" and the second is that for anchoring reasons VaR for leading to higher risk taking.

VaR is not subadditive: VaR of a combined portfolio can be larger than the sum of the VaRs of its components.

For example, the average bank branch in the United States is robbed about once every ten years. A single-branch bank has about 0.0004% chance of being robbed on a specific day, so the risk of robbery would not figure into one-day 1% VaR. It would not even be within an order of magnitude of that, so it is in the range where the institution should not worry about it, it should insure against it and take advice from insurers on precautions. The whole point of insurance is to aggregate risks that are beyond individual VaR limits, and bring them into a large enough portfolio to get statistical predictability. It does not pay for a one-branch bank to have a security expert on staff.

As institutions get more branches, the risk of a robbery on a specific day rises to within an order of magnitude of VaR. At that point it makes sense for the institution to run internal stress tests and analyze the risk itself. It will spend less on insurance and more on in-house expertise. For a very large banking institution, robberies are a routine daily occurrence. Losses are part of the daily VaR calculation, and tracked statistically rather than case-by-case. A sizable in-house security department is in charge of prevention and control, the general risk manager just tracks the loss like any other cost of doing business. As portfolios or institutions get larger, specific risks change from low-probability/low-predictability/high-impact to statistically predictable losses of low individual impact. That means they move from the range of far outside VaR, to be insured, to near outside VaR, to be analyzed case-by-case, to inside VaR, to be treated statistically.

VaR is a static measure of risk. By definition, VaR is a particular characteristic of the probability distribution of the underlying (namely, VaR is essentially a quantile). .

There are common abuses of VaR:

1. Assuming that plausible losses will be less than some multiple (often three) of VaR. Losses can be extremely large.

2. Reporting a VaR that has not passed a backtest. Regardless of how VaR is computed, it should have produced the correct number of breaks (within sampling error) in the past. A common violation of common sense is to estimate a VaR based on the unverified assumption that everything follows a multivariate normal distribution.

## VaR, CVaR and EVaR

The VaR is not a coherent risk measure since it violates the sub-additivity property, which is

$$\text{If } X, Y \in \mathbf{L}, \text{ then } \rho(X+Y) \leq \rho(X) + \rho(Y).$$

However, it can be bounded by coherent risk measures like Conditional Value-at-Risk (CVaR) or entropic value at risk (EVaR). In fact, for $X \in \mathbf{L}_{M^+}$ (with $\mathbf{L}_{M^+}$ the set of all Borel measurable functions whose moment-generating function exists for all positive real values) we have

$$\text{VaR}_{1-\alpha}(X) \leq \text{CVaR}_{1-\alpha}(X) \leq \text{EVaR}_{1-\alpha}(X),$$

where

$$\text{VaR}_{1-\alpha}(X) := \inf_{t\in\mathbf{R}} \{t : \Pr(X \leq t) \geq 1-\alpha\},$$

$$\text{CVaR}_{1-\alpha}(X) := \frac{1}{\alpha} \int_0^{\alpha} \text{VaR}_{1-\gamma}(X) d\gamma,$$

$$\text{EVaR}_{1-\alpha}(X) := \inf_{z>0} \{z^{-1} \ln(M_X(z)/\alpha)\},$$

in which $M_X(z)$ is the moment-generating function of $X$ at $z$. In the above equations the variable $X$ denotes the financial loss, rather than wealth as is typically the case.

## References


- Coker, Frank (2014). Pulse: Understanding the Vital Signs of Your Business (1st ed.). Bellevue, WA: Ambient Light Publishing. pp. 30, 39, 42,more. ISBN 978-0-9893086-0-1.
- Virine, L. and Trumper M., Project Decisions: The Art and Science (2007). Management Concepts. Vienna, VA, ISBN 978-1-56726-217-9
- Finlay, Steven (2014). Predictive Analytics, Data Mining and Big Data. Myths, Misconceptions and Methods (1st ed.). Basingstoke: Palgrave Macmillan. p. 237. ISBN 1137379278.
- Siegel, Eric (2013). Predictive Analytics: The Power to Predict Who Will Click, Buy, Lie, or Die (1st ed.). Wiley. ISBN 978-1-1183-5685-2.

- Nigrini, Mark (June 2011). “Forensic Analytics: Methods and Techniques for Forensic Accounting Investigations”. Hoboken, NJ: John Wiley & Sons Inc. ISBN 978-0-470-89046-2.
- Harold A. Linstone, Murray Turoff (1975), The Delphi Method: Techniques and Applications, Reading, Mass.: Addison-Wesley, ISBN 978-0-201-04294-8
- Michael Adler, Erio Ziglio (eds.) (1996), Gazing Into the Oracle: The Delphi Method and Its Application to Social Policy and Public Health, London: Kingsley Publishers, ISBN 978-1-85302-104-6
- Berg, Bernd A. (2004). Markov Chain Monte Carlo Simulations and Their Statistical Analysis (With Web-Based Fortran Code). Hackensack, NJ: World Scientific. ISBN 981-238-935-0.
- Binder, Kurt (1995). The Monte Carlo Method in Condensed Matter Physics. New York: Springer. ISBN 0-387-54369-4.
- Doucet, Arnaud; Freitas, Nando de; Gordon, Neil (2001). Sequential Monte Carlo methods in practice. New York: Springer. ISBN 0-387-95146-6.
- Fishman, G. S. (1995). Monte Carlo: Concepts, Algorithms, and Applications. New York: Springer. ISBN 0-387-94527-X.
- Hartmann, A.K. (2009). Practical Guide to Computer Simulations. World Scientific. ISBN 978-981-283-415-7.

7

# Essential Aspects of Risk Management

The essential aspects of risk management are risk matrix, RiskLab and precautionary principle. Risk matrix is used during risk assessment and is used to define the level of risk that can be caused by an event while RiskLab is a research laboratory that conducts research on financial risk management. This chapter serves as a source to understand the major aspects of risk management.

## Risk Matrix

A risk is the amount of harm that can be expected to occur during a given time period due to specific harm event (e.g., an accident). Statistically, the level of risk can be calculated as the product of the probability that harm occurs (e.g., that an accident happens) multiplied by the severity of that harm (i.e., the average amount of harm or more conservatively the maximum credible amount of harm). In practice, the amount of risk is usually categorized into a small number of levels because neither the probability nor harm severity can typically be estimated with accuracy and precision.

A Risk matrix is a matrix that is used during risk assessment to define the various levels of risk as the product of the harm probability categories and harm severity categories. This is a simple mechanism to increase visibility of risks and assist management decision making.

Although many standard risk matrices exist in different contexts (US DoD, NASA, ISO), individual projects and organizations may need to create their own or tailor an existing risk matrix.

For example, the harm severity can be categorized as:

- Catastrophic – Multiple Deaths
- Critical – One Death or Multiple Severe Injuries
- Marginal – One Severe Injury or Multiple Minor Injuries
- Negligible – One Minor Injury

The probability of harm occurring might be categorized as 'Certain', 'Likely', 'Possible', 'Unlikely' and 'Rare'. However it must be considered that very low probabilities may not be very reliable.

The resulting Risk Matrix could be:

| | Negligible | Marginal | Critical | Catastrophic |
|---|---|---|---|---|
| **Certain** | High | High | Extreme | Extreme |
| **Likely** | Moderate | High | High | Extreme |
| **Possible** | Low | Moderate | High | Extreme |
| **Unlikely** | Low | Low | Moderate | Extreme |
| **Rare** | Low | Low | Moderate | High |

The company or organization then would calculate what levels of Risk they can take with different events. This would be done by weighing up the risk of an event occurring against the cost to implement safety and the benefit gained from it.

## An Example

The following is an example risk matrix with particular accidents allocated to appropriate cells within the matrix:

| | Negligible | Marginal | Critical | Catastrophic |
|---|---|---|---|---|
| **Certain** | Stubbing Toe | | | |
| **Likely** | | Fall | | |
| **Possible** | | | Major Car Accident | |
| **Unlikely** | | | Aircraft Crash | |
| **Rare** | | | | Major Tsunami |

## Problems

In his article 'What's Wrong with Risk Matrices?', Tony Cox argues that risk matrices experience several problematic mathematical features making it harder to assess risks. These are:

- Poor Resolution. Typical risk matrices can correctly and unambiguously compare only a small fraction (e.g., less than 10%) of randomly selected pairs of hazards. They can assign identical ratings to quantitatively very different risks ("range compression").
- Errors. Risk matrices can mistakenly assign higher qualitative ratings to quantitatively smaller risks. For risks with negatively correlated frequencies and severities, they can be "worse than useless," leading to worse-than-random decisions.
- Suboptimal Resource Allocation. Effective allocation of resources to risk-reducing countermeasures cannot be based on the categories provided by risk matrices.
- Ambiguous Inputs and Outputs. Categorizations of severity cannot be made ob-

> jectively for uncertain consequences. Inputs to risk matrices (e.g., frequency and severity categorizations) and resulting outputs (i.e., risk ratings) require subjective interpretation, and different users may obtain opposite ratings of the same quantitative risks. These limitations suggest that risk matrices should be used with caution, and only with careful explanations of embedded judgments.

Thomas, Bratvold, and Bickel demonstrate that risk matrices produce arbitrary risk rankings. Rankings depend upon the design of the risk matrix itself, such as how large the bins are and whether or not one uses an increasing or decreasing scale. In other words, changing the scale can change the answer.

Douglas W. Hubbard and Richard Seiersen take the general research from Cox, Thomas, Bratvold, and Bickel, and provide specific discussion in the realm of cybersecurity risk. They point at that since 61% of cybersecurity professionals use some form of risk matrix, this can be a serious problem. Hubbard and Seiersen consider these problems in the context of other measured human errors and conclude that "The errors of the experts are simply further exacerbated by the additional errors introduced by the scales and matrices themselves. We agree with the solution proposed by Thomas et al. There is no need for cybersecurity (or other areas of risk analysis that also use risk matrices) to reinvent well-established quantitative methods used in many equally complex problems."

## RiskLab

RiskLab is a laboratory that conducts research in financial risk management. The first was created in 1994 at *Eidgenössische Technische Hochschule Zürich* in Zurich, Switzerland. In 1996, another one was created independently at the University of Toronto, this time sponsored by the private company Algorithmics Incorporated.

Shortly afterwards, and also in partnership with Algorithmics Inc, others were created in Munich (1997), at Cornell University (1998), at Cambridge University (1998), at the Universidad Autonoma de Madrid (2000), and at the Cyprus International Institute of Management, in Nicosia (2001). Risklab China Research Center was also created in 2006. Further, in 2013, a Finnish section of Risklab was independently created at Åbo Akademi University in Turku and Arcada University of Applied Sciences in Helsinki. In 2010, growing out of the RiskLab international network, RiskLabs built the strategic alliance named RiskLab Global. The ethos of all existing RiskLabs is a fusion of academic research, industrial innovation and governmental oversight in financial risk management.

RiskLab-Toronto, a divisional center at the University of Toronto at Mississauga (UTM), was featured in *Research Means Business*, a directory of "*cutting-edge research leading to industrial innovation and the creation of new business enterprises*".

In October 2007, The RiskLab was awarded the NSERC Synergy Award for Innovation. The award was delivered by Dr. Colin Carrie, Parliamentary Secretary to the Minister of Industry, on behalf of the Honourable Jim Prentice, Minister of Industry and Minister responsible for the Natural Sciences and Engineering Research Council of Canada (NSERC), and by Dr. Suzanne Fortier, President of NSERC.

### Global Organization Structure

RiskLab Toronto, Canada Chapter, Headquarter Institution: University of Toronto, Ryerson University

Members:

- Luis A. Seco, Professor of Mathematics, University of Toronto; Director of RiskLab - Toronto; President and CEO of Sigma Analysis and Management Ltd.
- Desheng Dash WU, Ph.D., Affiliate Professor and Managing Director, RiskLab - Toronto, Director of Risklab China Research Center.
- Marcos Escobar, Marcos Escobar Añel, Associate Professor, Ryerson University
- Pablo Olivares, Assistant Professor, Ryerson University
- Sebastian Ferrando, Professor, Ryerson University

## Precautionary Principle

The precautionary principle (or precautionary approach) to risk management states that if an action or policy has a suspected risk of causing harm to the public, or to the environment, in the absence of scientific consensus (that the action or policy is not harmful), the burden of proof that it is *not* harmful falls on those taking an action that may or may not be a risk.

The principle is used by policy makers to justify discretionary decisions in situations where there is the possibility of harm from making a certain decision (e.g. taking a particular course of action) when extensive scientific knowledge on the matter is lacking. The principle implies that there is a social responsibility to protect the public from exposure to harm, when scientific investigation has found a plausible risk. These protections can be relaxed only if further scientific findings emerge that provide sound evidence that no harm will result.

In some legal systems, as in Law of the European Union, the application of the precautionary principle has been made a statutory requirement in some areas of law.

Regarding international conduct, the first endorsement of the principle was in 1982 when the World Charter for Nature was adopted by the United Nations General Assembly, while its first international implementation was in 1987 through the Montreal Protocol. Soon after, the principle integrated with many other legally binding international treaties such as the Rio Declaration and Kyoto Protocol.

## Origins and Theory

The concept "precautionary principle" is generally considered to have arisen in English from a translation of the German term *Vorsorgeprinzip* in the 1980s.

The concepts underpinning the precautionary principle pre-date the term's inception. For example, the essence of the principle is captured in a number of cautionary aphorisms such as "an ounce of prevention is worth a pound of cure", "better safe than sorry", and "look before you leap". The precautionary principle may also be interpreted as the evolution of the "ancient-medical principle" of "first, do no harm" to apply to institutions and institutional decision-making processes rather than individuals.

In economics, the Precautionary Principle has been analysed in terms of "the effect on rational decision-making", of "the interaction of irreversibility" and "uncertainty". Authors such as Epstein (1980) and Arrow and Fischer (1974) show that "irreversibility of possible future consequences" creates a "quasi-option effect" which should induce a "risk-neutral" society to favour current decisions that allow for more flexibility in the future. Gollier et al. (2000) conclude that "more scientific uncertainty as to the distribution of a future risk – that is, a larger variability of beliefs – should induce society to take stronger prevention measures today."

## Formulations

Many definitions of the precautionary principle exist: Precaution may be defined as "caution in advance," "caution practised in the context of uncertainty," or informed prudence. Two ideas lie at the core of the principle:

1. an expression of a need by decision-makers to anticipate harm before it occurs. Within this element lies an implicit reversal of the onus of proof: under the precautionary principle it is the responsibility of an activity-proponent to establish that the proposed activity will not (or is very unlikely to) result in significant harm.

2. the concept of proportionality of the risk and the cost and feasibility of a proposed action

One of the primary foundations of the precautionary principle, and globally accepted definitions, results from the work of the Rio Conference, or "Earth Summit" in 1992. Principle No. 15 of the Rio Declaration notes: "In order to protect the environment, the precautionary approach shall be widely applied by States according to their capabilities. Where there are threats of serious or irreversible damage, lack of full scientific certainty shall not be used as a reason for postponing cost-effective measures to prevent environmental degradation."

The 1998 Wingspread Statement on the Precautionary Principle summarises the principle this way: "When an activity raises threats of harm to human health or the environment, precautionary measures should be taken even if some cause and effect relationships are not fully established scientifically." The Wingspread Conference on the Precautionary Principle was convened by the Science and Environmental Health Network.

The 2 February 2000, Commission of the European Communities, *Communication from the Commission on the Precautionary Principle*, noted that, "The precautionary principle is not defined in the Treaty, which prescribes it [the Precautionary Principle] only once – to protect the environment. But in practice, its scope is much wider, and specifically where preliminary-objective-scientific-evaluation indicates that there are reasonable grounds for concern that potentially dangerous effects on the environment, human, animal or [and] plant health may be inconsistent with the high level of protection [for what] chosen for the Community."

The 29 January 2000 Cartagena Protocol on Biosafety says, in regard to controversies over GMOs: "Lack of scientific certainty due to insufficient relevant scientific information ... shall not prevent the Party of [I]mport, in order to avoid or minimize such potential adverse effects, from taking a decision, as appropriate, with regard to the import of the living modified organism in question."

## Application

The application of the precautionary principle is hampered by both lack of political will, as well as the wide range of interpretations placed on it. One study identified 14 different formulations of the principle in treaties and nontreaty declarations. R.B. Stewart (2002) reduced the precautionary principle to four basic versions:

1. Scientific uncertainty should not automatically preclude regulation of activities that pose a potential risk of significant harm (Non-Preclusion PP).

2. Regulatory controls should incorporate a margin of safety; activities should be limited below the level at which no adverse effect has been observed or predicted (Margin of Safety PP).

3. Activities that present an uncertain potential for significant harm should be subject to best technology available requirements to minimise the risk of harm unless the proponent of the activity shows that they present no appreciable risk of harm (BAT PP).

4. Activities that present an uncertain potential for significant harm should be prohibited unless the proponent of the activity shows that it presents no appreciable risk of harm (Prohibitory PP).

In deciding how to apply the principle, analysis may use a cost-benefit analysis that factors in both the opportunity cost of not acting, and the option value of waiting for further information before acting. One of the difficulties of the application of the principle in modern policy-making is that there is often an irreducible conflict between different interests, so that the debate necessarily involves politics.

## Strong Vs. Weak

*Strong precaution* holds that regulation is required whenever there is a possible risk to health, safety, or the environment, even if the supporting evidence is speculative and even if the economic costs of regulation are high. In 1982, the United Nations World Charter for Nature gave the first international recognition to the strong version of the principle, suggesting that when "potential adverse effects are not fully understood, the activities should not proceed." The widely publicised Wingspread Declaration, from a meeting of environmentalists in 1998, is another example of the strong version. Strong precaution can also be termed as a "no-regrets" principle, where costs are not considered in preventative action.

*Weak precaution* holds that lack of scientific evidence does not preclude action if damage would otherwise be serious and irreversible. Humans practice weak precaution every day, and often incur costs, to avoid hazards that are far from certain: we do not walk in moderately dangerous areas at night, we exercise, we buy smoke detectors, we buckle our seatbelts.

According to a publication by the New Zealand Treasury Department,

The weak version [of the Precautionary Principle] is the least restrictive and allows preventive measures to be taken in the face of uncertainty, but does not require them (eg, Rio Declaration 1992; United Nations Framework Convention of Climate Change 1992). To satisfy the threshold of harm, there must be some evidence relating to both the likelihood of occurrence and the severity of consequences. Some, but not all, require consideration of the costs of precautionary measures. Weak formulations do not preclude weighing benefits against the costs. Factors other than scientific uncertainty, including economic considerations, may provide legitimate grounds for postponing action. Under weak formulations, the requirement to justify the need for action (the burden of proof) generally falls on those advocating precautionary action. No mention is made of assignment of liability for environmental harm.

Strong versions justify or require precautionary measures and some also establish liability for environmental harm, which is effectively a strong form of "polluter pays". For example, the Earth Charter states: "When knowledge is limited apply a precautionary approach ... Place the burden of proof on those who argue that a proposed activity will not cause significant harm, and make the responsible parties liable for environmental harm." Reversal of proof requires those proposing an activity to prove that the product, process or technology is sufficiently "safe" before approval is granted. Requiring proof of "no environmental harm" before any action proceeds implies the public is not prepared to accept any environmental risk, no matter what economic or social benefits may arise (Peterson, 2006). At the extreme, such a requirement could involve bans and prohibitions on entire classes of potentially threatening activities or substances (Cooney, 2005). Over time, there has been a gradual transformation of the precautionary principle from what appears in the Rio Declaration to a stronger form that arguably [by whom] acts as restraint on development in the absence of firm evidence that it will do no harm.

## International Agreements and Declarations

The World Charter for Nature, which was adopted by the UN General Assembly in 1982, was the first international endorsement of the precautionary principle. The principle was implemented in an international treaty as early as the 1987 Montreal Protocol, and among other international treaties and declarations is reflected in the 1992 Rio Declaration on Environment and Development (signed at the United Nations Conference on Environment and Development).

## "Principle" Vs. "Approach"

No introduction to the precautionary principle would be complete without brief reference to the difference between the precautionary principle and the precautionary approach. Principle 15 of the Rio Declaration 1992 states that: "in order to protect the environment, the precautionary approach shall be widely applied by States according to their capabilities. Where there are threats of serious or irreversible damage, lack of full scientific certainty shall be not used as a reason for postponing cost-effective measures to prevent environmental degradation." As Garcia (1995) pointed out, "the wording, largely similar to that of the principle, is subtly different in that: (1) it recognizes that there may be differences in local capabilities to apply the approach, and (2) it calls for cost-effectiveness in applying the approach, e.g., taking economic and social costs into account." The 'approach' is generally considered a softening of the 'principle'.

"As Recuerda has noted, the distinction between the 'precautionary principle' and a 'precautionary approach' is diffuse and, in some contexts, controversial. In the negotiations of international declarations, the United States has opposed the use of the term 'principle' because this term has special connotations in legal language, due to the fact that a 'principle of law` is a source of law. This means that it is compulsory, so a court can quash or confirm a decision through the application of the precautionary principle. In this sense, the precautionary principle is not a simple idea or a desideratum but a source of law. This is the legal status of the precautionary principle in the European Union. On the other hand, an 'approach' usually does not have the same meaning, although in some particular cases an approach could be binding. A precautionary approach is a particular 'lens' used to identify risk that every prudent person possesses (Recuerda, 2008)

## European Commission

On 2 February 2000, the European Commission issued a Communication on the precautionary principle, in which it adopted a procedure for the application of this concept, but without giving a detailed definition of it. Paragraph 2 of article 191 of the Lisbon Treaty states that

*"Union policy on the environment shall aim at a high level of protection taking into account the diversity of situations in the various regions of the Union. It shall be based on the precautionary principle and on the principles that preventive action should be taken, that environmental damage should as a priority be rectified at source and that the polluter should pay."*

After the adoption of the European Commission's Communication on the precautionary principle, the principle has come to inform much EU policy, including areas beyond environmental policy. As of 2006 it had been integrated into EU laws "in matters such as general product safety, the use of additives for use in animal nutrition, the incineration of waste, and the regulation of genetically modified organisms." Through its application in case law, it has become a "general principle of EU law."

## France

In France, the Charter for the Environment contains a formulation of the precautionary principle (article 5):

When the occurrence of any damage, albeit unpredictable in the current state of scientific knowledge, may seriously and irreversibly harm the environment, public authorities shall, with due respect for the principle of precaution and the areas within their jurisdiction, ensure the implementation of procedures for risk assessment and the adoption of temporary measures commensurate with the risk involved in order to preclude the occurrence of such damage.

## USA

On 18 July 2005, the City of San Francisco passed a Precautionary Principle Purchasing ordinance, which requires the city to weigh the environmental and health costs of its $600 million in annual purchases – for everything from cleaning supplies to computers. Members of the Bay Area Working Group on the Precautionary Principle including the Breast Cancer Fund, helped bring this to fruition.

## Japan

In 1997, Japan tried to use the consideration of the precautionary principle in a WTO SPS Agreement on the Application of Sanitary and Phytosanitary Measures case, as Japan's requirement to test each variety of agricultural products (apples, cherries, peaches, walnuts, apricots, pears, plums and quinces) for the efficacy of treatment against codling moths was challenged.

This moth is a pest that does not occur in Japan, and whose introduction has the potential to cause serious damage. The United States claimed that it was not necessary to test each variety of a fruit for the efficacy of the treatment, and that this varietal testing requirement was unnecessarily burdensome.

## Australia

The most important Australian court case so far, due to its exceptionally detailed consideration of the precautionary principle, is Telstra Corporation Limited v Hornsby Shire Council [2006] NSWLEC 133 (24 March 2006) .

The Principle was summarised by reference to the NSW *Protection of the Environment Administration Act 1991*, which itself provides a good definition of the principle:

"If there are threats of serious or irreversible environmental damage, lack of full scientific certainty should not be used as a reasoning for postponing measures to prevent environmental degradation. In the application of the principle... decisions should be guided by: (i) careful evaluation to avoid, wherever practicable, serious or irreversible damage to the environment; and (ii) an assessment of risk-weighted consequence of various options".

The most significant points of Justice Preston's decision are the following findings:

1. The principle and accompanying need to take precautionary measures is "triggered" when two prior conditions exist: a threat of serious or irreversible damage, and scientific uncertainty as to the extent of possible damage.

2. Once both are satisfied, "a proportionate precautionary measure may be taken to avert the anticipated threat of environmental damage, but it should be proportionate."

3. The threat of serious or irreversible damage should invoke consideration of five factors: the scale of threat (local, regional etc.); the perceived value of the threatened environment; whether the possible impacts are manageable; the level of public concern, and whether there is a rational or scientific basis for the concern.

4. The consideration of the level of scientific uncertainty should involve factors which may include: what would constitute sufficient evidence; the level and

kind of uncertainty; and the potential to reduce uncertainty.

5. The principle shifts the burden of proof. If the principle applies, the burden shifts: "a decision maker must assume the threat of serious or irreversible environmental damage is... a reality [and] the burden of showing this threat... is negligible reverts to the proponent..."

6. The precautionary principle invokes preventative action: "the principle permits the taking of preventative measures without having to wait until the reality and seriousness of the threat become fully known".

7. "The precautionary principle should not be used to try to avoid all risks."

8. The precautionary measures appropriate will depend on the combined effect of "the degree of seriousness and irreversibility of the threat and the degree of uncertainty... the more significant and uncertain the threat, the greater...the precaution required". "...measures should be adopted... proportionate to the potential threats".

## Philippines

A petition filed 17 May 2013 by environmental group Greenpeace Southeast Asia and farmer-scientist coalition Masipag (*Magsasaka at Siyentipiko sa Pagpapaunlad ng Agrikultura*) asked the Appellate court to stop the planting of Bt eggplant in test fields, saying the impacts of such an undertaking to the environment, native crops and human health are still unknown. The Court of Appeals granted the petition, citing the precautionary principle stating "when human activities may lead to threats of serious and irreversible damage to the environment that is scientifically plausible but uncertain, actions shall be taken to avoid or diminish the threat." Respondents filed a motion for reconsideration in June 2013 and on 20 September 2013 the Court of Appeals chose to uphold their May decision saying the *bt talong* field trials violate the people's constitutional right to a "balanced and healthful ecology." The Supreme Court on 8 December 2015 permanently stopped the field testing for Bt (Bacillus thuringiensis) talong (eggplant), upholding the decision of the Court of Appeals which stopped the field trials for the genetically modified eggplant. The court is the first in the world to adopt the precautionary principle regarding GMO products in its decision.

## Corporate

The Body Shop International, a UK-based cosmetics company, included the precautionary principle in their 2006 Chemicals Strategy.

## Environment and Health

Fields typically concerned by the precautionary principle are the possibility of:

- Global warming or abrupt climate change in general
- Extinction of species
- Introduction of new and potentially harmful products into the environment, threatening biodiversity (e.g., genetically modified organisms)
- Threats to public health, due to new diseases and techniques (e.g., AIDS transmitted through blood transfusion)
- Long-term effects of new technologies (e.g. health concerns regarding radiation from cell phones and other electronics communications devices)
- Persistent or acute pollution (e.g., asbestos, endocrine disruptors)
- Food safety (e.g., Creutzfeldt–Jakob disease)
- Other new biosafety issues (e.g., artificial life, new molecules)

The precautionary principle is often applied to biological fields because changes cannot be easily contained and have the potential of being global. The principle has less relevance to contained fields such as aeronautics, where the few people undergoing risk have given informed consent (e.g., a test pilot). In the case of technological innovation, containment of impact tends to be more difficult if that technology can self-replicate. Bill Joy emphasised the dangers of replicating genetic technology, nanotechnology, and robotic technology in his article in *Wired*, "Why the future doesn't need us", though he does not specifically cite the precautionary principle. The application of the principle can be seen in the public policy of requiring pharmaceutical companies to carry out clinical trials to show that new medications are safe.

Oxford based philosopher Nick Bostrom discusses the idea of a future powerful superintelligence, and the risks that we/it face should it attempt to gain atomic level control of matter.

Application of the principle modifies the status of innovation and risk assessment: it is not the risk that must be avoided or amended, but a potential risk that must be prevented. Thus, in the case of regulation of scientific research, there is a third party beyond the scientist and the regulator: the consumer.

In an analysis concerning application of the precautionary principle to nanotechnology, Chris Phoenix and Mike Treder posit that there are *two forms* of the principle, which they call the "strict form" and the "active form". The former "requires inaction when action might pose a risk", while the latter means "choosing less risky alternatives when they are available, and [...] taking responsibility for potential risks." Thomas Alured Faunce has argued for stronger application of the precautionary principle by chemical and health technology regulators particularly in relation to $Tio_2$ and ZnO nanoparticles in sunscreens, biocidal nanosilver in waterways and products whose manufacture, handling or recycling exposes humans to the risk of inhaling multi-walled carbon nanotubes.

## Resource Management

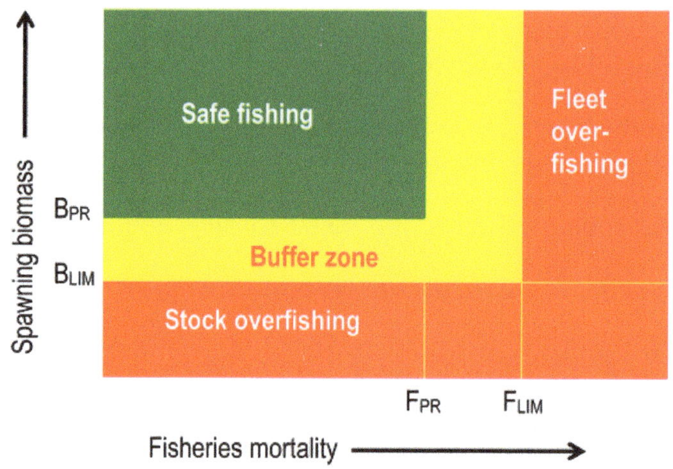


The Traffic Light colour convention, showing the concept of Harvest Control Rule (HCR), specifying when a rebuilding plan is mandatory in terms of precautionary and limit reference points for spawning biomass and fishing mortality rate.

Several natural resources like fish stocks are now managed by precautionary approach, through Harvest Control Rules (HCR) based upon the precautionary principle. The figure indicates how the principle is implemented in the cod fisheries management proposed by the International Council for the Exploration of the Sea.

In classifying endangered species, the precautionary principle means that if there is doubt about an animal's or plant's exact conservation status, the one that would cause the strongest protective measures to be realised should be chosen. Thus, a species like the silvery pigeon that might exist in considerable numbers and simply be under-recorded or might just as probably be long extinct is not classified as "data deficient" or "extinct" (which both do not require any protective action to be taken), but as "critically endangered" (the conservation status that confers the need for the strongest protection), whereas the increasingly rare, but probably not yet endangered emerald starling is classified as "data deficient", because there is urgent need for research to clarify its status rather than for conservation action to save it from extinction.

If, for example, a large ground-water body that many people use for drinking water is contaminated by bacteria (e-coli 0157 H7, campylobacter or leptospirosis) and the source of contamination is strongly suspected to be dairy cows but the exact science is not yet able to provide absolute proof, the cows should be removed from the environment until they are proved, by the dairy industry, not to be the source or until that industry ensures that such contamination will not recur.

## Criticisms

Critics of the principle use arguments similar to those against other formulations of technological conservatism.

## Internal Inconsistency – applying Strong PP Risks Causing Harm

Strong formulations of the precautionary principle, without regard to its most basic provisions that it is to be applied only where risks are potentially high AND not easily calculable, applied to the principle itself as a policy decision, may rule out its own use. The reason suggested is that preventing innovation from coming to market means that only current technology may be used, and current technology itself may cause harm or leave needs unmet; there is a risk of causing harm by blocking innovation. As Michael Crichton wrote in his novel *State of Fear*: "The 'precautionary principle', properly applied, forbids the precautionary principle." For example, forbidding nuclear power plants based on concerns about risk means continuing to rely on power plants that burn fossil fuels, which continue to release greenhouse gases. In another example, the Hazardous Air Pollutant provisions in the 1990 amendments to the US Clean Air Act are an example of the Precautionary Principle where the onus is now on showing a listed compound is harmless. Under this rule no distinction is made between those air Pollutants that provide a higher or lower risk, so operators tend to choose less-examined agents that are not on the existing list.

## Blocking Innovation and Progress Generally

Because applications of strong formulations of the precautionary principle can be used to block innovation, a technology which brings advantages may be banned by precautionary principle because of its potential for negative impacts, leaving the positive benefits unrealised.

The precautionary principle has been ethically questioned on the basis that its application could block progress in developing countries.

## Vagueness and Plausibility

The precautionary principle calls for inaction in the face of scientific uncertainty, but some formulations do not specify the minimal threshold of plausibility of risk that acts as a "triggering" condition, so that any indication that a proposed product or activity might harm health or the environment is sufficient to invoke the principle. In *Sancho vs. DOE,* Helen Gillmor, Senior District Judge, wrote in a dismissal of Wagner's lawsuit which included a popular worry that the LHC could cause "destruction of the earth" by a black hole:

Injury in fact requires some "credible threat of harm." *Cent. Delta Water Agency v. United States*, 306 F.3d 938, 950 (9th Cir. 2002). At most, Wagner has alleged that experiments at the Large Hadron Collider (the "Collider") have "potential adverse consequences." Speculative fear of future harm does not constitute an injury in fact sufficient to confer standing. *Mayfield*, 599 F.3d at 970.

8

# Various Risk Management Softwares

There are many econometric techniques that help in the process of financial risk modeling. Actimize provides prevention of financial crime and also provides risk management products and services to the financial service industry. Alternatively, the risk management software included in this chapter are PillarOne.RiskAnalytics, LogicManager and sureID. This section will provide an in-depth understanding of risk management softwares.

## Actimize

Actimize, Inc., a wholly owned subsidiary of NICE Systems, provides financial crime prevention, compliance and risk management products and services to the financial services industry. Primarily headquartered in New York City, United States, Actimize sells its software to firms and regulators worldwide. Its revenue is expected to cross the $100 million mark in 2010. Service providers and channel partners include Checkfree, FNIS, MasterCard, Pershing, IBM and Unisys.

### Products

NICE Actimize has core offerings across all financial crime prevention and compliance areas built on a unified reporting and case management platform. Actimize is known for its use of analytics and modeling techniques that uncover anomalous financial transactions, like fraud, money laundering and market manipulation.

Additionally NICE Actimize provides Know Your Customer/Client Due Diligence (KYC-CDD), FATCA compliance and Enterprise Risk Case Manager solutions.

### Customers

NICE Actimize has more than 300 clients including all top 10 global banks and many financial services industry regulators. Customers include Bank of America, Barclays, BB&T, Citi, Capitalone, Comerica, CFTC, HSBC, MasterCard, Capital One, E*Trade Financial Corporation, Mizuho, RBS, Amundi, Société Générale, The Vanguard Group, UBS and Morgan Stanley.

As an example, banks use Actimize card fraud prevention solutions to block fraudulent credit card transactions as they occur, whether at a point of sale, automated teller machine, online or over the phone. Similarly, financial institutions and securities trading firms also use Actimize products to uncover suspicious transactions that may indicate illegal money laundering and capital market manipulation.

## History

In 1999, Actimize was founded in Silicon Wadi, an area with a high concentration of high-tech industries in the coastal plain in Israel, similar to Silicon Valley in California by Israeli ex-army colleagues who specialized in business intelligence and data warehousing. The company focused its attention on building packaged trading compliance, anti-money laundering and fraud prevention software solutions for the financial services industry. Actimize was acquired by NICE Systems (NASDAQ: NICE) in July 2007 for $280 million and has grown into one of three of NICE's main lines of business.

NICE Systems shares are traded on NASDAQ as well as on the Tel Aviv Stock Exchange; where it is part of the TA-25 Index. NICE Total cash and equivalents as of December 31, 2009 were $548.5 million, with no debt.

In June 2009, Actimize acquired the assets of Syfact, a pioneer in enterprise investigative case management solutions. Actimize acquired rival anti-money laundering software vendor Fortent for $73.5 million in August 2009. In October 2008, Actimize acquired ATM and debit card fraud detection models, analytics technology and a data consortium with billions of ATM / debit transactions from BasePoint.

## Accolades

Chartis recognized NICE Actimize as the category leader for financial crime risk management technology in its 2014 RiskTech100® rankings. NICE Actimize was also recognized as the "Category Leader" for Financial Crime Solutions in the 2014 Chartis RiskTech Quadrant®. NICE Actimize was selected as a "Best-in-Class" provider in three categories, in CEB TowerGroup's "2013 Know Your Customer" Anti-Money Laundering Technology Report. The three categories in which the NICE Actimize Customer Due Diligence solution received a "Best in Class" designation were for "Initial Validation", "Compliance Operations" and "Enterprise Support". NICE Actimize was positioned as a Leading Vendor in the 2013 Aite Group Trade Surveillance Compliance Market Impact Report. The report highlights the NICE Actimize surveillance and communications solutions, including the breadth of its offerings and quality of its analytics. Actimize has been named Most Innovative Anti-Money Laundering (AML) Solution Provider by Financial-i magazine, rated as the only "Strong Positive" in Gartner's MarketScope for Enterprise Fraud Management, ranked atop Gartner's Magic Quadrant for Web Fraud Detection two years in a row, identified by Datamonitor as the only financial crimes vendor out of 29 reviewed with core competencies across all AML and fraud detection areas, named as a 'Leader' in Celent's "Automated Wealth Management Compliance Solutions" report for its Sales Practices solution, with high score for "breadth of functionality", "advanced technology", "largest live client base" and "depth of client services" and Bank Technology News recognized Actimize as a "Top 25 Innovator" for its Insider Fraud solution.

# PillarOne.RiskAnalytics

PillarOne.RiskAnalytics is a risk modeling tool for the European insurance industry, constructed in response to the EU Solvency II Directive. It is distributed as cross-platform open source software. Developed since 2008 by the "PillarOne community", the tool is intended to provide insurance companies with the tools to build their own internal models to evaluate their risks, in order to assess their capital requirements.

## History

With the upcoming Solvency II regulations for the European markets came the need of modeling risk for most of the European insurance companies. The PillarOne project was initiated with the aim of developing an open source risk modeling software which satisfies both typical users and the bodies which audit and regulate them. Consequently, transparency plays a major role. Markus Stricker and Stefan Kunz, et al. are developing the software in cooperation with PillarOne community members. Work began in 2008 and led to the first software releases a few months later. Since then, PillarOne. RiskAnalytics is being further improved.

## Scope

The project's main objectives are:

- To build an open source risk modeling tool for insurance companies which can be used as stand-alone as well as multi user client–server version
- To provide a rich business logic library which can be used to build partial as well as full internal models for Solvency II, ALM, reinsurance optimization
- To encourage the exchange on actuarial modeling and the development of standards

The main target users are actuaries, risk managers, risk controllers, auditors and regulators in the insurance industry.

## Features

PillarOne.RiskAnalytics is developed for building and analyzing partial internal and internal risk models.

- Deterministic or stochastic models
- Post simulation calculation of key figures such as VaR, TVar, volatility, etc.
- Components for modeling non-life underwriting portfolios, claims distributions (attritional, frequency severity for single per risk and cat), reinsurance contracts, dependency modeling
- Sample models
- Template models
- Hierarchical, tabular presentation of results and drill down to single iterations
- Zoomable graphics on the simulation result level and on the single iteration level
- Comparable results and parametrisations
- Batch runs
- Parameter validation support
- Period and cut-off date modelling possible

All PillarOne applications are built on the same IT application framework and offer

- Data validation
- Data versioning
- Can be deployed as stand-alone or as multi user client–server application
- Auditable (if deployed in client–server mode)
- Authorization and authentication (LDAP or ActiveDirectory integration in client–server mode)
- Reporting engine (pdf, hmtl, and excel-output)
- Copy-paste interaction with MS Office

## Technical Details

PillarOne.RiskAnalytics is a cross-platform open source software available for all major operating systems supporting Java. It is distributed as open source software under the General Public License v3. PillarOne.RiskAnalytics is based on a number of other open source projects:

- Grails, which provides the IT application stack including the Spring Framework and the Hibernate OR mapping for the database back-end

- Jasper for the reporting engine
- Quartz for scheduling tasks

The presentation layer for the GUI is built with an ultra-light client framework. It is not an open source product, but the developer licences have been donated to the project.

The roadmap for future developments is published on PillarOne's issue tracking website.

## Development

- v1.0 – Released on 10.7 2010More than 100 pages of documentation available, data validation service, a multi-company insurance group model.
- v0.6 Released on 14 April 2010Editing multi-dimensional parameters, performance, surplus in dynamic models
- v0.5 Released on 12.2.2010Business logic: Reserve Risks. Application features: Compare views for parameters and results, batch run, modularization with plug-ins
- v0.4 – Released on 13.9.2009Data-driven model extensions; performance improvement for database access and simulation engine.
- v0.3 – Released on 09.04.2009Changes: performance improvements, more chart options, multi period modeling, report generation and better installer.
- v0.2 – Released on 16 January 2009Changes: Focus on usability of the application and new reinsurance contracts and copula components.
- v0.1 – Released on 28 October 2008Changes: modeling infrastructure to run Monte-Carlo simulations and initial business logic library to build partial internal models for property and casualty in a Solvency II context.

## Background

The software is built and developed by the PillarOne community, which is a group of software developers, insurers, re-insurers, auditors and consultants. The community's name PillarOne is derived from the Solvency II regime, which is divided in three pillars. Pillar 1 describes the quantitative requirements. Generally binding rules derived from the principles will govern the calculation of the minimum capital requirement (MCR) and the solvency capital requirement (SCR) using the so-called standard formula. It will no longer be sufficient for insurers simply to respect simple rules as in the past, as the responsibility for applying the new rules will rest with them. They will be obliged to evaluate their risks and will need effective, process-based risk management to do this. Since all insurers in the European markets have to obey the rules of Solvency II by 2012, the companies are facing the imminent question whether to build (partial) internal models on their own, or use the standard formula. PillarOne.RiskAnalytics is intended to provide insurance companies with the tools to build their own internal models.

## Logic Manager

LogicManager, Inc. is an Enterprise Risk Management software provider, and the author of the RIMS Risk Maturity Model for Enterprise Risk Management. LogicManager is based in Boston, Massachusetts and was listed as a top vendor in ERM and eGRC software by Forrester Research in 2014 and 2016.

### History

Founded in 2005 by CEO Steven Minsky, LogicManager offers a Software-as-a-Service ERM/eGRC platform of scientifically validated Enterprise Risk Management decision and diagnostic tools for corporate governance, risk and compliance. Their patent-pending taxonomy technology is used by over 2000 customers worldwide.

### Platform and Services

LogicManager's ERM software aids risk professionals in identifying, mitigating and monitoring their organization's risk portfolio. The company's patent-pending taxonomy technology allows users to view existing relationships between risks in order to identify root causes of risks and how they affect strategic goals. LogicManager offers a range of point GRC solutions, as well as complete eGRC or ERM platforms, along with ERM consulting and support services.

The software is designed to identify redundant or overlapping activities automatically, and provide direct connections to performance management through the adoption of standards and reuse of information. As reported by The CIO Review, users can expect to see results within 90 days.

### RIMS Risk Maturity Model

The RIMS Risk Maturity Model for Enterprise Risk Management was co-developed by LogicManager and the Risk and Insurance Management Society in 2008. The RMM is an online assessment that helps users benchmark the progress of their ERM program. Scores on the RMM range from 1-5, with scores of 3 and above representing the presence of a mature ERM program. Scoring is based on a company's performance along 7 key performance attributes, which consist of 25 success factors and 68 key competency drivers.

In 2008, a research study concluded that, at the 95% confidence level, there was a positive correlation, which indicated the existence of a direct relationship, between higher RMM scores and higher business.

In 2014, a study of RMM data, entitled "The Valuation Impact of Enterprise Risk Management Maturity," was published in The Journal of Risk and Insurance by a research team from Queen's University. This study provided statistical evidence of up to a 25% public valuation premium for firms that reach mature levels of enterprise risk management, as measured by the Risk Maturity Model.

### Awards and Recognition

- In 2016, Forrester awarded GRC software vendor LogicManager with a perfect score in Customer Feedback and the second highest score in Product Vision and Strategy.
- In 2014, Forrester selected LogicManager as the governance, risk, and compliance vendor with the highest marks in customer satisfaction, ease-of-use, and price.
- In October 2014, The CIO Review chose LogicManager for its list of the 20 Most Promising Compliance Technology Solution Providers.

## SureID

SureID, formerly named Eid Passport, is a privately owned high-assurance identity management company based in the U.S. state of Oregon. Founded in 2000, the company operates a system primarily used by the U.S. military and large organizations to manage the identities of vendors and third-parties. Headquartered in Hillsboro, the 500-employee company had revenues of about $40 million in 2014.

### History

Steve Larson came up with the idea behind the company in 2000 when Bryan Nelson of Wavetrend Technologies Ltd. approached Unicru Inc., where Larson was the chief executive. Nelson, CEO of Wavetrend, inquired if Unicru could use Wavetrend's long-range radio-frequency identification scanning technology. Unicru's business model could not incorporate the technology, but Larson thought of a way the technology could be used in a similar fashion, and spun off what was then Eid Access. "Eid" stands for either employee or electronic identification; the name is not a reference to the Islamic holidays. While Unicru focused on automated background checks for employers, Eid would be used to provide similar assurances for vendors at retail outlets and other locations, and allow for easy access and tracking of the vendors. Originally, the company hoped to generate revenue by 2002, but Eid did not earn revenue until 2004.

In 2003, Eid Access was named as one of two winners, with Phoseon Technology the other, of the Portland, Oregon-based *Business Journal*'s Oregon Business Plan Competition. At the time, the company was located in Beaverton, Oregon, and had 22 employees, while its board of directors included people such as retired general Merrill McPeak. In June 2003, Kroll invested $2 million in the company for a 19 percent ownership stake, as well as taking on the background checks that are a part of the Eid system. Also in June, company president Larry Neitling went back into retirement, and Ed Hahn was named president of Eid. Eid changed its name in July 2003 to Eid Passport from Eid Access.

The company first installed its system in retail stores in the Chicago, Illinois, area in April 2003, starting with K-Mart stores. Revenue forecasts in 2003 called for $19 million for the fiscal year ending in 2004 growing to $67 million the following year, at which point Eid planned to make a profit. In August 2005, Ralph E. Eberhart, a retired United States Air Force general, was appointed to the company's board of directors. By October 2005, Eid had grown to 30 employees, but was still not profitable. By March 2007, Eid had grown to 53 employees and expected to have revenues of $18 to $24 million that year. Politician Tom Ridge was added to the company's board of directors that year as well, after the company had raised a total of $30 million in capital since its inception. Former United States Coast Guard admiral Thomas H. Collins was also on the board at that time.

Headquarters in Hillsboro

The company obtained a patent in 2009 for its business method. C&H Patriot Security, based in Virginia, was acquired by Eid in October 2009. For 2009, Eid had revenues of $6.6 million, and the next year had grown to 75 employees. Eid filed a lawsuit against Intellicheck Mobilisa Inc. in November 2009, accusing the competitor of anti-competitive behavior after Intellicheck bought Positive Access Corp. and canceled that company's license with Eid. Eid later expanded the suit to include false advertising. In July 2010, the United States District Court for the District of Oregon denied a motion to dismiss the suit.

Eid added a support office in Minot, North Dakota, in 2011. The company announced they would relocate the corporate headquarters from near Washington Square in Tigard to Hillsboro. Eid's new 72,000-square-foot (6,700 m²) headquarters are along the Sunset Highway in a three-story brick building that formerly housed an office of Credence Systems Corporation. At the time, revenue had grown from $10 million in 2010 to $30 million in 2011, and the company had added almost 100 jobs during that time, and planned to hire 100 more. The new office officially opened in August 2012 with a ceremony featuring board member Tom Ridge along with U.S. representatives Kurt Schrader and Suzanne Bonamici, as well as Hillsboro politicians. At the time of the opening of the new headquarters, Eid had 250 employees company-wide with satellite offices in Washington, D.C., and the support center in Minot. In 2015, EiD added 63,000 square feet (5,900 m²) of space by leasing an adjacent building to allow for growth from 330 employees.

In September 2015, Eid Passport, Inc., changed its name to SureID, Inc., citing the new name as a better reflection of its mission to providing identity management solutions to organizations and individuals. The company announced an investment from Goldman Sachs of $25 million in November 2015.

## Products

The company currently has three product offerings: RAPIDGate, RAPIDGate-Premier and VendorPassport. SureID signs-up retailers or other facilities, and then installs equipment at the individual locations that include radio-frequency identification (RFID) scanning equipment. The retailer or facility then requires its vendors to use the system, at which point the vendors submit each of their employees to an SureID background check. Upon passing the background check, the vendors are issued identification cards by SureID that include RFID technology. These cards can be read by the equipment from up to 300 feet (91 m) away. Then, when vendors enter a location, the system tracks when they arrived and left.

Fees are generally charged to the vendors for using the system, allowing for little in the way of expenses for the retailer or other location implementing the system. However, vendors only need to pay the fees once per employee per year, as the system then allows tracking of the same vendors at other retailers that also use the product. SureID then charges an annual fee to the vendor for both the company and each vendor employee to ensure both are still in good standing. Customers have included the United States Marine Corps, Manpower Inc., K-Mart, and Norwegian Cruise Lines.

## Awards

Inc. Magazine included Eid Passport on its Inc. 5000 List of the fastest growing companies in America in 2011, 2012 and 2013.

In June 2013, the *Portland Business Journal* named Eid Passport one of the fastest-growing private companies in Oregon and Southwest Washington for the fourth consecutive year.

In May 2013, Eid Passport founder Steve Larson was named a finalist for the Ernst & Young Entrepreneur of the Year Award in the Pacific Northwest.

In 2012 and 2013, Government Security News named Eid Passport a finalist in its annual Homeland Security Awards Competition.

9

# Risk Management: A Global Overview

The organizations and institutes working for risk management are Risk and Insurance Management Society, Institute of Risk Management, Global Association of Risk Professionals and Financial Risk Manager. Risk and Insurance Management Society is an association that dedicates itself to the practice of risk management. It has a number of nonprofit charitable entities and 3500 industrial entities. The chapter on organizations and institutes working for risk management offers an insightful focus, keeping in mind the subject matter.

## Institute of Risk Management

Institute of Risk Management (IRM) is a risk management professional education and training body. It was established in 1986, as a not-for-profit company limited by guarantee, and is governed by a Board of Directors elected from members with specialist non-member support. It has around 6000 members in more than 100 countries and has over 500 students studying risk management at any time. It takes a broad view of risk management as a discipline to be applied in all organisations, public and private, and from all sectors, covering risks of all types.

The Institute provides both taught and distance learning education, training and professional development in risk management at a range of levels. IRM Membership is recognised worldwide as the sign of a risk management professional and is achieved through examination and relevant experience.

The Institute is the only organisation currently offering vocational post-graduate level qualifications designed from the ground-up to meet the challenge of Enterprise Risk Management (ERM). Many other bodies run short courses focussed on individual areas of risk (e.g. insurable risk, risk in banks, health and safety, project risk, disaster recovery etc.) and in some cases there is the option to take an additional ERM paper but only IRM offers dedicated ERM qualifications.

### Membership Grades

- Fellow (FIRM) – Open to members who can demonstrate accredited practical experience, a record of personal professional development and proven contribution and support to the Institution

- Member (MIRM) – Requires completion of Institute's Diploma programme or equivalent qualification and a minimum of three years work experience
- Certified Fellow (CFIRM) and Certified Member (CMIRM) - additional award for members and fellows who can also demonstrate practical experience in line with IRM's professional standards
- Graduate (GradIRM) - Requires completion of Institute's Diploma programme or equivalent qualification recognised by the IRM
- Specialist (SIRM) - Requires formal qualification of the applicant in a risk specialism - e.g. audit, health and safety, risk financing, environment, project management, business continuity etc.
- Certificant (IRMCert) – Completion of the Institute's Certificate programme
- Student – Open to all candidates registered for the Institute's examinations
- Affiliate – Open to anyone with an interest in risk management. Discounted rates are available to groups of 10 or more. Affiliate membership is free to university students on IRM approved courses

## IRM Courses

- The International Diploma in Risk Management – A challenging post graduate professional qualification, usually taken over 3–5 years and completed via distance learning. It is recognised worldwide as the sign of a risk management professional.
- The International Certificate in Risk Management – This practitioner-level qualification provides a sound foundation in risk management theory and practice. It can be taken as a stand-alone course or as an introduction to the IRM Diploma. It is offered on a distance learning basis and takes 6–9 months to complete, with two intakes each year.
- Risk Management in Financial Services – focuses on ERM in banking and insurance, offered on a distance learning basis and takes 6–9 months to complete, with two intakes each year.
- Fundamentals of Risk Management – This two-day training programme provides a broad introduction to the subject of risk management. It aims to improve knowledge and practical skills in the identification, assessment and control of business risk, and provides an introduction to ERM and ISO 31000.

These qualifications are moderated by a panel of leading educationalists drawn from universities and business schools across the world. The qualifications are delivered by means of distance learning but the written examinations are taken in person and can be arranged virtually anywhere in the world.

### IRM Publications

The IRM is responsible for the 2002 Risk Management Standard in conjunction with The Association of Insurance and Risk Managers (AIRMIC) and ALARM, the National Forum for Risk Management in the Public Sector. The standard is available free of charge in 17 world languages. IRM has also issued free guidance notes on the implementation of ISO 31000 and on Risk Appetite, Risk Culture, Cyber Risk, Extended Enterprise, Competition Law and Creating Value from Insurer Risk Models.

## Risk and Insurance Management Society

The Risk and Insurance Management Society, Inc. (RIMS) is a professional association dedicated to advancing the practice of risk management. It was founded in 1950, and is headquartered in Manhattan. It publishes the industry-focused *Risk Management* magazine.

RIMS represents more than 3,500 industrial, service, nonprofit, charitable and governmental entities. The Society serves more than 10,000 risk management professionals around the world. There are 79 chapters across the United States, Canada, Mexico, and Japan.

The RIMS Risk Maturity Model is an online assessment tool for enterprise risk management (ERM). Developed in 2006, it has been recognized as a best practice framework by several National Organizations. Over 2,000 corporates and organizations have baselined their ERM maturity with the RIMS Risk Maturity Model.

Given appropriate experience and educational background, RIMS offers the certification RIMS-CRMP (*RIMS Certified Risk Management Professional*) and the professional designations CRM (*Canadian Risk Management*) and RF (*RIMS Fellow*); various intermediate designations are available via certification exams.

## Global Association of Risk Professionals

The Global Association of Risk Professionals (GARP) is a not-for-profit organization and the only globally recognized membership association for risk managers. With more than 150,000 members from 195 countries, GARP's mission is to advance the risk profession through education, training, and the promotion of best practices globally.

In the areas of financial and energy risk management, GARP sets the global standard in professional designation with the Financial Risk Manager (FRM®) and Energy Risk Professional (ERP®) certifications. Through its educational programs, in-person and online events, and worldwide chapters, GARP promotes best practices in risk management and supports professional and career development for risk managers.

## Financial Risk Manager (FRM) Designation

The Financial Risk Manager (FRM) designation is the most globally respected and widely recognized certification for financial risk management. Currently, there are more than 30,000 FRMs practicing worldwide in 141 countries and territories globally. The FRM designation is the globally recognized standard for those who manage risk. Certified FRMs are part of an elite, global network, and are valued by top employers across diverse businesses. They are represented at nearly every major banking institution, government regulator, consulting firm and financial services institution around the world. Certified FRMs have achieved positions such as Chief Risk Officer, Senior Risk Analyst, Head of Operational Risk and Director of Risk Management.

Anyone can register to take the FRM Exam. FRM certification is awarded after a candidate has passed two rigorous multiple choice exams (FRM Exam Part I and Part II) and demonstrated two years of relevant work experience. Candidates must take the FRM Exam Part I before taking Part II. Certified FRMs are strongly encouraged to earn 40 hours of Continuing Professional Development (CPD) every two years to maintain the latest best practices in risk management.

## Energy Risk Professional (ERP) Designation

The Energy Risk Professional (ERP) designation is the first and only global certification for energy professionals. The ERP Program delivers a crucial framework for thinking critically about the entire energy value chain. Certified ERPs represent major energy companies, financial institutions with direct and indirect investments in energy, consulting and technology firms with energy-related practices, and government agencies.

ERP Certification is awarded after a candidate has passed a rigorous, two-part practice-oriented exam designed to test fundamental concepts associated with the complex physical and financial risks inherent in the major energy markets, candidates must also demonstrate two years of relevant work experience in order to become an ERP. To maintain their certification, ERPs must also be an active Individual Member of GARP and earn 40 hours of Continuing Professional Development (CPD) every two years to keep up to date with industry developments and practices. Anyone can register to take the ERP Exam.

## Financial Courses

Financial education begins with risk courses from GARP. Designed for both experienced professionals and those new to the risk field, GARP's courses help candidates begin and advance their careers in risk.

- Foundations: Level 1 is a self-guided eLearning course that provides an introduction to the fundamental areas of financial risk. The course pays special attention to the ways in which financial institutions operate and the impact of international regulations. Ideal for candidates who are new to risk management, Foundations provides a broad overview of risk-related topics such as credit, market, operational, insurance risk management, and the Basel Committee on Banking Supervision's regulatory principles (Basel Accords).
- Risk and Regulation: Level 2 is a four-part, self-study course designed with mid-level risk professionals in mind, and builds upon the concepts covered in the Foundations course. The course offers a detailed analysis of the industry's current methodologies, and gives a comprehensive review of governance structures, market, credit, operational risk, and asset and liability management. Risk and Regulation teaches candidates to understand the issues related to the identification, assessment, and mitigation of risks, and prepares them to handle risks in the workplace. The course culminates in a formal exam administered by Pearson VUE, and candidates who successfully pass will be awarded the GARP Risk and Regulation certificate. Candidates do not need to complete the Foundations: Level 1 course before taking the Risk and Regulation Series: Level 2.

## Continuing Professional Development (CPD)

With risk management constantly evolving and new standards emerging every day, GARP's CPD Program is structured to accommodate the diverse needs and career demands of an FRM or ERP. The program is designed to deliver a broad range of accessible programming to all FRMs and ERPs, regardless of personal time constraints or geographic location.

GARP partners with more than 40 organizations to bring participants a multitude of pre-approved programming. CPD Activity Providers are vetted through the CPD committee and deliver a broad range of professional development opportunities.

## Events

GARP events are designed to advance the practice of risk management by preparing risk professionals to make better business decisions. Conferences, conventions, executive briefings and master classes showcase the latest in international risk management thinking and inform participants of best-practice strategies. GARP events include active involvement of the world's respected international risk management practitioners, regulators, academics, and consultants who actively share their wealth of experience in open dialogue.

## Conferences, Forums, and Master Classes

Produced in collaboration with the GARP Content Committee, events are highly educational, practice-driven forums focusing on current market concerns, new regulations, and educational topics that affect the role of risk managers on a daily basis. These meetings present a valuable outlook on best practices in risk management and are designed to give experienced risk professionals the opportunity to debate, discuss, and share their diverse points-of-view on emerging topics.

## Executive Meetings and Custom Events

Executive meetings and custom events program are devised to facilitate open and informed dialogue among qualified risk professionals on current and emerging issues in risk management. Supported by a sole sponsor, GARP's executive meetings are invitation-only sessions facilitating uncensored and respectful dialogue on current and controversial topics. They may be structured as open or closed meetings depending on desired participant interaction and access.

## Membership

GARP Membership has developed around a culture of best practice shared by its FRMs, ERPs, staff, and a global community of professionals and practitioners committed to financial and energy risk management. Members who are a part of GARP's risk-focused community have access to expert knowledge and global networking opportunities, which is the benefit of GARP's deep connectivity with industry and academia. In 190 countries around the world, GARP members work in regional and global banks, asset management firms, insurance companies, central banks, securities regulators, hedge funds, universities, large industrial corporations and multinationals.

GARP Membership is held at the individual level, and because there are no technical requirements or qualifications for membership, there is no application process. Membership is elective and achieved through registration with the Association and the registrant chooses the Membership Type which best suits his/her needs. Premium memberships are established on a rolling calendar basis for a 12-month term. GARP Members are expected to act in accordance with the GARP Code of Conduct.

## Membership Types

- Individual: Individual Members have access to a premium collection of knowledge and networking benefits. These include GARP's Risk Intelligence website; discounts on risk education offerings, events, and learning materials; a monthly member newsletter, and exclusive offers from strategic partners. FRMs and ERPs who maintain their GARP Membership enjoy a more extensive set of benefits and a preferential fee.

- Student: Student Membership is available for those who are enrolled in a full-time program at a recognized accredited academic institution. Student Members are entitled to the same package of benefits as Individual Members, with the exception of the right to vote on GARP matters, and are offered a price more in alignment with their finances. With few exceptions, FRMs and ERPs are not eligible for Student Membership.

- Affiliate: Affiliates have basic access to a subset of benefits at no cost. They may attend GARP chapter meetings, receive certain newsletters and reports, participate in industry-sponsored webcasts, and use GARP's Career Center, but without the premium features associated with membership. Affiliate status never expires, and Affiliates can always upgrade to Individual Membership.

More details regarding GARP Membership, prices, features and benefits, are available here

## Chapters

Created for members, by members, GARP's global chapter network is a core benefit to being a part of the GARP community. With 76 Directors representing 58 chapters in 34 countries around the world, GARP's Professional and University Chapters position members to make new contacts, gain new knowledge about important topics, and stay on the cutting edge of risk management. As a member of the GARP community, members may attend chapter meetings anywhere in the world.

## Academic Partners

GARP's Academic Partnership Program was created to help colleges and universities improve their risk management course offerings. The program offers a wide range of benefits for academic institutions, and combines rigorous instruction with practitioner-driven insight to ensure that students are prepared for the demands of the global financial industry.

## Risk Manager of the Year Award

Each year, GARP presents the Risk Manager of the Year award to an individual, or group of individuals, who have advanced and influenced the financial risk profession.

## Risk Managers of the Year:

- 2015: Craig Broderick, Chief Risk Officer, Goldman Sachs

- 2013: Robert B. Litterman, Partner and Chairman of the Risk Committee and Advisory Panel, Kepos Capital LP

- 2012: Brian Leach, Head of Franchise Risk and Strategy, Citi
- 2011: Aaron Brown, Head of Risk Management, AQR Capital Management
- 2010: Dr. Hugo Bänziger, Chief Risk Officer, Deutsche Bank
- 2009: Liu Mingkang, Chairman, The China Banking Regulatory Commission
- 2008: Dr. Rene' M. Stulz, Everett D. Reese Chair of Banking and Monetary Economics, The Ohio State University
- 2007: European Central Bank
- 2006: Robert J. Shiller, Stanley B. Resor Professor of Economics, Department of Economics & Cowles Foundation of Research in Economics, Yale University
- 2005: E. Gerald Corrigan, Managing Director, Goldman Sachs
- 2004: Jacques Longerstaey, Managing Director, Putnam Investments
- 2003: Michael Gordy, Senior Economist, Division of Research, Board of Governors of the Federal Reserve, Washington, DC
- 2002: Mark Wallace, MD, Head of Strategic Business Development and Ian Drew, Chief Credit Officer from UBS Warburg
- 2001: Glenn Labhart, Chief Risk Officer, Dynegy Inc.
- 2000: William Martin, Global Head of Risk Management, The Royal Bank of Scotland Group
- 1999: Thomas Wilde, Director, CSFB
- 1998: Robert Mark, Senior Executive Vice President, Chief Risk Officer, Risk Management, CIBC
- 1997: James Lam, President & CEO, Enterprise Risk Solutions (Oliver Wyman)

## GARP Board of Trustees

Architect, Market Risk Management and Analysis, Goldman Sachs

- Ken Abbott, Americas Chief Risk Officer, Barclays Capital
- Richard Apostolik, President and CEO, GARP
- Laura Dottori-Attanasio, Senior Executive Vice-President and Chief Risk Officer, CIBC
- Ben Golub, Chief Risk Officer, BlackRock, Inc.
- Bradford Hu, Chief Risk Officer, Citigroup
- Andrew Kuritzkes,Executive Vice President and Chief Risk Officer, State Street Corporation
- Stuart Lewis, Chief Risk Officer, Member of Management Board & Group Executive Committee, Deutsche Bank
- Michelle McCarthy, Managing Director, Risk Management, Nuveen Investments
- Lewis O'Donald, Group Chief Risk Officer, Nomura Holdings, Inc.
- Lisa Polsky, Executive Vice President and Chief Risk Officer, CIT
- Riccardo Rebonato, Professor of Finance, EDHEC
- Jacob Rosengarten, Chief Enterprise Risk Officer, XL Group plc
- Jonathan Stein, Chief Risk Officer, Hess Corporation
- Peter Tufano, Peter Moores Dean and Professor of Finance, University of Oxford

## Financial Risk Manager

The Financial Risk Manager (FRM) designation is an international professional certification offered by the Global Association of Risk Professionals. To be awarded the FRM designation, a candidate must complete a rigorous two-part, practice-oriented examination that covers the major topics in financial risk management, demonstrate two years' professional work experience in financial risk management, and meet other requirements.

### FRM Designation

The FRM is a qualification for risk management professionals, particularly those who are involved in analyzing, controlling, or assessing potential credit risk, market risk, and liquidity risk as well as non-market related financial risks. FRM holders perform a broad variety of functions related to risk management within investment banks, asset management firms, as well as in corporations and government agencies. Top employers of FRM holders include global financial services firms Deutsche Bank, HSBC, and UBS, as well as auditing firms KPMG, Ernst & Young (EY) and PricewaterhouseCoopers (PwC). The FRM designation specification is disclosed on the U.S. Financial Industry Regulatory Authority (FINRA) education website where the FRM certificate program is shown on the FINRA guide to designations. The FRM and PRMIA's PRM are often compared as being the two definitive risk management designations in the industry.

## History and Growth

GARP first awarded the FRM designation in 1997.

Candidate enrollment in the FRM program has grown rapidly: between 2001 and 2010, registration increased at a compound annual rate of more than 25%.

Growth has occurred not just in the United States but also in Europe and Asia: today, more than 70% of FRM holders reside outside of the United States. Top territories of residence for FRM holders include the United Kingdom, Switzerland, Singapore, and Hong Kong.

While the financial crisis of 2007–2010 resulted in a dramatic downturn in overall financial services employment, the effect has been opposite in the field of risk management: the bankruptcy of Lehman Brothers and the collapse of other large financial institutions underscored the need to accurately price the risk inherent in 21st-century financial products and markets. The financial crisis has given a greater role to financial risk professionals, and driven further demand for skilled financial risk managers and the FRM designation.

As of February 2012, GARP has more than 125,000 registrations for the FRM Exam from 129 countries around the world. There are over 28,000 Certified FRMs practicing worldwide. The FRM is a globally recognized benchmark certification program for financial risk managers, and is considered to be the de facto global qualification in the practice of financial risk management.

## Dispute

In 2000, two founders of Global Association of Risk Professionals filed paperwork to shut down the non-profit GARP and replace it with a new for-profit corporation with the same name. Some former regional directors of GARP left and adopted a similar business model to offer Professional Risk Manager(PRM) certification. In October 2001, GARP has returned to a not-for-profit organization until now.

## Requirements

The basic requirements for becoming certified as a Financial Risk Manager include passing scores on both the Part I and Part II exams, as well as a minimum of two years' full-time work experience in financial risk management related positions including portfolio management, risk consulting, and other fields.

## Curriculum

The FRM curriculum is based on a candidate body of knowledge as defined by the Global Association of Risk Professionals. The FRM Committee, a panel of leading risk practitioners, develops and oversees the FRM program. The FRM curriculum emphasizes the practical applications of risk management theory, and ensures that candidates have firm knowledge of the major areas of financial risk management.

The FRM syllabus is dynamic and changes every year to reflect recent events in the global financial markets.

To maintain qualification, Certified FRMs are also recommended to enroll in Continuing Professional Education Program. All participants are required to complete 40 credits of continuing education every 24 months after enrolling in the program. Credits are based on a 60 minute hour; one credit per hour.

## Exams

The FRM exams are intended to thoroughly assess a financial risk manager's ability to measure and manage risk in a real-world environment. The FRM exams are administered on a single day twice a year, on the third Saturdays in May and November. The FRM exams are administered on paper. All questions are multiple choice; each question has four answer choices. There are no penalties for wrong answers. The questions in the exams are structured in the context of situations that financial risk managers face every day. The information needed to answer each question is contained within the question or vignette. Only certain models of Texas Instruments (BA II Plus) and Hewlett Packard (10B II, 20B, and HP-12C) calculators may be used. In addition to the official curriculum materials from GARP, study materials for the FRM exams are available from a number of third party providers. GARP recommends 150–200 hours of study for each part of the exam.

## Transition to a Two-part Exam

In November 2009, the FRM exam was offered for the last time in a one-level ("full") examination format.

Beginning with the May 2010 exam window, the FRM Exam transitioned from a one-part to a two-part exam: FRM Part I and FRM Part II.

Each exam consists of a single four-hour session. Candidates may choose to sit for both parts on the same day; however, if a candidate fails Part I their Part II exam will not be graded.

## Part I Exam

The Part I exam is administered on FRM exam days in a single four-hour session from 8:00 am to 12:00 pm.

The Part I exam covers core areas of risk management, such as quantitative analysis, financial markets and products, and essential risk modeling.

The exam consists of 100 multiple-choice questions, and tests a candidate's knowledge base in four main topic areas, weighted as follows:

| Weight | Topic |
|---|---|
| 20% | Foundations of Risk Management |
| 20% | Quantitative Analysis |
| 30% | Financial markets and Products |
| 30% | Valuation and Risk models |

## Part II Exam

The Part II exam is administered on FRM exam days in a single four-hour session from 2:00 pm to 6:00 pm.

The Part II exam covers specific topics on the practical implementation and execution of measurement and management of market, credit and operational risk, as well as a section covering current issues in financial markets.

The exam consists of 80 multiple-choice questions, and tests a candidate's knowledge base in five main topic areas:

| Weight | Topic |
|---|---|
| 25% | Market Risk Measurement and Management |
| 25% | Credit Risk Measurement and Management |
| 25% | Operational and Integrated Risk Management |
| 15% | Risk Management and Investment Management |
| 10% | Current Issues in Financial markets |

## Historical pass rates

The FRM exams are considered to be among the most challenging in finance: fewer than 25% of candidates are able to clear both Part I and Part II exams on first attempts.

# Permissions

All chapters in this book are published with permission under the Creative Commons Attribution Share Alike License or equivalent. Every chapter published in this book has been scrutinized by our experts. Their significance has been extensively debated. The topics covered herein carry significant information for a comprehensive understanding. They may even be implemented as practical applications or may be referred to as a beginning point for further studies.

We would like to thank the editorial team for lending their expertise to make the book truly unique. They have played a crucial role in the development of this book. Without their invaluable contributions this book wouldn't have been possible. They have made vital efforts to compile up to date information on the varied aspects of this subject to make this book a valuable addition to the collection of many professionals and students.

This book was conceptualized with the vision of imparting up-to-date and integrated information in this field. To ensure the same, a matchless editorial board was set up. Every individual on the board went through rigorous rounds of assessment to prove their worth. After which they invested a large part of their time researching and compiling the most relevant data for our readers.

The editorial board has been involved in producing this book since its inception. They have spent rigorous hours researching and exploring the diverse topics which have resulted in the successful publishing of this book. They have passed on their knowledge of decades through this book. To expedite this challenging task, the publisher supported the team at every step. A small team of assistant editors was also appointed to further simplify the editing procedure and attain best results for the readers.

Apart from the editorial board, the designing team has also invested a significant amount of their time in understanding the subject and creating the most relevant covers. They scrutinized every image to scout for the most suitable representation of the subject and create an appropriate cover for the book.

The publishing team has been an ardent support to the editorial, designing and production team. Their endless efforts to recruit the best for this project, has resulted in the accomplishment of this book. They are a veteran in the field of academics and their pool of knowledge is as vast as their experience in printing. Their expertise and guidance has proved useful at every step. Their uncompromising quality standards have made this book an exceptional effort. Their encouragement from time to time has been an inspiration for everyone.

The publisher and the editorial board hope that this book will prove to be a valuable piece of knowledge for students, practitioners and scholars across the globe.

# Index


**A**

Acceptable Risk Criteria, 151

Actimize, 283-285

Asset Pricing, 177-182, 185, 200

Asset-specific Required Return, 182

Audit Risk, 45, 49, 75, 151

**B**

Balance Sheet Risk, 170-171

Basic Mathematical Foundation, 142

Black-scholes Equation, 243, 245-246, 252, 256

Black-scholes Model, 243-244, 251, 253-256

Business Recovery, 22

Business Risks, 47-48

**C**

Capital Asset Pricing Model, 177-178, 180-181, 200

Cash Flow Risk, 171

Casualty Actuarial

Society Framework, 77

Common Alerting Protocol, 31, 163, 166-168

Composite Risk Index, 7

Confrontation Crisis, 19

Contingency Plan, 24, 69, 163, 165-166

Control Self-assessment, 236-240

Coping Strategies, 88, 92-94

Corporate Social Responsibility, 172

Credit Risk, 1, 12, 37, 39, 51, 53-56, 98, 195-196, 301, 304

Crisis Leadership, 21, 25-26, 30, 32

Crisis Management, 17-18, 21, 23, 25-32, 75, 164-165

Crisis of Deception, 20

Crisis of Malevolence, 20

Customer Retention, 197-199

**D**

Decision Models, 197

Delphi Method, 210-212, 214-215, 267

Descriptive Models, 196

Direct Marketing, 197, 199

Dragon King Theory, 122

**E**

Efficient Frontier, 183-184

Enterprise Risk Management, 12, 15, 64, 76, 78-79, 83, 101, 104, 156, 161, 178, 187-189, 288-289, 293, 295

Establishing The Context, 4-5, 100

Event Chain Methodology, 177-178, 189, 191

Event Chain Methodology

Phenomena, 191

Event Chains, 189-191

**F**

Fault Tree Analysis, 13, 136-137, 139, 162, 187

Financial Risk, 35, 39, 48, 50, 52, 76-77, 82, 98-99, 121, 257, 263, 268, 270, 283, 293, 296-297, 299, 301-303

Financial Risk Management, 76, 98-99, 121, 257, 263, 268, 270, 296, 301-303

Flood Risk Assessment, 153-156

Foreign Investment Risk, 51

Fraud Detection, 195-196, 199-200, 206, 284

Fuel Price Risk Management, 99-101

**I**

Industry Adoption, 188

Interest-rate Curve, 256

Internal Audit Role, 81

It Risk, 15, 36-37, 52, 57, 59-60, 64, 76, 101-102, 104-106, 109, 116, 119-120, 152

It Risk Management, 64, 76, 101, 104-106, 116, 119-120

**L**

Linear Regression Model, 201

Logicmanager, 79, 178, 187, 283, 288-289

**M**

Megaprojects, 14-15, 75, 152

Mitigation Strategies, 91

Monte Carlo Simulations, 190, 219, 223, 225, 267

**N**

Naïve Bayes, 208

Neural Networks, 206-207

## O
Operational Implementation, 157, 159-160
Operational Risk, 12, 15, 37, 48, 52, 54-57, 76-77, 85, 94, 98, 160, 238, 296-297, 304
Operational Risk Management, 15, 54-55, 57, 76, 94, 98, 238
Orm Software, 98
Own Risk And Solvency Assessment, 156-157, 159

## P
Potential Risk Treatments, 8
Precautionary Principle, 268, 271-281
Predictive Analytics, 194-195, 197-201, 206, 208-209, 266
Predictive Models, 194, 196-197, 199, 209
Probabilistic Risk Assessment, 38, 130, 132, 138, 177, 186-187, 200
Probit Regression, 203
Project Management, 2, 14, 60, 86, 102, 120, 152, 189, 230-232, 294
Project Risk Management, 14, 76, 86-87, 177, 200, 233

## Q
Quantitative Analysis, 42, 190, 263, 304

## R
Resource Management, 280
Rims Risk Maturity Model, 79, 178, 187-188, 288, 295
Risk, 1-89, 91-192, 194-247, 249-304
Risk Analysis, 8, 11, 13, 36, 42, 65, 84, 87, 96, 103, 105-106, 108-109, 111, 120, 132, 145-146, 224, 227, 231-234, 270
Risk Assessment, 3, 6-8, 11, 15, 37-38, 40-43, 69, 74-75, 78, 81-82, 94-95, 99-100, 103, 105-113, 120, 130, 132-134, 138, 145-156, 176-178, 186-187, 195, 200, 235, 237, 268, 276, 279
Risk Breakdown Structure, 230-234
Risk Communication, 16, 115, 120, 132, 145
Risk Management Insight, 59, 120
Risk Management Methodology, 103-104, 116, 119
Risk Management Programme, 176
Risk Management Tools, 87, 177
Risk Matrix, 133, 268-270
Risk Mitigation, 7, 10, 91, 106, 113-115, 132, 191
Risk Monitoring, 94, 106, 115, 130, 231
Risk Pool, 174
Risk Register, 14, 111, 177-178, 192, 194
Risklab, 268, 270-271

## S
Sampling Risk, 49
Sarbanes-oxley Act, 70, 76, 81, 98, 237
Scenario Analysis, 5, 171, 241-242
Scope Exclusions, 56
Security Market Line, 179-181
Short Stock Rate, 256
Signal Detection, 21-22
Social Responsibility, 163, 171-174, 271
Social Risk Management, 76, 88, 93
Social Risks, 89
Society for Risk Analysis, 145
Software Evolution, 153
Solvency, 54-55, 57, 156-161, 187, 285, 287-288
Structural-functional Systems Theory, 25

## T
Technological Crisis, 19
The Volatility Smile, 255
Time Critical, 95-96

## V
Value At Risk, 12, 53, 102, 131, 257, 266
Var Risk Management, 261